Word of God
Words of Men

The Use and Abuse

of Scripture

Word of God
Words of Men

The Use and Abuse

of Scripture

A. Daniel Frankforter

Hampshire, England
Cleveland, Ohio

First published by Circle Books, 2011
Circle Books is an imprint of John Hunt Publishing Ltd., Laurel House, Station Approach,
Alresford, Hants, SO24 9JH, UK
office1@o-books.net
www.o-books.com

This book edition is a licensed adaption and condensation of Faith Practices(r) on-line program for groups,
published by The Pilgrim Press, Cleveland, Ohio. To utilize those fuller materials, which include leader
instructions and group activities, please see www.FaithPractices.org.

For more titles in this series, see www.Circle-Books.com.

ISBN: 978 1 84694 534 2

Design: Stuart Davies

Printed in the UK by CPI Antony Rowe
Printed in the USA by Offset Paperback Mfrs, Inc

We operate a distinctive and ethical publishing philosophy in all areas
of our business, from our global network of authors to production
and worldwide distribution.

CONTENTS

For my brothers:
David and Larry

I

The Central Issue

I am the Lord your God . . . . You shall have no other gods before me.
You shall not make for yourself an idol, whether in the form of anything
that is in heaven above, or that is on the earth beneath, or that is in the
water under the earth. You shall not bow down to them or worship
them; for I the Lord your God am a jealous God, punishing children for
the iniquity of parents
    — Exodus 20: 2-5[1]

Whenever I hear a brother Christian talk in such a way as to show that
he is ignorant of these scientific matters and confuses one thing with
another, I listen with patience . . . . The danger lies in thinking that
such knowledge is part and parcel of what he must believe to save his
soul and in presuming to make obstinate declarations about things of
which he knows nothing.[2]
    — St. Augustine of Hippo

Faith's Endangered Reputation

Religion can addle minds, and faith can corrupt character. This
charge is depressingly easy to document. Consider, for instance,
the field of literature. If novels and plays were purged of the
stock characters who travel faith's highway to Hell, the West's
literary canon would shrink significantly. Plots could not
function without the hypocritical cleric whose veneer of piety
cloaks a perverted soul; the priggish church elder whose sole
pleasure is sour contempt for all that is lovely and delightful; the
haughty moralist whose self-worth derives from condemnation
of others; the opportunistic evangelist who exploits the
desperate and the naive; or the true believer who, with arrogant

self-confidence, claims an understanding of God's will that destroys his humanity. The mirror that literary art holds up to life may distort reality, but its exaggeration and mockery also illuminate unpalatable truths.

It is undeniable that people of faith have sometimes done great damage to individuals and to communities. Wars, crusades, witch trials, inquisitions, persecutions, tortures, and holocausts have all been dedicated to God. It would be of some comfort if there were signs that the human species is maturing and outgrowing the religious prejudices and dogmatism of earlier generations — that the sins of faith are fading into the past. Such, however, is not the case, for religion's power to nourish violence, hate, and ignorance is as great as ever. We have only to consider the Muslim minority that celebrated the slaughter at the World Trade Center and the Christian majority that demanded bloody vengeance for its destruction. We have only to reflect on the numerous followers of the Prince of Peace who endorse fighting terrorism with terrorism. We have only to ponder the motives of the "religious values" voters who are eager to persecute sexual minorities, block fields of scientific research, the academic freedom of educational institutions, and pass legislation that will compel others to conform to their beliefs.

American Christians in particular have trusted in the goodness of faith, and they have been ridiculed for their simplistic "faith in faith" — a vacuous religiosity that renders them vulnerable to manipulation. President Dwight D. Eisenhower spoke for many of his fellow citizens when he said: "Our form of government makes no sense unless it is founded in a deeply felt religious faith, and I don't care what it is."[3] President Eisenhower's assumption that all religions lay a foundation for democracy by endorsing similar moral values, universal human rights, tolerance, and good citizenship reflected a time in American history when there was little acknowledged religious diversity in the country. In the 1950s a long tradition that equated some sort of liberal Protestantism with the "American way of life" was unchallenged. Catholic, Jewish, and Protestant minorities were expected to accept outsider status in exchange for toleration.

This is no longer true. Powerful religious organizations have emerged to fight for implementation of very specific faith agendas. Many American Christians, who confidently claim to know the mind of God, believe they have a duty to impose their understanding of God's will on "God's Country" and on other nations that seek its help.

Although some Americans may have had to pay a price for their constitutional right to freedom of religion, the country's individualistic culture nurtures an environment that is inhospitable to dogmatism — in the long run. From time to time, groups of Americans are carried away by enthusiasm for narrow-minded leaders or causes, but the country's deep commitment to personal freedoms usually inspires a corrective reaction. This may explain the results of a recent survey of religious attitudes conducted by the Pew Forum.[4] Despite the prominence of dogmatic religious leaders and movements in the late 20th century, the Pew survey discovered that 68% of Americans believed that there is more than one true way to interpret their faith tradition. That is, they did not equate belief in God with allegiance to a particular set of beliefs about God. They did not think, for instance, that all Catholics or all Protestants should have to embrace all the moral and doctrinal teachings of their brands of Christianity. This suggests that the vast majority of Americans may not be entirely comfortable with attempts by the country's "religious right" to write its views into American law.

Although the Pew survey finds that 63% of American church-goers did not believe that their churches should endorse political candidates, some clergy have openly challenged laws that forbid them to turn the pulpit into a soapbox. Many others routinely skirt the line by condemning positions while avoiding naming the politicians associated with those positions. Religion is a powerful motivator, and the temptation to use it to rally support for a cause or a leader is strong. History shows how dangerous this is, for religion easily convinces people that they have the right to sacrifice not only themselves, but others, in service of their God.

America is often said to be the most religious of Western nations, but the poll data cited to support this claim are difficult to interpret. Because Americans traditionally have associated patriotism with belief in God, many religious polls are distorted by what social scientists call the "social desirability bias." This bias arises from our tendency, when asked a question, to give what we assume to be the "right" or "good" answer rather than expose ourselves to criticism by saying what we truly believe. Shielding the interviewee from the interviewer (*i.e.*, by computer surveys instead of phone calls or face-to-face encounters) helps diminish this effect. Such polls suggest that "hard core" religious faith may be less widely held than previously reported — and that it may be beginning to decline. Indeed, the political activities of some conservative Christian groups may be contributing to what some recent surveys suggest is a diminishing respect for religion.

At the root of the issue is a war for control of the Bible that has been underway for at least two centuries. During these years liberal or modernist scholars have done much to penetrate the mysteries of the Bible's historical origin, but conservative and fundamentalist Christians have succeeded in persuading the masses that their supernatural faith is the only "Bible-based," and therefore true, understanding of Christianity. Not only do they claim an exclusive right to call themselves Christians, they insist that their reading of the Bible speaks for God.

Andrew Sullivan, a religious commentator who generally favors the right, has lamented the public's growing tendency to equate Christianity with harshly judgmental right-wing political stances on (among other things) abortion, homosexuality, and feminism.[5] He has proposed erecting a "big tent" for Christianity by repudiating attempts to equate it with any particular political position, and he has coined the word "Christianism" to describe the position of those for whom religion is a political ideology. Not surprisingly, his article led one of its readers (no doubt speaking for many) to challenge his right to call himself a Christian, given that he did not accept what the reader claimed were "the tenets that define Christianity in the first place, [what] we know . . . through Scripture, . . . what ultimately defines Christianity."[6]

The Hebrew prophets and many Christians would take issue with Sullivan's call to divorce faith from politics. Throughout history some sincere believers have retreated from the world into quietism, but more have acted on the assumption that biblical faith strives to redeem the world through pursuit of the divinely mandated goals of love and justice. Problems arise, however, whenever their struggle involves means that are anything but expressions of Christian love and the prophetic passion for justice.

Historically, atheism has never held much appeal for Americans, but this may change if the public is persuaded that a narrow-minded and repressive form of faith is its only alternative. A 2003 Harris poll reported that 79% of Americans were "absolutely" or "somewhat" certain of God's existence. By 2006 that percentage had shrunk to 73%.[7] In the same period the number of convinced atheists, increased from 9% to 11%.

This drift toward skepticism or unbelief doubtless has multiple causes, but European history provides a clue to one of them. The more problematic faith becomes, the greater the temptation simply to reject the whole religious enterprise. During the 18th and 19th centuries, many European churches were "establishments" that sided with oppressive regimes and class systems to oppose reforms that, when they were ultimately implemented, liberated the masses. Because history linked the Christian religion with values and traditions that Europeans had struggled hard to cast off, Christianity came to be seen as an outdated, irrelevant artifact — an impediment to progress and public well-being. As a consequence, in Britain today more people worship in mosques than in the country's Anglican churches.[8] If America is headed down the path that Europe has trod, it may be because conservatives and fundamentalists are succeeding in convincing the masses that to be "true to the Bible" they must reject science, ignore the dictates of reason and common sense, and embrace social attitudes that increasingly appear unjust and outdated. Many would conclude that if this is the case, faith calls for an unreasonable sacrifice that is not worth making.

Americans are showing increasing interest in religion's critics, particularly in the advocates for the so-called "New Atheism." Books by hostile commentators such as Christopher Hitchens, Richard Dawkins, Daniel Dennett, and Sam Harris have sold well, and their authors have attracted major media attention.[9] The titles of their best sellers proclaim their contempt for faith in no uncertain terms. Dawkins dismisses religion as a *God Delusion*. Dennett speaks of *Breaking the Spell*. Harris eagerly anticipates the *End of Faith*. And Hitchens boldly claims that *God is Not Great,* adding *Religion Poisons Everything*. For these men the lessons of history and recent experience are clear. It is not simply that faith may occasionally misfire and motivate destructive acts; faith is simply a bad thing in and of itself. If this were a sane and rational world, they argue, there would no place for religion — and we would all be safer and happier for its absence.

Religion's defenders object that this a classic case of tossing faithful believers out with their holy water, but an adequate response to faith's critics requires more than insisting on the virtue of soaking in the baptismal pool. Another watery analogy would suggest that you have to drain your swamp if you want to defeat your alligators.

Because Christians should be careful never to overestimate their own virtues, they ought always to take critics of their faith seriously. Humility requires them to acknowledge the dismal aspects of their religion's history and to ponder the troubling question that should haunt every believer: Why is it that people who aspire to be good and faithful servants of God do bad things — and do them with the best of intentions and the clearest consciences? The New Atheists and their fellow travelers have concluded that religion itself is the root of the problem. Christians have been too ready to ignore this charge and simply dismiss the evil done in the name of faith as an aberration outweighed by the good that religion does. They may cite St. Paul's lament: "Now if I do what I do not want, it is no longer I that do it, but sin that dwells within me . . . making me captive to the law of sin that dwells in my members" (Romans 6:20,23). However, no responsible exegete would argue that Paul intended to encourage sinners to use sin as an excuse for continuing to sin. Paul's point was that religion is human behavior and, therefore, is as vulnerable to perversion as everything that reflects imperfect human nature. But people who would be faithful to the Bible's God can never be content to leave it at that. To do so is to give religion's abusers a pass, to take sin more seriously than grace, and to ignore the prophet Amos's warning (5: 21-24) that faith can become an obstacle to its own goals.

Religious people need to be aware that every faith's sword has two edges. The world's survival may depend on their acceptance of the fact that they can no longer afford to indulge — in the name of God — passions that feed authoritarianism, self-righteousness, vicious factionalism, oppression, abuse, murder, genocide, and yet-to-be-imagined atrocities.

7

The Protestant Temptation

The Bible does not have much to say about God's sense of humor, but Protestant Christians better hope that He has one — as well as an appreciation for irony. In their desire to be faithful to God's Word, Protestants often break God's first commandment[10] by lapsing into the sin of idolizing the Bible. When they make no distinction between the Bible as words and the Bible as Word of God, they slip into the error of venerating a product of human hands as if it were God Himself.

Protestantism's powerful temptation to the sin of bibliolatry springs from the circumstances of its origin. The pioneers of the Protestant Reformation justified their secession from the Catholic Church by appealing to the authority of the Bible. For them, the Bible took the place of the pope and the tradition of the Church as the final arbiter of faith. The Roman Catholic position was (and is) that divine revelation is conveyed by the Bible while continuing to unfold within the history of the Church. Catholics point out that the Church existed before the Bible. If there had been no Christian congregations, there would have been no need for a New Testament and no one to write it. Why, therefore, it could reasonably be argued, should revelation end with the closing of the biblical canon? Why should the Bible be regarded as anything more than the record of one phase in the evolving story of God's interaction with His people? Why should new truths (*e.g.*, Purgatory, seven sacraments, the Immaculate Conception of Mary, papal infallibility, *etc.*) not continue to be revealed to the Christian community?

Luther, Calvin, and other Reformation leaders countered the papacy by charging that Rome's reliance on tradition led to innovations that corrupted and perverted the Christian faith. They believed that if you accepted the possibility of adding novelties to faith and practice, there was no way to avoid the slippery slide into error and apostasy. They insisted that the only way to restore the authenticity and integrity of the Church was to

8

return to the beliefs and practices of the first Christians — the record of which is to be found only in the New Testament. The Reformers saw the Bible as a timeless standard against which all generations of Christians had to test themselves so as to avoid compromising the authenticity of their faith. They knew, of course, that the Church had written the New Testament, but for them this guaranteed rather than compromised the Bible's claim to unique authority. Later generations of Christians could not find any more reliable guide for faith than that provided by those who bore the earliest witness to God's revelation in Christ

Some Reformers were stricter than others in applying the Bible's standards. Luther was inclined to tolerate post-biblical traditions so long as they did not conflict with his understanding of "primitive" (New Testament) Christianity. The Swiss Reformers took a harder stance. They argued for the elimination of everything that could not be authenticated as a belief or custom of the early Church. There was, therefore, plenty of room for disagreements among Protestants even though they all claimed to be guided by the same texts. There was general consensus on the sacraments, for the New Testament specifically mentions only two: Baptism and Eucharist. Many other issues were, however, open to debate. For instance: Was religious art acceptable or condemned as a form of idolatry; could newly composed hymns be used in congregational worship, or should Christians only sing Psalms?

The fact that most Protestants claim to be guided solely or primarily by the Bible has not prevented Protestantism from becoming a contentious movement riven by disputes and disagreements. To resolve these differences partisans often search out passages of Scripture that they believe substantiate their beliefs and refute those of their opponents. This method of arguing almost inevitably leads to the abuse of Scripture, for it tempts people to rip the Bible's verses out of context and treat each as if it were an eternal divine edict. When the Bible is treated in this way, it degenerates into a list of orders from God, and Christian faith becomes as blindly legalistic as the Judaism of the Pharisees whose practices Jesus criticized. The Gospels' message of grace and Paul's proclamation of freedom from the law then cease to be heard.

Given that so much hinges for Protestants on how they use the Bible, they need to think long and hard about its authority and method of interpretation. But the Protestant situation is not unique and not unique to religion. Questions about appropriate interpretation arise for anyone who attempts to live within confines set by a historical document. Americans, whose government operates according to principles laid down over two hundred years ago in their nation's Constitution, are familiar with the mixed blessings of a "sacred" text. An authoritative document serves a community as an anchor by safeguarding core values and encouraging continuity of development. But given that such documents are always rooted in the historical eras that produced them, changing circumstances alter the context for their interpretation. This can have troubling consequences. For instance, the authors of the U.S. Constitution's second amendment believed that it was important for citizens to have the right to bear arms in order to protect their freedoms. However, the Constitutional Convention could not have anticipated what that would mean for massive urban populations equipped with guns the likes of which no one in the 18th century ever imagined. The arms the nation's founders knew were single shot, muzzle-loaded rifles and dueling pistols. It is reasonable to wonder if they might have written a somewhat different second amendment if they had heard the sound of rapid-fire automatic weapons on the streets of Philadelphia.

The Bible, no matter what its readers think about the role divine inspiration may have played in its composition, confronts Christians with similar problems of interpretation. What, for instance, are they to make of a sacred epistle that urges slaves to "obey your earthly masters with fear and trembling, in singleness of heart, as you obey Christ" (Ephesians 6:5)? This and many other passages clearly endorse an institution that the ancient world accepted without question but which the modern Western world has come to regard as morally repugnant. Despite the fact that the Bible so clearly condones slavery that many who fought the Civil War sincerely believed slavery to be a divinely ordained condition, few Christians now would argue that obedience to God's Word requires them to restore the antebellum South's "peculiar institution." With respect to this social issue at least, the moral sensitivities and the values of modern Christians are superior to those of the Bible's authors.

Granting a document authority over conscience and reason is risky, for the guiding hand of the past can become a dead hand. America's founding fathers wisely made provision for amending the Constitution so that it could be adjusted from time to time to assure that it continued to serve its fundamental purpose: the preservation of what the Declaration of Independence claimed were "God-given" and "inalienable" (if somewhat vaguely specified) rights. Should Christians have a similar privilege with respect to the Bible? Should it be subject to "amending"?

Many sincere Christians would answer this question with a resounding "No!" They believe the Scriptures to be unique among historical documents, for they assume that, unlike the Constitution, the Scriptures were somehow revealed by God without any need to compromise with the limitations of our mortal nature. The Bible is, therefore, timeless, of absolute authority, and so plain that it does not need interpretation. To read the Bible, they insist, is to understand it — a theological position sometimes summarized on bumper stickers as: "God said it; I believe it; that settles it." The only challenge for students of the Bible, such Christians believe, is not how to understand its text, but how to muster the will to do what it says.

The most extreme version of this point of view holds that the

Bible is literally the words of God, inerrant and eternal. This theory appeals to sizeable numbers of people, for it cuts through the confusion associated with the search for faith. Americans have a reputation for impatience with complexity and subtle argument. Their attraction to quick, easy fixes inclines them to religious movements that claim that faith is simply the decision to cling to a belief no matter what challenges it. This thesis also appeals as a democratic, and therefore American, principle. It implies that no arduous training or difficult intellectual work is required in order to qualify to speak with authority about what the Bible says. Anyone can decide for him- or herself what it teaches. No elite company of effete scholars or greedy priests can boast of special access to knowledge of God's will or sit in judgment on the opinions of ordinary believers. If a question should arise, it can easily be resolved simply by searching out verses of Scripture that seem to speak to it. God's Word is law, but unlike human laws, it is couched in ordinary words that have the same meanings they have in ordinary conversation. All that a good Christian needs to do is hear and obey. Unfortunately, what these Christians often believe they hear as the voice of God is only the echo of their own firmly held opinions.

Christians who take this extreme position on biblical interpretation are a minority, but "softer" versions of this approach to the Bible are widespread. The members of this camp view the Bible as if it were a mix of human and divine elements, and they practice a kind of selective reading that arbitrarily distinguishes between passages that are literally God's "eternally true and always applicable" words and those verses that are human accretions that can safely be set aside.[11] This, however, offers no escape from the necessity of deciding how to interpret and explain the authority of what remains. It simply shrinks the size of the text while leaving open the question of how the remaining (allegedly essential) portions function as the Word of God.

The Interpretation Wars

Given the commanding role that the Bible plays in authenticating faith and practice for Protestants, disagreements about how the Bible should be interpreted may be the chief cause of upheaval within and among Protestant denominations. Quarrels ranging from esoteric, metaphysical and doctrinal disputes to squabbles over social issues and codes of personal morality can usually be traced to debates about "what the Bible says." These discussions are usually inconclusive because of fundamental disagreements about how the Bible should be read.

Historical and cultural circumstances have enthroned some form of biblical literalism in the minds of vast numbers of Americans. Fundamentalism and literalism are such powerful forces in American popular religion that many people automatically assume that they represent the only truly faithful approach to reading the Scriptures. It is, therefore, hardly surprising that the United States is the only Western nation in which arguments still rage over teaching Charles Darwin's theory of evolution. In some surveys of the general public almost half the respondents have claimed to believe that Earth is less than 10,000 years old.[12] Even more say that they believe that the Bible was dictated by God. This inevitably leads them to assume that the Christian faith requires people to believe things about the natural world and the cosmos that are ancient misconceptions and contrary to findings supported by mounds of scientific evidence.

Although biblical literalism claims to provide a secure foundation for a sturdy faith, the attempt to read the Bible literally creates more problems than it solves. Despite the fact that many conservative Christians claim to hold to a literal reading of the Scriptures, none does so consistently. To do so would require asserting that God has eyes, ears, hands, and male organs, for the Bible says this about Him. Even determined literalists and fundamentalists recognize that sometimes the Bible's language is poetic and metaphorical. The real issue, therefore, is where one draws the line in deciding which texts must be taken literally and which can be interpreted as meaning something other than what they plainly say.

Part of literalism's appeal is its promise of an escape from the burden of assuming personal responsibility for how one interprets the Bible. However, it fails to deliver on that hope when it confronts passages that literal readings turn into self-contradictory absurdity. For instance, in Deuteronomy (27:17-19) the Hebrews are ordered to "remember what Amalek did to you on your journey out of Egypt, how he attacked you." They are told that after they are settled in their new land, they "shall blot out the remembrance of Amalek from under heaven; do not forget." To obey the order not to forget to forget is unavoidably to remember what one is to forget. Also, given that this passage (and the earlier reference to Amalek's treachery in Exodus 17:8) is part of the Word of God that "shall not pass away," the admonition to forget is the sole reason why "the remembrance of Amalek" is not blotted out today.

The most glaring flaw in literalism is its unwillingness to admit the obvious: every act of reading involves interpretation. This is inescapable, for there is no understanding without interpretation. For instance, Christians who consult the Standard (*i.e.,* King James) translation of the Ten Commandments (Exodus 20:13) read: "Thou shalt not kill." But Christians who use the New Revised Standard Version of the Bible read God's words as, "You shall not murder." Most people make a distinction between killing and murdering. One might kill in self-defense or by accident, and such acts are not treated, at least in courts of law, as murder. But there are gray areas. The Bible often decrees the death penalty as a punishment for crimes. But the execution of a defenseless condemned criminal shares some of the features of murder — which is why medieval executioners asked forgiveness from those whom they were about to behead and modern firing squads used multiple riflemen to diffuse responsibility for the "hit." The Old Testament God is also a warrior deity who occasionally orders His armies to commit genocide (Joshua 6:21) — that is, the murder of non-combatants such as an enemy's infants, children, and women. Given that the Bible's translators have made different decisions about the meaning of the Hebrew word found in the sixth commandment (*i.e.* "kill" versus "murder"), what is its "literal" meaning — particularly in light of the rest of the orders God gives in the Scriptures? What at first glance looks like a simple, straightforward admonition is, on reflection, anything but simple — as military and prison chaplains will testify.

To defend their literal readings of the Bible, literalists have to do violence to the texts they claim simply to be reading (not interpreting). If every line in the Bible is literally the Word of God, every line must be both true and significant. To be true, every line in the Bible must also be consistent with every other. Contradictions would mean that some of the text is true, but incompatible verses are not — and that would mean that God is either confused or deceptive. All the Bible's verses must also be assumed to bear profound spiritual meaning. If they did not, God would appear to indulge Himself in idle, pointless chatter.

Any reader who attempts to defend the Bible's consistency and the elevated spirituality of all its verses can do so only by twisting and supplementing its words — by *rewriting* the sacred text to make it conform to human expectations. Anyone who begins reading the Bible at the beginning is immediately confronted with the problem of the Bible's consistency.[13] Genesis 1:11 says that "the earth put forth vegetation" on the third day of creation and that God made "humankind" as His final act on day six (Genesis 1: 27-28). Genesis 2:5-7 says that God "formed man from the dust of the ground" at a time "when no plant of the field was yet in the earth and herb of the field had yet sprung up" — that is, on the third day, not the sixth.

To render contradictions like this one apparent rather than

real, literalists supplement the text with interpretive assumptions that are not in the text itself. They might, for instance, argue that Genesis 1:27, which says that males and females were created simultaneously is really skipping over the details of separate creations for males and females described by Genesis 2. The former is a kind of summary of the latter. This might bring the two accounts closer together, but still fails to reconcile all their differences (e.g., the references to the origin of vegetation). But the primary problem with such explanations is that in the name of preserving the literal meaning of the text, they fundamentally supplement and rewrite the text to make it conform to human demands for consistency. This not only changes the Bible; it may also divert the reader from the point the original text intends to make. An inescapable self-contradiction lies at the basis of literalism. If the Bible is literally true, it should need no interpretation. But demonstration of its literal truth always necessitates (often very elaborate) interpretation.

It is equally difficult to defend the proposition that every line in the Bible, as God's inspired word, is equally profound and equally spiritually elevating. Genesis 12:10-20 tells a tale that is difficult to reconcile with standards of morality that conservative Christians believe are grounded in the Bible. These verses describe a situation that led Abram to prostitute his wife Sarai to Egypt's pharaoh. Sarai was so desirable that Abram was afraid that other men would kill him to possess her. Therefore, he passed his wife off as his sister and negotiated a handsome price for her services in pharaoh's harem. When God then sent plagues to punish pharaoh for falling for Abram's lies and unwittingly committing adultery, Sarai is returned to Abram, and the happy couple (a pimp and his prostitute!) leave Egypt much the richer for their escapade. The scam worked so well that Abram tried it again (with less success this time) on Abimelech, king of Gerar (Genesis 20:2-16), and it became something of a family tradition. Abram's son Isaac flirted with the same scheme (Genesis 26:6-11).

These stories make sense as examples of a common kind of folk tale — an entertaining narrative in which a clever ancestor turns the tables on a powerful superior and gets away with it. But who would argue that they represent Abram and Isaac as spiritual or ethical role models? If read literally, they would provide divine sanction for husbands to sell their wives' sexual favors.

For thousands of years rabbis have been laboring to find spiritual meaning in texts that on their surfaces are perfectly clear, but which seem morally ambiguous, odd, funny, or too trivial to merit God's attention. For instance, in Deuteronomy (25:11-12) God is reported saying: "If men get into a fight with one another, and the wife of one intervenes to rescue her husband from the grip of his opponent by reaching out and seizing his genitals, you shall cut off her hand; show no pity." One cannot help wondering why this strange scenario played out so often in ancient Israel that it required God's special condemnation. Rabbis explained that it was really an admonition to women not to embarrass men by intervening in their fights and that the punishment was actually a monetary payment, not the loss of a hand.[14]

"You shall have no other gods before me"

If literal readings of the Bible are either impossible, inadequate, silly or fraudulent, why belabor the issue? The unsustainable nature of literalism is so obvious that all attentive readers should surely and inevitably discover that fact for themselves. This, however, is plainly not the case. Large numbers of Christians and members of other faiths live with the dangerous illusion that they have access to the literal words of God. Their belief has horrific consequences for individuals, threatens the stability of societies, and is a chief contributor to "faith's endangered reputation."

Partisans of the West's major faiths (Judaism, Christianity, and Islam) should be especially alert to the dangers of literalism and fundamentalism, for all three, as offshoots of a single "Abrahamic" tradition, have a unique propensity for engendering conflict. Despite the fact that they agree that God commands them to pursue the virtues of love, mercy, charity, and justice, they all have lamentable records of inspiring hatred, intolerance, and violence. Not only have they often turned against each other, but each has spawned divisive factions and waged vicious internal conflicts. All three are monotheistic "religions of the book." They claim access to an omnipotent divine power through a sacred text.[15] How they use (or abuse) that text is, therefore, the key to the impact they have on the societies in which they function.

A strength is a source of power, and power brings temptation. The strength of the Abrahamic tradition is monotheism, and monotheism's temptation is intolerance.[16] Polytheism, by contrast, is inclined to be inclusive. It holds that the more gods we honor, the better our chances of covering all supernal bases. If, however, there is only one god, that fact is vitally important to uphold. Tolerance of other faiths implicitly accords legitimacy to their error. It betrays God by casting doubt on His existence and betrays one's fellows by allowing them to persist in sins for which they will suffer tragic, eternal consequences. Many Christian societies in many ages have judged infidelity to their concept of God a capital offense.

A monotheistic faith's inclination to intolerance is greatly increased when literal interpretation is mandated for its holy book, for literalism infects the faithful with a fearfully presumptive arrogance. It leads them to lay claim to powers that belong to God alone. Whether they admit it or not, individuals who believe that they possess God's very words are claiming the right to exercise God's authority. If they can quote God's words, they can speak for God. When they speak for God, they act as God.

Not only does literalism bestow unwarranted power on the

Bible's readers, it also frees them from responsibility for what they do. The more compassionate among them might say that they wish that things were different, but their condemnation of others is not a matter of choice. They have no option. God has spoken, and faith requires them to do as God commands, no matter the consequences. There is no compromising what God has decreed in Scripture. God's will is plain, and it is law. God, therefore, is responsible for what happens when His faithful servants obey.

This offers an open invitation for "good Christians" to do bad things. If it were up to them, some might wish to be tolerant, but God has left them no choice. God has, for instance, condemned homosexual acts, so homosexuality must be a sinful choice, not a natural orientation. God has condemned extramarital sex, so the unwed mother is a sinner. A given homosexual, an unwed mother, or a fornicator might be a sympathetic individual, but that is irrelevant. The best that "good Christians" can do, given God's laws, is "to hate the sin while loving the sinner." There is more self-justification than charity in such a stance. Anyone who has been on the receiving end of this specious simulacrum of compassion will testify that it is indistinguishable from condemnation, discrimination, and persecution.

Over a century ago Susan B. Anthony lamented that religious people so often lay the responsibility for their acts of prejudice and persecution at the feet of God. She said, "I distrust those people who know so well what God wants them to do, because I notice it always coincides with their own desires."[17] Anthony's "distrust" should strike all who have witnessed the rise of religiously motivated terrorism in the 21st century as too mild a verb.[18]

The overt fundamentalism that motivates terrorists and religious extremists is not the only form of literalist abuse to which the Bible is subjected. A casual or "soft" literalism infects many Christians, particularly in America. Dedicated fundamentalists approach the Bible with preconceptions that predetermine what they find in it, but they do read it. The casual Christian "literalists," on the other hand, prefer to "worship" the Bible rather than read it. They assume that it says things that it does not say and take it for granted that it blesses their opinions and prejudices. When the Bible, rather than the God to whom it points, becomes an object of veneration, it serves as the sort of idol it condemns. Like an idol, it is sometimes assumed to have magical powers. It may invite superstitious uses (*e.g.*, random searches for oracular hints in its verses), or it may discourage serious thought about the text (on the assumption that objective analysis is blasphemy).

The tendency to look on the Bible as a sacred object may help to explain one of the puzzles of American religious behavior. As noted above, huge numbers of Americans claim to be biblical literalists. That is, they tell pollsters that they believe that the Bible records the words of God, but they also admit to those pollsters that they do not read it. It seems odd that people who think that they have at hand a communiqué from God would not bother to open their divine mail. What could be more important than finding out what God says?

Many American Christians believe that they know what God says without having to read the Bible. After all, they live in a "Christian" country. So long as they respect the Bible, affirm its sacred origin, do their duty as citizens, and generally try to "be good," they must be living according to Biblical principles. Conversely, anyone who departs significantly from middle-class morality and the American way of life must be a sinner.

Of course America is not formally a Christian nation, but religion sometimes plays a larger part in American politics than in the politics of countries that have religious establishments. The role that Christianity has played in shaping American identity, American institutions, and American policies means that anyone who hopes to understand the country needs to consider its religious history — and that history's persistent flirtation with emotional, authoritarian expressions of faith.

America's myth of national origin draws heavily on biblical imagery. America is said to be God's special land, a "city upon a hill,"[19] and "the last, best hope of earth."[20] The *National Hymn*, which was written for the centennial of the Constitution of the United States and which is sung in many churches on patriotic holidays, speaks of God as "our ruler" and prays for "Thy Word [to be] our law." Americans see themselves as God's final chosen people, commissioned to save the world and to set an example of freedom for all nations. They take it for granted that, as God's special servants, they are entitled to prosper and dominate.

The religious cast of American culture is a legacy from its foundation. Many of the European immigrants who settled the American colonies saw themselves as religious refugees who had fled to "the wilderness" to find the freedom to worship God as the Bible commands. They identified with the ancient Hebrews, and even justified driving the native Americans from their land by recalling how God ordered the Hebrews to dispossess the Canaanites. Their divine mission was to clear a field on which to establish the "American way of life," which eventually came to be understood as the customs of the white, middle-class, Bible-believing (Protestant) family.

Therefore, despite a Constitution that prohibits mandating any religious test for political office, candidates have learned to advertise the fact that they are people of faith. At political rallies they conclude their speeches by invoking God's blessing. They campaign at "prayer breakfasts," and they lard their addresses with biblical references. President-elects have voluntarily added the phrase "so help me God" to the oath of office mandated by the Constitution, and most have taken that oath with their hands on a Bible, claiming the Bible's God as their witness.[21] In American political life, the Bible serves as *the* sacred object that validates the nation, its mission, and its values. The Bible is less a source of guidance[22] than a holy icon that reassure's the nation that it has God's backing.

In recent years fears have been mounting in some religious circles that the God-ordained American way of life is being undermined by ethnic diversity[23] and rampant secularism. The result has been an increasing call for the public display (*i.e.,* ritual veneration) of the Bible and acknowledgment of its role as the guarantor of essential American values.

The fear of those who sense a threat to the country's religious underpinnings has a basis in a situation that is changing. Although America has always been home to a variety of Christian groups, for much of the country's history most of these have been variations on a common (Calvinist) type. The result was a general consensus of opinion on the Bible's importance and its general message. No one used to object, therefore, if textbooks in public schools drew their lessons from the Bible and the school day began with readings from the Scriptures and prayers "in the name of Jesus". Students recited the pledge of allegiance to the American flag along with the Lord's Prayer. Patriotism and Protestant piety throve in a symbiotic relationship that few once thought to question.

This age of innocence ended in the 1960s, when increasing numbers of groups and individuals began to insist on rigorous enforcement of the Constitutional prohibition of state-mandated religion. Prayer and Bible reading disappeared from the public schools, and the stage was set for a major struggle over the role that the Christian faith should play in American society. As in the 1920s when the Darwinian theory of evolution set religious conservatives and liberals to battling over the nation's soul, advocates for opposing positions on the role of religion in American public life forced test cases into the courts.

Some of the more ingenious of the test cases involve the right to display copies of the Ten Commandments in government buildings. What makes this a contentious issue is the difficulty of characterizing the commandments. They certainly derive from a religious text, the Hebrew Bible,[24] and a few of them demand acknowledgment of God. However, they articulate principles of justice that are fundamental to many secular legal and moral codes. It might be argued that it makes sense to post a commandment prohibiting murder in a courthouse where murderers are tried, convicted, and punished. But parties that object to displaying the commandments argue that the true intent of their opponents is to associate the Bible with the country's foundational legal documents and thereby inch America closer to declaring itself a Christian nation. Moses' tablets could become the proverbial camel's nose poking under the Constitution's tent.

When cases involving the right to display the Ten Commandments are appealed to the Supreme Court, they are, ironically, decided in a building whose eastern pediment features a statue of Moses with his tablets. Despite this architectural legacy, the Supreme Court has thus far leaned in the direction of prohibiting similar displays in other government buildings. In 1980, for example, it struck down a state law that required Kentucky's public schools to post copies of the commandments. This, however, did not definitively decide the issue, for being required to do something and being permitted to do it are quite different things. Therefore, new cases were launched to discover the limits of the permissible. In June of 2005 the Supreme Court ruled against posting copies of the commandments — this time in Kentucky's courthouses — even when these were accompanied by other historically influential legal documents (e.g., the Magna Carta).

This raised the issue of what to do about some quite substantial displays that had been in place at some courthouses for a long time. In 1956, Cecil B. de Mille released an epic film version of Moses' story called *The Ten Commandments*. His studio's promoters and some private individuals who were inspired by the film raised money for public monuments depicting Moses' tablets. In 1961, the Fraternal Order of Eagles erected a six-foot tall granite replica on the grounds of the Texas state capitol. The courts decided that because its presence there had gone unchallenged for over 40 years, it could remain. Time had blunted its religious significance by integrating it into the historical context of the capitol's grounds. Its role as an artifact documenting a period in American history overwhelmed its status as a religious text.

Such was not the case for a newer monument. In 2001, Roy Moore, an Alabama judge, installed a 5,300 pound granite model of the Ten Commandments in his state's supreme court building. In 2003, when federal officials ordered him to remove it, he refused — with the result that he was removed from office, taking his "rock" with him. This made him something of a martyred hero to the religious right and encouraged his ambition to run for the office of governor. The weighty object that was the bone of contention was then placed on a flatbed truck and dispatched on a tour of America to rally support for his cause.

No one involved in Judge Moore's project seemed to have noticed the theological contradiction involved in inviting the public to turn out to venerate Moses' mobile stone tablets. If they had read what was written on those tablets, they might have noticed that high on the list of the divine mandates is a prohibition against making "for yourself an idol, whether in the form of anything that is in heaven above, or that is on the earth beneath, or that is in the water under the earth" (Exodus 20:4). Although this was surely not what they intended, it was what they did — as ancient pagans would instantly have recognized. Pharaoh's Egyptians, who gathered to venerate the image of Amon-Ra as it was carried through the streets of Thebes, would have spotted a kinship with the Christians who paid their respects to Alabama's granite tablets as they passed by on their flatbed truck.

This whole episode might be dismissed as a farcical example of the law of unintended consequences — a result of excess zeal undermining its own principles. After all, any readers of the Bible should be able instantly to spot a graven image — particularly if they were focusing their attention on the story of Moses. Moses' displeasure with idolatry even led him to grind a graven image to powder, mix it with water, and force his people literally to consume the object of their misdirected faith (Exodus 32:20). Were Moses still around, Judge Moore's supporters might have been condemned to a massive dose of "salts."

Idolatry is a perennial threat to biblical religion, for the kind of God the Bible describes is difficult to conceptualize. People find worship easier when they have a tangible anchor for their faith. Ancient pagans sculpted images of gods in human and animal form. Jews, despite being acutely mindful of the Torah's prohibition of idolatry, still dress Torah scrolls in velvet robes and silver ornaments and carry them about in ritual procession. Orthodox Christians kneel before icons. Catholics venerate images of saints, relics of martyrs, and the consecrated host enshrined in a golden monstrance.

Protestants share this human appetite for something that brings God down to earth and projects Him into our realm, but the Reformation stripped them of every sacred object but the Bible. By default therefore, the Bible literally became the center of worship in many Protestant churches. In the ancient Middle East gods were pictured standing on pedestals or mounted on animals. The virility of Canaanite deities was symbolized by imagining them mounted invisibly on the backs of bulls (the Bible's much maligned golden calves). The Ark of the Covenant served as the throne for an invisible divine presence the Hebrews called Yahweh. Protestants give central place in their sanctuaries to pulpits or tables on which huge Bibles lie permanently splayed. The Protestant faithful are terribly tempted to think of God as somehow captured between the covers of *the* book.

Ensuring the appropriate use for that book is, therefore, a matter of great importance not just for the private lives of America's Protestants and other Christians. Given the influence the book has on validating American policies, how it is understood may be of global significance.

A Bible conceived as the Word of God is far less vulnerable to abuse than a Bible that is literally thought to be the words of God. The former sheds the light of revelation only when inspired by God's grace, but the latter is totally under human control and subject to human manipulation. Anyone who claims to be able to speak God's words — no matter how worshipfully and respectfully — usurps God's place. A faith that is guided by a relationship with a living God produces fruit quite different from that of a religion governed by a dead text — by a collection of some 700,000 words credited to a deity who last spoke 2,000 years ago.

A faith that is a living relationship is not likely to produce a believer who claims absolute knowledge of God's will. Even a human spouse, if wise, learns never to presume to speak for his or her mate, and good friends always honor the right of their companions to represent themselves. People who believe that they can speak for God by quoting Scripture all too easily abrogate to themselves the authority to enforce God's will. The striving for heaven that begins by quoting God's "words" ends in the hellish journey of the suicide bomber.

It takes humility, patience, and hope to discern God's Word in a Bible that is read as the product of the prayers, meditations, and insights of untold generations of ardent searchers for meaning and purpose. If Christians are to avoid the temptation to commit the kinds of horrendous acts that have so often brought faith into disrepute, they need to resign themselves to living within their human limitations. God is not held captive in a book and cannot be compelled to speak by quoting the words of a book. With the Spirit's guidance God's Word shines through those words, but it should never be forgotten that those words are the words of people who have struggled (sometimes magnificently but always imperfectly) to hear God's "still, small voice" (I Kings 19:12).

NOTES

1   Unless otherwise indicated, the Bible is quote in the New Revised Standard Version (Zondervan, 1989).

2   Augustine, *Confessions*, translated by R. S. Pine-Coffin (NY: Penguin Books, 1961), p. 96.

3   Quoted in: Randall Balmer, *God in the White House: A History* (NY: HarperCollins e-Books), p. 147.

4   Pew Forum on Religion and Public Life, "U.S. Religious Life Survey" (June 23, 2008), http://pewforum.org;category Index.aspx?id=80&pages8 (accessed 19 July 2010).

5   Andrew Sullivan, "My Problem with Christianism: A Believer Spells Out the Difference Between Faith and a Political Agenda," *Time* (May 15, 2006), p. 74.

6   Letter to the Editor signed by Martyn Whittaker, *Time* (June 5, 2006), p. 12.

7   Financial Times/Harris Poll (December 20, 2006), "Religious Views and Beliefs Vary Greatly by Country." http://www.harrisinteractive.com/news/allnewbydate.asp?n ewsID=1131 (accessed 19 July 2010).

8   Ruth Gledhill, "Churchgoing on Its Knees as Christianity Falls Out of Favour," *The Sunday Times* (May 8, 2008), timesonline.co.uk/tol/comment/faith'article3890080.ece.

9   Religion has been receiving so much bad press that some scholars have felt called to defend not a specific faith, but the concept of faith itself: Huston Smith, *Why Religion Matters: The Fate of the Human Spirit in an Age of Disbelief* (NY: HarperCollins, 2000); John F. Haught, *God and the New Atheism: A Critical Response to Dawkins, Harris, and Hitchens* (Louisville, KY: Westminster/John Knox, 2008).

10   The verses from Exodus 20 quoted at the head of this chapter

11   Prominent Americans, such as Thomas Jefferson and Elizabeth Cady Stanton, have been moved to edit the Bible so as to cut out the "chaff" and reduce it to its "core" elements.

12   This may explain why as many as 45% of Americans claim to believe in Creationism. See: A. J. Jacobs, *The Year of Living Biblically* (NY: Simon and Schuster, 2007), p. 57.

13   The Creation stories and the Book of Genesis are dealt with in greater detail in chapter 6.

14   Discussion of this passage and its rabbinic interpretation is found in: A. J. Jacobs, *The Year of Living Biblically*, pp. 111-112.

15   "Perhaps the strangest claim ever made for any written document in history is that its words are or somehow contain the 'Word of God.' Such an assertion assumes that God is a very human-like being." John Shelby Spong, *The Sins of Scripture: Exposing the Bible's Texts of Hate to Reveal the God of Love* (Harper San Francisco, 2005), p. 142.

16   See: Jonathan Kirsch, *God Against the Gods: The History of the War Between Monotheism and Polytheism* (NY: Penguin Group, 2004).

17 Susan B. Anthony, speech to the National American Women's Suffrage Association in 1896 during a debate over Elizabeth Cady Stanton's *Women's Bible*. See: Jack Humberman, *The Quotable Atheist* (NY: Nation Books, 2007), p. 13.

18 See: Mark Juergensmeyer, *Terror in the Mind of God* (Berkeley and Los Angeles, CA: University of California Press, 2000).

19 John Winthrop, the image is drawn from a sermon ("A Model for Christian Charity") he preached in 1630 on Matthew 5:14,"You are the light of the world. A city built on a hill cannot be hid." Alan Heimert and Andrew Debaco, eds., *The Puritans in America: A Narrative Anthology* (Cambridge, MA: Harvard University Press, 1985), pp. 89-92.

20 Abraham Lincoln, message to Congress, December 1, 1862.

21 Protests were raised when a Muslim congressman recently took the oath of office with his hand on the Qu'ran.

22 Many people have wondered how Americans reconcile their passionate devotion to individualistic capitalism and their professed Christian values. The former would seem to encourage selfishness and the latter self-sacrifice. Some religious leaders have prospered simply by insisting (against the evidence) that Christianity is capitalism and that its practice leads to wealth and success. What has recently been characterized as the "Prosperity Gospel" is only a new name for an old heresy that has enjoyed surges of popularity throughout American history.

23 It was once unthinkable that a Catholic could be elected to

the American presidency. That barrier fell in 1961 with the election of John F. Kennedy, but it is still the case that one must be at least a nominal Christian to make a serious bid for the White House. The false claim that Barach Obama is a Muslim was cited by many American voters as a reason for opposing his run for the presidency.

24 The Bible records them in two slightly different versions in Exodus 20:1-17 and Deuteronomy 5:6-21. Most of the principles they endorse are not unique to the Bible.

2

A Polarized Faith

Should mainline churches choose to remain as they are . . . their survival in the long run seems extremely doubtful. They could sputter on for decades without orthodox Christianity, of course, appealing to an assortment of professors, radical feminists, and vegetarians. But their appeal would be increasingly minimal.[1]
— Thomas C. Reeves

Whether true or not, men have always believed in "unscientific concepts," and these beliefs often are the real "facts" which shape their destiny.[2]
— Max I. Dimont

The Gathering Storm

American society entered an era of accelerating change during the second half of the 20th century. Immigration and differing birth rates among ethnic groups increased the diversity of the country's population, and successful civil rights movements had implications for the nation's balance of political power. White and Protestant Christian majorities, whose dominance had never previously been challenged, awakened to the realization that they were headed for minority status. Some Americans were alarmed, for they saw this as a threat not only to their self-interests, but to what they regarded as their nation's authentic identity.

The changing demographics prompted debates about the characteristics of a "true American," and this raised the issue of the role that religion has played (and should or should not play) in shaping American values. The country that the Founders knew when they drafted the Constitution had a fairly homogenous culture. It was dominated by people with British and north European backgrounds, most of whom professed some form of Protestantism. Therefore, it is reasonable to wonder if the Founders, who enshrined freedom of religion in the Constitution, ever imagined that this situation might change — that Americans might not always share a common set of "Christian values." Given the European example, they understood how contentious and divisive religious differences can be, but did they (under the influence of 18th-century rationalism) believe that Americans would outgrow the kind of religion that had kept Europeans fighting among themselves for two centuries? Did they naively trust that all "true" religions would ultimately converge? If this was their assumption, did the Constitution they wrote unwittingly commit their homeland to a dangerous course by stripping its government of the power of "prohibiting the free exercise" of religion?

In reality, American courts have seldom hesitated to intervene whenever judges conclude that the religious practices of a minority (e.g., polygamy, animal sacrifice, etc.) are at odds with generally accepted standards of behavior.[3] Whenever the constitutionality of their rulings has been challenged, the state's power has usually been upheld. But afterward, little may be done to enforce the court's interpretation of the law. A spirit of "live-and-let-live" prevails unless a group pushes the limits. Polygamy, for instance, has been tolerated if it does not involve suspicion of sexual exploitation of minors.

Some Americans, however, who would favor taking a stronger and more rigorously consistent stand. Rather than confine religious regulation to the extreme behavior of peripheral groups, they would have the United States openly embrace a Christian identity and alter its Constitution to mandate their understanding of Christian principles. Such a step would lift the lid from a veritable barrel of irascible worms, for it would force

Americans to agree on an answer to a question that has threatened to divide them since the nation's founding: *What kind of Christianity is American?*[4]

The rigorous moralism and intellectualism of colonial New England's Puritans did not spread to other regions of the country, and the Enlightenment rationalism of the Virginian Deists who played major roles in the revolutionary government never held much appeal for the American masses. At significant periods in the country's history, large numbers of Protestant Americans have considered the Christianity of Roman Catholics (a papal monarchy) to be incompatible with the principles of American democracy. The various Orthodox Christian communities also cherish ethnic roots (Greek, Russian, Serbian, Armenian, *etc.*) that suggest that being something more than generically American is essential to their faith.

The most powerful religious influence on the formation of early American identity was a species of Protestant evangelicalism. Camp meetings proliferated during the Federal Period, and the denominations that enthusiastically adopted the camp meeting style (*e.g.*, the Methodists, Baptists, and Presbyterians) were most successful in spreading institutionalized religion to what had previously been a largely unchurched nation. Evangelical piety flourished during the 19th century, for it suited the sentimentality of the Victorian era and was congruent with the middle-class values of an increasingly prosperous and upwardly mobile Protestant, if multi-denominational and unofficial, establishment. Evangelicals dominated leadership of the major religious associations, and their faith inspired mass movements backing major social reforms (*e.g.*, abolition of slavery, temperance, and compulsory public education) that transformed American society.

Not all evangelicals were cast in the same mold. Distinctions emerged, and toward the end of the 19th century, a form of "liberal Christianity" began to attract a following. It favored a more formal, less emotional style of worship than was favored by many evangelicals, and it advocated a different approach to working for the Kingdom of God. Generally speaking, evangelicals hoped to reform society by saving people one at a time — by persuading individual sinners to make decisions for Christ that would transform their behavior. Liberals, on the other hand, approached the salvation of individuals through the restructuring of society — by attacking the institutions, traditions, and prejudices that they believed fostered self-destructive behaviors. Liberal Christians fought corporations and political machines, supported labor unions, and tried to legislate and enforce what they understood to be responsible codes of conduct.

The early 20th century saw the rise of the Social Gospel, a liberal theology centered on the Old Testament prophets' call for social justice and Jesus' assertion that the poor and defenseless are closest to God's heart. The Social Gospel placed the struggle to improve this world ahead of preparing for a world-to-come. It sometimes implied that the path to heaven was a perfected American way of life. When the confident optimism that characterizes the American spirit led liberal Christians to overplay their hands, they cultivated utopian dreams and ignored the Bible's darker warnings about the pervasive nature of sin. Progress in science, technology, and education encouraged their assumption that humanity could be perfected and that heaven could be brought down to Earth. All that was needed was hard work, self-discipline, and good strategic plans for government and social service agencies.

Eventually, however, it became clear that when Christianity's ethical ideals are detached from its message of sin, grace, and redemption, the faith degenerates into shallow socialism. Although Marxism and 20th-century communism were ardently anti-religious, some liberal Christians found much in them to admire. As a result, many of their fellow Americans began to have serious reservations about liberal Christianity. The carnage of the world wars raised up a generation of "neo-orthodox" theologians who corrected the excessive optimism of the Social Gospel by renewing an emphasis on the cross and the costliness of grace.

While all this was going on, American evangelicals also began to sing from a new hymn book. Throughout most of the 19th century they had been confident that religion, science, and democracy were working together for the good of humanity.[5] But as liberals began to challenge the evangelicals' long-standing dominance of American religion, evangelicals' outlook darkened. In particular, they feared that ideas that liberals embraced — namely, Darwin's theory of evolution and new critical techniques for interpreting the Bible's texts — were undermining the foundations of faith. It seemed that science, which some had assumed would assist faith in bringing in the Kingdom of God, had suddenly turned on them. Science had declared war on religion, and they, therefore, were obliged to make a choice (rather than seek a compromise) between faith and reason.[6]

American Christianity had always had "conservative right" and "liberal left" wings. Tension between their partisans had divided some denominations (*e.g.*, most notably, the Presbyterians) and spawned a few heresy trials of prominent clergy, but the two opposing camps usually managed to coexist without much difficulty. With the start of the new century, however, things escalated toward a showdown. Distinctions between liberals and conservatives grew sharper as they began to compete for control of America's *de facto* Protestant establishment.

Between 1910 and 1913 a series of privately funded pamphlets, *The Fundamentals*, was published for free distribution "to every pastor, evangelist, minister, theological professor, theological student, Sunday school superintendent, YMCA and YWCA secretary in the English-speaking world."[7] The authors of *The Fundamentals* claimed that in order legitimately to claim to be a Christian one had to affirm five ideas that, they alleged, were indispensable to the faith tradition: 1) that literal reading of the Bible yielded inerrant information, 2) that Jesus was born of a virgin, 3) that God required Jesus' death as payment for sin, 4) that Jesus' body was physically resurrected, and 5) that all of his miracles were historical events. Curiously absent from the list of "fundamentals" was any reference to what Jesus himself said was fundamental to faith:

> You shall love the Lord your God with all your heart, and with all your soul and with all your mind. This is the great and first commandment. And the second is like it, you shall love your neighbor as yourself. On these two commandments depend all the law and the prophets (Matthew 22:37-40)

The five fundamentals were inspired less by a desire to summarize the Christian faith than to challenge the willingness of religious liberals to tailor their theology to accommodate the new sciences. The fundamentals were all ideas that liberal scholarship had called into question as incompatible with reason and modern points of view.

The Fundamentals found an enthusiastic readership, and the pamphlets launched a "fundamentalist" movement that leapt across denominational lines. Fundamentalism could be easily conjoined with a type of evangelicalism that valued experiential religion more highly than theological understanding, and its appeal owed much to the anti-intellectualism and suspicion of scholarly elites that is a persistent feature of American popular culture. Fundamentalism and evangelical Protestantism have had great success (even in some well-educated circles) recruiting followers with the promise that the simple faith of humble folk can banish doubt and chart a clear path through the complexities and disorienting relativism of life in the "post-modern" era.

Americans tend to denigrate intellectuals (*e.g.*, "egg heads" and "policy wonks") and admire plain speakers, but they do not respect fools. In the first half of the 20th century, fundamentalists blundered into a situation that exposed them and their conservative Christian allies to widespread ridicule. In 1925 a law prohibiting the teaching of the theory of evolution in Tennessee's public schools was tested in the infamous "Scopes Monkey Trial." The courtroom hosted a media circus, and the nation followed with glee as Clarence Darrow made a laughingstock out of the fundamentalists' champion, William Jennings Bryan.

The humiliation was so great that fundamentalists retreated from public view for decades. They abandoned the struggle for control of the major Protestant denominations and withdrew into a world of their own — a bastion of Bible colleges and independent churches. A new (to the modern, if not to the medieval, era) doctrine spread through their ranks. The confident evangelicals of the 19th century had embraced a post-millennialism, a doctrine that anticipated the world's redemption and transformation. A darker pre-millennial vision held more appeal for the 20th century's marginalized fundamentalists. It predicted a long era of painful struggle as history drew to a violent end and confirmed the fundamentalists' suspicion that the hostile, corrupt world that mocked their faith was beyond saving. The task of the true believer, they concluded, was to hunker down and avoid contamination from the world while waiting for an angry, vengeful God to fulfill the Bible's apocalyptic prophecies. The pre-millenialists pined for "the Rapture," a scenario for the last days created by piecing together texts from different parts of the Bible. They believed that God's faithful remnant was to be lifted ("raptured") into the sky to escape the suffering that was to be justly inflicted on Earth's sinful hordes.

Disaffected conservative Christians were content to sit on the sidelines of American public life until the 1960s, when a convergence of events and movements spurred them to action. They suddenly reversed course, left the safe confines of their independent churches, entered the realm of politics, and openly declared their intention to rescue America from the forces of "secular humanism" and scientific modernism. Christian fundamentalism asserted itself in the West just as Islamic fundamentalism began to make its power known elsewhere in the world.

America's religious right was roused to action by developments that it perceived as threatening the very survival of Christianity in America and, therefore, of the role that America was to play as God's chosen instrument in the drama of salvation. By the 1960s the surging power of popular culture — of television, films, and new genres of music — had begun to breach the defenses of conservative enclaves and nudge the country in directions that were anathema to the right. Free love movements, drug cultures, rock-and-roll sensuality, and paeans to self-indulgent excess of all kinds undermined values that many conservative Christians assumed were essential to the pursuit of personal salvation and the preservation of the divine mandate that made America "the last, best hope of earth."[8] A surging youth movement contributed to the anxiety of religious conservatives by encouraging challenges to parental authority. An anti-war movement offended their sense of patriotic duty and love of country. Southern states (where the largest number of evangelical and fundamentalist groups was to be found) were particularly agitated by a civil rights movement that indicted the morality of what many cherished as their traditional way of life. A feminist movement seemed set on subverting what they believed to be *the* Christian concept of the family and gender relations — as did a gay-rights movement that religious conservatives feared was designed to make converts to a "lifestyle" that the Scriptures, they claimed, explicitly condemned.

The catalyst that may have done most to galvanize action by Christian conservatives was the Supreme Court's decision in 1962 to ban prayer in the public schools. A series of additional cases soon followed further limiting religious activities, displays, and instruction. And the *Roe vs. Wade* decision in 1973, which affirmed abortion rights, only confirmed conservative Christians in their belief that Satanic powers were assaulting God's chosen country.

The North's victory in the Civil War had established the Democratic Party's dominance over the South, the evangelical heartland. The Republican Party, heir to the hated Lincoln's legacy, was slow to make inroads into the South. It drew leaders from a northern elite and support from the prosperous folk who affiliated with the mainline Protestant denominations. The Civil Rights Act of 1964 altered these long-standing affiliations. When five Southern states, which had not been in the Republican column since the Civil War, switched sides in that year's presidential election, an alliance between right-wing politics and right-wing religion was born. This was arguably the most significant development in late 20th- century American politics.

The rise of an assertive religious right in the late 20th century, like the emergence of fundamentalism in the early years of that century, increased both the political and religious polarization of American society. The news media have accustomed Americans to think of their country as divided between blue (liberal Democratic) and red (conservative Republican) states — although shifting allegiances in the 2008 presidential election rearranged colored maps and prompted some regions to be described as "purple". Spokespersons for the right fulminate against the machinations of a "liberal establishment" that frustrates the will of a silent, but allegedly conservative, majority. Advocates for the left warn that "a vast right-wing conspiracy" poses a growing threat to American liberties.

Political allegiances have become so closely associated with religious positions that whether a church's congregation is perceived as leaning right or leaning left may now be the most important factor in determining an individual's decision to affiliate with it. Duane Murray Oldfield notes:

> A strong case can be made that denominational differences are losing their import and that cross denominational splits between religious liberals and conservatives are coming to replace them as the fundamental cleavages in American religious life . . . . Americans, it is argued, are dividing into more distinct conservative and liberal camps; the religious center is not holding.[9]

When a society's center weakens, willingness to cooperate diminishes, compromise becomes difficult, leadership stalemates, and hostility intensifies. Religious divisions are particularly troubling when they enter the political realm, for principles of faith absolutize conflict. Religion turns what is essentially a fight for the advantage of one group over another into a struggle to destroy all impediments to God's will. The stakes in such campaigns rise so high and the consciences of those who fight them remain so clear, that no price can seem too great to pay and no strategy too extreme to adopt in pursuit of victory. History is filled with examples of individuals and nations driven to madness and self-destruction by the presumption that they were empowered to act for God.

The Strength of the Right: Cloaked Accommodation

The division between right and left in America is not trending toward an equal split of the population. Although the American "middle" is quite large, conservatives are far more confident of their appeal to the masses than are liberals. While many politicians and less exalted citizens proudly embrace the conservative label, the partisans of the left often avoid using the term *liberal*. *Progressive* has become the adjective of choice for the left and its causes. Conservative politicians and religious leaders brand liberals as elitists and claim that the majority of ordinary Americans favors their agenda. Questions seldom arise about the patriotism of conservatives, but liberals find themselves on the defensive — accused of hostility to the "real America."

Despite the right's claim that the media is controlled by liberals, conservatives dominate politically oriented talk-shows on radio, and virtually all religiously themed television caters to conservatives. Evangelical and fundamentalist groups are also much more successful than liberals at blurring the line between church and state. They publish so-called "voters' guides" to marshal support for right-wing politicians and programs and then distribute them through church networks. Religious groups (*e.g.*, Focus on the Family) function as unofficial adjuncts to right-wing political campaigns, and conservative politicians, who solicit support from the religious right, have cavalierly skirted laws governing church-state relations. When Ronald Reagan first ran for the presidency in August of 1980, he journeyed to Texas to address the Religious Roundtable, a large body of conservative Christian leaders. After being introduced by a Baptist minister as "God's man," he told the assembly, "I know you can't endorse me, but I want you to know that I endorse you and what you are doing."[10] Reverend Jerry Falwell, pastor of the hyper-conservative Thomas Road Baptist Church of Lynchburg, Virginia, then reminded those in attendance that although their organization could not endorse a candidate without losing its tax exempt status, he hoped that they would vote for the "Reagan of their choice."[11]

It is instructive to compare this cynical flaunting of the intent of the law — an act that passed without legal consequences for Falwell and others — with the response to a sermon preached by Rev. J. Edwin Bacon at All Saints Episcopal Church, Pasadena, California, on October 31, 2004. On the eve of another presidential election, Rev. Bacon's meditation imagined a conversation involving Jesus Christ, George W. Bush, and John Kerry. He did not endorse a candidate. He acknowledged that thoughtful people could take opposing points of view, and he encouraged his hearers to vote according to their best lights. A few months later, however, the Internal Revenue Service informed the church in which he had preached that it was suspected of having forfeited its tax-exempt status by engaging in political advocacy and that an inquiry was being initiated. The process dragged on for two years and cost the congregation $200,000 in legal fees. In the end the church retained its tax-exemption, but the case only confused guidelines governing freedom of speech from pulpits.[12]

It may not be irrelevant to note that All Saints Episcopal, Pasadena, is one of California's major, overtly liberal congregations. Its reputation is apparently what drew the ire of a conservative administration, for the IRS did not act against the First Baptist Church of Springdale, Arkansas, where, on July 4, 2004, the Rev. Ronnie Floyd, the megachurch's pastor, had preached an overtly partisan sermon. Rev. Floyd (who later sought the presidency of the Southern Baptist Convention) specifically lauded the policies of the Bush administration, criticized John Kerry, and used the church's audio-visual equipment to highlight his message's patent enthusiasm for George W. Bush.[13]

The clergy who serve liberal mainline congregations might be excused if they sometimes seem dispirited and unsure. Many of them must view their preaching as a "still, small voice" that struggles to compete with a thunderous cacophony of opposing religious messages from conservative sources. None of the liberal clergy is to be found thriving at the head of a wealthy television ministry. None has received an invitation to the White House to serve as personal chaplain to the nation's leader. Few are solicited for endorsements by political candidates.[14]

The fact that liberal clergy are given scant attention by politicians may not be unrelated to the decades of declining membership reported by their denominations. Many commentators have blamed the pastors themselves for the fading popularity of the traditions they represent. In their defense, clergy find it hard to argue that they are hapless victims of a rising tide of unbelief in American society. The fading stars of their mainline denominations dim in the powerful light cast by the rising sun of the independent, conservative megachurch phenomenon. Religious institutions featuring campuses, lavish facilities, thousands of members, and multifaceted programs run by large professional staffs are springing up in every part of the country.

Thomas C. Reeves has argued the case for those who believe that the mainline denominations are declining because their leaders are out of step with the majority of Americans. The traditionally dominant (and allegedly liberal) denominations are losing ground, he insists, because a gap has opened between their laity and their clergy.[15] He believes that the latter are stuck in the outdated trendy movements of the 1960s and have no firm convictions and no commitment to the core doctrines of the Christian faith. He writes:

> Here we are at the root of things: the submission of liberal Protestantism to a secular gospel rests upon a failure to accept the essentials of the Christian faith. . . . [T]he first and most critical step in halting the slide of the mainline churches is the restoration of their commitment to orthodox theology. Everything else depends upon that . . . [and] orthodoxy requires faith in an all-powerful God who was and is capable of the miraculous. Christianity without miracles is dead, and its founder and the apostles madmen.[16]

Because the mainline churches, in Reeves' opinion, shy away from asserting the supernaturalism affirmed in their traditional creeds and doctrines and fail to place moral demands on their members, they have nothing to offer potential recruits that these individuals cannot find in a secular club. These churches, therefore, appear (and are) spiritually irrelevant. People, Reeves persuasively argues, are drawn to churches that give meaning to their lives by making demands on them and taking firm doctrinal stands. The mainline denominations fail at this because they have watered down their theologies and compromised their ethical teachings. The crucial point, according to Reeves, is whether or not there is "truth, supernaturally revealed in Christianity, that lies beyond our present understanding of things, truth that is unchanging and absolutely vital to our present and future?"[17]

R. Albert Mohler, ninth president of Southern Baptist Theological Seminary, makes a similar argument and poses a question that liberals ought seriously to consider. Like Reeves, he claims that relativism in theology and ethics explains the failure of the mainline churches "to remain 'relevant.'" They have blurred the distinction between a life of faith and a life guided by secular values by backing off from the Bible's assertion that Christ is the only path to salvation and by compromising "Christian principles" to accommodate "permissive sexuality." Conservatives' churches have flourished, Mohler says, because they "maintain clear boundaries between belief and unbelief." He warns that "without a firm grasp of the gospel, a bold commitment to Biblical authority, and a clear vision for evangelism, churches and denominations are destined for decline and eventual dissipation." Conservative churches are growing, he insists, because they resist the forces of modernism that, by denying supernaturalism, promote secularism. "Once the churches have been thoroughly secularized," Mohler asks, "what value remains in church membership and denominational identification?"[18]

Liberal Christians need to address the claim (made by Reeves, Mohler, and many others) that an individual's only option is to embrace supernaturalism or surrender to secularism. They need to make clear how an authentic biblical faith can be built on a foundation that accommodates science, historical-critical interpretations of Scripture, and reason. To do so, they need to clarify the relationship between God's Word and the Bible's human words.

Conservative Christians insist that liberal interpreters rob the Scriptures of their authority and clear the way for relativism. By twisting traditional Christian beliefs to make them accommodate current moral and intellectual fads, they rob the Bible of its function as the fixed anchor for a timeless faith.

The promise of a viable alternative to "wishy-washy" liberalism is doubtless an effective recruiting tool for the religious right. People long for certainty and are impatient with qualifiers and complications. They are drawn to leaders, movements, and organizations that scorn complexity and confidently propose simple answers for complex questions. Many people have willingly surrendered their autonomy and acquiesced to authoritarianism to achieve certainty. A sense of relief accompanies submission to a leader or ideology, for submission offers escape from the guilt of doubt and from the responsibility of making decisions for oneself. It is tempting to hearken to promises that peace of mind can be instantly achieved simply by mustering the will to believe. Many popular religious leaders have taken their cue from a phrase that has been derived (with questionable accuracy) from the works of Tertullian, a 3rd-century Latin preacher: *Credo quia absurdum* ("I believe because it is absurd.").[19] They refuse to entertain any challenge to their beliefs and take pride in declaring that their faith overcomes the need for rational support or evidence.

Doubt can sometimes be suppressed by refusing to acknowledge it. Doing so may actually feel like a virtuous act — a muscular embrace of Christian humility. Tertullian's insistence that faith need not account for itself in the court of reason nor be troubled by contradictions, inconsistencies, or lack of evidence is seductive. It can seem preferable to the daunting task of trying to figure things out for oneself. To attempt to do so, after all, is to risk the possibility of creating a private religion that is nothing more than a projection of the self. There is, however a third possibility — a critical relationship with a faith tradition. The choice is not between living in an ancient house that provides inadequate shelter or tearing the old place down to erect an insubstantial new structure. Renovation, renewal, and updating offer a more promising option.

Religious conservatives often insist that their faith is true because it is based on a superior respect for tradition. The past can certainly be a source of wisdom, and respect for tradition counters a dangerous tendency of the human ego — the inclination to regard oneself as the center of the universe and the final arbiter of what is right and wrong. By honoring tradition we acknowledge that we did not make the world that shapes our lives and that the world does not exist to serve us. We acknowledge that we live amidst tides of phenomena with which we must come to terms. Tradition also comforts us with the assurance that we do not face life's perennial challenges alone or unarmed. Others have trod this path before us and left us a legacy of hard-won lessons from which we might draw guidance. As the medieval schoolmaster, Bernard of Chartres, is reported to have said: "We are like dwarfs riding on the shoulders of giants. We see more and farther than the giants — not because we are physically or intellectually their superiors, but because we have been lifted up by their great stature."[20]

Tradition alone, however, is not enough. Living creatively in the present requires more than blind allegiance to the past, for the world is a kaleidoscope of shifting circumstances. It is commonly said that those who do not know the past are condemned to repeat it, for people do have a depressing tendency to make similar mistakes again and again. But in truth the past never repeats itself. People who claim enduring relevance for their religious tradition need to think seriously about what they are claiming. What is the nature of the authority that a faith tradition can legitimately exercise?

This is a central issue for faiths such as Judaism, Christianity, and Islam, for they are governed by Scriptures that ground them in the distant past. When faithful people try to live strictly within the confines of the early worldviews described in sacred texts and apply the teachings of these texts literally, they may actually subvert the tradition their texts are intended to preserve. For Christians to insist that their faith requires them to adhere to the beliefs and values of the first century is to deny that their faith is a living thing. This runs counter to the history of their faith, for Christianity has inspired a great deal of moral progress over subsequent ages by insisting that its adherents evolve and pursue ever higher standards of love and justice.

The modern world would be a far worse place if the closing of the biblical canon had ended the possibility for progress and social development. Had that been the case, today's Christians would still, like those of the New Testament era, be blind to the immorality of things such as slavery, torture, and imperialistic war. Perhaps the best evidence for the claim that Scripture is divinely inspired is the power that Scripture has to foster a faith that is fundamentally self-critical and, therefore, progressively self-transforming. This is why biblical faith remains alive and enduringly relevant. Time and again, the study of the Bible has inspired people to greater moral sensitivity than is expressed in many of its individual verses.[21] The Bible as a whole has an effect that is greater than the action of its parts. Appropriation of the Judeo-Christian tradition requires the will to be guided by the past while exercising the courage to transcend it.

Although religious conservatives make much of their dedication to unchanging Christian principles and their opposition to "the world," their rhetoric does not conform with their practice. Their thriving megachurches pride themselves on a "contemporary" style of worship consciously designed to conform to their customers' demands. The result is often less a celebration of biblical faith than a fusion of popular culture with vacuous religiosity. These churches dispense with traditional creeds and the theologically demanding texts of traditional hymnody and deliberately blur the distinction between prayer and entertainment. Their congregants cheer sermons condemning the sins of "the world" while surrendering to the erotic throb of a rock band and singing "praise songs" that are carols to carnality. Given what transpires in a hard-rocking megachurch, it is bizarre to hear conservatives indict mainline clergy for the sin of tailoring the gospel to the fads of the world.

It is also the case that, despite what often seems to be assumed, the biblical literalism endorsed by Christian conservatives is not faithful to the way Christians have traditionally read the Bible. Literalism is a fairly recent development in the history of the Church. Its roots go back less than two centuries, and it was specifically repudiated by the Bible's early Christian interpreters. The missionaries who converted the Roman Empire were acutely aware that many educated pagans were put off by the Bible's rough literary style and by some of its cruder, more colorful stories (*e.g.*, I Samuel 18:24-27). They were also puzzled by its many inconsistencies. They solved both these problems by employing allegorical interpretation to reveal deeper meanings than were apparent when texts were read literally. The Bible's seeming deficiencies so troubled St. Augustine of Hippo that he was unable to come to faith until the allegorizing sermons of St. Ambrose of Milan persuaded him that the Bible had a profundity that literal reading had not disclosed.

Contemporary Christian conservatives often dismiss allegorical exegesis — claiming that it is simply a way to make a text mean whatever an interpreter wants it to mean. That is indeed a potential problem with allegory. But the odd thing is that the conservatives who are most insistent on literal interpretation of the Bible are also the people who are most inclined to invent elaborate allegorical interpretations of books such as Daniel and Revelation. Allegory is an indispensable handmaiden for devotees of biblical prophecy. It is their key for unlocking the secrets of the end times.

The Weakness of the Left: Condescending Cowardice

Religious conservatives prosper by claiming to defend the American way of life by recalling the nation to its authentic Christian nature. They claim to oppose the modern secular world while actually accommodating many of its prejudices and appetites. To confirm the rightness of their cause, they call attention to the shrinking membership roles of mainline denominations, and they claim that these churches are declining because their liberal clergy have abandoned "biblical" preaching. They have conformed the Bible's message to the demands of science and "modernism." Therefore, their exegesis of Scripture has brewed a weak tea that has no power to energize faith. Liberal Christianity is alleged to have emasculated the true biblical message by denying its supernatural elements. The result is the promotion of relativism and skepticism instead of faith. People find little spiritual nourishment in such churches and gravitate toward the "strong meat of the gospel" served up by conservative ministries.

Conservatives are justified in accusing their liberal competitors of weakness, but they may not have correctly identified the source of the left's malaise. Sociologists Andrew Greeley and Michael Hout have tested the conservatives' claim that liberals are losing a popularity contest with conservatives and that mainline denominations are bleeding members to the opposition.[22] They write:

> Most observers . . . assume that the conservative churches are growing because of conversions from the mainline churches. The conservatives, it is said, have a strong appeal for American Protestants because of their emphasis on traditional evangelical teachings. The mainline clergy have sent their flocks elsewhere by some combination of liberal politics

and "feel-good" religion. By their collective reckoning, the growth of the conservative denominations represents a reaction against "excessive liberalism" in which people raised in mainline denominations register displeasure with the (supposed) liberal ethos of mainline Protestantism by leaving to join denominations that emphasize the conservative beliefs they share.[23]

Greeley and Hout claim, however, that their research has uncovered "no evidence of massive conversions of mainline Protestants (or Catholics) to the conservatives, despite contrary claims by the conservatives."[24] For one thing, the conservatives' argument that 1960s liberalism is to blame for the decline of the mainline denominations makes no sense given that the demographic shift in favor of conservativism began well before the 1960s. Greeley and Hout also point out that the rate of conversion from mainline to conservative denominations has not changed significantly for at least 75 years — and that this rate is not high.[25]

Greeley and Hout's study concludes that the growth of the religious right and the decline of the left has little to do with the respective orientations of their clergy. It is, they argue, primarily a function of birthrates: "for most of the 20th century, women in conservative Protestant denominations had more children than women in mainline denominations did. The larger families gave conservative denominations such a huge demographic advantage that it explains seventy percent of the conservative upsurge."[26] Much of the remaining difference can be accounted for by the growing social acceptability of conservative faith. Whereas at one time upwardly mobile evangelicals tended to mark the acquisition of middle-class status by leaving their marginalized groups and joining a mainline denomination, this ceased to be the case in the 1970s and 1980s. In the current American environment conservative Christians "are more defiant and less apologetic about their faith than they used to be . . . ."[27] Their religious affiliation is no longer regarded as *declassé*.

Furthermore, Greeley and Hout have found no difference in the ability of mainline denominations and conservative groups to retain the loyalty of their young:

New adult members of conservative congregations are coming from the conservative Protestant homes they were raised in. Their parents were conservative Protestants, and now that they have reached adulthood, they are too. Mainline denominations do almost as well at socializing their young. The advantage goes to the conservative denominations because they start with more children; conservative Protestant women have more children than other Protestant women do. The raw power of demography joins with the staying power of religious socialization to produce growth for conservative denominations.[28]

The hard fact of "differential fertility" means that relatively larger numbers of conservative young are on track for having larger numbers of children. Consequently, Greeley and Hout predict that "the Protestant population will continue to shift in a conservative direction for many years to come, even if no further changes in their underlying behaviors occur."[29]

Despite the fact that Greeley and Hout find no evidence for a mass exodus from the mainline denominations caused by dissatisfaction with the liberalism of out-of-touch leaders, mainline clergy might want to reconsider their recruitment strategies. If, as Greely and Hout suggest, the mainline denominations are shrinking in relative size because of the lesser fertility of their clientele, their leaders need to take care not to alienate their base in the mistaken belief that they are losing sheep to the seductive appeal of the conservative fold.

Many mainline congregations have been tempted to embark on "church growth" strategies that call for them to ape the practices of conservative megachurches. Shrinking congregations reasonably conclude that they need to change their behavior if they hope to survive — and many assume that the most obvious thing to do is to become more like the groups whose popularity they envy. This seems plausible on the surface, but it is seriously flawed strategy for evangelism. If people want what the religious right offers, many congregations do an excellent job of providing it. But a mainline church that tries to find a compromise between its historical traditions and the novelty that has come to be known as "contemporary Christian worship" runs a double risk. Its "blended worship" may diminish its appeal to its core constituency and still be rejected as an inferior product by the kind of potential customer who is attracted to the glittery productions of a megachurch. Rather than play to a competitor's strength, it is wiser to build on one's own.

Church growth strategies often focus on plans for reformatting worship. But a serious attempt at renewal must involve more than deciding to fire the organist and hire a drummer. The central issue for any Protestant "reform" should be a thoughtful reconsideration of how the Word of God is taught and lived. That means coming to a clear understanding of how the Bible serves as the Word of God that inspires and nurtures faith. The true weakness of mainline clergy may be their lack of courage in boldly preaching and teaching what they truly know and believe about the Bible.

For well over a century, a gulf in biblical literacy has been widening between clergy and laity. The professional educations that clergy in the mainline denominations receive have given them a perspective on the Scriptures that they are often reluctant to share with their congregations. The way for their denominations to begin rebuilding the strength and integrity of their parishes, therefore, may be to clarify and communicate their understanding of how the Scriptures function as the Word of God. At least one major mainline denomination considered (but did not embrace) this option.

The United Methodist Church has published a professional journal for its clergy called *The Circuit Rider*. The title honors the itinerant clergy who, in the 18th and early 19th centuries, began the work of frontier evangelism that, for a time, made Methodism America's largest (and, as some historians have claimed, most American) Protestant denomination. Instead of settling down and serving a single congregation for an extended period of time, circuit riders circulated through the sparsely settled countryside gathering people from scattered farmsteads for occasional services of worship.

The legacy of mobility Methodist pastors have inherited from their circuit-riding predecessors is now more theoretical than real, and most of them have much better educations than were available to the men on horseback. Journals, such as *The Circuit Rider*, were designed to provide them with information they need to discharge their professional responsibilities. Given the specialized nature of the intended readership, such journals can have the air of a conversation among insiders. Their articles tend to be positive, encouraging, upbeat, and seldom self-critical. However, the featured article for the April 1994 issue of *The Circuit Rider* was a striking exception. It did not focus on a strategy for improving some pastoral function or church activity. It called for the denomination's clergy boldly to rethink their preaching and teaching ministries. It implied that a lack of courage, or excess of caution, had resulted in a *de facto* conspiracy among clergy to leave the laity in ignorance.

The issue's cover depicted a book (labeled "Bible Commentary") bound by knotted strings that were beginning to come unraveled. Blazoned across the top of the page in inch-high letters was: "It's Time for You to Tell the Truth." The point was that significant numbers of Methodist clergy had not been leveling with their people about their understanding of the Bible and the time had come for them to do so.

The author of the article, J. Phillip Wogaman, was not an

outsider, a maverick, or a peevish critic with an axe to grind. He was the senior minister of one of Methodism's most prominent urban congregations, Foundry United Methodist Church in Washington, D.C. His article reflected strong feelings, but it was not the hasty product of an angry impulse. It grew out of six years of reflection on an event that had transpired at the 1988 General Conference (*i.e.*, national meeting) of the United Methodist Church. Reverend Wogaman pondered for a long time before going public with his concerns.

In 1988 the delegates to United Methodism's General Conference had been asked to clarify the denomination's position on the authority of Scripture by adopting the following statement: "[W]e recognize that Scripture contains both authoritative witness to the Word of God and expressions of human and cultural limitation."[30] This cautiously worded proposal would have put Methodism on record as opposing Biblical literalism and fundamentalism. It implied that care had to be taken, when teaching and preaching the Bible, to distinguish the timeless Word of God from the time-bound human words of the priests, prophets, poets, letter-writers, historians, preachers, and story-tellers whose works are collected in the Scriptures. It acknowledged that the Bible's numerous authors wrote from the perspectives of many different historical periods, that they had a variety of concerns and motives, and that they tailored their messages for diverse audiences. Of necessity, these people wrote with their contemporaries in mind, not 21st-century readers.

Given that Protestantism is founded on the belief that Scripture is the supreme guide for the faith and practice of Christians, if there is anything that a Protestant denomination ought to be able to do, it is to state, without ambiguity or uncertainty, its understanding of the authority of Scripture. The General Conference of 1988, however, failed to muster enough votes to pass the statement that was intended to make the denomination's position clear — nor did the assembly suggest any modifications or substitutions that would achieve that objective. It chose not to raise the issue and thereby to leave the denomination's position ambiguous. A decision not to decide is, nevertheless, a decision, and decisions have consequences.

It was not the failure of the proposal that was the primary thing that troubled Reverend Wogaman and motivated him to write his article six years after the event. What concerned him was the knowledge that many of the people who voted against the proposal admitted that they thought that what the proposal said was correct. They simply did not think that it was politic to say so. Privately, they were willing to admit that they understood the Bible to be a complex document — not a product of divine dictation but of human efforts to respond to God. They feared, however, that a public affirmation of this fact would constitute "a shock treatment to our people."[31] It was, they decided, best to let sleeping Christians lie.

The schools that trained Methodist clergy were reputable scholarly institutions. The denomination's seminaries prepared candidates for ordination by teaching them to read the Bible in the original languages and by acquainting them with the techniques of the various methods of text criticism. Most graduates entered on their pastorates with a firm grounding in Biblical scholarship and exegetical technique. But Reverend Wogaman's blunt message to his colleagues ("It's time for you to tell the truth!") implied that responsible leaders of the United Methodist denomination believed that many of its clergy were failing to use their educations to educate the laity who were in their charge. Clergy with modern understandings of the Bible were content to leave their flocks with premodern worldviews they did not share. This meant that fundamental dishonesty characterized the relationship between those pastors and their people. Like medieval Catholic clergy, they were tacitly endorsing two different Christian belief systems: one for the educated elite and another for the masses. This condescending attitude was, of course, one of the abuses of clerical power that had inspired the Protestant Reformation. It is not hard to imagine how Luther and Calvin would view its resurgence in a denomination considered to be "mainline" Protestant.

Clerical posts (with the exception of staff positions at a few megachurches) are not generally regarded as stepping stones to wealth and power, and people who choose a clerical career usually do so knowing this. Their professional rewards derive from the fulfillment of serving others. Men and women with such vocations are torn when circumstances pressure them to shy away from telling the truth. They know that in the "best of all possible worlds" one should always speak the truth, but as mature adults they have enough experience to understand that this imperfect world does not offer an ideal environment for truth-telling. They fear that by doing so they might undermine the faith of the faithful and ultimately do more harm than good.

Despite the importance of "telling the truth," it is understandable that clergy, who spend years in graduate school laboring to acquire even a basic understanding of arcane biblical scholarship, are loath to try to educate their congregations. Forty-minute Sunday school classes, twenty-minute sermons, and a Bible study group for the motivated few offer scant opportunities for passing on what has taken professionals so much time and effort to learn. It is tempting to let well enough alone and hope that the whole issue of what is meant when the Bible is called the Word of God never comes up. However, ignorance is never safe.

The fact that there are practical considerations that clergy need to take into account before deciding "to tell the truth" is undeniable. American churches are voluntary organizations. As such, they are dependent on offerings freely contributed by their members. When pastors challenge their congregations, they risk alienating some individuals. This can cause funds to dry up, membership rolls to shrink, and opponents to threaten the continuation of ministries. Standing up for the truth is often costly, and truths that challenge well-established, if ill-founded, beliefs are particularly difficult to proclaim. They can trouble peaceful congregations, promote schism, and cost leaders their careers. It is tempting, therefore, for clergy to rationalize avoidance of contentious issues. They convince themselves that their pastoral duty to nurture community is more important than the risky attempt to educate their flock by driving it into the thickets of biblical scholarship. The easiest way, a shepherd may conclude, to keep the full component of sheep in the fold is never to say anything that would offend a sheep.

The temptation for clergy to dissimulate, avoid, obfuscate, or pretend neutrality is strong. But St. Paul warns that the gospel is a "rock of offense" (Romans 9:33 KJV). A church that fears giving offense lacks the clarity of purpose and will to lead, and the church that chooses not to lead is thereby condemned to follow. It becomes a pawn, not a player, and it is swayed by forces that it ought to oppose or reform.

When alternatives are unattractive, the wisest strategy is to search for a middle ground. But this is a hard and perilous undertaking that inevitably (as striving for growth always does) causes conflict. A church that fears offending anyone, however, is a church committed to the pursuit of irrelevance. Irrelevance purchases peace, but it is the peace of a slow, lingering death.

Conservative critic Thomas C. Reeves notes, "[N]umerous polls and studies point to an important fact: great numbers of people stay away from churches simply because they do not see them as relevant to their lives." But it is by no means certain that, as he claims, the irrelevancy of these churches can be traced to a "liberal Protestantism" that "has become so secularized and indistinct that it cannot compete successfully with an abundance of causes and activities that many find more valuable."[32]

It is worth at least considering that if a parish church is declining into irrelevancy, the reason may not be the "liberalism" of its position, but simply its unwillingness "to tell the truth" and build a sound foundation for its faith. People become bored and indifferent when they intuit an element of falsity in the messages they hear. If they sense that something is being kept from them or that their leaders are not being straight with them, they wander off to seek better company elsewhere. People respond to high expectations, and the relevance of faith to their lives may only become clear when faith challenges their under-standing and as well as their conduct. Conservative churches have long understood the value of placing demands on people. This may be the most important lesson they have to teach the liberal clergy who envy their success.

When mainline churches shy away from "telling the truth" about the Scriptures, their timidity yields the high ground to bold proclamations of faith emanating from the religious right. This allows the right to hijack Christianity, and Christianity comes generally to be viewed as a religion defined by conservative social and political values, moralism, emotionalism, and anti-intellectualism. The situation has already reached the point where the right has virtually co-opted the term "Christian." When the proverbial "Man-on-the-Street" is asked if he is a Christian, he assumes that he is being asked if he has been "born again" and if he affirms literal interpretation of the Bible. Polls report that approximately 30% of Americans are willing to state that they have been born-again and that they endorse literal readings of the Scriptures.[33] The image of a good Christian that dominates popular culture is the image of an evangelical biblical literalist. However, if this continues to be the standard definition of Christianity, the faith may doom itself to pointless culture wars and ultimate irrelevancy.

The vote taken at the 1988 General Conference of the United Methodist Church was not just a minor episode in Methodist history. It was symptomatic of a long-standing and wide-spread reluctance of leaders of mainline Protestant churches to face up to the responsibility of educating their people. If their hope is that by leaving the masses in ignorance they can preserve the people's allegiance, they gamble on a risky strategy. When they fail to teach the Scriptures according to their best lights, they have nothing all that interesting, useful, or convincing to say. Instead of helping people toward a firm scriptural grounding on which to build a faith that comes to terms with the modern world (the discoveries of scholarship and the challenges posed by critical thinking), they lapse into vacuous equivocations. Such rhetoric cannot compete with the right's bold, simplistic call to "turn back to the Bible," embrace "traditional family values," and be "born-again" with a commitment to the "fundamentals" of Christian supernaturalism.

People ardently desire certainly and conviction, but they need to remain alert to the dangers inherent in the lust for certainty. Countless tyrannies, atrocities, and genocides have sprung from the perverse faith of "true believers" (i.e., persons who by a "triumph of the will," totally commit themselves to the service of a sacred or secular ideology). Such people are dangerous. Recent history has made this obvious, but most Americans tend to associate the current risk solely with Muslim fundamentalism. It is, however, a feature of religious fundamentalism of all kinds. Both Christian and Muslim fundamentalists are anti-life and pro-death in so far as they are contemptuous of the world and indifferent to its survival.[34] Sadly, their actions end by opposing the essential thrust of the religious traditions they profess, for they minimize the importance of scriptural mandates — found in both the Qur'an and the Bible — that call for people of faith to practice mercy and forgiveness and to work for justice, peace, and universal well-being. Both regard as inevitable a bloody struggle that will culminate in the victory of "their god" over his opponents.

Like Muslim extremists, some right-wing Christian leaders develop a following by cultivating paranoia. They insist that "true Christians" (themselves and their adherents) are a persecuted minority — a faithful remnant — engaged in a desperate struggle with the all-encompassing, satanic liberalism of modern civilization. "The world" allegedly has such hatred for them that they "have become the Jews of the 21st century."[35] But unlike Germany's Jews (and the Church's martyrs), this time God's elect are determined not to end up on a cross.[36]

The first Christians were recruited from synagogues that were places for serious study as well as prayer. Christian clergy are called to preach and provide the sacraments, but they are also admonished to teach. Should they fail in this duty, some of those whose spiritual wellbeing is in their care will flee to the false prophets who claim that willful ignorance is the route to the security of faith. Others will give up on Christianity as a serious option, shake sanctuary dust from their sandals, and turn their backs on the whole religious enterprise. The result for everyone will be failure and loss. Therefore: "It is time for you to tell [or seek] the truth."

A few Christians may make it safely from the cradle to the grave without ever confronting doubt, but most will at some point in their lives be challenged to a wrestling match by Jacob's angel. No thinking individual can go through life without puzzling over the morality of God. Why are babies born deformed or destined to know only pain in a brief existence that is nothing but a struggle to die? Why is genocide permitted? Why is nature a realm where "acts of God" wreck havoc? Why do good people suffer? It is a rare believer who will never have a personal reason to cry: "Lord, what have I done to deserve this?" Faith will inevitably be tested, and when it is, a faith that rests on ignorance will quickly reveal itself for what it is: self-delusion. The challenges to belief and, therefore, to the survival of America's mainline Protestant churches (and perhaps to Christianity itself) are today much more powerful than they were when the Methodist General Conference met in 1988. Both the examined and the unexamined life pose dangers to faith, but risks are less for the former than the latter. The best hope for navigating an era of confusion and alarming prospects is to confront reality and trust in a sincere effort to speak the truth.

NOTES

1   Thomas C. Reeves, *The Empty Church: The Suicide of Liberal Christianity* (NY: The Free Press, 1996), p. 208.

2   Max I. Dimont, *Jews, God, and History* (Mentor, Penguin Group, 1962/1994), p. 24.

3   Marci A. Hamilton, *God vs. Gavel: Religion and the Rule of Law* (NY: Cambridge University Press, 2005), David M. O'Brien, *Animal Sacrifice and Religious Freedom* (Lawrence, KS: University Press of Kansas, 2004). Courts have often made a distinction between freedom to believe, which is absolute, and freedom to act on a belief, which is limited. For many religious people, however, the freedom to believe without the freedom to follow a belief is no freedom at all.

4   Although American Christianity has most often been associated with Protestantism, even that category provides too broad a tent for *true* Christianity as it is defined by some American religious leaders. On a broadcast of the TV program, the 700 Club (January 14, 1991), Pat Robertson dismissed America's prominent mainline Protestant denominations, saying: "You say you're supposed to be nice to the Episcopalians and the Presbyterians and the Methodists, and this and that and the other thing. Nonsense! I don't have to be nice to the spirit of the Antichrist." See: Rob Boston, *Pat Robertson: The Most Dangerous Man in America* (NY: Prometheus Books, 1996), p. 143.

5   "The late 19th century . . . marked a high point for American evangelicalism, as the progress of the church and nation appeared to go hand in hand." Duane Murray Oldfield, *The Right and the Righteous: The Christian Right Confronts the Republican Party* (NY: Rowman and Littlefield, Inc., 1996), p. 14.

6   George M. Marsden, *Fundamentalism and American Culture: The Shaping of Twentieth-Century Evangelicalism, 1870-1925* (NY: Oxford, 1980), pp. 11-26.

7   *The Fundamentals*, volume 1 (The Bible Institute of Los Angeles, 1917), preface.

8   Abraham Lincoln, Address to Congress, December 1, 1862.

9   Oldfield, *The Right and the Righteous*, pp. 32-33.

10   Robert Marus and Greg Warner, "Ronald Reagan's Ascent to Office Paralleled Rise of Religious Right" http://www. abpnews.com/2034.article (accessed 7 July 2008).

11   Oldfield, *The Right and the Righteous*, p. 117.

12   The IRS condemned Bacon's sermon as "a one-time intervention in the presidential race," but refused a request to clarify the criteria for its judgments. CBS News posting, September 24, 2007 http://www.cbsnews.com/stories/ 2007/09/24. (accessed 20 July 2010).

13   "Ronnie Floyd, on Fox News, Discusses Pulpits and Politics," August 2, 2004 http://www.bpnews.net/bpnews (accessed 20 July 2010).

14   Steven Waldman (editor-in-chief of Beliefnet.com) cites a significant piece of evidence for the rightward drift of American religious views and the fact "that America has actually become less inclusive and pluralistic over time." He notes that the custom of asking a clergyman to offer prayer at a presidential inauguration began in 1937. Until 1989 the tradition was to honor American pluralism by asking representatives of different faiths to bestow blessings. But in 1989 the task was assigned to a single individual, America's religious superstar, Billy Graham. He cautiously used inclusive language in his prayers, but in 1997 he offered an explicitly Christian prayer, a practice that has continued. See: Steven Waldman, "The Power of Prayer," *The Wall Street Journal* (January 17-18, 2009), W-1, W-2.

15   The same charge is made by Glenn H. Utter and James. L. True, *Conservative Christians and Political Participation* (Santa Barbara, California: ABC Clio, 2004), p. 15

16   Reeves, *The Empty Church*, p. 175.

17   *Ibid.*, p. 3.

18   Mohler's article, "America's Vanishing Protestant Majority — What Does It Mean?" was originally issued on August 9, 2004, and reprinted online on June 23, 2006, "in light of the actions this week of the Episcopal Church USA and the Presbyterian Church (USA)"; archived at: www.Albert Mohler.com/2005/07/08/americas-vanishing-protestant-minority-what-does-it-mean (accessed 7 July 2010).

19   Tertullian, *De Carne Christi* V, 4: *"certum est, quia impossible"*

20   John of Salisbury, *Metalogicon* (1159)

21 As Scott Sanders discovered, the Bible can disappoint readers who expect it consistently to reflect the influences of a morally and spiritually elevating faith. He writes: "Anxiety over the fate of the world drove me back to the Bible, where I noticed how often the cry for God's mercy toward the faithful is accompanied by the cry for vengeance toward enemies. In the Psalms, for instance, the songs of love are shadowed by songs of hatred . . . . Time and again the Psalmist pleads with God not merely to chastise but to extinguish the foe . . . . Paul described the work of Christ as a prolonged siege against unbelievers, culminating in final victory for the only Son . . . . From beginning to end, while preaching forgiveness and love, the Bible envisions a God given to intolerance and spite." [Scott Russell Sanders, *A Private History of Awe* (NY: North Point Press, 2006), p. 173.]

22 See the arguments cited above by Thomas Reeves and Albert Mohler.

23 Andrew Greeley and Michael Hout, *The Truth about Conservative Christians: What They Think and What They Believe* (Chicago: University of Chicago Press, 2006), p. 24.

24 *Ibid.,* p. 103-104.

25 *Ibid.,* p. 104.

26 *Ibid.,* p. 105.

27 *Ibid.,* pp. 108-109.

28 *Ibid.* p. 110.

29 *Ibid.,* p. 112. If conservative religion continues to correlate

with right-wing political agendas, this has clear implications for future shifts of power in American government.

30 J. Phillip Wogaman, "It's Time for You to Tell the Truth," *The Circuit Rider*, April (1994), p. 4.

31 *Ibid.*

32 Reeves, *The Empty Church*, p. 171.

33 Gallup polls have sometimes estimated that the number of self-professed biblical literalists in American society was as high as 38%. See also: Roger Doyle, "Sizing up Evangelicals," *Scientific American* (March 2003).

34 "Literalism, it should be clear is more than 'just' a philosophy of language. It is capable of creating and destroying worlds. It closes the door on confusion and uncertainty but also on what could be called the salvation of accident, the ways in which contingency facilitates freedom, allowing people to move in multifarious directions, a feeling as necessary for language as it is for life itself — for life, that is, to be felt as life." Anne Marie Oliver and Paul F. Steinberg, *The Road to Martyrs' Square: A Journey into the World of the Suicide Bomber* (NY: Oxford University Press, 2005), p. xxii.

35 Michael Horowitz, senior fellow of the Hudson Institute, in an address to an audience of evangelicals at a "War on Christians" conference, cited in: *Time* (April 10, 2006), p. 19. Pat Robertson said something similar in an interview with Molly Ivins in 1993: "Just like what Nazi Germany did to the Jews, so liberal America is now doing to the evangelical Christians . . . . More terrible than anything suffered by any

minority in history." www.geocities.com/campitolhill/7027
/quotes.html (accessed 20 July 2010).

36 In the context of the current "war on terror," siege mental-
ities are developing in all the Abrahamic faiths. Muslims
believe that the West has again mounted a "crusade" aimed
at the destruction of Islam, and conservative Christians
anguish over what they perceive to be a surging tide of Islam
worldwide. The fears of the latter are excessive. Philip
Jenkins' research into the spread of Christianity in the
Developing World has led him to the conclusion that "it is
Christianity that will leave the deepest mark on the twenty-
first century." See; Philip Jenkins, "The Next Christianity,"
The Atlantic (7 October 2003).

3

God is Love?

More people have been killed in the history of the world in conflicts over and about religion than over any other single factor. Religion has so often been the source of the cruelest evil.[1]
— John Shelby Spong,

Jesus said more about Hell than He did about Heaven[2]
— Jerry Falwell

I want you to just let a wave of intolerance wash over you. I want you to let a wave of hatred wash over you. Yes, hate is good . . . . Our goal is a Christian nation. We have a Biblical duty to conquer this country.[3]
— Randall Terry

Law, Faith, and Conscience

Judaism, Christianity, and Islam are products of an intellectual revolution that took place during what the German philosopher Karl Jaspers dubbed "the Axial Age" or the pivot point in the history of human consciousness.[4] Between 800 and 200 BCE, remarkable thinkers appeared in China, India, Persia, Palestine, and Greece: Confucius, Buddha, Zarathustra, the Hebrew prophets, and the Greek philosophers. Karen Armstrong, an expert in the field of comparative religions, has succinctly described how they set the world on a new spiritual course:

The Axial Age marks the beginning of humanity as we now know it. During this period, men and women became conscious of their existence, their own nature and their limitations in an unprecedented way. Their experience of utter

67

impotence in a cruel world impelled them to seek the highest goals and an absolute reality in the depths of their being. The great sages of the time taught human beings how to cope with the misery of life, transcend their weakness, and live in peace in the midst of this flawed world . . . .

The Axial sages scrutinized the old mythology and reinterpreted it, giving the old truths an essentially ethical dimension. Morality had become central to religion. It was by ethics, not magic, that humanity would wake up to itself and its responsibilities, realize its full potential and find release from the darkness that pressed in on all sides. . . . All were convinced that there was an absolute reality that transcended the confusions of this world . . . and sought to integrate it within the conditions of daily life.[5]

The Bible affirms that the goal of life is to realize the moral potential that distinguishes human beings from other living things. It makes this point at its beginning with a startling assertion: "Then God said, 'Let us make humankind in our image, according to our likeness'" (Genesis 1:26). The bestowal of God's "likeness" on a creature implies that the Creator is more than incomprehensible power. He has moral intent. He desires love and demands justice. Possession of His image makes it possible for His human creatures to have just and loving relationships with Him and with one another. This is the lesson that Hebrew prophets found in Israel's sacred history and that Christians discovered at the heart of the mystery of the cross.

Each testament has a great verse that offers the same simple summation of the Bible's message. In the Hebrew Scriptures the prophet Micah (6:8) asks, "What does the Lord require of you but to do justice, and to love kindness, and to walk humbly with your God?" In the New Testament (Matthew 22:37-40) Jesus says, "You shall love the Lord your God with all your heart, and with all your soul, and with all your mind. This is the greatest and first commandment. And a second is like it: You shall love your neighbor as yourself. On these two commandments hang all the law and the prophets."

Moral awareness gives humanity the ability to be "humane," but it can also have the opposite effect. As soon as human beings are mature enough to distinguish right from wrong, they develop a capacity for guilt and shame. They sense the burden of responsibility for their actions and experience anxiety about the consequences of their decisions. Even young children show great ingenuity in devising schemes to avoid accountability. They lie, shift blame, and invent self-justifying excuses.

People are defenders of freedom in theory, but less enthusiastic about its exercise in practice — hence, society's preoccupation with making and enforcing laws. Laws are usually thought of as a means for holding people accountable for how they use their freedom, but laws can also assist them in avoiding responsibility for their actions.

Jesus had much to say about people who try to live faithful lives by obeying sacred laws. He insisted that faithful obedience to God demands much more than that. Consider, for instance, the conversation he had with a sincerely pious young "millionaire." (The story is told in three of the Gospels: Mt. 19:16-22; Mark 10:17-22; Luke 18:18-23.) The youth approached Jesus expecting praise, for he had done a very difficult thing. He had kept all the Torah's many laws all his life. The response he got from Jesus was not what he anticipated. Jesus told him that keeping the law was all well and good, but if he hoped to be perfect, he had to go further and give all his wealth to the poor. Jesus' intention was not to add a 614th law to the Torah. He was simply pointing out that laws cannot definitively define the life of faith. God's true "law" is the one that Jeremiah said is written on the heart. Given that the heart does not rest easy with anything short of total selflessness, however, it is tempting to avoid its demands by focusing on the Bible's hundreds of specific laws.

Laws are not a problem in themselves, for freedom is impossible without the stable societal structures laws provide. But problems develop when human beings make obedience to law an end in itself and forget what laws strive to achieve. Laws are accountable to higher, transcendent principles that create the gap that always exists between the "spirit" and the "letter" of the law.

Many Christians (especially those who claim that every one of the Bible's words is imbued with God's eternal authority) are inclined to read the Bible as if it were a law book. But they cannot escape doing so selectively. Were they to implement every rule and example the Bible records, their lives would be even more circumscribed than those of the most rigorous Orthodox Jews. The Jews, after all, only have the laws of the Torah; Christian legalists also have whatever might be gleaned from the New Testament. If they were to restore all the Bible's practices (e.g., slavery, stoning, sabbatical redistribution of property, etc.) they would find themselves at odds with American law, justice, and standards of morality.

The Bible is a veritable storehouse of laws — some 613 in its first five books alone. The temptation to reduce faith to a life lived "according to God's laws" is understandable, for believers have both a desire to do God's will and a degree of uncertainty about what that requires of them. Laws are useful guides, but also occasions for sin when people foist responsibility for their actions onto their laws. What the law mandates and what morally sensitive individuals "feel" to be right can be different things.[6]

Some Christians have tried to narrow the field of their moral obligations by retreating from the world into communities governed by their own versions of God's laws (their models for "the kingdom of God on Earth"). They eschew responsibility for the world at large and concentrate on their own redemption. More commonly, however, Christians attempt to utilize principles of faith to reform and redeem the world.

When principles of faith are ossified as civil laws, they inevitably fall far short of perfectly realizing the goals of love and justice. Often this effort fails because people easily succumb to the temptation of identifying God's will with their self interest and claiming God's authority for their own agendas. But even individuals who are models of saintly selflessness do damage when striving to obey what they believe to be "God's law." The much revered Roman Catholic nun, Mother Theresa, who devoted her life to caring for the impoverished victims of India's overpopulation, believed that birth control was contrary to God's law. Rather than trying to limit population growth in that desperately overcrowded land, she offered to take in all the children indigent families could not support — a promise she had no realistic hope of keeping. Unrestrained population growth will outstrip not only the resources of charity but those of Earth itself.[7] Care for individuals, no matter how important, well-intended, and passionately pursued, has always proved to be an inadequate response to systemic sources of mass suffering. Sexual ethics that were life-affirming in eras when the human species struggled with high mortality rates become life-destroying as the specter of overpopulation looms.

Many Christians who claim that society should be governed by God's law should consider what life in modern America would be like if only a small part of the law recorded in the Scriptures (*e.g.*, the Book of Leviticus) was enforced in this country.[8]

American diets would have to be radically altered to meet kosher requirements:

Flesh that touches any unclean thing shall not be eaten; it shall be burned up (Leviticus 7:19);

You shall eat no fat of ox or sheep or goat (7:22);

You must not eat any blood whatever, either of bird or of animal (7:26);

No person among you shall eat blood, nor shall any alien who resides among you eat blood (17:12);

From among all the land animals, these are the creatures that you may eat. Any animal that has divided hoofs and is cleft-footed and chews the cud — such you may eat. But . . . you shall not eat . . . the camel, . . . the rock badger, . . . the hare, . . . [and] the pig . . . . Their carcasses you shall not touch[9] (11: 2-8);

These you may eat, of all that are in the waters. Everything in the waters that has fins and scales . . . . Everything in the waters that does not have fins and scales is detestable to you (11:9, 12);

These you shall regard as detestable among the birds — eagle, vulture, osprey, buzzard, kite, raven, ostrich, nighthawk, sea gull, hawk of any kind, owl, cormorant, water hen, stork, heron, hoopoe, bat (11:13-19);

among the winged insects that walk on all fours you may eat those that have jointed legs above their feet (11:21)[10]

Decisions that are now private choices would be mandated as public policy. For instance, all male babies would have to be circumcised at the age of eight days:

On the eighth day the flesh of his foreskin shall be circumcised (12:3)

Male ejaculation and female menstruation would be regard as polluting:

If a man has an emission of semen, he shall bathe his whole body in water, and be unclean until the evening. . . . . If a man lies with a woman and has an emission of semen, both of them shall bathe in water, and be unclean until the evening (15:16, 18);

When a woman has a discharge of blood that is her regular discharge from her body, she shall be in her impurity for seven days, and whoever touches her shall be unclean until the evening. Everything upon which she lies during her impurity shall be unclean . . ." (15:19-20);

You shall not approach a woman to uncover her nakedness while she is in her menstrual uncleanness (18:19)

No work or shopping would be allowed on the seventh day of the week (i.e., Saturday), and the nation would have to observe an annual Day of Atonement:

Six days shall work be done; but the seventh day is a sabbath of complete rest, a holy convocation; you shall do no work (23:3);

This shall be a statute to you forever: In the seventh month, on the tenth day of the month, you shall deny yourselves, and shall do no work, neither the citizen nor the alien who resides among you. . . . . it is a statute forever (16:29, 31)

Every workman would have to be paid at the end of each workday:

you shall not keep for yourself the wages of a laborer until morning (19:13)

No hybrid stock could be bred — and no one could wear a shirt or dress woven from different kinds of thread:

> You shall not let your animals breed with a different kind; you shall not sow your field with two kinds of seed; nor shall you put on a garment made of two different materials (19:19)

Male grooming standards would have to change. Barber shops and the Gillette corporation would experience reduced commerce:

> You shall not round off the hair on your temples or mar the edges of your beard. (19:27)

Tattoo parlors would be closed, and all Christians who had crosses, pictures of Jesus, or "God is love" slogans inked into their flesh would have to report to plastic surgeons to have them erased:

> You shall not . . . tattoo any marks upon you (19:26)

The young could be prosecuted if they failed to stand up when an elder entered a room:

> You shall rise before the aged (19:32)

Capital punishment would become mandatory:

> Anyone who kills a human being shall be put to death.(24:17)

And capital punishment would apply to a wide range of offenses:

> — for astrologers and fortune tellers:

A man or a woman who is a medium or a wizard shall be put to death; they shall be stoned to death (20:27)

— for adulterers (including several prominent American evangelists):

If a man commits adultery with the wife of his neighbor, both the adulterer and the adulteress shall be put to death (20:10)

— for anyone who takes the Lord's name in vain:

One who blasphemes the name of the Lord shall be put to death; the whole congregation shall stone the blasphemer. Aliens as well as citizens . . . shall be put to death (24:16)

— for anyone who curses one of his parents:

All who curse father or mother shall be put to death (20:9)

Anyone who reads astrology columns in the newspaper would be considered cursed by God and driven into exile:

If any turn to mediums . . ., I will set my face against them, and will cut them off from the people (19:6)

Mutilation would become the punishment for infliction of an injury:

Anyone who maims another shall suffer the same injury in return (24:19)

Individuals would be held financially responsible for all of their relatives:

If any of your kin fall into difficulty and become dependent on you, you shall support them (25:35).

And they would have to assume the burden without feeling resentment:

You shall not hate in your heart anyone of your kin (19:17)

Slavery would be restored to the American continent, so long as it involved only persons defined as "aliens:"

it is from the nations around you that you may acquire male and female slaves. You may also acquire them from among the aliens residing with you . . . . You may keep them as a possessions for your children after you, for them to inherit as property (25:44, 46).

Few Americans would favor altering the nation's laws to bring them in line with the biblical decrees cited above, for modern societies have values and moral sensitivities never imagined by ancient Middle-Eastern peoples. No reasonable person would dispute that humanity has made ethical progress since the eras of Abraham and Moses. Given that much of this progress has been inspired and guided by the Bible's admonitions to love others, forgive wrongs, and pursue justice, it is perverse to take contrary passages out of historical context to justify hate, discrimination, and persecution.

The Bible is amply supplied with tales of bloodshed, abuse, incest, anger, spite, and vengeance. But the Bible as a whole has led many Jews and Christians to question death penalties, slavery, gender discrimination, sexual abuse, war, economic exploitation, social prejudice, jingoism, and all forms of inequality. The Bible has been the most effective agent for undermining some of its own alleged "commandments."

Many conservative Christians are willing to dismiss some Biblical mandates (*e.g.*, those cited above from Leviticus and the ritual prescriptions in Numbers and Deuteronomy) as irrelevant while insisting that others, which are mixed in with them, are eternally binding. Setting aside texts that relate to the tabernacle and the Temple is easy to rationalize, for these institutions no longer exist. But many biblically mandated practices, such as wearing fringes on one's garments (*e.g.*, Numbers 15:37-39), could easily be followed, but are not. The basis for deciding which verses are no longer important and which are still to be enforced is usually little more than a feeling, a prejudice, or a convenient preference. Few Christians, either conservative or liberal, pay any attention to Jesus' condemnation of divorce: "Whoever divorces his wife and marries another commits adultery against her . . ." (Mark 10: 11). But many insist loudly on the constraints that Pauline letters place on women and Leviticus on male homosexuals.

Conservatives often claim that they have no choice but to be faithful to what God has plainly said in Scripture. They insist that any alternative interpretations proposed for controversial texts are only attempts to make God's clear word conform to sinful human preferences. But there is no reading without interpretation; even deciding to read a text literally is to choose an interpretation. Even Orthodox rabbis, who insist that every word in the Bible is true and inspired by God, support that belief by going to great lengths to explain why a morally troubling text does not mean what it literally means.[11] Literalists and fundamentalists deceive themselves when they assume that they can quote the very words of God from the Bible. Such self-deception corrupts their characters and places others at serious risk.

Homosexuality and God's Law
No issue better illustrates this than the campaign the religious right wages to combat what it claims is "the homosexual

agenda" — an alleged conspiracy by alleged perverts to undermine family life and morality. Despite much evidence to the contrary, some Christians doggedly insist that homosexuality is a lifestyle choice, not a natural sexual orientation. They have no option, for only if it is a choice can it be branded a sin. If it is a natural attraction, it must be one of God's gifts.

The religious right has backed political campaigns to deny homosexuals minority protections and legal support for the kind of stable family ties that heterosexual marriage is said to maintain (soaring divorce rates notwithstanding). However, the disproportionate passion that surrounds the issue suggests that, for many, opposition is driven by personal revulsion more than by fidelity to the Bible. After all, the Bible says little about homosexuality and a great deal about the sin of failing to care for the poor, but no comparably vigorous campaign for the elimi- nation of poverty has yet emerged from the right.

Christians who for whatever reasons are opposed to homosex- uality eagerly cite biblical condemnations of homosexual practices. But the Bible offers them little ammunition, and they often assume that it says much more than can be substantiated by a careful reading of its texts. For instance, the Bible condemns specific acts, not a sexual orientation — a concept that was unknown in the ancient world.[12] All but one of the oft quoted verses appear to apply only to males.[13] Some of the passages that are cited as damning homosexuality actually say nothing about sex.

Take for instance the story of Sodom and Gomorrah (Genesis 19). The word "sodomite" was coined during the Middle Ages as a label for a person who committed any one of a number of prohibited sexual acts (*e.g.*, bestiality, heterosexual anal penetration, *etc.*). Today it is most used as a derogatory term for a male homosexual. This limitation of the word's meaning was inspired by a misunderstanding of the reason for God's anger with the people of Sodom — an error prompted by ignorance of the story's original context.

The Sodom episode is part of a larger narrative involving divine messengers who come to Abraham to assure him that Sarah will bear him a son. After lunching with Abraham, the angels proceed to Sodom where Abraham's nephew Lot has taken up residence. Lot offers them shelter in his home, but that evening a hostile crowd gathers outside his house and calls for the strangers to be turned over. When Lot refuses, God prevents Sodom's men from storming Lot's house by striking them blind. The following day Lot, his wife, and his daughters flee the city, and it is destroyed.

The crux of the tale is punishment of a sin — but what sin? For a modern reader it seems strange that the story says so little about the specific reason for God's extreme anger. But for the ancient Hebrews (for whom the story was written) Sodom's transgression would have been obvious and hardly in need of emphatic identification. It was Sodom's failure to honor God's demand that protection and hospitality be extended to strangers and sojourners.[14]

The mistaken understanding of the sin of Sodom as a sexual act derives in part from the text's use of the ambiguous word *ya'da*, "to know." The word appears over 900 times in the Hebrew Scriptures. In a small number of cases the context implies knowledge acquired through sexual contact, but most often the reference is simply to learning something. For modern readers the Sodom and Gomorrah story raises the specter of illicit sex when it says that Lot offered his *virgin* daughters to the crowd in place of his guests. The reference to the girls' virgin status turns the modern mind to thoughts of sex, but for an ancient reader it would only have signaled their youth and vulnerability.

To assume that the "Sodomites" were male homosexuals who lusted for the unknown men who were Lot's guests is a bit of a leap. It is even odder to assume that, if they were, Lot's plan was to divert them from their objective by offering them girls to ravish. Why would male "homosexuals" be tempted by an offer of women? And what kind of a father would consider doing what Lot proposes? Why does the story represent this as the behavior of a good, God-fearing man?

The ancient Israelites would not have been puzzled by Lot's behavior, for they knew the sacred duty that the story was intended to illustrate. Ancient societies had no international treaties, no consulates, and nothing to provide security for individuals once they left the protection of family, tribe, or homeland. Their safety depended entirely on promises of "hospitality" from natives of the places they visited. The word *hospitality* has been trivialized in modern usage. For us it conjures up the offer of a cup of coffee or a dinner invitation, but in the ancient world it entailed extremely serious obligations. The Homeric Greeks called it "guest-friendship." The relation of guest-friend was a formal bond passed down in families from generation to generation. In Homer's *Iliad* two warriors who duel at the battle of Troy cease fighting and exchange armor after a recitation of their respective lineages reveals that their ancestors were guest-friends. The ancient Hebrews honored similar customs. Leviticus 19:10 instructed Hebrew farmers to leave gleanings in their fields and vineyards for "the poor and the alien," and Leviticus 19:33 went much further, decreeing: "you shall love the alien as yourself."

In ancient societies, the promise of protection to an outsider laid a serious obligation on a host. The Sodom story illustrates how serious this obligation was and what could be at stake. The point of the story is that Lot must choose between his duty to defend his guests and his responsibility to the weakest, most vulnerable members of his family, his virgin (*i.e.*, too young to be married) daughters. Lot makes what the ancient world regarded as the right choice. He places the safety of his guests before that of his kin. The sin of the men of Sodom was their failure to respect the stranger, not homosexual lust,[15] and Lot's virtue is revealed by the length to which he was willing to go to honor the sacred obligation of hospitality.

If homosexual rape had been an implied threat to the strangers who were Lot's guests (as it may be to a traveler in a similar story found in Judges 19), the ancient hearers of the tale would have assumed that the motive of the men of Sodom was not lust, but power — the intent to subjugate the outsiders whom Lot, an outsider himself, had brought into their city. On ancient battlefields warriors sometimes anally penetrated those whom they defeated. The act was the ultimate demonstration of their superior strength and their opponents' utter submission. In the Greek and Roman world a man's reputation was not threatened by homosexual acts so long as he took the "male" role and penetrated his partner.[16] Society's only rule was that he not compromise his masculinity by behaving like a woman. To rape another soldier was literally to unman him.

Persons who insist that the Sodom story is a lesson about sexual morality ought to be seriously troubled by its conclusion. After Lot flees Sodom, he commits incest with his daughters and sires his own grandsons, the ancestors of the Moabites and Ammonites (Genesis 19:30-38). If a threatened homosexual act was enough to inspire God to rain down fire on Sodom, what might God have done to punish Lot for impregnating his own daughters? Plainly the authors of these stories were much less preoccupied with sex than many of their modern readers. Their intent was not to make some point about father-daughter relations, but to explain the kinship ties that were assumed to exist among the Moabites, Ammonites, and Hebrews.

Some of the common misconceptions of what some biblical texts say originate from ignorance of ancient customs. Others can be traced to errors by early English translators. The authors of the Standard Version (i.e., "King James Version") were respon-sible, knowledgeable scholars, but in the 17th century, when they worked, much less was known about ancient manuscript sources, practices, and languages than is known today. Many of their "best guesses" about the meaning of some texts now appear clearly wrong; others are certainly problematic. This should give pause to Christians who insist that the translation of the Bible that King James authorized for his subjects' use is not a mere "version," but is God's inerrant word. The beauty of the Standard Version's language is undeniable, and it continues to influence more accurate translations by better equipped scholars. But those who rely on it need to remember that the English language is constantly evolving and that the antique wording of the KJV may be in error or prompt misunderstandings.

Some passages from the Hebrew Scriptures that have been assumed to condemn homosexuality belong in the category of potential mistranslations. Deuteronomy (23:17 - 18) says that a Jewish female may not serve as a *kadeshah* or a male as a *kadesh*. The terms refer to women and men who had some function in the pagan fertility religions that were common in the ancient world. Because these people were associated with cults for which sex was a religious concern, the Bible's early English translators called them prostitutes. This, however, is a loaded word based on unsubstantiated conclusions. No one knows what the role of a *kadesh* or *kadeshah* was. In II Kings 23:7, Josiah's reform of Judaism is said to have involved "breaking down the houses of the male temple prostitutes [*kadeshim*] that were in the house of the Lord, where the women did weaving for Asherah." Asherah was the goddess wife of a male god. A male priest who served a goddess would not have promoted fertility by acting as a homosexual prostitute. More likely, he would simply have been her priest. If ritualized sex was involved, he would have taken the role of a male god in rituals with a female priestess to reenact the "sacred marriage" of the deity and her consort.

If the verses relating to Sodom and the *kadeshim* are eliminated, the only texts in the Hebrew Scriptures that clearly condemn homosexuality are two from the Book of Leviticus. They are found mixed in with many laws that, as noted above, Christians blithely dismiss as irrelevant. They are:

You shall not lie with a male as with a woman; it is an abomination (18:22)

If a man lies with a male as with a woman, both of them have committed an abomination; they shall be put to death (20:13)[17]

Steven Greenberg, a gay Orthodox rabbi, argues that the scope of these prohibitions is much narrower than often assumed. A close translation of the first verse, he says, would read: "And with a male you shall not lie the lyings of a woman: it is a *toevah*."[18] Why, he asks, does the law not simply say, "You shall not lie with a man"? "The lyings of a woman" is an odd phrase. The only passages comparable to it are references in the Book of Numbers (31:18, 35) to women who have experienced "the lying of a male" (*i.e.*, sexual penetration). Leviticus, therefore, may only intend to condemn males who submit to penetration ("the lyings of a woman"), as was the rule, as noted above, in Greek and Roman cultures. This, the rabbi points out, is far from the blanket condemnation of homosexuality (female as well as male) that is assumed by many modern Jews and Christians to be God's law. Its purpose doubtless had less to do with mandating standards of sexual morality than with acculturating males and females in the symbiotic roles that preserved ancient patriarchal tribes.

In the New Testament, Jesus is not reported to have said anything about homosexuality. In Matthew 15:19, where he lists the behaviors that proceed "from the heart" and defile a man, fornication is mentioned, but, despite Jesus' obvious familiarity with the laws of Leviticus, he makes no reference to homosexuality. The New Testament verses that might refer to homosexuality are all from letters by (or imputed to) St. Paul. In I Corinthians 6:9-11, Romans 1:26-27, and I Timothy 1:10, Paul condemns the *malakoi* ("soft," "effeminate"?) and the *arsenokoites* ("male - bedding"?). The meanings of both terms are obscure. *Malakoi* in other ancient texts refers to people who are lazy and do not work. The Septuagint, the ancient Greek version of the Torah, uses *arsenokoites* to translate *kadesh* — the mysterious pagan figure whose religious function is unclear. In some ancient sources the word seems to refer to pimps, which might explain its use by the Septuagint's Jewish translators as a hostile characterization of the priests who presided with priestesses over fertility cults. The word does not appear in ancient erotic literature in reference to homosexual behavior. In short, although the Hebrew Scriptures cast aspersions on some kinds of homosexual behavior and Saint Paul appears to have believed that homosexual acts were a consequence of idolatry's distortion of natural human appetites, the Bible is far less concerned with the issue than many contemporary Christians seem to be.

Women and God's Law
Just as some biblical texts have been all too freely and hastily read as justifications for condemning homosexuals, other verses have been used to denigrate women. The ancient Jews, like most ancient peoples, took patriarchy for granted. They knew no other way of life and assumed, therefore, that patriarchy was natural and just. The Bible describes God as the ultimate patriarch — the spouse to whom "feminine" Israel owed faithful love and service. The Jews traced their origin as a people to a single patriarch (Abram), and the Bible's Creation myths rooted the beginning of human society in patriarchy.

Genesis 2:4 — 3:24 (the Bible's second Creation story) has probably had more influence on Western concepts of gender than any other passage in Scripture (or literature). It contrasts starkly with Genesis 1: 1 — 2:4 (the Bible's first Creation story). In the first story God creates males and females simultaneously and bestows His divine image on both of them. The first Creation story ends with God's statement of satisfaction: "God saw everything that he had made, and indeed, it was very good" (Genesis 1:31). The world was a perfect place.

But the world of human experience is not a perfect place. It is often not even "very good." It is filled with suffering, violence, and death. The second Creation story provides an explanation for the discontinuity between God's plan and our reality. In doing so, its authors made some assumptions about early human societies that we now know to be incorrect. For instance, they posited farming as the original human condition. But, in reality, human beings wandered the face of the planet for eons before farming and herding economies began slowly to appear. Humans have sustained their species by hunting and gathering far longer than by farming.

The second Creation story confronts what theologians call "the problem of evil:" Why does evil exist in a world made by an omnipotent, benign divinity who has declared creation to be good? The second Creation story excuses God from complicity in the human tragedy by tracing the origin of the evils that plague human existence to the power that creatures who were made in God's image had to rebel against Him.

Many people who read the tale conclude that it points the finger of blame specifically at its female protagonist. She is the one the serpent tempter approaches. She is the first to eat from the tree that God has forbidden her to touch, and she gives its fatal fruit to her (curiously uncurious and passive) mate. As a result, sin severs the originally intimate relationship between God and His human creatures, and they are driven from the Garden of Eden to live in a world distorted by their rebellion. Each is condemned to bear a different burden as the consequence of sin. The male will labor endlessly to wrest a living from the recalcitrant soil, and the female will suffer the pains and burdens of motherhood.

If this story is read simplistically as literal history, it seems to indict females, make them responsible for the existence of human misery, and justify their subordination to males. Tertullian (fl. c. 200 CE), the first major Latin Christian theologian, made this case against women in the bluntest possible language. In a sermon on the topic of vanity, which he addressed primarily to the women in his congregation, he ordered them to contemplate the massive burden of guilt that was their heritage from the first of their kind. He said that each woman should be:

> walking about as Eve mourning and repentant, in order that by every garb of penitence she might the more fully expiate that which she derives from Eve — the ignominy, I mean, of the first sin, and the odium (attaching to her as the cause) of human perdition. . . . . And do you not know that you are (each) an Eve? The sentence of God on this sex of yours lives in this age: the guilt must of necessity live too. *You* are the devil's gateway: *you* are the unsealer of that (forbidden) tree: *you* are the first deserter of the divine law: *you* are she who persuaded him whom the devil was not valiant enough to attack. *You* destroyed so easily God's image, man. On account of *your* desert — that is, death — even the Son of God had to die.[19]

Literal interpretations of the second Creation story, like Tertullian's, have had (and continue to have) tragic consequences for many women. If, as they might imply, women are responsible for all the difficulties men face in life, males and females are, in a primal sense, enemies. Women are dangerous to men. Consequently, they must be confined, disciplined, controlled, and compelled to submit to their male superiors.

This interpretation of the text provided a cogent explanation for the actual condition of most ordinary women in the ancient world.[20] Hardly anywhere did women even begin to approach equality with men, and nowhere did females routinely dominate males.[21] It seemed obvious, therefore, that women were destined by God and nature to play the inferior role in society. The lessons of common sense and Scripture were substantiated by rational hypotheses. Aristotle, the Greek philosopher and natural scientist, argued that the female was a deformed male.[22] Girls were born, he claimed, when something went wrong with a biological process that was designed to create boys. The female's contribution to the birth of children, he claimed, was that of an incubator and supplier of raw material; creative energy and form were the gift of her mate.

Because female subordination has been so common and is still so widespread, many Jews and Christians read the second Creation story as taking precedence over the first. Following St. Paul, they cobble together bits and pieces of both accounts to make one that is not in the Bible. Instead of males and females being simultaneously created and endowed with the image of God (Genesis 1:27), Adam and Eve are separately created — and only Adam gets "the image." This lead Paul to represent Adam as the true primal "mother," the first human and the one from whom Eve was created. That provided Paul with a neat explanation for the ancient world's belief that nature intended men to take all public roles and that women ought to confine themselves to the domestic sphere — and veil themselves when it was necessary for them to leave the house:

> For a man ought not to have his head veiled, since he is the image and reflection of God; but woman is the reflection of man. Indeed man was not made from woman, but woman from man. Neither was man created for the sake of woman, but woman for the sake of man. For this reason a woman ought to have a symbol of authority on her head . . . .
> (I Corinthians 11:7-10)

I Timothy, a pseudo-Pauline letter, draws similar, if more extreme, implications from the second Creation story:

> Let a woman learn in silence with full submission. I permit no woman to teach or to have authority over a man; she is to keep silent. For Adam was formed first, then Eve; and Adam was not deceived, but the woman was deceived and became a transgressor. Yet she will be saved through childbearing, provided they continue in faith and love and holiness, with modesty. (I Timothy 2:11-15)

Conservative Christians in America have opposed feminism on these and other scriptural grounds. A statement of faith published by the Southern Baptist Convention directs "a wife to submit herself graciously to the servant leadership of her husband."[23] In 2000 the convention reconsidered its own practices and voted to exclude women, including those previously ordained, from the pastoral office.

The larger concerns of the Bible (i.e., to inspire love and the pursuit of justice) serve to raise doubts about the abusive uses of specific biblical texts. So it was for Paul. His rearing as a male in the ancient Roman world made him uncomfortable with the idea of women asserting themselves in public. He also feared that this would cause scandals that would create obstacles to missionary work. His reading of the second Creation story helped convince him that Christian women should, therefore, conform to the custom of the time and veil themselves. But his deeper understanding of the faith gave him second thoughts. He sensed a conflict between preaching woman's inferiority while proclaiming a new order of grace and freedom in which "there is no longer Jew or Greek, there is no longer slave or free, there is no longer male and female" (Galatians 3:28). He cautioned his readers to remember that "in the Lord woman is not independent of man or man independent of woman. For just as woman came from man, so man comes through woman; but all things come from God" (I Corinthians 11:11-12). Ultimately, Paul dismissed the issue of veiling a woman while she prayed in public as a matter of choice, not law. The most significant thing is that he (unlike the author of I Timothy) did not challenge the right of women — veiled or unveiled — to pray and to prophesy on an equal footing with the males of his congregations.

The second Creation story is amenable to interpretations quite different from the one Tertullian gave it — interpretations more in line with the gender equality that Paul alludes to in Galatians and I Corinthians. (However, this requires acknowledgment of the mythic nature of Genesis 2 — 3.) The deity in the second Creation story resembles a Zeus or a Marduk. He experiments and tinkers as he creates, and he is not omniscient. He walks in gardens to enjoy cool evening breezes and has to question his creatures in order to discover where they are and what they have done. The story is delightfully dramatic and entertaining, but it cannot be taken literally as a description of the God who thunders at Job: "Where were you when I laid the foundation of the earth?" (Job 38:4)

The second Creation story recycles material from primitive myths and legends that circulated widely in the Middle East long before the Bible was written.[24] But the important thing is not the sources of the tale, but how the Bible's authors reshaped the material they borrowed to guide meditation on the human condition. The "man" who is made first in this story is not a male in the ordinary sense. He and God's creation are incomplete (*i.e.*, not yet "good"), for God decides that "it is not good that the man should be alone" (Genesis 2:18). To complete him, "he" is divided into two new kinds of beings: a male and a female. "He" is not fully human and creation itself is not finished until God's culminating act, the fashioning of "woman." To read the story otherwise is to imagine God creating the first man with genitals for which God had not yet imagined a purpose![25]

The ascending order of events in the process of creation seems to suggest that the "woman," whose appearance was creation's crowning event, was originally the "man's" superior. That would be consistent with the fact that the serpent chose to tempt her rather than him. The Bible takes sin with absolute seriousness. It never allows sin to be excused as a mistake, an error, or the consequence of weakness or ignorance. People sin through abuse of their power — the freedom of self-determination that God gives them. The serpent, therefore, attacks at the top by tempting the pinnacle of God's creation to rebel against Him. The "man" in the story acts the part of a subordinate. He does what he is told and eats what the "woman" gives him without argument, question, or discussion.

The first sin then reverses the order of creation. The "man" who (as Genesis 2:5 implies) had always been intended "to till the ground," finds that the task that should have been his fulfillment has become his curse (Genesis 3:17-19). For the woman, pain is added to childbirth and, as a further affliction, she is told that the man "shall rule over" her (Genesis 3:16) — a condition that apparently was not God's original intent. If, as seems plausible, the story is meant to explain patriarchy, it also condemns patriarchy as a consequence of sin.

Jesus' relationships with women supports this interpretation of the second Creation story. Jesus, a man conceived without the sin that spawned patriarchy, shows a concern and respect for women that mystifies his disciples. They do not understand why he pays so much attention to women, and they fear that his behavior will cause scandal. Women respond with an insight into Jesus that long eludes his male disciples. Women are the first people to recognize and witness to Jesus' messianic identity. In Mark's Gospel (14:3-9) an unnamed woman mysteriously appears to anoint Jesus on the eve of his passion. Anointing was a ritual for enthroning kings, and the woman's act proclaims Jesus' role in salvation history before any of his disciples grasped it or he acknowledged it — which may be why Jesus said, "Truly I tell you, wherever the good news is proclaimed in the whole world, what she has done will be told in remembrance of her" (Mark 14:9). Women are also (for Mark) the sole witnesses of Jesus' crucifixion, the first to discover his empty tomb, and the first of his followers to receive the news of his resurrection. They were the first human beings, therefore, to receive the grace of faith — the first Christians. Jesus, the second Adam (I Corinthians 15:45-48), reversed the consequences of sin and brought about a new creation in which Eve took the place that God initially intended for her.

St. Paul, who although saved by grace remained a sinner (Romans 7:19), had a similar, if less perfect, relationship with women. Paul may have been an inspired spokesman for faith, but he was not God incarnate. He was a man of his time and place. If his faith was radical, his personal inclinations were conservative. Paul's authentic letters reflect the thoughts of a man who was torn between the patriarchal conventions of his world and his belief that men and women were equals in the faith. The advice he gave women was colored by his all-too-human fear that the supreme mission of the Church — to make as many converts as quickly as possible — would be impeded if Christian women gave free reign to their freedom and behaved in ways that offended the sensibilities of their contemporaries. But in Paul's dealing with individuals, he acknowledged some women as equals. In Philippians 4:3, he urged support for Euodia and Syntyche, "for they have struggled beside me in the work of the gospel, together with Clement and the rest of my co-workers." In the last chapter of his letter to the Romans, Paul sent greetings to twenty-eight people, ten of whom were women.[26] Some he specifically mentioned as sharing his ministry: Phoebe ("a benefactor of many and of myself as well"), Prisca and Aquila ("who work with me in Christ Jesus"), Tryphaena and Tryphose ("workers in the Lord"), and Andronicus and Junia ("prominent among the apostles,[27] and . . . in Christ before I was"). Numerous other women are mentioned in his letters and in the Book of Acts as having hosted (possibly "lead") congregations in their homes.

The Earth and God's Law

Just as some people use biblical texts to justify abuse of God's creatures, others cite them to justify misuse of God's creation. Religious conservatives who oppose the work of environmentalists and the funding of programs to limit population growth have often quoted the Genesis Creation stories when dismissing the concerns of "liberal tree-huggers." The world, they argue, was made for our use, and God has given us a mandate to exploit it: "Be fruitful and multiply, and fill the earth and subdue it; and have dominion over the fish of the sea and over the birds of the air and over every living thing that moves upon the earth" (Genesis 1:28). A literal reading of this key verse reduces it to the level of a license from God for His undisciplined children to run riot on the earth. But those who respect the Bible as a sacred text should anticipate more profundity in what it strives to teach.

First: The verse has a context that tends to be overlooked. It is part of the first Creation story, which describes a world that has not yet been damaged by humanity's sinful rebellion. It discusses the world that God created and declared "good," but that world is not the "real" world of the second Creation story — the historical world into which Adam and Eve are driven when they leave the Garden of Eden. This world is a more problematic place than the one envisioned as God's ideal. Its inhabitants must struggle against want ("cursed is the ground because of you; in toil you shall eat of it all the days of your life; thorns and thistles it shall bring forth for you," Genesis 3:17-18). And nature itself challenges the dominion God gave to his human creatures: "he [the man] will strike your head, and you [the serpent] will strike his heel" (Genesis 3:15).

English translations of God's mandate in Genesis 1:28 pair

"multiply . . . and subdue" with the exercise of "dominion." *Dominion* is the prerogative of a *dominus,* someone who has "lordship." Lordship entails both privilege and responsibility. Lords have power over their subjects, but that power is granted them so that they can protect and provide for others. If the common English translations accurately reflect the intent of the Hebrew original, "dominion" does not grant license to rape the earth. It charges those who bear God's image with responsibility for His creation's continued well being.

Dubious readings of the first Creation story are used to sanction rampant exploitation of the environment, but the most serious threat that abuse of the Bible poses to life on Earth comes from the influence of verses that were written much later. They reflect novel ideas that emerged during the years that spanned the closing of the Hebrew canon and the composition of the New Testament.

The Book of Daniel, the last addition to the collection of documents that became the Hebrew Scriptures, added the idea of the apocalypse to the biblical tradition. *Apocalypse* means something that is "uncovered" or "disclosed," but in the religious context it refers specifically to supernaturally revealed information about the *eschaton* (*i.e.,* "last things," the end of the world). The end is imagined as a violent destruction of the old order and the subsequent creation of a perfect new world. It is God's final judgment on humanity's sins, the ultimate moral accounting that fulfills the demands of divine justice. Even the dead will be raised to face the consequences of their actions, and eternal punishments and rewards will be handed out in accordance with God's will.

Apocalyptic literature signaled a major change in the thinking of the ancient Jews. It began to take hold about the time that "the period of inspiration" (the era during which the Hebrew Scriptures were composed) was coming to an end. Although the Book of Daniel introduced it into the Scriptures, the Jews regarded most of the other ancient texts that touch on it as having less authority than the Scriptures. Together these books constitute a collection called the Apocrypha (the "hidden").[28] The Apocrypha's books are invaluable for tracing the evolution of Jewish thought between the close of the Hebrew Scriptures and the composition of the New Testament — and for understanding the context for Jesus' earthly mission and the birth of the Church.

Apocalyptic thought gained ground as the Jews of the post-Exilic era meditated on their desperate situation and God's promises to Abraham. Through Abraham, God had promised the Jews a triumphant future: "I will make of you a great nation, and . . . in you all the families of the earth shall be blessed" (Genesis 12:2-3); "count the stars . . . So shall your descendants be" (Genesis 15:5). For centuries the Jews assumed that these prophecies would be fulfilled in the course of ordinary events. That is, the Jews would found a great, prosperous, and powerful nation that would play a prominent role in world history. There was no talk of a life after death in which fidelity to God would ultimately be rewarded. The reward for fidelity and the punishment for faithlessness were expected to be meted out in ordinary time. Israel was God's partner in history, and God's will was revealed by what happened to Israel's people in this life. When they were obedient to God, they prospered (e.g., they conquered Canaan and established an independent kingdom). When the people sinned, they were punished (e.g., driven into exile).

That was the point at which the Jews' original expectation for their nation's future began slowly to change. A small number of Jews returned from "the Exile" that followed the Chaldaean destruction of Israel in 587 BCE to re-establish Jerusalem and the temple, but their community did not flourish. And as the years passed, it became increasingly difficult to hold on to the hope that the tiny Hebrew nation could somehow grow strong enough to match the great gentile empires that dominated the ancient world. Jews were few and gentiles many.

The alternative was either to lose confidence in God's power and faithfulness or to assume that God had a different plan for His people. Faith dictated the latter course and raised expectations that God, at a time of His choosing, would intervene in history to vindicate His people's trust in the promises He had made to their father, Abraham.

Isaiah 24 — 27, which was written after Jerusalem fell to the Babylonians in 587 BCE, records an early phase in the Jews' rethinking of their future. Isaiah predicted that God would "lay waste the earth and make it desolate" (Isaiah 24:1) and that this purging of the sins of humanity would clear the way for a new state of Israel. The scattered Jews would miraculously be recalled to Jerusalem, and the restoration of their nation would be a blessing for the whole Earth (*i.e.*, "fill the whole world with fruit"):

> In days to come Jacob shall take root, Israel shall blossom and put forth shoots, and fill the whole world with fruit. . . . On that day the Lord will thresh from the channel of the Euphrates to the Wadi of Egypt, and you will be gathered one by one, O people of Israel. And on that day a great trumpet will be blown, and those who were lost in the land of Assyria and those who were driven out to the land of Egypt will come and worship the Lord on the holy mountain at Jerusalem. (Isaiah 27:6, 12-13)

A few verses scattered among the works of other prophets (particularly Ezekiel and Zechariah) express similar hopes for God's intervention in history, but the Bible did not describe that intervention in specifically apocalyptic terms until the Book of Daniel appeared.

The Book of Daniel, which dates from the mid-2nd century BCE, is much younger than the other texts of the Hebrew Bible.

It was written at a time when the Jews of Palestine were oppressed by Greek kings who had succeeded to a portion of Alexander the Great's empire. Daniel is a kind of novel.[29] The story it tells is set during the period of the Jews' exile in Babylon (some 400 years before the book's composition). The book's adventure tales, dream interpretations, and predictions were designed to encourage the Jews of the 2nd century to resist pressure from their Greek overlord to assimilate to gentile culture.

Although Daniel makes clear, if veiled, references to the reign of the Greek king Antiochus IV (r. 175-163 BCE), countless generations of readers have insisted that its strange images and mysterious citations of numbers were really intended as coded messages for their own day. Most intriguing for readers who erroneously assume that biblical prophecy is fortune-telling is the rumor that Daniel contains a clue to the date that God has ordained for the destruction of the world. Many such dates for the Apocalypse have been derived from the books of Daniel and Revelation. Obviously all have been wrong thus far, but this does not stop hordes of Christian conservatives from assuming that Jesus did not mean it when he said, "about that day and hour [when 'Heaven and earth will pass away'] no one knows, neither the angels of heaven, nor the Son, but only the Father" (Matthew 24: 35, 36). Their appetite for new predictions based on elaborate interpretations of Daniel and Revelation continues unabated. Their eagerness for the end to come in their own time is also suggestive of an unhealthy (and un-biblical) preference for death over life.

Apocalyptic prophecies appealed greatly to an oppressed Hebrew minority that was struggling to keep faith in its divine destiny. The authors of Daniel and many of the books of the Apocrypha insisted that the God of Abraham was still in control of history and that His promises to His people would be fulfilled. It was troubling, however, that as the years passed so many of the faithful died — some of them as martyrs — before witnessing the long-delayed fulfillment. Confidence in God's justice led to the conviction that somehow the faith of the departed would be rewarded, and this encouraged a hope that had not previously been a part of Hebrew tradition — the belief that the dead would be resurrected for a final accounting.[30] The task of God's people in the context of the oppressive Greek and Roman empires was simply to persist, to preserve their faith, and to endure until God, in His own time, dramatically intervened to vindicate them.

This vision of the triumph of a faithful remnant over ungodly worldly powers has appealed to many religious minorities other than the Jews who originally conceived it. Among these were the first Christians. Apocalyptic expectations underlie much of the New Testament. Jesus is quoted as warning of a future Apocalypse (Matthew 24:29-35), and Paul led his converts to believe that the "end times" were not far off (I Thessalonians 3:13-18).

Mark, the oldest of the four canonical Gospels, depicts Jesus as an apocalyptic messenger and offers this succinct summary of his teaching: "The time is fulfilled, and the kingdom of God has come near; repent, and believe in the good news" (Mark 1:15).[31] When Jesus' disciples asked him when the climax of history would come, he warned them to be constantly vigilant and on guard and expanded on the horrors of the end times. He predicted "suffering, such has not been from the beginning of the creation that God created until now, no, and never will be" (Mark 13:19). Matthew's Gospel (chapter 24) added numerous specifics: wars, famines, earthquakes, and increased persecution of the faithful. Matthew also warned that the end would come as unexpectedly as a flash of lightning stretching from the east to the west and that it would be accompanied by alarming celestial phenomena: the sun and moon would fade and "the stars will fall from heaven." The culmination of these pyrotechnics would be the appearance of "the Son of man coming on the clouds of heaven with power and great glory." Similar verses found in Luke's Gospel (chapter 21) added the warning that the faithful should expect to "be betrayed even by parents and brothers, by relatives and friends . . . ."

Although Matthew said that "the Son" did not know the date of the Apocalypse (Matthew 24:36), Mark implied that he believed it to be near and Luke greatly narrowed the scope of Jesus' prediction: "But truly I tell you, there are some standing here who will not taste death before they see the kingdom of God" (Luke 9:26-27).

Paul, too, suspected that some of his contemporaries would live to witness the end times (I Thessalonians 4:17). It only stood to reason: Jesus was the Christ, the Messiah who was God's final redemptive act in history, and after the Messiah appeared nothing more remained to be done than to bring the great drama of creation to its divinely ordained conclusion.

Apocalyptic expectations introduced a powerful strain of asceticism into early Christianity. Paul's advice to the Corinthians on issues of sex and family life was premised on his belief that the end was near. "It is well," he wrote, "for a man not to touch a woman" (I Corinthians 7:1), and the celibate apostle added: "I wish that all were as I myself am" (7:7). This was a departure from the ancient Hebrews' concern for the preservation of the people of Israel, and it disregarded the ordinance (in Genesis 2:24) that a man leave his parents, take a wife, and "become one flesh" with her. The time for the responsibilities of family life (*i.e.*, to "be fruitful and multiply," Genesis 1:28), Paul believed, was at its end. Only minimal preparations were needed for a future that was likely to be brief.

Traditional Judaism, had maintained that God was committed to participating in the history of this world and that He cherished this world. Jews had always prayed for the blessings of many children and a long life lived in a context of peace and plenty. But preoccupation with the apocalypse turned some Jews (notably a group called the Essenes) and many Christians away from the world of ordinary human values. They denigrated their "flesh" as belonging to a sinful material realm that was condemned to pass away. They believed that creation — far from being "good" — had become hateful to God, and God was set upon its destruction. It followed, therefore, that God's people ought to subdue their bodily appetites, for these things bound them to the doomed material world and distracted them from the eternal life of the spirit.

When carried to an extreme, these views were condemned by the Church as a "Gnostic" heresy. Gnostics believed that there were two cosmic forces at war in history. One represented matter and the other spirit. Some argued that the God of the Old Testament, who created the material world, was a demon opposed to the spiritual divinity revealed in Christ. The Church rejected this by embracing the Hebrew Scriptures and their respect for the creation and its God. But many of Paul's letters and the New Testament's later epistles suggest how difficult it was for the early Christians to resist the seductions of Gnosticism.

For centuries a Christian ideal has been the saint whose heroic acts of self-denial utterly defeat the flesh. Asceticism has declined as a popular religious practice in the modern West. Although many conservative Christians believe that "flesh and blood cannot inherit the kingdom of God" and that their earthly bodies will soon be replaced by heavenly bodies (I Corinthians 15:35-55), they still consider the flesh worth investing in. They have opened Christian gyms and compounded energy bars made from ingredients mentioned in the Bible. The medieval saints who gloried in destroying their bodies and making themselves physically repulsive would be puzzled indeed to meet a Christian physical trainer who proudly displays his sculpted physique and markets his protein shakes.

The body may arguably be better served now than it was in

the heyday of apocalyptic religion, but its material environment is fairing far less well. Thanks to ramped up rates of consumption and wasteful squandering of resources, Western societies are literally living apocalyptically — that is, "as if there were no tomorrow." Some conservative Christians are contemptuous of conservation programs. They argue that efforts to conserve show either a lack of faith in God's ability to provide or a misplaced concern for a material realm that should be used up and hastened to destruction. Secular values of radical individualism and unfettered free enterprise are often combined with right-wing religious beliefs to fuel resistance to proposals for confronting environmental problems. There is little reason to respect, conserve, and care for the material world if this world is dismissed as an arena of sin that has no future.

Fascination with the Apocalypse has grown in America as conservative religion has surged. Serious political commentators have speculated in print about the influence that apocalyptic beliefs might have on the policies of some American presidents,[32] and the immense popularity of Tim LaHaye and Jerry B. Jenkins' "Left Behind" novels and films suggests how intrigued the masses are with the possibility that Earth is hastening to its end. It might seem strange that wealthy, comfortable Americans should be attracted to the idea of the obliteration of a world that has treated them so well, but Americans have a well cultivated taste for spectacles of destruction, death, and devastation as entertainment. The Apocalypse is ready made to serve these fantasies.

The religious conservatives who are most eager for the approach of the Apocalypse (and willing to do what they can to hasten its arrival) do not fear the pain they believe it will entail, for they do not expect to suffer any of its negative consequences. They pin their hopes for escape on an elaborate fantasy called "the Rapture." The Rapture is the emergency evacuation that God's elect expect when the Apocalypse suddenly breaks into history. The plot for the unfolding of the Rapture has been created by cobbling together a number of literally interpreted passages from different parts of the Bible. Its thesis is neatly stated on a bumper sticker: "In case of the Rapture this vehicle will be unattended."

Paul, when describing the end times to his Thessalonian converts (I Thessalonians 4:15-18), gave free reign to his imagination. He pictured "the Lord himself" descending from heaven with a loud cry at "the sound of God's trumpet."[33] The trumpet's blast would awaken "the dead in Christ" (about whose fate the Thessalonians had asked Paul). And those "who are alive, who are left, will be caught up in the clouds together with them to meet the Lord in the air; and so . . . will be with the Lord forever." Paul often indulged in poetic language and imagery. If he intended his words to the Thessalonians to be taken literally, we can only wonder how he reconciled their bodily assumption into heaven with his insistence to the Corinthians (I Corinthians 15:44) that heavenly life is lived in a spiritual body.

Luke (17: 30-35) said nothing about raising the dead or a trumpet. He stressed the speed with which the saved and the damned would suddenly be separated, and, if he is read literally, he also believed that the Apocalypse would happen after dark ("on that night there will be two in one bed; one will be taken and the other left"). The sheep will rapidly part from the goats, but Luke does not promise sheep ascent into the clouds.

Matthew's Gospel (chapter 24) slows things down and describes the end times as stretching out for an extended period. First, false messiahs are to appear to tempt the faithful to defect. Then there will be wars, famines, and earthquakes. Jesus' followers will be tortured, put to death and "hated by all nations." As a consequence, many will fall away, and dissension will break out in their ranks. But those who persevere "will be saved." Far from being suddenly raptured into heaven to enjoy a safe seat from which to enjoy the torment of the sinners who have been "left behind," Matthew believes that the only comfort "the elect" can anticipate is that these days of agony will be cut short for their sake — else, the text says, "no one would be saved."

Rapture enthusiasts have combined elements from, and ignored inconsistencies among, these texts to produce a narrative that owes far more to human invention than to divine inspiration. They have, with the help of the books of Daniel and Revelation, created an elaborate chain of events involving among other things Jerusalem, a restored temple, the emergence of an Antichrist, the migration and conversion of Jews, and a great battle at Armageddon. But this slicing and dicing and reassembling of texts is not a faithful reading of the Bible. It is a perverse attempt to rewrite it. To conflate diverse verses ripped from context in order to create a single complete and self-consistent narrative is to prefer a fantastical invention to the Bible as we have it.

When bits and pieces are carved out of the Scriptures and stitched together to support a reader's agenda, the result is usually disastrous for the Bible's core messages. If the Christian religion is to have any integrity, it cannot be based on a text that has been chopped into pieces and reassembled for purposes other than its own. The Word of God shines through the words of Scripture only when readers respect the complexity, contradictions, and historical limitations of those words. To substantiate this claim, we need to allow the Bible to teach us how to read.

NOTES

1   Spong, *The Sins of Scripture*, p. 204.

2   Jerry Falwell, Sermon (March 12, 2006), at: http://sermons.trbc.org/20060312.html (This is a dubious claim given that Matthew lists only four relevant passages,

and Luke and Mark only one — a repetition of one of Matthew's. In John's Gospel Jesus never uses the term. In all cases the reference is to the Hebrew *sheol*, the realm of the dead, not a place of punishment.)

3   *The News Sentinel*, Fort Wayne, Indiana (August 16, 1993), quoted at: www.geocities.com/capitolhill 7027/quotes.html (accessed 20 July 2010).

4   See: Karl Jaspers, *Way to Wisdom*, 2nd ed., trans. by Ralph Manheim (New Haven, CN: Yale University Press, 1954).

5   Karen Armstrong, *Buddha* (NY: Penguin Group, 2001), pp. 11, 19.

6   This is not an insight unique to religious traditions. The ancient Greek playwright Sophocles explored it powerfully in his play *Antigone*.

7   The evidence currently available suggests that the modern human species appeared in Africa about 130,000 years ago, and for most of its history its numbers increased quite slowly. World population did not reach one billion until the end of the 18th century CE. It had doubled by the early decades of the 20th century, and by the end of that century was inching toward seven billion.

8   For a witty, but serious, account of a similar experiment see: Jacobs, *The Year of Living Biblically*.

9   So much for the pigskin that is integral to the football games beloved by many a conservative Christian.

10   Bugs would make an alarming, but scripturally validated,

addition to a church tureen dinner.

11 James L. Kugel (*How to Read the Bible : A Guide to Scripture, Then and Now*, NY: Free Press, 2007, p. 269) notes that ancient rabbis argued that the biblical standard of justice, "an eye for an eye," actually mandated monetary compensation, not mutilation, for injury. Otherwise a blind person who injured someone's eye could not fulfill the law, and there can be no situation in which God's law could not be fulfilled. Faith in the literal truth of Scripture, therefore, required that Scripture not be literally interpreted.

12 The word *homosexual* was only coined in the last half of the 19th century. It seems to have originated with a German scholar, and may not have appeared in English until 1897.

13 The exception is Romans 1:26-27, where Paul says that God punished idolaters, both male and female, by causing them to lust for members of their own sex.

14 The Torah contains several passages ordering the ancient Israelites to care for strangers in commemoration of the fact that they once lived as aliens in the land of Egypt.

15 This is the interpretation of the tale found in Ezekiel 16:49-50, and it was Jesus' understanding of the story (see Matthew 10:14-15 and Luke 10:7-6). But in the legal context provided by the civilized Roman Empire, the hospitality rules of early, tribal societies faded from memory. The Letter of Jude (verse 7) proposed a sexual interpretation for Genesis 19, but not one that had anything to do with homosexuality. It compares the behavior of the rebellious angels in the Noah story who "left their proper dwelling" with that of the people of Sodom and Gomorrah. Both, allegedly, sought *sarkos heteras*

("strange flesh"). The reference is to "the sons of God" who bred with "the daughters of humans" and created the corrupt order that God swept away in the Great Flood (Genesis 6:1 — 7:23). Jude saw the sin of Sodom as the desire of men for sex with a different order of beings — with the angels (not men) who visited Abraham and Lot.

16 See: Kenneth James Dover, *Greek Homosexuality: Updated and with a New Postscript* (Cambridge, MA: Harvard U. Press, 1989, c. 1978), and Craig A. Williams, *Roman Homosexuality: Ideologies of Masculinity in Classical Antiquity* (NY: Oxford University Press, 1999).

17 Jean Hardisty, *Mobilizing Resentment: Conservative Resurgence from the John Birch Society to the Promise Keepers* (Boston, MA: Beacon Press, 1999), p. 41, notes that some contemporary Americans favor the literal application of this text: "In the early 1980s, a leader of a California Moral Majority chapter called for the death penalty for homosexuality."

18 Steven Greenberg, *Wrestling with God and Men: Homosexuality in the Jewish Tradition* (Madison, Wisconsin: The University of Wisconsin Press, 2004), pp. 79ff.

19 Tertullian, "On the Apparel of Women, Book 1. Introduction," translated by the Rev. S. Thelwall, http://www.newadvent.org/fathers/0402. (accessed 20 July 2010).

20 See: Averil Cameron and Amélie Kuhrt, *Images of Women in Antiquity* (Detroit, Wayne State University Press, 1983).

21 Archaeologists dismiss stories about ancient matriarchal societies as myths that owe more to male fantasies and

imaginations than to memories of actual communities. Modern feminist theories about a matriarchal phase in human social development are rooted in the writings of a 19th century theorist, J. J. Bachofen (*Das Mutterrecht*, Stuttgart: Krais and Hoffmann, 1861), and largely dismissed by anthropologists.

22 Aristotle, *The Generation of Animals* 737a25-28.

23 "The Baptist Faith and Message" (Southern Baptist Convention, 2000), http://www.sbc.net/brm/bfm2000.asp (accessed 7 July 2010).

24 The ancient Sumerian *Epic of Gilgamesh* first introduces us to the serpent who deprived humanity (the hero, Gilgamesh) of a magic plant that conferred the gift of eternal life. Likewise Genesis's association of the first woman with a rib probably derives from a story about a Sumerian goddess who was created to heal a god's rib and whose name was similar to a word for *mother*.

25 Medieval scholars debated whether Adam had a navel, for having never been born, his navel would have served no purpose. Given that God would not have created something that had no use, Adam must have had a smooth belly. This line of reasoning could also be used to argue that the first "man" was not a male, for he would have had no use for the sex organs that define masculinity. If so, it is reasonable to conclude that when Eve was created so was Adam.

26 Karen Jo Torjesen, *When Women Were Priests* (HarperSanFrancisco, 1993) provides this count and a survey of the women mentioned by name in the New Testament.

27 Italics added to call attention to the fact that here Paul appears to rank a woman with the apostles and, therefore, with himself.

28 Catholic Christians have tended to make more use of the Apocrypha than Protestants. The Apocrypha may be found bound with the canonical texts in some Catholic editions of the Bible. See chapter 7 for further discussion.

29 The Hebrew scholars who assembled the Scriptures assigned its books to three classes: the Torah (foundational law and history), the Prophets (state history and prophetic teachings), and the Writings (miscellaneous materials: Psalms, wisdom literature, and novellas such as the Book of Esther). Daniel was placed in this last category and, therefore, not regarded as a work of history or the kind of prophecy derived from history.

30 The 12th chapter of the Book of Daniel contains the only discussion of this topic in the Hebrew Scriptures.

31 Some theologians have argued that the kingdom whose arrival Jesus announced was not an apocalyptic event, but that Jesus' claim was that God's lordship was arriving through him and his followers and already challenging and transforming the abusive secular systems of exploitation that dominate human history. See: Marcus J. Borg and N. T. Wright, *The Meaning of Jesus: Two Visions*, (NY: HarperCollins, 2007), pp. 189-196). However, verses in Mark's Gospel report Jesus using vividly apocalyptic imagery in his preaching (Mark 13:24-26).

32 Sidney Blumenthal, "Apocalyptic President," *The Guardian*, 23 March 2006.

[33] Paul might have been inspired by the trumpet reference in Isaiah 27:13, but Isaiah envisioned the restoration of Israel and a universal blessing, not the destruction of the world.

4

Learning to Read

It is characteristic of this sacred book [the Bible], or religious literature, that in it the religious element emerges directly out of the crude stuff of human life as it is lived in its many phases[1]
— C. H. Dodd

Truth is what stands the test of experience.[2]
— Alfred Einstein

[Fascism] bases itself on loneliness, on the experience of not belonging to the world at all, which is among the most radical and desperate experiences of men. . . . [I]n this situation man loses trust in himself as the partner of his thoughts . . . [and develops an] extreme contempt for facts[3]
— Hannah Arendt

Following or Forcing

The Bible teaches those who accept it on its own terms how it should be read. The crucial thing is to avoid imposing preconceptions on it. This is difficult for people who have a long acquaintance with the Bible. Passages become so familiar that they no longer speak for themselves. Readers automatically assume that they already know what it has to say. When the Bible is read in this way, there is little reason to read it. The Bible is no longer itself. It simply serves as a mirror to reflect its readers back at themselves.

Readers should reflect on this each time they open the Bible. For if they are not mindful of the kind of book they are reading, they run the risk of misunderstanding it. To mistake a novel for a history book is to acquire a distorted view of the past. To mistake a partisan political tract for an objective analysis of a situation is to allow oneself to be manipulated. To accord a collection of folk remedies the authority of a medical textbook may be to endanger one's health. To fail to comprehend how the Bible conveys the Word of God is to endow human words — despite their limited historical and cultural contexts — with the authority of the transcendent divine Word.

Before readers launch into the Bible, therefore, they should pause to reflect on what they anticipate. Will it be a book that can be read like an ordinary book, or does it require special handling? How is it organized? Is the pattern of its organization significant? Does it have a narrative line? Must its contents be read in sequential order, or can it be dipped into randomly? Is it a collection of diverse materials or a unified composition? What is its subject? What is its purpose? Who was it written for? What kind of information can it be expected to provide? Was its writing motivated by the same concerns that prompt its reader to read it? Are the questions the reader expects it to address the questions it was intended to answer?

The first two chapters of the Bible's first book demonstrate how the book has to be read. The Bible begins at the beginning — with an account of creation. But instead of opening with a single creation story, which is how a historical account of Earth's origins would begin, the Bible offers two Creation stories that are contradictory and differ so much in style, vocabulary, and organization that they hardly look like they belong together in the same book.

The first Creation story describes creation as a somewhat abstract logical process. It posits a chaotic "sea" of pure, undifferentiated being that is reduced to order in stages of increasing specificity. Its Creator is omnipotent and transcendent. Things spring into existence at His Word. The second Creation story, however, is quite literally down-to-earth. Its language is concrete, and it features colorful characters — one of whom is God

Himself. It tells a tale rather than framing a philosophical model. The God of the second story is almost as limited as His human creatures. He enjoys walking about gardens enjoying cool evening breezes. People can hide from Him, and He has to ask them to confirm His suspicions about their misconduct.

In the first story, each of God's acts builds on the one that precedes it to create a perfect whole. There are no blunders, no tentative steps, no revisions, and the result is "good." God sets lights in the sky, separates the waters from dry land, and furnishes that land with plants and animals — fully setting the stage before he calls human beings (male and female) into existence. But in the second story the plants and animals follow the creation of the "man," and humanity is engineered in two phases. The "man" is molded from the "dust of the ground" at a time "when no plant of the field was yet in the earth and no herb of the field had yet sprung up." His "partner," whose creation God does not appear to have originally planned, enters the story after "every animal of the field and every bird of the air" has been examined and rejected as a suitable companion for "the man."

None of God's human creatures is named in the first Creation story. God creates humankind, not two individual people. But in the second Creation story God creates two nameable human beings with distinct personalities. Names indicate individual identities, but most also have meanings. These names are gendered stereotypes. "Adam" derives from *adamah* ("earth," the material from which he is made and with which he is condemned to struggle for his food). "Eve" comes from *Hawwāh* ("breath" or "life", the gift she bestows when giving birth).

Many of the Bible's readers try to turn the two quite different Creation narratives into one. They do so because they assume that if the Bible is to be believed, it must be "true," and there is only one way to be true. A trustworthy Bible must accurately describe events that really happened (*i.e.*, history) and be logically consistent in what it says about these events. Readers who impose this arbitrary standard of integrity on the Bible deny its conflicts, gaps, contradictions, and confusions. They believe that they must defend the text by explaining these things away. To do so, they have to lard the Bible with assumptions and additions they invent to make it conform to their demand for coherence and plausibility. Rather than accept it as it is, they rewrite it. Although they would be horrified at the charge, they treat the Bible as if it were an inferior piece of work, a hack job in need of a good editor.

Not only is it presumptuous to rewrite the Bible, but rewriting produces a mutilated text that has no claim to divine authority. It is much more respectful of the Bible to accept it as it is and humbly to ponder what its puzzling features might mean. At the very least, Genesis's two contrasting accounts of creation indicate that the Bible is not much concerned with the kinds of questions that many people would expect an account of creation to cover if they were writing it — the kinds of issues dealt with by historians, geologists, astronomers, and a host of scientific specialists.

If the Bible is pressed for information that it is not designed to provide, all kinds of distracting, unanswerable questions arise. How could there be "evening" and "morning" marking the first three days of creation[4] before the sun and moon appeared on the fourth day "to separate the day from the night" and serve as "signs . . . for days"? Given that "the man and his wife" had to rely on God to make "garments of skin" for them, did God also make tools to equip "the man" to "till . . . and keep" the garden? If "the man" and "the woman" had remained in Eden, would they have had children or was sex one of the consequences of sin? Would any being be a "human" being if it had no moral sense — no "knowledge of good and evil"? If the man and woman originally had no such knowledge, how did they know that it was wrong to disobey God and eat the fruit of the forbidden tree? If they had no such knowledge, were they really responsible for their actions? And why did God forbid them to eat of only one of Eden's special trees, "the tree of the knowledge of good and evil"? The "tree of life" also grew in the garden. Its fruit would have enabled them to "live forever." To prevent that God expelled them from the garden. Does that mean that they were created mortal — that they had always been destined for death — that death is not the consequence of sin (as I Corinthians 15: 21 states), but the fate God always intended for humankind? Death obviously did not first become their fate on the day when they ate the forbidden fruit, for why would there have been a "tree of life" in the garden if there was no death? Was the serpent more honest than God in dealing with this issue? God warned "the man" that if he ate of the forbidden tree, "in the day that you eat of it you shall die." But the serpent told "the woman" that this was not the case, and the serpent was correct. "The man" did not die that day, but lived for 930 years — at least 800 of which transpired after his expulsion from Eden (Genesis 5: 3-5).

Readers who insist that the opening chapters of Genesis be understood literally as stories about real persons and events invite the kinds of questions that expose the Bible to ridicule. The Creation narratives can be made to look like history only when they are trimmed and supplemented by unsubstantiated speculation. The outcome of this process is quite a different Bible than the one that history has bequeathed us. It is an idol we have fashioned to worship in the place of God's Word.

Idolatry is not a sin confined to the ancient pagan world. Idol worship begins whenever people substitute something human for the divine. Even the most sincere readers of the Bible have to be on guard against it, for the human ego is such that people find it hard to resist making themselves the center of its stories. We want the Bible to be about us — our world, our history, our concerns, our interests, our questions. But the Bible is sacred because it is not primarily about us; but about God.[5] It is a theological text, and *theology* means "knowledge of God."

The first line of the Bible identifies the book's subject and principle actor: "In the beginning God . . . ." The intent of the passages that follow is not to explain the universe, but to indicate what sort of transcendent reality faith maintains frames its existence. As an account of the creation rather than the Creator, Genesis 1:1-31 does not work well. Earth, for instance, is said to bring forth vegetation that bears fruit (Genesis 1:12) before the sun is created "to separate the light from the darkness" (Genesis 1:18). Logically, the sun would have had to come first, for plants need its light to fulfill their divine mandate (*i.e.,* to bear seed and fruit). As a theological account of creation, however, the first Creation story makes complete sense. Its God imposes order on chaos by working from the general to the specific. He is, therefore not only powerful, but His actions have intelligible order and purpose. They culminate in the creation of beings who are in His image and, therefore, capable of knowing Him. For human beings to make a god in their image is one thing, but quite a different thing for God to make humankind in His.

The Bible's Language

To refuse to read the Bible in a truly literal fashion — that is, to be lead by its texts rather than to compel them to conform to our expectations — is to try to turn it into an ordinary book. To refuse to recognize and respect its contradictions, complexities, metaphors, and poetic images is to deny its sacred character and mistake it for a mundane text. But no ordinary book could do what the faithful believe that the Bible does — that is, convey the Word of a transcendent God.

Ordinary (if specialized) language suffices to enable natural scientists to talk meaningfully about the universe.[6] But to talk about the Creator of the universe language has to break loose from bondage to the ordinary. Ordinary language functions by distinguishing one thing from another. Words are defined by stating the limits of their application. *Dog* can be used for some purposes but not for the same ones as *cat*. But the God of the Bible is not a thing among things, a god among gods, a member of a class of similar beings. His reality transcends the kind of reality that permits multiplicity. This makes it impossible to talk about Him in any literal way, for human languages derive from reified concepts (*i.e.*, from our interaction with things and the generalized concepts we abstract from our experience of things).

This may be the point of the mysterious answer that God gave to Moses when Moses asked God for His name (Exodus 3:13-15). English translators have struggled with ways to render the *tetragrammaton*, the Hebrew consonants that spell God's "name," YHWH.[7] The term has variously been said to mean something like: "I am that I am," I am who I am," "I am what I will be," *etc.* The puzzle the word poses for our understanding is a warning that God cannot be named in the ordinary sense, for the purpose of a name is to distinguish something from others like itself. God's uniqueness as the transcendent Other puts Him beyond naming. God's existence is His "name," for nothing like Him *is*.

God's unique reality means that language has to be transformed in order to talk about Him. It must be tricked into pointing beyond its ordinary frames of reference. Theological language is poetry's cousin. Theologians, prophets, and mystics (like poets) rely on metaphor, analogy, allegory, contradiction, and paradox, for that is the only way they can avoid the error of appearing to speak directly about God. To use literal language about God is to turn God into an idol by treating Him as a thing among things.

Idolatry is serious business, for idolatry promotes false religion, which can have terrible consequences. The Latin root of the word *religion* (*religare*, "to reconnect") implies that the purpose of religion is to ground people in a reality fundamental to their own (*i.e.*, to restore them to what they truly are). When people mistake the nature of the reality they strive for, they form a relationship that is either futile or destructive. They commit to a faith that fails them or leads them to betray their own humanity.

Some religions have assumed that the natural world is the only reality that exists and that the human challenge is to manage a relationship with its forces. Ancient people had no knowledge of what caused earthquakes, storms, sickness, victories, defeats, floods, feasts, famines, blessings, and curses. The obvious assumption was that these phenomena were the result of wills similar to, but far more powerful, than our own. Because human beings could know little about the minds and motives of gods, the worship that helped them navigate life's challenges was designed to placate the mysterious divine forces by offering them the sorts of inducements — sacrifices, gifts, service, and flattery — that succored favor with human superiors.

The faith that produced the Bible signaled a radical break with religion of this kind, for it witnessed to a God who was not the world, either in whole or in any of its parts. Its God was conceived as the Creator who was at "the beginning" of the world. He was the transcendent "Other" who called the universe into being. He was not part of what He made — a captive of His own creation. Idolatry is not possible in the Bible's religion, for its God cannot be engaged as a being among beings.

The exalted nature of the God implied by the opening chapters of Genesis might seem to doom prospects for religion of any kind. How can people connect or "reconnect" with a deity who is not part of their existence? How can such a God even be said to exist given that He creates existence itself?

The ancient Jews believed that knowledge of God would not be possible if God did not take the initiative to provide it. The Creator could not be searched out or stumbled across by human explorers, for He is not part of the realm He creates. God is known only because He chooses to have a relationship with the creatures He makes for this purpose. The Bible does not explain why God wants such a relationship, but it does say when, where, and how that relationship began. Knowledge of God did not begin with creation. The Bible's God is not revealed by natural phenomena. Psalm 19:1 claims that "the heavens are telling the glory of God," but "the heavens" do not lead to an encounter with God. Many people have been awestruck by the majesty of the universe without coming to any understanding of the Bible's God or even faith in His existence.

Nature is the domain of objects, but God is the supreme subject. He has no objectivity. He cannot be known in the way that people know passive things. Passive things can be discovered and examined at will, for they have no power over themselves. Subjects, however, are never found. They are known only when they offer themselves to be known or, in theological language, when they reveal themselves.

Revelation is not a kind of knowledge unique to the experience of God. The only way in which any subjective being can be known by another is through revelation — the process by which a subject "opens" or "gives" itself to another. Unlike the Bible's God, human beings are both objects and subjects. They can be partially understood objectively. They can be physically measured, probed, dissected, and analyzed. But their interior lives, the subjective consciousnesses that are the essence of their humanity, can be known only if they choose to reveal them. Also, revelation cannot occur unless what a subject offers is accepted. Most people have had the experience of opening themselves to others only to discover that their gift was not received.

Subjects are not found in nature, for nature is the product of laws. The same causes always have the same effects. Subjects are revealed in unique interactions — through relationships created by individual decisions to give and to receive. Relationships are not fully realized in an instant as the result of a single experience. They unfold over time as the products of shared experiences. They belong to history, not nature — to the realm of things that are unique because they are governed wills, not laws.

The Bible's God is unknown until He enters history. But He is no more a prisoner of history than of nature. He chooses which history He will use for the purpose of revealing Himself. The Bible's premise is that God's self-revelation began when He approached a man named Abram (later, Abraham), the founder of the Hebrew people.[8] The Bible says nothing about why God chose Abram. (God does not have to explain Himself.) But the Bible is very specific about the kind of relationship that God offered Abram (and his descendants). God did not command or enslave Abram. He invited Abram to join Him in a covenant (*i.e.*, contract) — a partnership. If Abram promised exclusive loyalty to God, God would make Abram the father of a great nation that would be "a blessing" to all peoples.

Given the disparity between God and a man, a covenant might seem to be a surprising vehicle for their relationship. But the Bible mentions several occasions on which God binds Himself in covenants with His creatures.[9] This is how God honors His image in their humanity. A covenant is an agreement between free agents — between subjects. Children and mental incompetents cannot enter into covenants, for they do not have the power to dispose of themselves. They are "subject to" the wills of others. God does not force acquiescence. That would be to treat His creatures as if they were objects. His desire is for a relationship, not an instrument.

Abram entered into his covenant with God in the expectation that God would fulfill His promise to give him numerous descendants. His offspring would become, in Moses' terms, a "chosen" people[10] with a special mission The Bible does not explain why God opted to invite the Hebrews into a unique relationship — other than to say that He "loved" them (Deuteronomy 7:8). It does not claim that the Hebrews were more deserving of, or better equipped for, this role than other people. The Bible is, however, clear about the task for which the Chosen People were chosen. They were called to be the means by which God made

Himself known to the world. The unfolding history of their relationship with God was to be the vehicle of God's self-revelation to the world. They were to serve as a "light unto the nations to open the eyes that are blind" (Isaiah 42:6).[11]

The Bible's authority rests on its claim to be the record of God's use of the history of the Jews (and, for Christians, of Jesus of Nazareth) to reveal Himself. The Bible is an account of a *sacred* history that begins not with creation, but with the events narrated in the 12th chapter of Genesis (*i.e.,* with the appearance of Abram). Before Abram's covenant there are no Chosen People, no sacred history, and, therefore, no accounts of events revealing God. The Creation stories (and the colorful tales of floods and towers that follow in Genesis' first eleven chapters) cannot to be read as part of sacred history. They are a theological prolegomena to sacred history.

Many a book opens with an introduction that serves to prepare its readers for the task ahead. The early chapters of Genesis serve this function. They set the scene for Abram's appearance by drawing on the only sources that purported to describe the world before sacred history began: the legends that were the part of the general cultural legacy of the ancient Middle East. The Bible never represents the Hebrews[12] as the original, or even one of the world's most ancient, peoples. The land that they believed God deeded to Abram's children was previously occupied by Egyptians, Hittites, Canaanites and others. Many generations passed before the Hebrews reached a level of cultural development comparable to that of the older societies with which they had contact. Therefore, when they speculated about the remote past and about human origins, they did not begin with their own memories, but drew on myths far older than the stories of Abram. These borrowed tales were, however, not simply told; they were reworked as vehicles for what history had taught Abram's descendants about his God.

Myths are not history, but they are also not fictions that have no claim to credibility as sources of information about the Bible's God. Myths have a kind of objectivity, for they are not invented. They are inherited.[13] They emerge as a people's cultural legacy evolves. Narrators may sometimes adapt and retell them, but they have a certain "fixedness." They describe what a community "knows" to be true about itself. They have a relationship with history, for they are distilled from hard-won lessons of life experience. They preface history without being historical. Given that human curiosity about the past far exceeds information from the past, myth satisfies the need for a point of origin. But the line between myth and history is not always clear. Myth overlaps history, for scant memories of remote eras invite fleshing out by legend.

Because the Bible derives its insights into God from sacred history, its readers should not expect everything it records about God to form a single, consistent image of the divine. Historical information accrues over time. New experiences deepen understandings and alter previous points of view. Given that portions of the Bible were written at different times over a span of centuries, the Bible should be expected to say contrasting, sometimes contradictory, things about God.

Interpreting what the Bible says about God also requires taking into account the fact that the Scriptures are not just the product of what God revealed. They were also formed by what God's human partners were prepared, at various stages in their cultural development, to receive. Noah's God delighted in sniffing the smoke of burnt offerings (Genesis 8:20). But the God the prophet Amos knew was much more concerned for the poor than for sacrifices (Amos 5:22-23) — and Paul's God was entirely finished with the temple's bloodstained altar. Abram's God was willing to spare a city if ten good men could be found in it (Genesis 18:32). The God Joshua (Joshua 6:17:21) and Saul (I Samuel 15:3) served was a ferocious deity who ordered genocides. But, through Jesus, God warned that "all who take the sword will perish by the sword" (Matthew 26:52).

The many contrasting images of God that are found in the Bible reveal as much about the maturing of God's partners in the covenant relationship as they do about God.[14] God's Word is always heard by human agents who have to make of it what they can. The Bible, as a depository of their responses, is one of humanity's great projects — the record of a long struggle to work out the meaning of existence in a theistic context. It reflects on a portion of a continuing journey toward an uncertain destination, a journey that at times meanders into strange territory and requires course corrections. Rather than a map charting a single route to a fixed goal, the Bible is a pilgrim's journal filled with encouragement and advice for those who would join its quest.

The Bible's Development

Even a casual browser will not fail to notice that the Bible is more a library than a book — not a single, through-written volume, but a collection of different kinds of texts by different authors from different periods. Its component parts were produced and originally circulated as separate items, and it was a long time before they were gathered together, accorded sacred status, and listed in the orders in which readers expect to find them today.

Modern Christians are accustomed to a Bible that is bound as a single volume, but this is a fairly recent convention. Hebrew scribes wrote on scrolls (rolls of papyrus or parchment some twenty to thirty feet long). They were wound around rods, and readers had to unroll them to find the passages they wished to consult. Because it would have been impossibly unwieldy to inscribe the entire Bible on a single scroll, the Scriptures (*i.e.,* "writings") were literally plural — a collection of separate scrolls. Many people and communities probably had only a few of the sacred books, and they may not have filed these in any particular order. Codices (stacks of sheets stitched together as pages for what we now think of as a book) only began to replace scrolls in the 2nd century CE. The innovation was widely adopted by Christian scribes, but the earliest extant codices containing the whole New Testament date no earlier than the 4th century CE.[15]

Jews and Christians are "people of the book," but they were practicing their faiths long before the Bible was fixed in form and content. The Hebrew Scriptures accumulated piecemeal for over half a millennium. What constituted Judaism changed, therefore, and evolved as the collection of Hebrew sacred materials grew. All Jews did not always agree on what should be regarded as Scripture, and they did not all interpret their common texts in the same way. Judaism has always been, therefore, not one thing, but several. Similarly, the four Christian Gospels were originally written for different Christian communities, and their authors did not intend them to be read together as they are today. A congregation that knew only the Gospel of Mark could not have understood Christianity in the same way as a congregation that used only the Gospel of John.

Change can never be regarded as apostasy for religious traditions that draw their insights from sacred history. History is a record of changing events and changing interpretations of events. Even if "sacred history" (*i.e.*, "the period of inspiration") is believed to have closed with the authorship of the last item added to the Scriptures, revelation's evolutionary process implies that faith is a dynamic phenomenon. Openness to growth and adaptation is essential to its nature. Groups of believers (*e.g.*, Orthodox Jews, Amish Christians, *etc.*) do try to stop faith's development, they can do so only by choosing an arbitrary point in history as its final stage. Even then, despite sacrifices, harsh disciplines, and acceptance of minority status, they find they have to compromise with modernity to some extent. There is no way to step outside of history.

The thirty-nine books of the Hebrew Scriptures (the Jews' *Tanakh* and the Christians' Old Testament[16]) come from many sources and time periods. The New Testament's much smaller collection of twenty-seven items only spans about three-quarters of a century but still testifies to a diversity of Christian beliefs. In addition to these things, which compose the core of the biblical *canon* ("rule" or "standard"), fourteen other ancient documents constitute a collection called the Apocrypha ("the hidden").[17] They were included in the Septuagint, the ancient Greek translation of the *Tanakh*, that was used by the authors of the New Testament. However, the medieval rabbis responsible for the modern Hebrew canon (the Masoretic text[18]) regarded them as "deuterocanonical" (of "secondary authority") and did not count them among the Scriptures. Christians disagree about their status. Protestants generally ignore them. Roman Catholics include most of them in their translations of the Bible, and the Orthodox traditions vary in the opinions of different books. All contemporary Christians, therefore, do not agree about what constitutes *the* Bible.[19]

The Bible's component parts are also organized in different ways by Jews and Christians. The Jews group their sacred books in three categories: the Law (Torah), the Prophets (*Nevi'im*), and the Writings (*Kethuvim*). The Torah (or the Pentateuch — the "Five Books") contains the oldest material and probably reached something like its current form as Hebrew scribes labored to preserve their traditions during the "Babylonian Exile" (the years after the Chaldaean destruction of the kingdom of Judah in 587 BCE). The books of Ezra and Nehemiah, which tell the story of the post-exilic attempts to rebuild Jerusalem and its temple, contain the earliest references to "the book of the law of Moses, which the Lord had given to Israel" (Nehemiah 8:1). The impetus to define that law may have come in part from the Persian government that overthrew the Chaldaeans, ended the Exile, and ordered the restoration of "the house of God at Jerusalem" (Ezra 6:9). A letter from the emperor Artaxerxes empowered Ezra, "a scribe skilled in the law of Moses" (Ezra 7:6), to "appoint magistrates and judges who may judge all the people . . . who know the laws of your God; and you shall teach those who do not know them" (Ezra 7:25). It took a long time for the Torah to assume its present form,[20] but it had probably acquired canonical status by the 4th century BCE. The earliest references to the *Nevi'im* and *Kethuvim* come from the second half of the 2nd century BCE. The *Kethuvim* may not have been fully established until the Christian era.

The Hebrew Bible does not list its contents in the same order as the Christian Old Testament. The organizational differences have theological significance. The last books in the Hebrew canon are I and II Chronicles, which survey sacred history and conclude with the decree of the Persian king, Cyrus the Great, that ended the Exile and ordered the rebuilding of Jerusalem and the temple. The Hebrew Bible thus concludes by looking forward to the fulfillment of God's promise to restore the nation of Israel. The Christian Old Testament, on the other hand, ends with words of the prophet Malachi that early Christians believed predicted the imminent arrival of the Messiah: "The messenger of the covenant in whom you delight — indeed he is coming, says the Lord of hosts" (Malachi 3:1). Malachi's prophecy serves as a transition to the Gospels and their claim that Jesus of Nazareth was the "messenger" whose arrival Judaism anticipated.

Although the books in modern Bibles sometimes bear the same names as those that circulated in the ancient world, they do not all have exactly the same content. Prior to the 15th century CE all books were individually copied by hand. This meant that many changes were introduced into texts either accidentally or on purpose. Careless or marginally literate scribes made mistakes, and editors made what they regarded as justifiable additions and emendations. Given that there were never very many copies of any work in existence, any manuscript (no matter what its quality) could (if it was the one that survived to serve as the model for a school of copyists) have great influence on the version of the book that has come down to us. Thanks to time's random winnowing, an inferior manuscript could replace more accurate copies and become the ancestor of the modern received text.

Hebrew texts were especially vulnerable to confusion, for Hebrew was originally written only with consonants and (like other ancient languages) without any punctuation or spacing between words. It was not until the Middle Ages that a desire to ensure the accuracy and consistency of copies led to the invention of "vowel points" to guide the pronunciation and identification of words. The difference of a single letter could significantly alter the meaning of a text.[21] Modern scholars try to correct errors in transmission by comparing manuscripts that have survived from the ancient world, but this is not always possible. With the exception of rare finds, such as the biblical books discovered among the Dead Sea Scrolls,[22] many books are represented only by fragments (if that) of early copies. The evidence is clear, however, that there was significant variation among ancient manuscripts. Some of the Hebrew texts from which the Greek Septuagint translations were made in the 3rd to 2nd centuries BCE diverged significantly from the versions in use today.[23]

Although Christian manuscripts were drafted in Greek (and the Greek alphabet added vowels to consonants), Christian texts share many of the problems that cast doubt on the accuracy of Hebrew books. It was not until well into the medieval era that scribes began to use spaces between letters.[24] Readers in the ancient world had to decide on their own where the breaks came between words and sentences, and this could lead to serious confusion. How, for instance, should one read: "GODIS-NOWHERE' — as "God is nowhere" or as "God is now here"?[25]

Imposing modern conventions of punctuation on ancient manuscripts also has the potential to mislead the Bible's readers. For instance, in common English translations of the story of Abraham and Isaac, Abraham appears less than truthful on a couple of occasions. When he and his son part from their companions to offer the sacrifice that God has ordered, Abraham says that after he and Isaac have worshiped, "we will come back to you" (Genesis 22:5). At this point, however, it was Abraham's firm expectation that only one of them would return. Having fibbed once, readers might wonder if Abraham lied again when his boy asked him where the lamb was for the burnt offering. The current English translation (the NRSV) quotes Abraham as saying: "God himself will provide the lamb for a burnt offering, my son" (Genesis 22:8). But knowledgeable readers will recall that there was no punctuation in the ancient Hebrew text and that the present tense of the verb *to be* is sometimes not written but assumed in Hebrew sentences. In that case, the proper translation of the passage might be: "God himself will provide. The lamb for the burnt offering [is] my son."[26] This has the virtue of representing Abraham as leveling with his boy. It also has theological appeal in that it represents Isaac, like his father, willingly acquiescing to God. Ambiguity about the meaning of the text also exists in the English translation. The comma that the translators inserted could mean that "my son" is the person Abraham addressed (the vocative),which is how most people probably read it. But given that a comma can indicate words in apposition, perhaps Abraham said "the burnt offering — my son." In both the Hebrew original and English translations the correct literal meaning of the passage remains elusive.

Early Christian writers complained that the copies of the sacred texts at their disposal were plagued by ambiguities, careless scribal errors, and willful editorial alterations. One of the Church's earliest and most influential theologians, Origen (182-251 CE), was so concerned about the differences he noted in manuscripts that he might be said to have pioneered textual criticism. In a huge work entitled *Hexapla* he compared the Hebrew text of the Old Testament with four different Greek translations.

In Origen's day there was still no any agreement among Christians on the contents of a New Testament. Theological controversies also contributed to the confusion of texts and the process of their transmission. The early Christian centuries were rife with doctrinal disputes, some of which can be traced back to the first generation of Christians. Paul's letter to the Galatians, for instance, was motivated by his eagerness to condemn preachers "who are confusing you and want to pervert the Gospel of Christ." Paul condemned these people in no uncertain terms: "if anyone proclaims to you a Gospel contrary to what you received, let that one be accursed!" (Galatians 1:6-9)

Given competition for converts among missionaries and the different messages that were preached in the early Church,[27] the temptation to forge a text or tinker with a manuscript to bring it into line with one's side in a controversy must have been strong. Forging and tinkering explain some of the peculiarities of the current canonical text. For instance, scholars have been puzzled by what looks like a contradiction between St. Paul's practice and his message. Paul praises many women for working with him to promote the faith. He even called one an "apostle" (Romans 16:7). But elsewhere in letters ascribed to him he clearly condemns women for asserting themselves in public. Some of the harshest of these admonitions are found in I Timothy (2:8-15). Most scholars agree, however, that this epistle has been falsely attributed to Paul and that it comes from the pen of a Christian of a later generation. I Corinthians, however, is authentically Paul's work, and it has a few verses (14:34-36) that seem to support what I Timothy represents as Paul's teaching. Scholarly editions of the New Testament warn their readers that confusion in the manuscript tradition raises questions about the authenticity of these verses. They interrupt the flow of Paul's letter. In verses 14:31-33 Paul discusses the role of a prophet in a Christian congregation — a topic that continues with verse 37. Verses 34-36, which order women not to speak in church, look like a digression, and in some early manuscripts they follow verse 40, not verse 33. The suspicion is that a scribe, who was familiar with I Timothy, may have added them to his copy of Paul's letter to clarify what he believed was Paul's intent. In I Corinthians Paul urges his congregants to maintain seemly order in their meetings by prophesying in turn and not all at once. The scribe who copied the text may have wanted to make it clear, on the basis of I Timothy, that Paul was thinking here only of men. He was concerned that the verse might be read as opening the way for women to claim a turn as prophets and teachers. Perhaps the scribe's additions were originally only jotted into the margin of his version of the text as a clarifying note, and copyists subsequently integrated it into different manuscripts in different places.

The New Testament books were clearly altered during the process of their transmission to us. Many of the documented changes are insignificant, but some raise serious questions. The Gospel of John, for instance, comes to a logical conclusion with chapter 20,[28] but today the Gospel has a final 21st chapter that does not quite fit. In chapter 20 the resurrected Christ appears to his disciples in a house (apparently in Jerusalem) and empowers them to judge the world and forgive its sinners. But in chapter 21 the apostles seem to have forgotten this and returned to their secular occupation as fishermen on the Sea of Galilee. Did Jesus appear to his followers in Jerusalem on the evening of the same day that the empty tomb was found, and did they immediately come to faith in his resurrection (John 20)? Or were they so disappointed by his crucifixion that they returned home to take up their old way of life and then were converted by a resurrection experience in Galilee (John 21)?[29]

The end of the Gospel of Mark poses an even greater puzzle. Most scholars believe that Mark is our earliest Gospel and a major source for the Gospels of Matthew and Luke. The earliest manuscripts of the Gospel conclude with what is now verse 16:8.

That suggests that Mark's original text ended with the announcement by "a young man" that Jesus had been raised from the dead and a promise that he would appear to his disciples in Galilee. The women who received this message are said to have suppressed it out of fear (*i.e.*, they "said nothing to anyone, for they were afraid"). A Gospel that ended with the promise, but not the report, of a resurrection appearance — and no description of how the news spread — must have disappointed some readers and motivated copyists to correct these apparent defects. No fewer than two new endings — a shorter and a longer — were added to Mark's draft. Significant issues hinge on what one thinks about the authority of these endings. In the last one, for instance, we are told hat believers will not be harmed by drinking poison or by the bite of lethal snakes. Is it truly one of Jesus' teachings?

As numbers of allegedly Christian documents multiplied, the issue of their authenticity arose. Novel interpretations and inventions posed a threat to the possibility of a coherent Christian faith.[30] This point was driven home in the mid-2nd century, when a wealthy merchant named Marcion joined the church in Rome and threatened to take it into strange theological waters. Marcion was troubled by "the problem of evil." How, he wondered, could the loving and redeeming God manifested in Jesus be reconciled with the Hebrew Bible's judgmental Creator of a world rife with suffering and injustice? Marcion's solution was Gnosticism, the heresy of positing two opposed principles — one of spirit and the other of matter. Marcion argued that the Hebrew Creator was not the beneficent deity revealed in Christ, but an evil demon who imprisoned spirits in a prison of flesh. Jesus had taken material form to awaken souls to their true nature and to free them to return to the divine light. Marcion insisted that this position was supported by the Apostle Paul's letters and the "original" (*i.e.*, his edited version of) Luke's Gospel.

Challenges like Marcion's necessitated making decisions about which texts Christians should trust to guide their faith, but the Church had no central leadership with the authority to create and police standards. At one time scholars thought that the Hebrew canon had been decreed in 90 CE by a council of rabbis that met to reorganize Judaism after the Romans sacked Jerusalem and destroyed the temple. It now seems more likely that the three categories of the Hebrew Scriptures acquired their sacred status separately and the process of their canonization was well underway long before the end of the 1st century CE. The Jewish historian Josephus (*ca.* 37 − 95) claimed that his people had twenty-two sacred books, which he assigned to three categories: the laws of Moses, the teachings of the prophets, and four books of hymns and advice on how to live. Apart from the Torah, the books named for prophets, the Psalms, and probably the "wisdom" texts (Proverbs and Ecclesiastes), the content of Josephus's version of the *Tanakh* is uncertain. Some books that are now separate may have been combined with others in his day. Debate about the contents of the *Kethuvim* (Writings) continued well into the 4th century CE.

Christian documents began to appear in the decades after Jesus' crucifixion, but it was a long time before anyone conceived of a New Testament. No Gospels had yet been written when Paul and his fellow missionaries were founding the first churches. Paul never refers to a Gospel and probably did not anticipate the need for one. Early Christians gave no thought to supplementing the Hebrew Scriptures,[31] for they believed that they were living in the last days. Jesus was soon to return and bring history to its end.

But when time passed and the first generation of believers began to die off, Christians began to collect and record the stories about Jesus that were circulating in oral traditions. Little is known about the early stages in this development. It may be that the first step was simply to compile lists of Jesus' teachings. This is the form taken by the Gospel of Thomas, a non-canonical text that may be almost as old as the four canonical Gospels. Thomas's Gospel has no narrative structure or story line. It consists of 114 separate sayings or brief exchanges between Jesus and his apostles. These have no context or significant order. Many scholars believe that a similar document lies behind portions of the Gospels of Matthew and Luke. Matthew and Luke both used Mark's Gospel as a primary source, but they also shared a good deal of information not found in Mark. Scholars speculate that this came from a no longer extant text that they have named "Q" (*Quella*, German for "source"). In so far as Q can be reconstructed from Matthew and Luke, it seems to have been a list of Jesus' teachings.

Inevitably, saying and anecdotes imputed to Jesus were collected and given interpretative narrative frameworks. So many of these Gospels ("good news" proclamations) appeared in the early Christian centuries that almost everyone associated with Jesus was credited with one. In addition to two named for Thomas, there were Gospels attributed to James, Mary Magdalene, Nicodemus, Bartholomew, Peter, Philip, Judas, and others! Only four won universal acceptance as Scripture: Matthew, Mark, Luke, and John. But no one knows how they came to be written, how they circulated, or (given their differences) how they came to acquire canonical authority.

Internal evidence has enabled scholars to date the composition of the four canonical Gospels to the last third of the 1st century CE, but their authors are unknown. Traditions about the authorship of some of them were circulating by the 2nd century CE, but these are unreliable. Matthew's Gospel was thought to have been written by the tax collector who became one of Jesus' disciples. John's Gospel claims to rest on the testimony of "the beloved disciple," whom the Gospel never identifies. Mark's Gospel was alleged to be the work of the Apostle Peter's secretary, and Luke's Gospel and the Book of Acts were supposedly memoirs compiled by one of Paul's traveling companions.

There are good reasons to question all these identifications. None of the Gospels' authors claims to have witnessed the events he reports.[32] The earliest stories about Mark claimed that Mark wrote second hand — producing an account of what he remembered Peter saying sometime after Peter died. If this was the case, then the author of Matthew's Gospel was not likely one of Jesus' disciples, for Matthew derived much of his Gospel from Mark's work.[33] A disciple who had been one of Jesus' companions would not have relied on a Gospel written by someone who was only reporting what he remembered someone else saying about Jesus.

If Luke was an associate of Paul's, that relationship would not have provided him with any firsthand information about Jesus' ministry. Paul came to Jerusalem after Jesus' crucifixion, and he never met the historical Jesus. Paul is also adamant in his claim that his message did not derive from Jesus' apostles (Galatians 1:11-24), and Paul seems to have taken little interest in what Jesus did or said prior to his crucifixion and resurrection. His letters contain almost no information about Jesus' life and teachings.

John's Gospel is strangely reticent about naming "the beloved disciple" who "is testifying to these things and has written them" (John 21:24). He is obliquely identified as the man "reclining next" to Jesus at the Last Supper (John 23). He is said to have had a conversation with Jesus while Jesus hung on the cross — an unlikely scenario that is inconsistent with the report in Mark's Gospel. Given the vividly contrasting descriptions of Jesus in the Gospels of John and Matthew, both would not likely have been the memoirs of apostles. Of the two, the Jesus in John's Gospel is least likely to have been the historical individual who traveled with the Apostles. For the author of John's Gospel, Jesus' humanity is overwhelmed by his divinity.

It is highly unlikely that any of the Gospels can be traced to anything that Jesus' apostles wrote. They were men from the

Galilean peasant class and, therefore, were most likely illiterate. Their language would have been Aramaic, and they certainly would not have been capable of writing the kind of Greek in which the canonical Gospels were composed. The earliest Christian message was also urgently apocalyptic, and the expectation that the world was at its end would have eliminated any motive for producing a written record for future generations.

None of the Gospel authors imagined that one day his work would be read in conjunction with three other Gospels. Each Gospel was intended to be the only Gospel its readers would need. If Matthew had expected his readers to use Mark's Gospel he would not have incorporated almost all of Mark's content (and some of his words) in his own work. Also, if Matthew and Luke had been aware of each other's Gospels, they surely would have done more to coordinate their contents and remove conflicting reports. John's Gospel is so radically different from the other three that it must have been intended to stand on its own. It not only contradicts the others in reporting where and when Jesus did important things (e.g., the cleansing of the temple, the Last Supper, the date of the crucifixion, etc.), but its god-like Jesus does not much resemble the human Jesus of the other Gospels.

In addition to the four Gospels, the New Testament contains twenty-one letters . Tradition credited thirteen of these to St. Paul, but scholars have doubts about the authorship of six of those. Two other documents are in categories of their own: The Book of the Acts of the Apostles (which continues Luke's Gospel into the history of the early Church), and the Book of Revelation (an apocalyptic vision). Many other texts were candidates for the canon, but ultimately rejected (at least by most Christians) — the many Gospels mentioned above, a number of acts of apostles, and a great number of letters, apocalypses, and prophecies.

Little is known about how this mass of material was winnowed down to the twenty-seven items now commonly found in the New Testament. As early as the end of the 2nd century, Christians may have been drawing up lists of materials they thought were reliable. The earliest evidence for this is a fragmentary manuscript called the Muratorian Canon. It names twenty-two of the items in the modern New Testament along with a few noncanonical texts. Not until the end of the 4th century do we find lists of contents for the New Testament that match what we are accustomed to today. The earliest comes from a letter that Athanasius, bishop of Alexandria, circulated among the churches of his diocese in 367 CE. However, not all Christian leaders agreed with Athanasius. His contemporary, Eusebius of Caesarea, divided candidates for canonization into three categories: those that were universally accepted, those that were disputed, and those that should be rejected. The Book of Revelation, the Epistle of James, and some of the shorter letters were slow to win approval in some circles while other items (*e.g.*, The Shepherd of Hermas and epistles by Barnabas and Clement) retained their popularity for a long time. Universal agreement on the content of the New Testament has yet to be reached, for some groups in Africa and the Middle East still have slightly different canons than the one in general use. There has always, therefore, been some disagreement about what constitutes the New Testament.

The Bible's Translation

Debates about the Bible's authority revolve around what it means to say that the text was divinely inspired. Some conservatives view inspiration as verging on dictation, but the issue is hardly worth arguing. Even if the Bible was originally dictated by God, the text as we now have it has been severely compromised. If God once endowed the Bible with word-by-word accuracy, that would be of little relevance now. The fallible process by which we human beings have passed the text down over the centuries means that we can never be sure how closely our versions of the

Bible match God's "original."

The Bible that modern Christians read and trust as God's Word is a scholarly reconstruction, a carefully thought out "best guess" as to its earlier contents. A glance at the footnotes to a good modern edition (*e.g.*, the New Revised Standard) will verify this, for they indicate where the printed text diverges from specific "ancient authorities" (*i.e.*, manuscripts). Every page but one (p. 999) in the Zondervan 1989 edition of the New Testament (NRSV) has notes proposing alternative readings based on the testimony of ancient sources. Over 5,700 manuscripts of all or parts of the New Testament have been catalogued, and more may yet be discovered. No one has counted exactly how many variations for portions of the Scriptures are documented by these sources, but some scholars estimate that the number may be between three and four-hundred thousand. Bart Ehrman claims that "there are more variations among our manuscripts than there are words in the New Testament."[34]

Apart from uncertainty about the phrasing of some texts, scholars cannot always be sure about the meaning of some of the words in texts whose authenticity is not questioned (*e.g.*, Leviticus's *kadesh* or Paul's *arsenokoites*[35]). Readers of modern vernacular versions of the Scriptures are usually unaware of these problems. Translators of modern Bibles, even when they are uncertain about the meaning of some passages, have to render them in words their readers will understand. Once their work is printed and bound, it assumes an air of objective authority. It looks fixed and certain. Readers have no indication of how much speculation may have gone into drafting controversial passages.

Even the biblical text that has been reconstructed as accurately as possible by scholars is inaccessible to most American Christians. They are able to read it only in translation. (Many even choose to read it in paraphrased versions of translations.) If the Bible's readers are not fluent in early Hebrew,

Aramaic, and *koine* Greek, the Scriptures they study are at least once removed from their "original" versions.[36]

It should not be forgotten that a translation is an approximation of thoughts originally conceived in another language. One reason why English speakers have adopted so many words and phrases from other languages is that another language may more accurately capture a given idea (*e.g.*, many English words are needed for what the Germans say in one: *Schadenfreude*). Equivalencies between languages are never exact, for a word carries nuances and associations from the culture that coined it. The word for *dog* in a text from an Islamic culture that despises dogs resonates quite differently when translated into English and read in Britain, a country noted for dog fanciers.[37] Words also often alter meanings in public discourse. Few contemporary Americans would be puzzled if told that a certain "cool" Hollywood star is "hot," but Shakespeare, whose grasp of English was fairly good, might have been mystified by the statement. If it is difficult to grasp contextual nuances of meaning for modern languages, it is far more challenging to recapture them for the Bible's ancient tongues.

As for the words the Bible credits to Jesus, most readers of the Gospels are twice removed from what Jesus actually said. They read his worlds in a translation of a translation. The Gospels were written in Greek, but Jesus (a Galilean peasant who worked among Galilean peasants) would have spoken Aramaic. The only Aramaic words of his the Gospels quote are found in Mark 15:33. They are the last (and only) words Marks says that Jesus spoke from the cross: *Eloi, Eloi, lama sabachthani.* Mark translates them as: "My God, my God, why have you forsaken me?" If Mark's report is accurate, Jesus himself may have known the Scriptures only in a translation. His cry was a quotation of the opening line in Psalm 22, but in Aramaic, not Hebrew.

Men from the class from which Jesus and the Apostles came are not likely to have had much literary education. The Book of

Acts (4:13) says that Peter and John "were uneducated and ordinary men." Given the cost and scarcity of books in the ancient world residents of a poor village like Nazareth were not likely to have had copies of the Hebrew Scriptures. The Bible for Jesus and his fellows may have been an Aramaic oral tradition. A wide gap separated their intellectual world from that of the cultivated Greek speakers who wrote the New Testament. Jesus is known today only through a language he did not speak and through layers of cultural filters that affect understanding of what he meant.

Anxiety about the validity of translations is not a recent development. By the 3rd century BCE, many Jews were living in gentile communities and were more fluent in Greek than Hebrew. They wanted a version of the Scriptures in their vernacular tongue, but some feared that God's law could not be accurately conveyed by a language other than Hebrew. Greek translations did begin to appear, and the Egyptian pharaoh Ptolemy II Philadelphus (283-346 BCE) is said to have requested one for the famous library the Ptolemies sponsored in Alexandria. By the 2nd century BCE, a legend had sprung up to validate the authority of a Greek translation called the Septuagint ("the seventy"). The story was that seventy (or seventy-two) scholars had been commissioned to make this translation, and — working independently — they had all produced exactly the same text. In reality, the Septuagint grew piecemeal over a period of a century and a half. It was not completed until about 130 BCE, and some portions were executed more skillfully than others. Whatever its origin and accuracy, the Septuagint was the version of the Hebrew Scriptures used by the Greek-speaking authors of the Gospels.

The Gospel writers' reliance on the Septuagint may have given rise to a doctrine that is a key belief for some Christians, but which might not have occurred to anyone had Matthew and Luke worked with the Hebrew text. Matthew and Luke both claim that Jesus was born of a virgin who conceived him by the power of God. This was said to be the fulfillment of a messianic prophecy in Isaiah 7:14,[38] which Matthew's Gospel (1:23) quoted as: "a virgin shall conceive and bear a son."

Isaiah would probably have been surprised by Matthew's interpretation of his words for two reasons. First, Isaiah was thinking about the situation facing Ahaz, king of Judah (742-726 BCE), not the Messiah. He assured the king that by the time a soon-to-be-born child reached the age of reason, Judah would be delivered from its enemies, Damascus and Israel.

Second, Isaiah would have been puzzled by the inference Matthew drew from his reference to a pregnant woman. Matthew read Isaiah's verse in the Septuagint's Greek translation. In that version Isaiah's Hebrew word *alma* , the "young woman" who was to bear a child, was rendered by the Greek term *parthenos,* "virgin." The translation had implications that the original term did not. This prompts speculation that the story of the virgin birth might not have become part of the gospel if early Christians had worked from the Bible's original Hebrew text.

When the Roman Empire succeeded to the empires of the Greeks, its Latin language became the common tongue of many Christians. Pope Damasus (r. 366-384) recognized the need for a Bible in the Latin vernacular and persuaded a scholar named Jerome (340-420) to undertake a translation. Jerome completed the New Testament about 388 and then set to work on the Hebrew Scriptures. The result was the Vulgate (*vulgaris,* "common folk"), the Latin Bible authorized by the medieval Roman Catholic Church. After the fall of Rome's empire, knowledge of Greek virtually disappeared from Western Europe, Jerome's Latin Bible became *the* Bible.

During the Middle Ages Latin gave way to the modern European languages and survived as a tongue for scholars. Once again ordinary people thirsted for Bibles in their familiar languages, and unauthorized translations of the Vulgate began to appear. The Church feared that these would generate heresy, but rather than commission new translations, it made possession of a Bible in a vernacular a capital offense.

As levels of education rose and vernacular literacy became more common some of the Church's scholarly critics took things into their own hands. At Oxford, John Wycliff (ca. 1380-1384) produced an English version of the Vulgate for the masses. Efforts were made to suppress it, but the Protestant Reformation made access to the Bible one of its chief goals. Reformers claimed the Bible's authority for their programs, and this made it extremely important to establish the accuracy of its texts.

In the years leading up to the Reformation, the study of Greek returned to the curricula of Europe's schools, and scholars appeared who were able to work with manuscripts of the New Testament in its original language. In 1515, Erasmus, one of the greatest of the Renaissance "humanists," published a Greek New Testament. It was based on a couple of manuscripts from the 12th century that were of such inferior quality that he had to translate parts of the Vulgate into Greek to fill in their gaps. But this was regarded as the most authentic text of the New Testament available, and it became the basis for new vernacular translations.

In 1525 William Tyndale (ca. 1494-1536) published an English New Testament based on Erasmus's Greek edition. He then embarked on the Old Testament, but he was executed for heresy in 1538 before completing it. Tyndale's translations became the basis for the Bible King Henry VIII licensed for use in the Anglican Church, and in 1611 a commission established by King James I published the most influential of all English Bibles, the "Authorized Version."[39]

The "King James Bible" is a product of the Golden Age in English literature and a rhetorical masterpiece. But in terms of content and accessibility, it has flaws.[40] Many more ancient manuscripts are known today than were available to the fifty-four scholars who collaborated on its translation in the 17th century. Our understanding of the history of the Bible's composition and transmission has vastly increased, and this has, from time to time, necessitated reworking the Authorized Version.[41] The language in which it was written has also continued to evolve. James and his subjects were attuned to the elegant prose and poetry of Shakespeare's world. But no one today speaks in such phrases with such rhetorical flourishes or writes with such majesty and with such an archaic vocabulary.

For some Christians this is all to the good. The less the Bible sounds like ordinary speech, the more it seems like "words from God" ringing across the ages from the dawn of time. The more mysterious and obscure the text, the more holy it seems. But Christians are "people of the book," and a book fulfills its purpose only if it is intelligible to its reader.

Anyone who cherishes the hope of finding the *living* Word of God in the Bible must abandon the temptation to treat the Bible as a timeless artifact sealed in amber. The Bible is less a static thing than a generative phenomenon — the arc of a dynamic history. It can, of course, be treated like any ordinary text and mined for rules and theories that relieve its reader of the responsibility of freedom and self-determination. But on a reader who is willing to let it speak for itself it can have quite a different effect. Christian tradition is filled with stories of people whom the Bible took by surprise and whose lives were radically altered when some of its words suddenly rang with the Word of God.

NOTES

1 C. H. Dodd, *The Bible Today* (Cambridge, England: Cambridge University Press, 1960), p. 2.

2 Quoted in: E. L. Doctorow, *Creationists* (NY: Random House, 2007), p. 160.

3   Quoted in: Lauren Sanders, *Righteous: Dispatches from the Evangelical Youth Movement* (London: Viking/Penguin, 2006), p. 240.

4   The Hebrew tradition measures the day from evening to evening. The Sabbath begins at sundown on Friday and continues until sundown on Saturday. Genesis 1, therefore, follows this pattern: "there was evening and there was morning the first [second, third, fourth, fifth, sixth] day."

5   "Though it [the Old Testament] was a book of human destiny, the story belonged to God, His works of creation, His mercy, or His wrath. The story of God's covenant with His chosen people told how He rewarded or punished their response to His commands . . . . Though a work of many authors, it told a single theme — God's purposes." Daniel J. Boorstin, *The Seekers, The Story of Man's Continuing Quest to Understand His World* (NY: Vintage Books, 1999), p. 127.

6   But if pushed to the ultimate, language about the universe begins to lose its ordinary meaning. When the universe (space itself) is described as expanding or space is said to be curved, words begin to take on meanings that bridge the gap that usually separates the literal from the metaphorical.

7   YHWH is often supplied with vowels and rendered as Yahweh or Jahweh.

8   The Bible often identifies God as the God of Abram, Isaac, and Joseph, but never as the God of Adam, Seth, and Noah.

9   God covenants with His creation (Noah), with individuals (Abram and David), and with the Hebrew people (at Sinai). The word *testament* means *covenant*. When referring to their

Scriptures as the New Testament, Christians are claiming that God, through Jesus, established a new covenant with humanity in place of His former covenant with the Jews.

10 Deuteronomy 7:6: "For you are a people holy to the Lord your God; the Lord your God has chosen you out of all the people on earth to be his people, his treasured possession"

11 The concept of the "chosen people" introduced a complex theme into the Bible. God's concern is for all people, but the instrument He opts to use to reveal that fact is a special relationship with one specific group. That means that this group has to set itself apart and preserve its uniqueness. (Some scholars have argued that this was the reason for much of the law.) The great threat to God's plan is that His chosen people might lose their identity by assimilating gentile cultures. This concern introduced an element of chauvinism or, in a loose sense, "racism" into the Scriptures. The Bible clearly and often forbids intermarriage between the Hebrews and their gentile neighbors, for such unions threatened to obscure the dividing line between peoples and cultures. Aaron took Moses to task for marrying a Cushite woman (Numbers 12:1). On the eve of their entrance into Canaan, Moses himself warned the people: "Do not inter-marry with them [the Canaanites], giving your daughters to their sons or taking their daughters for your sons . . ." (Deuteronomy 7:3). The Hebrews who returned to Jerusalem from the Exile were ordered by Ezra to "send away" their foreign wives and the children they had by them (Ezra 10:3). When these passages are excised from their historical and theological contexts, the Jews appear to practice the kind of racism that has so often victimized them.

12 "Hebrew" may derive from *hapiru*, a word that seems to

mean a wanderer, a person who crosses boundaries — a nomad who has no fixed home or land of his own.

13   "The English word *myth* derives from the Greek *mythos*, which meant 'word' in the sense of a final pronouncement [*i.e.*, a declaration]. Its special meaning appears by contrast with the Greek *logos*, which meant 'word' in the sense of the truth that can be argued and demonstrated [*i.e.*, a proof]." Boorstin, *The Seekers*, p. 128.

14   If the changes are credited to God rather than to human understanding, God appears to have a curious biography. See: Jack Miles, *God: A Biography* (NY: Vantage Books, 1996).

15   The oldest complete manuscripts of the New Testament are the Codex Vaticanus and the Codex Sinaiticus (which also contains some noncanonical material). The oldest known Christian document is a small fragment of the Gospel of John that dates to the first half of the 2nd century.

16   Some of the books that are numbered separately in Christian Bibles are combined in the *Tanakh,* giving it a total of twenty-four books instead of the Christian thirty-nine. The contents are, however, the same.

17   For a discussion of the Apocrypha see chapter 8.

18   The Masoretes ("transmitters") were a school of Hebrew scholars from the 9th and 10th centuries.

19   The Bible derives its name from *biblia,* Greek for "small books." The word *biblia* comes from the name of an ancient city (Byblos) that was known for the export of writing materials.

20   Most scholars believe that it combines material from four or more sources whose integration required several major re-editings. For a discussion of scholars' theories about its origin see the next chapter.

21   The modern translation of the story of Jacob wrestling with an angel (Genesis 32:28) reads: "you have striven with God and with humans and have prevailed." But the difference of a single letter (which would explain the Septuagint version of this passage) would change the passage to: "you have struggled with God, and with men you will prevail." See: Kugel, *How to Read the Bible*, p. 595.

22   The first of the ancient manuscripts known by this title were discovered in a cave near the Dead Sea in 1947. Subsequent searches in the region recovered about 200 items from eleven caves. With few exceptions (*e.g.,* Isaiah), the biblical texts are not complete but represented only by fragments.

23   The Hebrew text of Jeremiah is "twelve percent longer than the Greek — a difference of some 2,700 words . . . [and] the chapters are ordered differently. . . . the Greek version of Job is also much shorter than the traditional Hebrew version; chapters 4 — 6 of the book of Daniel are substantially different in the Septuagint; and the Septuagint version of the story of David and Goliath is considerably shorter than the traditional Hebrew version." *Ibid.* pp. 594-595.

24   It was also in the medieval era that scholars began to divide the Bible's books into chapters and verses in order to make citation easier. The process of working out a system may have begun in the 13th century, but modern conventions of numbering developed only after standardized printed editions began to appear in the 16th century.

25 The example is Bart Ehrman's. See: Bart D. Ehrman, *Misquoting Jesus: The Story Behind Who Changed the Bible and Why* (NY: Harper Collins, 2005), p. 48.

26 Kugel, *How to Read the Bible*, p. 13.

27 Paul's epistles and most of the later letters in the New Testament show a growing concern to expose "false" preachers. The chief threat seems to have been the spread of Gnostic ideas among Christians.

28 "Now Jesus did many other signs in the presence of his disciples, which are not written in this book. But these are written so that you may come to believe that Jesus is the Messiah, the Son of God, and that through believing you may have life in his name."

29 Some scholars believe that John 21 may have originated as a report of the resurrection experience that brought Peter to faith. The earliest tradition about the resurrection appearances places them in Galilee, not Jerusalem.

30 Christians were very slow to take official stands on the contents of their Scriptures. The Roman Catholic Church did so at the Council of Trent (1545-1563) which it convened to respond to the challenge posed by the Protestant Reformation. Martin Luther agreed with the list of twenty-seven items it ratified for the New Testament, but he opposed the council's inclusion of fourteen books of the Apocrypha in the Old Testament. Trent's decision was guided by the fact that these books were part of the ancient Septuagint. Trent spoke for Roman Catholics, but no leader or council has ever had the authority to legislate for all branches of Christianity.

31 No one knows precisely what Jews of Jesus' day regarded as Scripture. The Hebrew canon was still in the process of formation.

32 The first person plural pronoun appears in a few chapters of the Book of Acts (cf. 20 — 21), which is a continuation of the Gospel of Luke. These passages may be the result of the author of Luke-Acts copying a source, such as someone's travel diary.

33 A minority of scholars has argued that Mark's Gospel derives from Matthew's. But this does not seem likely. Mark's Gospel omits Matthew's stories about Jesus' birth and, more significantly, Matthew's reports of resurrection appearances. Someone retelling Jesus' story would not have decided to omit crucial portions of it if they were available to him in his source.

34 Ehrman, *Misquoting Jesus*, p. 89-90.

35 For discussion of these terms, see the previous chapter.

36 Muslims take a firmer line on the status of translations than most Christians, for they believe that the Prophet's role was to serve as the conduit for God's final words. The only true Qur'an, therefore, is the Arabic original. Many Christian literalists, who like Muslims, believe that every word in their Bible is inspired by God, extend inerrancy to some translations and are not constrained by their ignorance of the Bible's languages from claiming the Bible's authority for their pronouncements.

37 Symbolic actions, like words, do not always translate exactly, or even closely, from one culture to another. The Iraqi

journalist who threw his shoes at an American president created a scene that played quite differently to Arab and American television audiences. What was for one a most serious insult was for another a partially comical gesture.

38   Many scriptural texts that the Jews had never read as having anything to do with the Messiah were interpreted as messianic prophecies by the authors of the Gospels. They also seem on occasion to have inferred things about Jesus' life from texts they believed were prophecies rather than deriving them from reports of what he had done and said.

39   Ironically the Bible is commonly called the "King James Bible," in honor one of England's most libertine monarchs.

40   For instance, modern editions of the Bible correct what scholars believe was a late editorial alteration of the Greek text of I John 5:7. The apparent motive for the rewrite was to provide the New Testament with at least one verse that overtly referred to the Trinity

41   It was reworked as the "Revised Version" in England in 1885 and as the "American Standard Revised Version" in the United States in 1901. This was updated in 1952 as the "Revised Standard Version," and in 1989 a "New Revised Standard Version" appeared. The modern editions build on all known manuscripts, not just those that were available to James' scholars in the 17th century.

5

The Hebrew Phase, Part I

Once upon a time, when the only authors were God and his prophets, stories were presumed to be true simply by the fact of being told.[1]
— E. L. Doctorow

That God created mankind, male and female, in his own image is a matter of faith. That our forebears strove for centuries to perfect themselves in the image of their God is a matter of historical fact.[2]
— Jack Miles

Beliefs are stronger than facts.[3]
— Elle Newmark

Sacred and Secular History

The Bible is analogous to a living thing in that it took time to achieve maturity and has never stopped evolving as it is passes from generation to generation and people to people. It got its start in the faith that God chose to reveal Himself through the *history* of a people who called themselves "the children of Abraham."

History is the study of unfolding time. Nature, on the other hand, is the study of the working of laws indifferent to time. History is concerned with change — with the exercise of wills at the intersection of freedom and necessity. No reader of the Bible should be surprised, therefore, to find it filled with changing points of view. What the primitive nomads who followed the Hebrew patriarchs believed about God should be expected to be quite different from what was taught by the sophisticated priests who served Israel's kings. The outlook of the subjects of a prosperous Hebrew kingdom would inevitably be altered by their experiences as exiles from their homeland. Despite aspirations to objectivity, every history is partly a hi-*story*. That is, it depends on creative insight to supply contexts for and propose linkages among the events it describes. It gives its elements meaning by integrating them into its "story."

There are different kinds of stories, and the Bible's stories might be thought of as acts in a drama that sweeps across eons. Its plot is not always easy to follow. The Bible argues with itself, leaves parts of tales untold, and does not follow a coherent path of development to a neat resolution. It delights in retelling tales in different ways, and does not resolve all its sub-plots.

The Hebrew Scriptures are the product of generations of reflection on the adventures of a people who claim a special relationship with God. The history of these "Chosen People" has a dimension of meaning not found in other histories, for it is not just their history. It is the vehicle God chose to reveal Himself. Like ordinary history, it can be divided into periods. Important developments cluster in some of these, and at other times nothing much transpires. And like all history, interpretation of the Bible's sacred history is subject to revision from the perspective of each generation.

Because large stretches of the Bible look like conventional historical narratives, they are often read that way. That is, readers assume that the Bible offers an accurate objective account of real people and real events. There was an Abraham. There was a Moses. There was an Exodus from Egypt. There was a David who built a great kingdom, and there was a Solomon of awesome splendor and wisdom.

Occasionally, a correlation is found between secular and sacred history in records from the ancient Middle East, and secular history does help clarify some of what the Bible reports. But analysis that stops at this level misses the point. The theological significance of a tale does not rise or fall with its historical verification. The crucial issue is why the story was told, for the telling is the source of the insight it offers into God.

The Bible's story of the adventures of the Chosen People begins when God approaches Abram, the first of the "patriarchs." Abram is introduced as a man without a country, an identity, or much in the way of prospects for a future. He is associated with the *Apiru* (*Hapiru* or *Habiru*[4]), a class of persons who lived on the periphery of the ancient world's settled regions. For Abram *Apiru* rootlessness was a new experience. The Bible says that he once had an urban home. He had been born in the city of Ur "of the Chaldaeans."[5] Ur, a Sumerian city near the headwaters of the Persian Gulf, had a history stretching back to the beginning of civilization.

Abram is sojourning near Haran when God first speaks to him. Haran was a caravan station north of Babylonia at the midpoint between the Tigris and Euphrates rivers. The time appears to be early in the 2nd millennium BCE. The city of Ur's III Dynasty (and the last Sumerian kingdom) collapsed about 2004 BCE. This occasioned considerable upheaval throughout the Middle East as refugees (like Abram) and invaders migrated up the Euphrates looking for places to settle.[6]

God and Abram enter into a covenant (*i.e.*, a contract). Abram vows exclusive loyalty to this unknown deity, and in exchange God promises that Abram's descendants will become a great nation. Abram then visits Canaan, the land that he is told will someday belong to his descendants. That, however, lay far in the future. In the interim Abram and his kin make their livings as pastoral nomads. They and their flocks drift about Canaan and the Negeb desert and occasionally wander into Egypt.

Abram's faith in his covenant partner was severely tested. God promised Abram numberless descendants, but Abram's wife Sarai did not bear a single child. Only after Abram and Sarai were so old that the conception of a child seemed impossible, did God condescend to confirm His power and fidelity. Sarai conceived and bore Isaac.

Apart from the famous story in which Abraham nearly sacrifices his son as an offering to God, the Bible says little about Isaac, the second patriarch. There are many more stories about Isaac's son Jacob, the third patriarch, whose twelve sons found the twelve tribes of Israel. Jacob's son, Joseph, ends this period in sacred history by winning permission for his people to settle on Egypt's northeastern perimeter in a district called Goshen.

Egyptian records confirm that it was not unusual for people from Canaan and the desert to enter Egypt during periods of famine. Canaanite agriculture depended on rainfall, but Egypt's farms were sustained by the Nile's floods. When drought afflicted Canaan, Egypt's irrigated fields still yielded food. Abram and Sarai had visited Egypt at times like this, but Joseph and his people come to live there.

There was a time in Egyptian history when groups of Semitic nomads, like Joseph and his brothers, might have been welcomed into Goshen and allowed to settle. Sometime after 1630 BCE the Egyptian delta was occupied by a people whom the Egyptians called the Hyksos ("foreign rulers"). The Hyksos seized the Egyptian delta and set up a kingdom under a pharaoh of their own. The Hyksos were not the Bible's Hebrews, but they were fellow Semites. If any Egyptian king might have welcomed Hebrews into Egypt, it would most likely have been a Hyksos pharaoh, who wanted to build up Semitic manpower reserves.

The Bible says that the Hebrews remained in Egypt for 430 years, but it reports nothing about this period. For nearly half a millennium God falls silent and there is no sacred history. The turning point came after a change in Egypt's government. The Bible says that "a new king arose over Egypt who did not know Joseph" (Exodus 1:8). If a new administration appeared that had no history of ties with Joseph's people, it was likely the dynasty founded by the native Egyptian ruler who drove out the Hyksos in 1550 BCE. The reunification of Egypt inaugurated what historians call the New Kingdom. The pharaohs of the New Kingdom pursued a more aggressive foreign policy than their predecessors. Prior to the Hyksos incursion, geography had adequately protected Egypt from foreign invasion, but the Hyksos ended that illusion. The New Kingdom's pharaohs understood the dangers of isolationism and opted for offense as the best defense. They embarked on wars of aggression that extended an Egyptian empire up the coast of the Mediterranean into Syria. This gave the land of Goshen, on Egypt's eastern frontier, new strategic importance as a military base.

The Bible says that the pharaoh enslaved the Hebrews and put them to work making bricks to build the "supply cities, Pithom and Rameses" (Exodus 1:11-14). Pharaoh's armies needed supply depots on Egypt's border, and as was customary in the ancient world, locals were pressed into labor gangs for the government projects in their neighborhood. The pharaoh during whose reign the Bible sets these events might have been Rameses II (r.1279-1212 BCE), ancient Egypt's most prolific builder.

At this point the Bible's long-silent God roused Himself and charged a man named Moses with leading the Hebrews out of Egypt. Moses is said to have been born a Hebrew but adopted and raised by an Egyptian princess. His name might have a link with Egyptian royal names (*e.g.*, Ra-*moses*, Thut-*moses*) or it could have a Hebrew root.[7]

God's admonition to the Hebrews to remember their identity as heirs to the promises He had made to Abraham launched one of the most important events in sacred history, the Exodus. Moses and his people set out for Canaan, their "Promised Land," on a journey that lasted an entire generation. They gathered at the foot of a mountain, which the Bible calls both Sinai and Horeb, affirmed their covenant with God, and received the first of the many laws "of Moses" that were to set them apart as God's special people.

After most of the members of the generation of Hebrews who

had fled Egypt died off,[8] God directed their children to cross the Jordan into Canaan. Canaan was occupied by powerful city-states that had long fended off incursions by desert nomads. But about 1230 BCE, there was an international crisis that would have created an ideal opportunity for bands from the desert to break into Canaan. The coastal districts of the eastern Mediterranean were invaded from the sea. Scholars debate the identity of the newcomers, whom the Egyptians simply called "Sea Peoples," but there is no doubt about the threat they posed to the Middle East. Egypt retreated to its former borders, and the era's other superpower, the Hittite Empire, was overthrown. To confront the Sea Peoples, the Canaanite cities would have diverted military resources from the Jordan Valley's desert frontier to the coast. The upheaval gave the Hebrews their chance to slip into Canaan. It was not long after this presumed event that we find the first extra-biblical confirmation for the existence of a people called Israel — on a stele listing enemies whom the pharaoh Merneptah (d. 1211 BCE) claimed to have exterminated.

After their entrance into Canaan, the twelve Hebrew tribes went their separate ways. They did not conquer or rule the land, but only settled in its unclaimed mountainous interior. They had no leader or centralized government and did not always cooperate militarily. What organization they had was provided by "judges," charismatic individuals whom God raised up to take control during periods of crisis. After each emergency passed, the judge faded from power, and the tribes reverted to their previous independence. This uneven leadership handicapped progress toward the formation of a state, and, the Bible says, the people tired of their weakness. They demanded that their religious leaders appoint a king (I Samuel 8:4-22). God yielded to their wishes and directed the prophet Samuel to anoint a man from the tribe of Benjamin named Saul.

The coronation of Saul (r. 1020-1000 BCE) was the first step toward the creation of a Hebrew state, but a kingdom was not securely established until the reign of his successor, David (r. 1000-961). David claimed the throne after Saul and most of his sons were killed in battle with the Philistines (former Sea People). David's kingdom was divided into two regions. The northern section (home to ten of the twelve tribes) was called Israel proper and the southern portion Judah. David established his capital at Jerusalem, where his son and heir, Solomon (r. 961-922 BCE), built the first of the Hebrews' temples. Solomon brought the young kingdom to a pinnacle of power and wealth, but Israel refused to acknowledge his heir, Rehoboam, and chose a rival king. Hostilities erupted, between the two Hebrew states. In 721 BCE Israel fell to the Assyrians, who, as was their custom, deported and scattered its inhabitants. Ten of the Hebrews' twelve tribes were thereby "lost" — that is, they were assimilated into other cultures and lost their identity. Consequently, composition of the Bible fell to Judah, the only surviving Hebrew state, and sacred history is written from its point of view. In 587 BCE, Judah went the way of Israel. The Chaldaeans of Babylon stormed Jerusalem, destroyed its temple, and carried off some of its people.

Loss of the Promised Land inaugurated a period in sacred history called "the Exile." It was an era of great importance for the formation of the Bible. During the Exile, Hebrew scholars created, collected, and integrated documents to preserve the memory of their people's history and the cult of the God called Yahweh. For the Jews (Judeans) this was the beginning of the *diaspora*, a "scattering" of their people around the world that has continued to the present day. For some Jews, however, the Exile lasted only about fifty years.

In 539 BCE, the Persian ruler, Cyrus the Great, conquered Babylon and added the Chaldaean lands to his empire. Most ancient peoples thought of gods as having territorial jurisdictions, and Cyrus wanted to ensure that all the gods relating to his new domain were properly honored. Because the Jews maintained that sacrifices to their God could be offered only at the site of His former temple in Jerusalem, Cyrus permitted some of them to return to Judah to rebuild and man its temple (538 BCE).

Progress in restoring Jerusalem was slow. The city was unfortified and surrounded by hostile neighbors. The completion of the new temple about 515 BCE made little difference. In 445 BCE a group of influential Jews won support at court for a second attempt at reviving the Jewish state. A priest named Ezra led a group back to Jerusalem, bringing financial aid and a sacred book that was to be the basis for building a new community. This may be the earliest reference to the Torah.

The chief threat to the survival of biblical faith during the "Second Temple Period" was the temptation with which the Jews had long struggled: the attraction of pagan cultures and their gods. To prevent assimilation Ezra ordered Hebrew males who had married gentile women to separate from their wives and children[9] and to take new wives from among their own people. From this point on, the struggle to preserve the identity of the Chosen People becomes a major theme of sacred history.

The Book of Daniel (the last book written for the Hebrew Scriptures) appeared in the second century BCE to encourage perseverance in this fight. In 336 BCE Alexander the Great had invaded Persia, and at the time of his death in 323 BCE he ruled an empire that stretched from the Aegean and Egypt to the Indus River valley. The Greek generals who carved up Alexander's empire into kingdoms for themselves believed that the best way to consolidate their holdings was to "Hellenize" their subjects — that is, to force them to assimilate Greek culture.

In 167 BCE the demands of the Greek king Antiochus IV prompted a Judean faction, under the leadership of Judas "Maccabeus" ("Hammer") of the priestly Hasmonean family, to take up arms. This was the situation to which the Book of Daniel alludes, despite its fictional setting during the Babylonian Exile. The Maccabees liberated Jerusalem from Greek control and ruled the tiny Jewish state until 63 BCE. At that point, the Romans appeared in the eastern Mediterranean, and "Judea" became a client kingdom within their empire. At this point the Hebrew Scriptures come to a close, and the books of the Apocrypha take up the tale.

Reflection and Reconsideration

There are times when secular history appears to confirm sacred history's narrative, but much has been learned (particularly from archaeology) that calls sacred history into question. This is true not only of discoveries but of their absence — that is, when intensive searches fail to find evidence that should be easy to uncover: (e.g., the places where the Bible says that Moses' people camped in the Sinai, remnants of Jericho's fallen walls, or any sign of Solomon's great kingdom). Common sense alone would be enough to discredit some of sacred history's claims. Is it likely, for instance, that the ancient Hebrews would have retained a separate ethnic identity after living in Egypt for 430 years? It took much less time for Israel's ten tribes to lose their identities after the Assyrians sent them into exile. When searching for evidence to verify biblical texts, the Bible's readers, like physicians, must guard against an error called "satisfaction of search,"[10] the inclination to leap to a premature conclusion to confirm the correctness of a preconception.

It is important and legitimate to search for archaeological and textual information with which to compare the Bible's narrative. This improves understanding of the environment from which the Bible emerged and helps with accurate interpretation. But if the hope is to use this material to confirm the literal historicity of the Scriptures and, therefore, the truth of faith, the effort is misguided. It ignores a crucial fact: Ordinary history is not a vehicle for revelation. That is the function of sacred or mythic history. History's sacred dimension is only visible through the lens of faith. Faith does not rest on the kinds of evidence that documents historical events.

Much has been discovered about the history of the Bible's composition. The process that brought it into existence was far more complex than what is involved in writing history. Sacred texts evolve as convictions tested by the historical struggles of generations crystallize as stories. These may involve the narration of history, but history passed through mythic memory. The intent is not so much to record the particular as to inspire insight into the universal, which is the reason for the continued relevance of a body of sacred literature.

This is the appeal of much that is found in the Torah, Judaism's most sacred text and the Bible's foundation document. Tradition credited the Torah to Moses, but many generations of scholars puzzled over its duplicate stories and inconsistencies. Why did Moses not write a more coherent text? Many readers simply have chosen to ignore the Torah's contradictions or invent elaborate schemes for reconciling them, but in 1883 Julius Wellhausen, a German professor of theology and oriental languages, argued for taking the Torah's textual challenges seriously. He suggested that they offered clues to the history of the Torah's authorship.

The first detail that led Wellhausen to his "Documentary Hypothesis" was something that had troubled Hebrew scholars for centuries. The Torah seems arbitrarily to switch back and forth between two names for God: Jahweh (Yahweh)[11] and Elohim.[12] No difference of meaning between the names could be found to account for how they were being used, and there was contradictory information in the Torah about their origin. Genesis 4:26 says that people began to call on God as Jahweh during the generation of Adam's grandson Enosh, but Exodus 6:3 says that this name was not revealed until God identified himself to Moses at the burning bush.

Wellhausen pointed out that if the passages that call God Jahweh are culled out from those that call Him Elohim, the Jahweh verses constitute a relatively complete narrative beginning with an account of creation (the second Creation story) and continuing down to the time of Moses. Most of the places mentioned in this "J" (for Jahweh) document, particularly those associated with Abram and the patriarchs, are located in Judah, the Hebrews' southern kingdom. The verses that use the name Elohim for God (the E document) look like they were selected to supplement the J account. They begin with stories about Abram and end with the Hebrews fleeing Egypt. In these verses Abram and the patriarchs are linked with places that belonged to the Hebrews' northern kingdom, Israel.

Wellhausen suggested that this could be explained if the biblical text, as it now stands, combines two formerly independent accounts of Hebrew sacred history. The J or Jahwist document would have been composed for the court of Judah and the E or Elohist document for the kingdom of Israel. When the Assyrians overwhelmed Israel, refugees from the northern kingdom probably brought its sacred scrolls to Jerusalem where they were integrated into Judah's version of sacred history.

The J-E document was subsequently augmented and edited to accommodate material from two other sources, D and P. The D or Deuteronomist source was allegedly inspired by a scroll that King Josiah's priests discovered during a renovation of Jerusalem's temple in 622 BCE. It guided an extensive program of religious reforms that the young king sponsored. The P or Priestly document was a collection of laws and other materials compiled by Hebrew priests during the Exile. It was also during the Exile that J, E, D, and P were worked together, and at the Exile's conclusion, the scribe Ezra brought the finished product, the "Five Books of Moses," back to Jerusalem to guide its restoration (Nehemiah 8).

Modern scholars have proposed many revisions and refinements of Wellhausen's Documentary Hypothesis. Some believe that J, E, D, and P were not all necessarily separate documents but perhaps only different stages of rewriting and expanding a text. The features of an oral tradition are so obvious in parts of the Torah that scholars debate how much the Torah owed to recitation and how much to literary composition. There is also argument about when the Torah reached the form it takes today.

Conservative Christians have rejected the Documentary Hypothesis and any claim that the Bible show signs of revision. James L. Kugel has succinctly summarized their argument:

> accepting the documentary hypothesis in any form means retreating substantially from the most basic idea of Scripture itself, that the Bible represents *words given by God to man* [italics supplied]. If God had something to say to different writers in different periods, he ought nonetheless to be basically the same God and say basically the same things[13]

What, Kugel wonders, should a reader conclude if D "frequently contradicts what is said in other parts of the Pentateuch"? If that were true, he insists, it would be impossible to defend the proposition that the Bible was inspired by God.

But if there are contradictions in the Bible (as there so evidently are), must a reader really conclude that it has no divine authority — or that contradictions would imply that God is a confused or careless deity? Might it not simply be that the contradictions in the Bible are meant to warn its readers that its text is *not* to be read as "words given by God to man" but as man's flawed apprehension of God's Word? Having a literally inspired text is, after all, no shield against the development of controversy about what it means.[14] Literalism demands the sacrifice of reason and commonsense in exchange for a false hope of certainty.

Only the most doctrinaire readers will deny the evidence that the Torah is the product of a long period of composing, integrating, and editing. And it is hard to argue that rewriting of this kind would not have occurred, for other books of the Bible clearly show their authors revising earlier sacred texts. I and II Chronicles, which were written after the Jews returned from the Exile, recycled material from the older books of Samuel and Kings. Their purpose was to create a new version of national history that would serve the prospects of the tiny, struggling, post-exilic Hebrew state.[15] This revised national history downplayed the achievements of David and Solomon as founders of a powerful, eternal kingdom to match a much diminished expectation for the country's future. Chronicles focused instead on the part the famous kings played in establishing the Temple and its rites. The authors of Chronicles no longer saw Hebrew history as tending toward the earthly triumph of a powerful nation. The Chosen People's mission was now simply to survive with their identity intact, to maintain the temple, and faithfully observe the law of the covenant until God intervened in history.[16] Sacred history, like the secular kind, follows a changing course.

The most radical reappraisal of Wellhausen's Documentary Hypothesis and the Bible's outline of sacred history may come from an interpretation of the archaeology of the Holy Lands that has been proposed by Israel Finkelstein and Neil Silberman. They write: "It is now evident that many events of Biblical history did not take place in either the particular era or the manner described. Some of the most famous events in the Bible clearly never happened at all."[17]

Finkelstein and Silberman place Deuteronomy (the D document) at the center of the theological movements that shaped the Torah's narration of sacred history. They question the traditional division of the Hebrew Scriptures that separates the Torah from the Nevi'im (Prophets), for they see the Book of Deuteronomy as the core of a "Deuteronomistic History" that has shaped both the Torah and the *Nevi'im*'s books: Joshua, Judges, I and II Samuel, and I and II Kings. They write:

> Archaeology has provided enough evidence to support a new contention that the historical core of the Pentateuch [Torah] and the Deuteronomistic History was substantially shaped in the seventh century BCE. . . . much of the Pentateuch is a late monarchic creation, advocating the ideology and needs of the kingdom of Judah, and as such is intimately connected to the Deuteronomistic History.[18]

The authors note that the Torah often "privileges" the kingdom of Judah. Many of its geographical references are Judean and conform to the extent of the kingdom as it existed in Josiah's day (*e.g.*, Joshua 15:21-62). Josiah's administration (r. 639-609 BCE) implemented reforms that were intended to strengthen his people's allegiance to their ancestral covenants with God. The reform program, which was spelled out in the Book of Deuteronomy (*i.e.*, "the repetition of the law"), asserted the Davidic dynasty's claim to sole legitimacy and designated the royal temple in Jerusalem as the only place where sacrifices could be offered to God. Documents on which the Torah was based were edited to justify the aspirations of Josiah's kingdom and support the rationale for its reform program. The lesson of sacred history, the Deuteronomist claimed, was that the Chosen People thrive when they are exclusively loyal to God and suffer when they lapse into idolatry. This model, the Deuteronomistic History, prevailed until the crisis of the Exile.

Genesis 49:10 goes so far as to claim that Judah's right to rule over all the Hebrews was acknowledged even before there was a Hebrew state. It quotes Jacob telling his twelve sons, the founders of Israel's twelve tribes, that "the scepter shall not depart from [your brother] Judah." God Himself is said to have confirmed this in a covenant with Judah's king David: "Your house and your kingdom shall be made sure forever before me; your throne shall be established forever" (II Samuel 7:16).

Finkelstein and Silberman argue that the primacy of Judah and its interests in the Torah and the books of the Deuteronomistic History point to Judah as the place where much of the Old Testament was either composed or significantly reworked. They also note that a community does not acquire literacy, methodical record keeping, and the skill to compose narratives until it reaches "a particular stage of social development" (i.e., "state formation, in which power is centralized in national institutions like an official cult or monarchy").[19] The archaeological evidence, they insist, indicates that Judah did not reach this stage until late in the 8th century BCE:

> Judah was a rather isolated and sparsely populated kingdom until the eighth century BCE. It was hardly comparable in territory, wealth, and military might to the kingdom of Israel in the north. Literacy was very limited and its capital, Jerusalem, was a small, remote hill country town. Yet after the northern kingdom of Israel was liquidated by the Assyrian empire in 702 BCE, Judah grew enormously in population, developed complex state institutions, and emerged as a meaningful power in the region.[20]

Prior to Israel's fall, Judah's poverty, its self-sufficient pastoral-agrarian economy, and its sparse population make it difficult to credit the Bible's claim that Jerusalem's king David had the resources and manpower he would have needed to conquer a great kingdom. There is also no evidence that in Solomon's day Jerusalem boasted anything like the monumental buildings that the Bible describes. An inscription dated to about 835 BCE testifies to the existence of a "House of David," but archaeology suggests that the Davidic kingdom was anything but a powerful state. According to Finkelstein and Silberman:

Judah remained relatively empty of permanent population, quite isolated, and very marginal right up to and past the present time of David and Solomon, with no major urban centers and with no pronounced hierarchy of hamlets, villages, and towns. . . . [T]enth century Jerusalem was rather limited in extent, perhaps not more than a typical hill village.[21]

If sacred history's story of a great Davidic kingdom that was divided after Solomon's death into two states is more fantasy than reality, how reliable is the Bible's description of other key events? Finkelstein and Silberman argue that there is no evidence for an ethnically distinct Israelite people who invaded and conquered Canaan — that is, no evidence for Moses' Exodus from Egypt, for the giving of the law at Sinai, and for Joshua's victorious campaign. "Excavations of the early Israelite villages," they say, suggest "that the people who lived in those villages were indigenous inhabitants of Canaan who only gradually developed an ethnic identity that could be termed Israelite."[22]

The rise of the Israelite villages in the Palestinian highlands is associated with the slow deterioration of Canaanite cites in the richer agricultural districts, but there is no sign of invasion or infiltration of Canaan by outsiders. What seems to have occurred was the gradual transformation (perhaps in response to changes of climate or economy) of local nomadic pastoralists into settled peasant farmers. Finkelstein and Silberman believe that "the emergence of early Israel was an outcome of the collapse of the Canaanite culture, not its cause. And most of the Israelites did not come from outside Canaan — they emerged from within it. . . [T]he early Israelites were — irony of ironies — themselves originally Canaanites."[23]

Instead of a great unified kingdom founded by David that split into two states of equal significance and cultural development after Solomon's reign, Israel had always been the more advanced and powerful region. It had agriculture resources and important trade links that Judah lacked, and Judah languished in poverty and insignificance until the fall of Israel created an opportunity for it to assert itself. The result was the dream and plan for a glorious Judean future that the framers of the Deuteronomistic History formulated for Josiah, Judah's ambitious royal reformer.

Arguments based on archaeological evidence are often difficult for both professionals and lay people to evaluate. The material evidence archaeology uncovers is always partial and incomplete. Archaeologists debate the dating of crucial discoveries. And there is always the possibility that new discoveries will overturn previously accepted theories. Some critics might argue that the revision of the outline of sacred history that Finkelstein and Silberman propose rests on a foundation of contentious evidence, but in the end this may not matter much. Faith in the Bible as the Word of God does not rise or fall on secular evidence for sacred history's narrative.

If the Bible is not a treatise on natural science, it is also not to be reduced to the level of a mere history book. Many passages blatantly puzzle their readers to force them to pause and reflect on possible distinctions between biblical literature and ordinary texts. The Bible presents us with contradictory data for Noah's flood (*e.g.*, the length of the inundation). It describes Moses' parting of the sea in different ways. After claiming that Joshua obliterated the Canaanites, it proceeds in both the books of Joshua and Judges to describe conflicts between the Hebrews and the Canaanites and domination of the Hebrews by the Canaanites they had supposedly obliterated. Instead of being the masters of Canaan, the Bible claims that the allegedly triumphant Hebrews remained virtually a Stone Age people as late as the era of Saul's kingdom. In I Samuel 13:19-22 we read:

Now there was no smith to be found throughout all the land

of Israel; for the Philistines said, "The Hebrews must not make swords or spears for themselves"; so all the Israelites went down to the Philistines to sharpen their plowshares, mattocks, axes, or sickles. . . . So on the day of the battle neither sword nor spear was to be found in the possession of any of the people with Saul and Jonathan; but Saul and his son Jonathan had them.

Readers who want to be faithful to the Bible's text cannot simply refuse to see these inconsistencies or try to reason them out of existence. If they have any respect for the Bible's integrity, they need to take this feature of the Scriptures seriously as part of the message of revelation.

Many well-intentioned Christians disagree and take it for granted, as Gleason Archer claims, that "if the biblical record can be proved fallible in areas of fact that can be verified [e.g., geology, history, etc.], then it is hardly to be trusted in areas where it cannot be tested [e.g., faith, ethics, and revelation]."[24] This, however, subjects the Bible to a test that is far from self-evidently legitimate. Jesus cautioned against putting God (His Word) to the test (Matthew 4:7), and those who would impose such a rigid test of reliability need to justify what they do. Their assumption that all truths are validated in the same way (e.g., by the standard of scientific objectivity) fails to recognize that there are different ways to "tell the truth" about what Archer admits are different "areas of fact." Is it likely that the methods used to verify my report about what I had for lunch will be the same as those used to confirm my profession of love for my wife?

The Bible's purpose is not to provide its readers with information they can find elsewhere and puzzle out on their own — like knowledge of natural phenomena or human history. The Bible's function is to reveal God, and revelation is the kind of information that cannot be seized, but only received. The stories the Bible uses to illustrate the relationship between God and His people may touch on real events in real time and place, but they are not captive to historical objectivity. Their function is less to record a past than to illuminate a present. There are points at which sacred history may intersect with what archaeologists and secular historians have discovered about the past. But the "history" the Bible narrates is a mythic history that applies to the "presents" in all eras. This is why many people for many centuries have found the Bible's account of the adventures of the ancient Hebrews relevant to their own lives. Sacred history is a triumphantly optimistic story of faith that nurtures hope — hope for liberation from oppression, hope that life is worth its struggles, and hope for ultimate fulfillment.

Sacred Catalyst

If the Bible had been designed to provide us with information about the natural world and human history, it would quickly have become irrelevant. Innate human curiosity drives an ongoing process of research and discovery that has moved us far beyond what was believed about the world when the Bible was written. At that point Earth was assumed to be the stable center of a three-tiered universe — the gods dwelt above and the dead languished beneath the land of the living. Christian literalists, who reject all the discoveries of modern geology, cosmology, and biology that do not conform with their reading of the Bible, undermine Christianity by making an outdated worldview the touchstone of faith. They invite ridicule for their faith tradition by insisting that to be a Christian one must, for instance, affirm that Earth is only 6,000 years old — despite all the evidence to the contrary. Any faith that requires its adherents to retreat into a long-vanished past cannot claim to be a living faith. Christians of this ilk are like the historical re-enactors who don antique costumes to enjoy the fantasy of living in a bygone era. The religion they cultivate is only a historical artifact.

If the Bible is not intended to be mined for information in the same way as an ordinary book, what is its purpose? To use an analogy from chemistry, it is living and relevant when it operates like a catalyst. It stimulates reflection and guides thinking about the challenge of living humanely (or, as Genesis audaciously claims, "in the image of God").

The world that human beings confront is constantly in the process of change. Ideas that served people adequately at one time fail them at another, for life's context is always revising itself. There are perennial challenges that face every generation, but the Bible's function is not to resolve these, for the search for meaning is the quest that makes human beings human. The Bible's ideal standards and absolute demands prompt and prod those who would give up the search or impose a false conclusion to it. When the Bible is used to end rather than drive striving, it becomes a weapon to subdue humanity and silence God.

Prolegomena

The way people live reveals the stance they take toward life on the continuum between trust and despair. The Bible opens by inviting its reader to entertain the possibility that the world is not a random accident, but an intentional creation. If so, what expectations might we have for life in such a world? Are its prospects more or less promising?

The two Creation stories that begin the Book of Genesis set the stage for the Bible's numerous reflections on the human condition. Neither of the stories is entirely original. The first relies on Babylonian myths, and the second is deeply indebted to Sumerian religious texts and the world's oldest superhero fantasy, *The Epic of Gilgamesh*.

Unlike some pagan creation myths, neither of the Bible's Creation stories is so presumptuous as to assert anything about the Creator's origin. God's being "in the beginning" (Genesis 1:1) is simply assumed, and it is senseless to speculate about what happened before "the beginning." A faithful reader learns to respect the Bible's agenda, follow its lead, and not flesh out its stories with fantasies to answer questions it does not address.

Theologians disagree about the intention of the opening lines of the first Creation story. Do they imply that God creates the universe *ex nihilo* (out of nothing) or that (like gods in other ancient myths) He imposes order on pre-existent being? It may make little difference, for nothing limits God's hand in crafting the kind of world He wants. No other reality dictates what He can and cannot do. He speaks; His will is done; and what is done He judges to be good. He makes no compromises that might help to explain what human beings regard as the world's imperfections, the sources of evil and suffering.

Genesis's Creator is "the transcendent Other." His reality precedes what we know as reality: the "heavens and the earth" — the dimensions of time (which ancient people marked by observing the heavens) and space. Like other ancient myths, Genesis pictures "the beginning" as "a formless void" on which the Creator imposes order. The chaos of formlessness is represented as a dark, watery depth (Genesis 1: 2). This "water" is not H_2O, which does not appear until the third day of creation when wet and dry are first separated. The primal "water" is a metaphor for pure being — existence without form and intelligibility.

Division and contrast give form to pure abstraction. God's first step is to create a division within being's "watery" flux. He separates "the light from the darkness." This is not the light that eyes perceive, which issues from the sun on the fourth day. This is the "light" that minds perceive — the light of intelligibility created by the possibility of distinguishing one thing from another. It is the start of the process that generates the ordered realm of being that we comprehend.

Genesis's first Creation story imagines the universe as the ancient Babylonians described it — as a protected bubble of order submerged within the sea of primal chaos. God's second act of creation is to establish this "dome in the midst of the waters," an ordered place sustained by God where life can exist. In the story of Noah's flood, when God decides to "blot out" His creatures, He reverses this process. He pierces the "dome" and allows the waters of chaos to stream in through the "windows of the heavens" and "the fountains of the great deep" (Genesis 7:11). God's third act of creation begins to shape the environment for life. Water is separated from dry land, and vegetation springs forth. Having established the ground beneath our feet, God's next, His fourth, creative act organizes the heavens over our heads. He calls forth the two "lights," the sun and moon, that "give light upon the earth" (*i.e.*, the light of vision). The heavenly lights separate day from night and govern the succession of seasons, days and years. They also serve as "signs," an allusion to the ancient belief that celestial bodies provided omens prefiguring events on Earth. Given that the heavenly bodies that govern the passage of time only appeared on the fourth "day," references to the "days "of creation must be metaphors for stages in God's creative process.

God's fifth act of creation is to populate the earth with a second category of life. The vegetation that sprang up on the third "day" is joined by one kind of animate life, the kind that "swims" (in water and in air). God's sixth and final creative act brings forth the other kind of animate life, the kind that travels on the ground. First to appear are "cattle and creeping things and wild animals" and then God's ultimate creature, "humankind in our [*i.e.*, God's] image, according to our likeness . . . ." Significantly, human beings do not get a separate day of creation to themselves. They share a day with the animals. God gives humans "dominion" over the earth, but the order of creation implies a kinship between humans and the animals they dominate. Both are products of the same phase in God's creative activity. Humanity's implied tie with the animal world is even closer in the second Creation story. It says that God initially searched among the animals for a "companion" for "the man"

He had created. There is nothing in either story about a special creation for humanity that rules out the possibility of an evolutionary origin for the human species. In fact, it is easier to make a case for evolution than for special creation from the Bible's text. Both arguments, however, would be anachronistic. They are sides in a modern debate that has no counterpart in the world of the Bible's authors.

With the appearance of a being capable of mirroring God Himself, the first Creation story says that God's project was finished. It might be significant that God is not described as calling the world into existence in a single spontaneous burst of creativity. Instead, God is said to have proceeded by logical steps from the most abstract and general (*i.e.*, the dimensions of time and space) to the most particular and individual (*i.e.*, the self-aware human being). If God had called everything into existence at once, God's power would resemble magic. A magician's tricks are meant to be mystifying and incomprehensible, but the Creator proceeds by logical steps that make sense and, therefore, imply a rational, intelligible force at work. The God of the first Creation story is a God who condescends to be known by the human creatures who share His image. As the patriarchs later discover, He is even be willing to be challenged, reasoned with, and sometimes persuaded.

God's openness to human understanding meshes neatly with what the first Creation story suggests was the ultimate purpose of His creative activity. God wills to have beings capable of relationship with Him, beings that can mirror the freedom and power He has demonstrated as the Creator — beings who are equipped to exercise the Creator's prerogative: "dominion."

The Bible's God resembles a human being, but the Bible does not anthropomorphize Him as pagan gods are anthropomorphized. Myths depict pagan gods as humans writ large. They preside over the forces of nature and are more powerful than their human worshipers, but they are constrained by the natural order within which they operate. The Bible's Creator limits Himself so as to interact with His creatures, but He is not limited by what He creates. Whereas most ancient people made gods in their own image, the Hebrews believed in a God who made them in His image. Instead of humanity diminishing divinity as it does in paganism; the Bible asserts that divinity has elevated the dignity of humanity.

With the creation of humanity God's plan was complete, and the Bible says that He "rested on the seventh day." Given that Psalm 121 asserts that God "will neither slumber nor sleep," God's rest in Genesis 1:2 must be a poetic way of asserting that the world He created was perfect. There was nothing left for Him to do. The text is also the Bible's first example of a kind of story that crops up often in the Torah, an etiology. An etiology is a tale told to explain something — in this case, to provide an explanation for Judaism's Sabbath observation. The custom of ceasing all labor on the seventh day (the Sabbath) of the week was probably not established in Judaism before the Exile (587-538 BCE), which may be when the first Creation story was written. The Documentary Hypothesis identifies it as one of the P (Priestly) document's contributions to the Torah.

The first Creation story ends with the claim that God made a perfect world, but that is not a satisfying conclusion from the human perspective. The world, as humans experience it, is far from perfect. A gap has obviously opened between the Creator's plan and our reality.

This is the issue that the second Creation story addresses. It is the Problem of Evil. Simply stated: If God is good and all-powerful, why does evil exist? Whatever the explanation, the Bible is clear about one thing. Human beings, not God, are responsible for the world's imperfections. The second Creation story asserts that human beings spoiled things by the use they made of the freedom God gave them to act independently of God. The story makes more sense, however, as a description of the human condition than an explanation for it.

The second Creation story, like the first, imagines creation taking place in stages, but it does not describe those stages in the same way. Here the creation of humanity is not simultaneous (male and female) on the final day of creation, but occurs in two phases: the first (the formation of "man from the dust of the ground") takes place before plants appear upon the earth (*i.e.*, on the third day of creation); and the second (the creation of "the woman") is the last thing God does. Once God had placed "the man" in Eden, His creative activity had seemed to be complete. Earth's rivers were flowing, its plants and animals were flourishing, and God's garden had "the man" to till it. But God then reconsidered His handiwork and decided that "the man" should have a companion. He considered each of the animals but found none suitable. Finally, He creates a woman from "the man's" rib. Once she appears, gender arises. "The man" becomes a male, a separate but similar being capable of union with her, and the story concludes with an etiology — an explanation for marriage.

The second Creation story's style suggests an origin in a literary environment quite different from the one that informed the first Creation story. Here God is tentative and "human." Unlike God in the first Creation story, God here proceeds by trial and error and does not anticipate the consequences of His actions. He is surprised by developments and reacts to what His creatures do.

Details within the story suggest where it was written. It describes four rivers flowing from Eden. Pishon circles Havilah (Arabia) and Gihon "the land of Cush" (Egypt and Ethiopia). The other two rivers are the Tigris and Euphrates. The author of the story locates the Tigris ("flows east of Assyria"), but simply names the Euphrates, which he (?) must have assumed would be known to his readers. The world he sketched extended no farther than the Tigris to the east, the Persian Gulf and Indian ocean to the south, and the Nile to the west.

The author of the second Creation story wrote for a people (like the Hebrews, but unlike other ancient peoples) who associated nakedness with shame. When the primal couple acquire the knowledge of good and evil, they become moral beings capable of feeling guilt and shame. The story's author took it for granted that the most shameful condition his readers could imagine finding themselves in was nakedness.

There are curious elements of the second Creation story that are not self-evidently part of what we might expect in such a tale. Why, for instance, should eating be chosen to represent humanity's fundamental rebellion against God? Why does the Bible postulate a "culinary theory of sin"? Why is the villain of the piece a serpent? And why does God make the woman only from the man's rib and not from a representative assortment of his body parts? After all, the man does describe her as "bone of my bones and flesh of my flesh" (Genesis 2:23).

Middle-Eastern legends that are far older than the Bible suggest probable sources for these details. The world's earliest known literature was produced by the Sumerians and preserved for us on clay tablets inscribed in cuneiform. In the Sumerian creation stories the goddess Ninhursaga curses the god Enki for eating some plants she creates. When he begins to die, the other gods persuade her to heal him. To do so, she conjures divine nurses to tend to each of his afflicted parts. Among them is Nin-ti, the "lady of the rib." In the Sumerian language *ti* had two meanings. As a noun it meant "rib," and as a verb it meant "to bring to life." By the time the legend had been retold in different languages and passed to the Hebrews, the pun on Nin-ti's name had been forgotten, but not its association of a rib with maternity (*i.e.*, "to bring to life"). The Sumerian "lady of the rib" became "the lady made from a rib."

A link between eating and death is established in another Sumerian legend, *The Epic of Gilgamesh*, where the serpent is added to the story. When Enkidu, the companion of the great king Gilgamesh of Uruk dies, Gilgamesh is forced to confront the fact that death will someday come for him. As a superhero, he is unwilling to accept this without a fight and embarks on a quest for the secret of eternal life. After many trials, he learns that a plant grows at the bottom of the sea that renews the youth of those who eat it. He manages to obtain this virtually inaccessible botanical wonder, but before he eats it, a serpent steals it and acquires the ability to be born anew (by shedding its skin). Gilgamesh is left with no choice but to come to terms with the inevitability of death and content himself with the ordinary human pleasures of food, drink, sex, and family. Eden's serpent does not seek the immortality he symbolizes in the iconography of the ancient world, but by tempting others to eat he causes them to forfeit any such hope.

If readers of the Bible forget that its subject is theology and search the Genesis Creation stories for history, all kinds of questions arise to undercut the Bible's credibility and distract from its purpose. When the Creation stories are read as myths, however, they do a superb job of setting the stage for sacred history by describing the world as the ancient Hebrews knew it. Their authors seem naively to have assumed that what they knew about the reality of life in their day had always been true and would forever be the universal human condition.

Ancient societies were all supported by agrarian economies. Sumerian myths claimed that it was the gods' desire for laborers to raise their food that motivated them to create human beings. A memory of this legend may hover over the second Creation story. Before the first "man" was created, Genesis (2:5) notes that "there was no one to till the ground," and God creates "the man" expressly for this purpose (Genesis 2:15). It almost looks like man was made for the Garden, not the Garden for man.

When God presents His other creatures to His gardener, "the man" demonstrates his authority over them by naming them. Subsequently, he asserts the same right over his new companion by "naming" her ("woman," not yet Eve). This etiology was Genesis's explanation for the gender relationships that characterized virtually all ancient societies. The punishments for sin that God ultimately inflicts upon the man and the woman do not change their roles; they only make them much less pleasant. The tiller of the earth is cursed by having his job become a sweaty struggle to wrest "bread" from recalcitrant ground. God faults him "because you've listened to the voice of your wife,"[25] and the woman is told that her husband "shall rule over you." A dominance relationship burdens both their lives, and the decree that they "become one flesh" (in a child) is shadowed by lust and the pains of childbirth.

This was, as far as the early Hebrews knew, the ordained order of things: men spent their lives struggling to feed families that women laboriously bore and nurtured. The farming and the child rearing were not, however, curses. The popular understanding of the Garden of Eden conjures up fantasies of Adam and Eve lolling about and taking their ease on an eternal vacation in paradise. But that is not what either of the Creation stories implies was God's intent for them. Both stories represent human life as having a purpose. Both give humanity the fearful responsibility of "dominion." In the first Creation story, the gift of God's image would not have produced passive creatures, for they would have been incapable of carrying out the order to "subdue" the earth. And in the second story, laziness and dependence would hardly have made Eden's "tiller" and his partner fit companions for the God who sought them out on His evening walks.

The Creation stories make more sense as descriptions of the human condition than explanations for it. Theologians, however, have not always been mindful of this when extrapolating dogmas from myths. One consequence has been the rise of a controversial doctrine positing something called "original sin" (i.e., sin at the point of origin). It explains the world's evil by asserting that Adam and Eve's sin permanently corrupted human nature. Consequently, every human being ever born has borne the guilt of sin from the moment of birth. This has led some Christians to view sex itself as a sinful act and caused many Christian parents the anguished fear that a sickly newborn might die before being "cleansed" of its sin by baptism. That in turn led to hypothesizing the existence of Limbo, an eternal abode for the not-quite sinless, if blameless, souls of infants. When reading the Bible launches a chain of increasingly speculative inferences like these, readers should pause to consider whether their reading is wandering away from the purpose of their text.

It is not likely that Genesis' opening chapters were intended to explain *why* the human condition is what it is. If that had been their purpose, then it ought to be possible to imagine a human condition that would be vastly improved if the events Genesis describes had not taken place. But what would human beings be like if the man and the woman had turned up their noses at the thought of eating fruit? Would they have been human without the knowledge of good and evil? If they had no moral awareness, could they have had any responsibility? Could they have had any potential for dignity or nobility? Could they have exercised just dominion if they had no sense of right and wrong? Would they have been anything more than brainless simpletons or bovine beasts? How could such creatures be in God's image?

A well-intentioned effort to defend God argues that God had to give the first humans freedom to make them human; they misused this gift; and this altered their natures so that they developed the "sin gene," which they transmitted to all their descendants. As atheists have pointed out, however, this hypothesis does not cast God in a very flattering light. Because two people sinned, God had to damn everyone — including unbaptized infants who are born only to be condemned? Little wonder that some people have found it impossible to love such a God.

Those who read the second Creation story in this way need to pause and reflect on the fact that it reports that Adam and Eve paid the penalty for their crime. Adam sweated in the fields, and Eve bore him children. Sentence passed; time served. Should that not have been the end of it? The fact that it was not can only imply that God is incredibly rigid and vindictive. Arguments intended to "justify the ways of God to man" have a distressing tendency to backfire.

If the theology (*i.e.* knowledge of God) of the Creation stories is to be compatible with what the rest of the Bible says about God's character those stories must be read as description not explanation or justification of the fact that life is hard. People labor to earn livings; they sacrifice to raise children; and their lives are upended by accidents and natural disasters. It can all seem like punishment — and injustice.

The Bible is a realistic book that does not shy away from taking a hard look at life and its moral quandries. It begins by saying, "This is the way things are." But then it asks, "What are you, the possessor of God's image, going to do about it?" People who have read the second Creation story as a condemnation to eternal sin have sometimes drawn the conclusion that all they can do is endure the consequences of sin and wait for salvation. But the Bible is filled with calls to action, reform, and service. It insists that people take responsibility for their lives and strive to better their world.

The ancient Hebrews cherished the hope that something like the peace and prosperity of Eden could be restored, and they believed that it was for this purpose that God had given them the law. The reward for obeying the law was not to come after death in a utopian heaven. It was to be experienced in life as it is lived here and now. The Hebrew Scriptures spend little time speculating about life after death. They assume that the appropriate realm for human concern is the earthly existence over which God has given people dominion. Why else would they have been given such authority? The prophets hammered away at this by insisting that God was less concerned with what His people did *for* Him than by what they did *to* one another. One of God's most surprising attributes is His concern for how His creatures deal with one another.

This becomes apparent once Adam and Eve leave the Garden of Eden for the real world, and their children begin to be born. At this point the Bible offers the first of its many genealogical lists — again to describe the world more than to explain it. Many a well-intentioned person has set out to read the Bible from cover to cover only to bog down in the boredom of wadding through seemingly endless lists of names. They wonder what the point can be and skip on to the next story. The function of the genealogies to which the Bible reverts again and again is to identify (and make connections among) the various peoples with whom the Hebrews interacted in sacred history.

The first genealogies involve the Cain and Abel story, which is more a tale about a clash of cultures than of individuals. Cain is a farmer, and his brother Abel is a herdsman. These were the ancient world's two major lifestyle options. Farmers settled down in villages and worked the land. Herdsman wandered with their flocks from pasture to pasture as the seasons changed. The story of Cain and Abel implies God's preference for herdsmen — the profession of the patriarchs.

Nothing is said about God requiring sacrifices, but Cain and Abel both assume that they should offer God a share of what they produced. Without explanation God accepts Abel's offering, but declines Cain's. Cain is enraged by the divine favoritism and kills his brother.

If read as history, the story raises unanswerable questions about God's motives. Its point is not that meat is the only acceptable sacrifice, for the Hebrews also offered "the bread of the Presence" to God (I Samuel 21:6). The story might be an etiology explaining the enmity that might have existed between nomadic herding and settled farming populations in the ancient Middle East.[26] If so, the early Hebrews were the "Abels," the wandering herdsmen whom the "Cains" drove away from their cultivated lands.

God punishes Cain, but he survives and sires lines of descendants.[27] This turns out to be of little significance, for the lineages of Cain and Abel are wiped out by the Great Flood. It is Noah, descendent of Adam's third son, Seth, through whom sacred history says that the human species descends. Theologically, the Cain and Abel narratives begin the Bible's transition from the myths of Eden to the narratives of sacred history. They make the point that the reality of the world in which human beings are called to be the images of a just and loving God is fratricide.

The Bible's somber warning about the prospects for goodness in this world leads directly from Abel's murder to Noah's Flood — a sign of God's nearly total disillusionment with His errant human image. The story of a universal flood that nearly wiped out humanity, like the second Creation story, draws on Sumerian myths found in *The Epic of Gilgamesh*. Some literalists cite this extra-biblical reference to the flood as confirmation of the flood's historicity, but there is no geological evidence for such an event and no need for one to account for the story. The Sumerians occupied an alluvial plain that flooded annually. This provided the water needed to farm in an arid region, but it also threatened to wipe out human communities. When the Sumerians imagined the destruction of their world, a great flood automatically came to mind.[28] Their story passed to the Hebrews who told it for their own purposes. In fact, two versions of the tale with different details were combined by the Bible's authors (which explains the contradictions found in the story of Noah's adventure[29]).

Attempts to read the flood story as history compound absurdities. The Bible says that the ark was 450' long, 75' wide, and 45' high. This would hardly provide sufficient space for pairs of every species "of the birds according to their kinds, and of the animals according to their kinds, of every creeping thing of the ground according to its kind" (Genesis 6:20). There would not begin to be enough room for the some 50,000,000 species that inhabit Earth — even without the fish and aquatic creatures God overlooked when He stated His intention "to make an end of all flesh" (Genesis 6:13). Given that food would also have had to be stowed on board for all the animals (and the puzzling fact that there was no provision of extra members of some species to feed the carnivores), the tale certainly does not pass muster as history. To insist on reading it as such is to miss its theological point.

For the Sumerians the flood myth offered assurance that their gods would not lose patience with the errant human species, forget their desire for offerings, and obliterate human kind. The Hebrews told the story for much the same reason. The Bible's version ends with God (like a Sumerian deity) smelling "the pleasing odor" of Noah's sacrifice and promising "nor will I ever again destroy every living thing as I have done" (Genesis 8:21). God formally confirms this promise by entering into a covenant with Noah "and every living creature of all flesh." The rainbow is set in the sky as its seal. The story is an etiology explaining rainbows, but it has a much deeper meaning than that. It is God's pledge of eternal commitment to His perennially disappointing creatures. This is the promise on which faith draws to live with optimistic confidence despite knowledge of pain, suffering, and injustice.

The story of Noah's flood reveals how different the Bible's God is from pagan deities. His anger with his human creatures is not fired by their neglect of Him, but by their wickedness (Genesis 6:5). He gave them dominion over a good creation, but this was not enough: "every inclination of the thoughts of their hearts was only evil continually" (Genesis 6:5). The experience of the flood does not change their nature. There is no indication that surviving the flood made Noah's descendants better people than those who had been swept away. Nor does God use the threat of future obliteration to frighten His creatures into compliance. In fact, He does the opposite. God acknowledges that "the inclination of the human heart is evil from youth," but He pledges not to give up on the creature whom He has made, as the Bible here reiterates, "in his own image" (Genesis 9:6). He commits Himself to a permanent partnership with humankind in sacred history. This is a new kind of God with a new kind of hope for human beings. His will is that they fight their evil tendencies and manifest the goodness and justice of the One whose image they bear. By living justly and charitably with one another, they serve Him.

After God's affirmation of His covenant with the world, only one thing remains to set the stage for Abram and sacred history's opening scene. A list of Noah's sons and their descendants supplies a kind of catalogue of the peoples of the world, and buried in this list is a prophecy. Noah had three sons, Shem, Japheth, and Ham. Ham violated a rule, which the Bible does not explain, by seeing "the nakedness of his father," something most sons occasionally do. Curiously, however, it is not Ham, but his son Canaan, who is punished for this transgression. Noah curses Canaan, saying the "lowest of slaves shall he be to his brothers" (Genesis 9:25). Canaan is, of course, the eponymous ancestor of the Canaanites whose country is to be ceded to God's Chosen People.

One more thing remains to be described about the world before history begins. The Bible premises a common origin for all human beings in God's creation, but it also acknowledges that diverse cultures and languages obscure all that humankind shares in common. Genesis 10 simply notes this as a fact of life and moves on. But reflections on the pagan customs of the Hebrews' Babylonian neighbors suggested a mythic etiology to explain the plurality of human tongues.

The ancient Mesopotamians erected artificial mountains called ziggurats as platforms for the temples that housed their gods. In a flat land a ziggurat provided a high place that was a fit home for a god, and it served as a means of communication between the human and divine realms. Its construction was an act of piety for its pagan builders, but the Bible's authors saw it as an arrogant attempt to scale the heavens. In the Bible's story God responds defensively to the construction of a great ziggurat, the Tower of Babel. He scatters its builders by scrambling their speech. The Bible's authors drew realistic details for their story from real ziggurats, for they claimed that Babel's architects used "brick for stone, and bitumen for mortar." The Mesopotamian plain provided little stone for building but abundant mud for bricks, and the oil-rich region produced tar to bind them together. The Babel story suggested a fanciful explanation for one of the world's important features, but it also served theologically as a warning to Noah's descendants not to presume on the privilege of God's covenant.

With the story of Babel, the Bible shifts from humankind in general to the people whom God singles out to serve as agents of His revelation. Scholars debate how much of what follows is mythic imagination and how much is historical memory, but for the Bible's theological purpose, there may be little need to distinguish between these. Understanding the message is more important than confirming its source, for the only confirmation applicable to revelation is faith.

NOTES

1   Doctorow, *Creationists*, p. 145.

2   Miles, *God: A Biography*, p. 3.

3   Elle Newmark, *The Book of Unholy Mischief* (NY: Atria Books, 2008), p. 255.

4   *Habiru* may be the root of the word *Hebrew*, but if so, the word originally did not indicate an ethnic group, but a social or economic condition.

5   Because the Bible identifies Ur as lying in Chaldaean territory, this story was probably written sometime in the 7th or 6th century BCE, long after the Hebrews had settled in kingdoms of their own. There were no Chaldaeans in the era in which Abram is represented as living. They ruled from 626-539 BCE.

6   Ur's passing marks the transition from the Early to the Middle Bronze Age (*ca.* 2000-1550 BCE).

7   Some scholars propose a verb ("to draw out") as the source of the name and see it as an allusion to the story of the infant Moses being "drawn out" of the Nile by the princess who found him floating in a basket. See: Israel Finkelstein and Neil Asher Silberman, *The Bible Unearthed: Archaeology's New Vision of Ancient Israel and the Origin of Its Sacred Texts* (NY: Simon and Schuster, Touchstone, 2002), p. 50.

8   The delay was a punishment for their sins.

9   The repudiation of the children reflects the custom of tracing Hebrew descent through the female line. There was no way to prove paternity in the ancient world, but maternal ties were obvious. Therefore, to guarantee the purity of the community, Hebrew men had to marry Hebrew women. To do otherwise, the Bible implies, was to run the risk that the paganism of non-Hebrew mates would undermine the Chosen People's exclusive commitment to Yahweh.

10   Jerome Groopman, *How Doctors Think* (NY: Houghton

Mifflin Co., 2007), pp. 169-170.

[11] This is the most commonly used transliteration of the Hebrew, but the vowel sounds are problematic, for ancient Hebrew had no symbols for vowels. Because German scholars were prominent pioneers of textual studies and J is pronounced as Y in German, Jahweh is sometimes written as Yaweh or as YHWH (to preserve the ancient practice of omitting vowels). The 17th-century translators of the King James Bible transliterated the Hebrew, inserted arbitrary vowels, and thereby invented the name Jehovah.

[12] *Elohim* is a plural form that is translated in the singular when it refers to the Hebrew's God and in the plural when context suggests pagan deities. Good English translations of the Bible make it clear where the two words for God are used in the Hebrew text by using "God" in the place of Elohim and "Lord God" to represent Jahweh.

[13] Kugel, *How to Read the Bible*, p. 299.

[14] Muslim history clearly illustrates how faith in the infallible inspiration of a text is no guarantee of its validity, for its meaning is always a function of how fallible human minds receive and understand it. In terms of its textual history, the Qur'an is a much simpler document than the Hebrew and Christian Scriptures. Its composition is much more recent (7th century CE) and credited to a single individual, the Prophet Mohammed. It was fixed in writing not long after the Prophet's death and was largely (but not entirely) unaffected by a tradition of manuscript transmission. Its words are believed by the faithful literally to have been dictated by God through the Prophet as His passive agent. Despite this, there is significant disagreement among

Muslims today about what the Qur'an commands. See: John L. Esposito and Dalia Mogahed, *Who Speaks for Islam?* (NY: Gallup Press, 2007). See also: Toby Lester, "What is the Koran?" *The Atlantic* (January 1999), http://www.theatlantic.com/doc/19901/Koran.

15   Kugel, *How to Read the Bible,* pp. 9-10.

16   Stephen Harris, *Understanding the Bible,* 7th ed. (NY: McGraw Hill, 2006), p. 280. Unlike the Christian Old Testament, the Hebrew Bible ends with II Chronicles and its report of the decree of the Persian king Cyrus that permitted the Jews to return to Jerusalem from the Exile specifically for the purpose of rebuilding its temple. The Hebrew Bible, therefore, ends with a hope for the restoration of God's Chosen People — but as a holy nation of priests, not as subjects of a powerful earthly kingdom.

17   Finkelstein and Silberman, *The Bible Unearthed,* p. 5.

18   *Ibid.,* p. 14

19   *Ibid.,* p. 22.

20   *Ibid.,* p. 43-44.

21   *Ibid.,* p. 132–133.

22   *Ibid.,* p. 98.

23   *Ibid.,* p. 118.

24   Gleason Archer, *Encyclopedia of Biblical Difficulties* (Grand Rapids, MI: Zondervan, 1982), p. 23.

25 God had not previously forbidden the man to submit to the woman or ordered the woman to obey the man. The man named her, but her creation completed him. Sharing the same bone and flesh, they were equal — and equally responsible. The man's passive acquiescence to sin was as guilty as the woman's active embrace.

26 Some anthropologists, however, believe that herders and farmers were more likely to live in a peaceful symbiotic relationship.

27 Cain's punishment is odd. He is made "a wanderer on the earth" (Genesis 4:14) which, as a herdsman, he already was. He is then credited with founding the first city (Genesis 4:16-17), the domain of the murderous opponents of the nomadic Hebrews. His descendants are the pioneers of civilized skills: metal workers and musicians. At one time there must have been a collection of stories about Cain, some of which are now lost. The "Song of Lamech" (Genesis 4:23-24), for instance, refers to Cain being "avenged," but no such tale now exists.

28 Today, our fantasies of destruction center on threats from outer space (aliens or asteroids) or backlash from technology (bombs, genetic accidents, and climate change).

29 For example: Genesis 7:17 says that "the flood continued forty days on the earth," and Genesis 7:24 says that "the waters swelled on the earth for one hundred fifty days." Genesis 7:2 says that God ordered Noah to take "seven pairs of all clean animals" and a single pair of all unclean animals onto the ark, but Genesis 7:8 reports that "of clean animals, and of animals that are not clean . . . two and two, male and female went into the ark with Noah, as God had commanded Noah."

6

The Hebrew Phase, Part II

the Bible's integrity and, in fact, its historicity do not depend on dutiful historical "proof" of any of its particular events or personalities . . . . The power of the biblical saga stems from its being a compelling and coherent narrative expression of the timeless themes of a people's liberation, continuing resistance to oppression, and quest for social equality.[1]

— Israel Finkelstein and Neil Silberman

I imagined the stories of ordinary black people merging with the stories of David and Goliath, Moses and Pharaoh, the Christians in the lion's den, Ezekiel's field of dry bones. Those stories — of survival, and freedom, and hope — became our story, my story; the blood that had spilled was our blood, tears our tears; until this black church, on this bright day, seemed once more a vessel carrying the story of the people into future generations and into a larger world.[2]

— Barack Obama

Patriarchal Origins

Sacred history begins with the story of God's approach to Abram (later Abraham), the first of the *patriarchs* and the founder of the Hebrew people. That a man named Abram actually existed or had the career the Bible describes for him is highly uncertain. Israel's prophets mention some of the later patriarchs (*e.g.,* Jacob), but not until the late 6th century BCE does one of them allude to Abraham. This has led James Kugel to wonder: "If he were well known as an ancestor of Israel in the eighth or seventh century . . . would not one of these prophets [the ones active during those centuries] have referred to him?"[3] Finkelstein and

Silberman speculate that because "[m]any of the stories connected with Abraham are set in the southern part of the hill country, specifically the region of Hebron in southern Judah,"[4] Abraham may have originated as a Judean cult figure. If so, it is clear how he might have come to be thought of as the first of the patriarchs. After the Assyrians destroyed the kingdom of Israel, Judah emerged as the leader of the Yahweh cult. The Deuteronomists who were dominant at the Judean court at the time reinterpreted sacred texts to bring them in line with Jerusalem's agenda. Stories that celebrated Abram as the founding father of the only surviving Hebrew kingdom would have been rewritten to forecast the rise of Judah and validate its political aspirations.[5]

Much in the Abram stories reads like retrospective history: a past created to support an agenda for the future. Abram is said to be a descendant of Noah's son, Shem, and, therefore, the beneficiary of the curse Noah laid on Ham's son, Canaan: "Blessed by the Lord my God be Shem; and let Canaan be his slave" (Genesis9:26). Abram's ancestry meant that even before God struck up the covenant with him and promised him the land of Canaan, his descendants had a right to dispossess and rule over the Canaanites. On Abram's first trip to Canaan he is said to have hallowed the places where the future kingdoms of Israel and Judah would have their cult centers. He first erected an altar at Shechem in Israel, and as he traveled on, he was blessed by Melchizedek, king of (Jeru)Salem and "priest of God Most High" (Genesis 14:19). This is likely not a historical memory, but a late invention. Nothing is said about Melchizedek's origin and how (having no previous relationship with Abram) he could have become a priest of the God who was to be revealed through the sacred history that was only beginning with Abram. The text is an etiology explaining the custom of tithing to support Jerusalem's priesthood, for it claims that following the blessing, Abram gave Melchizedek "one-tenth of everything."

Abram's adventures in Egypt prefigure the Exodus, the turning point in the history of his descendants. When Abram enters Egypt, he passes his wife Sarah off as his sister and receives a large bride price for her when she attracts the affections of Egypt's pharaoh. God punishes pharaoh's unwitting adultery with plagues until pharaoh learns the truth and orders Abram and Sarah to take the fortune they have extorted and leave Egypt. Centuries later, Moses also brings plagues down on pharaoh to open the way for Abram's descendants to "plunder the Egyptians" (Exodus 3:22) on their way out of Egypt.

Like David, the founder of the Hebrew kingdom, Abram is a warlord who defeats Judah's enemies. He inaugurates male circumcision as the sign of the Chosen People's covenant with God. He sires the ancestors of the Arabs as well as the Jews. And he wins formal recognition of his descendants' claim to Judean territory by purchasing a burial ground for his family at Hebron — a deal that is witnessed and confirmed by the Hittites who acknowledge him to be "a mighty prince among us" (Genesis 23:6).

The issue of whether or not Abram really existed is not all that important for the purposes of sacred history. The Bible's sacred history does not operate by the same rules as secular history. Its purpose is not to record what people have done, but what God has done. Its objective is not knowledge of the past for its own sake but interpretation of the past as a source of God's revelation. From this perspective Abram's stories have deep significance, for they represent him as the "hero of faith," a model or paradigm for all believers.

Theologians have coined the expression "leap of faith" to describe the transition believers make from doubt to trust. "Leap" acknowledges a disjunct between evidence and belief. Faith is not indifferent to evidence nor entirely devoid of a need for it. But the evidence available is never quite sufficient for the conclusion the believer draws. Faith involves a willingness to go further, or trust more, than an objective analysis of a situation might support.

Abram is the premier "leaper." Out of the blue, Yahweh (Jahweh), an unknown deity, confronts him with an offer and a challenge. He is asked to venture into strange territory simply on the basis of a promise of future rewards. And without hesitation or debate, he goes.

But Abram's behavior may be less remarkable than the behavior the Bible ascribes to God. Unlike other gods, Yahweh does not command; He invites. He does not overwhelm and insist on unconditional submission; He offers a conditional deal in which He voluntarily binds Himself by a contract (a covenant).

The covenant establishes the special relationship that the Bible claims exists between God and Abram's descendants, the Chosen People. But God also makes other covenants — with Noah, with the Hebrews before Sinai, and with King David. But Abram's covenant is key. Its importance is such that its terms are stated on four separate occasions. Initially, God promises Abram: "I will make of you a great nation and I will bless you, and make your name great so that you will be a blessing . . . [and] in you all the families of the earth shall be blessed" (Genesis 12:1-3). After Abram's blessing by Melchizedek, God explained what He meant by "a great nation:" "Look toward heaven and count the stars . . . so shall your descendants be. . . . To your descendants I give this land, from the river of Egypt to the great river Euphrates" (Genesis 15:5, 18). On the third occasion, as God is about to fulfill His promise to give Abram (here renamed Abraham) a son, God repeats the promise to "make you [Abraham, through his descendants] exceedingly numerous," and God imposes circumcision[6] "as a sign of the covenant" (17:2, 11). On the fourth and final occasion, after Abraham has shown his willingness to obey God even if it means sacrificing his son, God reaffirms His promises in more specific detail: "I will indeed bless you, and I will make your offspring as numerous as the stars of heaven and as the sand that is on the seashore. And your offspring shall possess the gate of their enemies, and by your offspring shall all the nations of the earth gain blessing for themselves" (Genesis 22:17-18).

These passages are often cited for what they say about the Jews' claim to be God's Chosen People. But what they say about God should not be overlooked. Despite His special relationship with Abraham's offspring, God is the universal deity. His intent is that all people be blessed by what He does through the agency of Abraham's descendants.

The thread that runs through the stories about Abraham is his anxious anticipation of the fulfillment of God's promise. This situation (which is common to all believers) provides the context for one of the Bible's most famous episodes: a warning about how difficult and risky faith can be. The fulfillment of God's side of the covenant depends on Abraham having a multitude of descendants, but his wife Sarah (Sarai) is unable to bear him even one child. After the two of them have grown old and all natural means have been exhausted, God intervenes and a single boy is born. It is solely through this son, Isaac ("laughter"[7]), that God's promises can be fulfilled. Years pass, and things look good. But as Isaac nears maturity and marriage (the Bible says that he is man enough to carry the load of wood to be used for his immolation), God does something unthinkable. He orders Abraham to sacrifice the son who holds the only promise for fulfilling the covenant. Abraham had previously reasoned with God to persuade Him to spare the city of Sodom if ten good men could be found in it (Genesis 18:23-33), but he makes no plea for his son's life. He simply packs wood, fire, and a knife and sets out with Isaac to the place God designated for the bloody offering. At the last minute God stays Abraham's hand and institutes a substitutionary sacrifice — an animal in place of a man.

This story has been interpreted in many ways.[8] Most readers today concentrate on its human side, on Abraham's behavior. But for an ancient Hebrew, the tale's most obvious message might have been what it implied about God. Modern people are shocked at the thought that a father might sacrifice one of his children for any reason at all — let alone on command from the Bible's God.[9] Child sacrifices were, however, quite common in the ancient world. Virtually all ancient peoples considered children to be the property of their parents. Parents had the right to expose infants to die if they did not want to raise them or they could sell their children into slavery to satisfy their debts. And many gods (including Yahweh, according to Leviticus 23:10) demanded the sacrifice of "first fruits" — the first sheaf of wheat from the harvest, the first lamb from the flock, and the first-born son (the one Yahweh claimed in the final plague He inflicted on Egypt). Abraham may have put up no fight for Isaac because he expected his new god, who had not yet revealed much about Himself, to make the same demand other gods made.[10] The point of the story in the ancient world, therefore, might not have been what Abraham was willing to do as an act of faith, which was not all that unusual, but revelation of how his God differed from other gods. God still required blood sacrifice, but of animals not humans.

Sacrificial rituals were universal in the religions of the ancient world. A god who was not worshiped in this way might, therefore, have been literally inconceivable to ancient peoples.[11] Attitudes change, however, as sacred history unfolds. Sacrifice was eventually limited to a single altar in Jerusalem and was discontinued after that shrine was destroyed by the Romans in 70 CE. Today most people are repulsed by the idea of the blood offerings that feature prominently in the Torah, but the impulse to sacrifice remains deeply ingrained. Christian liturgies speak of their bread and wine rituals as memorials of, or participations, in Jesus' bloody sacrifice on the cross.

After Sarah dies and is buried in Hebron, Abraham took a second wife who bore him seven more sons. They, however, are given "gifts" and sent away "to the east country." The legacy of a

Chosen People will not pass through their descendants. It falls to his two older sons, Isaac and Ishmael, to bury him, but only Isaac is heir "to all he had" (*i.e.*, the covenant). The Bible then passes over Isaac's reign as the second patriarch and skips to the end of his life. Even there, its focus is less on him than on the competition between his twin sons Esau ("hairy") and Jacob ("supplanter").

Many colorful stories that look like folk tales cluster in this portion of the Bible. Esau gives up his birthright as the elder son in exchange for a bowl of stew. Isaac, blind in old age, can't tell the difference between his son Esau's hairy arm and the pelt of a goat wrapped about Jacob's smooth extremity. Jacob's father-in-law tricks him into marrying the wrong sister, but Jacob gets his revenge. After Laban, his father-in-law agrees to give him all the animals born with spotted coats, he plants rods in front the stronger animals to cast shadows over them while they breed. This allegedly ensured that all the choice newborns would be "striped, speckled, and spotted"! (Genesis 30:37-39)

Jacob's chief contribution to sacred history was to sire the twelve brothers who are the founders of Israel's tribes. The sons of Leah, Jacob's first wife, create the southern tribes of Judah and the priestly tribe of Levi. The northern tribes trace their ancestry to Rachel, Jacob's second wife. His brother Esau, his sometime enemy, founds the nation of Edom (Idumea), which had a long history of hostility toward Israel. At one point King David conquered the Edomites (II Samuel 8:13-14), but they struck back decisively by assisting Nebuchadnezzar in the assault that destroyed Jerusalem and sent its people into the Exile.[12]

Jacob was given a hint about the role he was to play in sacred history when he fled Esau to take refuge with Abraham's kin who had remained behind in Haran. God appeared to him in a dream and sought his consent to the covenant God had previously made with Abraham. When he awoke, Jacob pledged allegiance to God — but only on condition that God provide him with food and clothing and bring him safely back to his father's land. Jacob then erected a pillar, anointed it with oil, and named the place Bethel or "House of God" (Genesis 28:22). The Hebrew faith that the Bible describes at this point still had much in common with pagan practices.

Jacob's second encounter with God was on his journey home. At a place he named Peniel ("Face of God"), he engaged in a nocturnal wrestling match with a mysterious "man." At the end of the match, the stranger crippled Jacob but acknowledged his worthiness as an opponent by giving him a new name: "You shall no longer be called Jacob, but Israel, for you have striven with God and with humans, and have prevailed" (Genesis 32:28). The tale is an etiology that explains Israel's name. Linguists believe that a more accurate translation of *Israel* would be "God reigns," but the definition the Bible gives better captures the spirit of the covenantal relationship between God and the Chosen People. They are not His slaves, but partners in a relationship that is often a struggle.

After this, sacred history moves quickly to the adventures of Jacob's youngest son, Joseph, his father's favorite. The Bible contains a number of stories in which a younger son (*e.g.*, Jacob himself) displaces an older brother. These tales established precedents for the leadership role to which the little kingdom of Judah staked a claim after the fall of its dominating "brother," the rich and powerful kingdom of Israel.

Joseph's jealous siblings sold him into slavery in Egypt where, thanks to the power God gave him to interpret dreams, he won the confidence of the pharaoh. Pharaoh made him the *de facto* ruler of Egypt, and he, in turn, made Pharaonic power absolute. Joseph filled the royal granaries during years of abundant harvests, and when famine struck, he forced the Egyptians to sell their land, their livestock, and finally themselves as slaves to pharaoh in exchange for food.[13] When the same famine drove his brothers into Egypt, he won them the right to settle on "the best of all the land of Egypt" (Genesis 45:20). With these fantastic tales, the Book of Genesis comes to an end and God falls silent. The Bible claims that there was no sacred dimension to Hebrew history for the next 430 years.

Exodus and Home Coming

By the end of Genesis God has chosen a lineage for the people with whom He will work, but they are not yet a people in the sense of having their own customs and defining characteristics. They know little about God, what He expects from them, and what will set them apart as a Chosen People. The Book of Exodus launches them on the path to nationhood and the realization of their destiny. In Genesis God primarily interacted with individuals, but in Exodus He is intimately and continuously present with His people. He travels with them in a portable shrine (the tabernacle) and literally leads their journey through Sinai's desert. He renews the covenant, but this time with all the people, not simply one of their leaders. He begins to issue commandments that spell out the terms of the covenant in unprecedented detail. The people begin to receive the law (*torah*) that sets them apart, keeps them together, and makes them a holy nation.

God's choice to lead His people's exodus from Egypt was a man named Moses. Sacred history provides him with a complicated background that owes much to myth and invention. It says that he was born a Hebrew, but raised a prince of Egypt. This unlikely development was allegedly the unintended by-product of Hebrew fertility. The Bible says that Hebrews were multiplying so rapidly that the pharaoh feared they would overwhelm Egypt. Therefore, he ordered the slaughter of all their male infants. This is improbable for at least two reasons. First, Egypt was the largest and most densely populated land in the ancient Middle East; and second, the logical way to limit population growth is to slaughter females, not males. What's more, the

Bible's claim that Moses' mother kept him safe by floating him in a basket in the crocodile infested Nile and that he was discovered there and taken home by a footloose Egyptian princess is not original. It comes from a story much older than the Bible. It was first told to explain the obscure origin of the world's first empire builder, an Akkadian king of Mesopotamia named Sargon (2371-2316 BCE). It was adapted for Moses, founder of the Hebrew nation, and finally attached to Rome's founders, Romulus and Remus.

The Exodus transpires in the realm of myth more than history, but that does not diminish its theological significance. With Moses, as with Abraham and others, God shows His power by doing great things through men who have no prospects, no gifts, no strengths, and no resources of their own. God chooses as his agent an orphaned refugee who brings little other than faith to the work he is called to do. Moses' success testifies to God's hand in the history of His Chosen People.

The Exodus narrative is filled with reports of miracles. Moses first hears God's voice issuing from a "bush"[14] that burned without being consumed. He is given the power to perform wonders in an attempt to impress pharaoh. When that strategy fails, he calls down a string of phenomenal curses on the Egyptians. After pharaoh finally gives in and allows the Hebrews to leave Egypt, Moses parts a sea for their crossing, drowns a pursuing army, brings water from rocks, and sustains his people by causing a mysterious food (manna) to appear on the ground each morning.[15] Moses erects a bronze statue of a serpent that has the power to cure victims of snakebite when they look at it. And he turns a rabble of slaves into a formidable army that wins numerous battles.

Much ingenuity has been wasted on proposing natural causes for Moses' plagues, sea crossing, and food supplies (*i.e.*, an algae bloom turning the Nile blood red; a shifting wind lowering sea levels; manna, a sap exuded by desert plants in response to temperature fluctuations, *etc.*). As with other attempts to turn sacred history into ordinary history, this only serves to distract the Scriptures' readers from their point. The Bible piles up miracles to assert in the strongest terms possible that God was at work in the history of His Chosen People. But thoughtful readers will ponder something surprising about the context for these miracles. They do not produce faith. They have no effect on pharaoh's religion or the beliefs of his people, and the Hebrews, who witnessed many more miracles than the Egyptians on their journey with Moses, quickly lose confidence in him and his God. They are quick to contemplate returning to Egypt and prone to revert to idolatry. When the Exodus account is read as history, the Hebrews appear to be remarkably obtuse or strangely susceptible to spells of mass amnesia. How could they doubt so many vivid demonstrations of God's power? Clearly faith must be bolstered by something more than mere miracles.

In the Gospels, as in the Hebrew Scriptures, miracles are often said to be responses to faith, not its cause. After Jesus performs a healing act, he sometimes gives the credit to the one he heals: "Your faith has made you whole." On at least one occasion (Luke 8:46-48), he healed someone he had not even noticed until after the miracle took place (a faithful woman healed herself simply by touching him). Matthew's Gospel reports that some of those who witnessed the miracle of the resurrected Christ "doubted" (Matthew 28:17). And in John's Gospel, the apostle Thomas is chided by Christ for refusing to believe unless his faith is verified by personal experience of Jesus' miraculous resurrection (John 20:29).

The central event in the Exodus journey is a meeting between God and His people at a mountain called both Sinai and Horeb.[16] During the year the Hebrews spent camped at its base, they received a crash course in the rules of their new life, their instruction in *torah* (*i.e.*, "law"). The only specific commandment God had given earlier (other than to keep faith with Him) was the order to circumcise all Hebrew males. Now, however, laws begin to multiply at a great rate.

Christians pay little attention to most of the Torah's 613 laws and tend to think of *the* law as little more than the Ten Commandments (or Decalogue). The Book of Exodus highlights these, for it implies that they were the only laws that God personally issued to His people. God Himself is even described as inscribing them on stone tablets.

Despite the attention they have attracted, the Ten[17] Commandments are a little underwhelming. They contain no surprises or dramatic revelations. The Bible provides us with two slightly different versions of them, one in Exodus 20:1-17and another in Deuteronomy 5:6-21. As laws, they are fairly obvious or self-evident requirements for maintaining the covenant relationship and a stable society. The first three remind the people of what they need to remember about their divine covenant partner. The remaining seven caution them about what they need to do if they want to survive as a community in covenanted relationship with God.

The purpose of the covenant was to establish an exclusive relationship between God and Abraham's descendants. Consequently, the first commandment is: "You shall have no other gods before me" (Exodus 20: 1-17). A careful reader will note that this did not prohibit belief in the existence of other gods. It only insisted that the Hebrews commit themselves to serve Yahweh exclusively. (Explicit monotheism is not clearly a Hebrew belief until the era of the prophets and the Exile.) The second commandment identifies Yahweh as a deity different from all others in the ancient world. He cannot be represented by an idol — by "the form of anything that is in heaven above, or that is on the earth beneath, or that is in the water under the earth." The third commandment is an admonition to respect the partner in the covenant by not invoking His name inappropriately. Ancient people believed that names conjure powers. God had shared something of importance with Moses when He condescended to tell Moses His name.

The remaining commandments are obvious. They are the rules that the members of every community must abide by if they are going to function as a community. A society would have no unity, peace, or order unless its members honored their elders,[18] punished murderers, respected marriage vows, forbade stealing, dealt honestly with one another, and restrained jealousy and covetousness. Nothing here would have struck Hammurabi or any ancient law-giver as a radical innovation or arbitrary decree.

Despite the exalted claims that some Christians make for the Ten Commandments, they are far from being a complete or even sufficient list of guides for a Christian life. Simple to state in theory and hard to apply in practice, it is uncertain whether they are meant for humanity in general or only for the Hebrews to whom they are explicitly given. For instance, do they forbid all killing or only killing of other members of the covenant community? If adultery is forbidden, is fornication permitted? Is coveting prohibited only for men, given that the tenth commandment cautions against coveting a neighbor's wife?[19] Glaringly absent from the list of ten is any mention of the love, charity, and obligation to care for the poor, defenseless, and weak that features large in the teachings of the prophets and Jesus. Reading the Bible literally is potentially pernicious as a strategy for dealing with its vast store of laws. It may be safer to the spirit of the Bible to keep one's attention firmly fixed on its forest rather than its trees — that is, on its fixed goal more than its evolving means. This seems to be what the prophet Micah (6:8) and Jesus (Matthew 22:39-40; Mark 12:29-31; Luke 10:27) taught when they summed up the law as a simple directive to love God and one's neighbor.

After the Ten Commandments are given, the Bible begins to pile law upon law. Some of these, particularly regulations governing slavery, are forbidden by the codes of modern

Western states. Capital punishment is decreed for a whole range
of offenses. Ancient societies lacked prisons and enforced justice
by fine, mutilation, and death. Although Moses' people were
pastoralists wandering the desert, some of laws they were
allegedly given during the Exodus apply only to settled farming
communities. They would have had no use for those until a much
later period in their history. A great deal of space is devoted to
specific directions for building and furnishing the tabernacle and
equipping it with priests. Exodus ends with God descending on
the tabernacle in the form of a cloud and taking personal
command of His people. At this point the Hebrews' theology and
worship practices were still quite similar to those of their pagan
neighbors. They have a kind of temple (a portable tent), which
despite prohibitions of idolatry, is inhabited in some way by the
presence of God. The "ark of the covenant," a box sheathed in
gold serves God as a throne and, like the throne of a human king,
is flanked by guards (two cherubim).

The Hebrews viewed the priesthood as a hereditary office
passed down in the tribe of Levi.[20] Hence the name of the Torah's
third book: Leviticus. It contains little narrative material and is
primarily a collection of laws relating to, or enforced by, priests.
The chief exception is the story of the ordination of Moses'
brother Aaron as the first chief priest. Many of the regulations
involve methods the Hebrew priests used for distinguishing
between acts and foods that were considered clean and unclean.
When individuals were polluted by unclean acts, they were
ordered to separate themselves from the community or from
religious activities for specific numbers of days and submit to
priests for purification. Leviticus makes a sharp distinction
between things that are holy and unholy, and many of its sins are
the result of crossing forbidden boundaries or polluting the
purity of things by mixing them together. The book's equation of
purity with homogeneity resulted in some strange regulations.
For instance, chapter 13, which lumps all skin conditions together

as "leprosy," says that if the skin is partially discolored, the infected person is unclean. But if the disease spreads over the entire body, he becomes clean!

The rationale for labeling some things clean and others unclean is not clear. Animals that have divided hooves and chew cuds are clean, but those who have only one of these characteristics are not. Acceptable seafood must have both fins and scales. Birds (among which bats are counted) are distinguished by species[21] rather than attributes, and a list of insects that are acceptable for dining is also provided. Much attention is given to sex. People are polluted by both semen and menstrual blood, and rules identify numerous kinds of incestuous relationships. Some rules ordered the transgression of other rules under certain circumstances. Normally a man was forbidden to marry a woman who had been his brother's wife (Leviticus 18:16), but concern for perpetuation of family lines overrode this. Deuteronomy 25:5-10 obligated a man whose brother had died before siring a son to impregnate his sister-in-law to create an heir for his brother. If he refused, the woman had a right to humiliate him publically by pulling off his sandal and spitting in his face.

Leviticus orders the celebration of several festivals that would meet with considerable resistance if attempts were made to enforce them by law today. In chapter 25 God orders all farming to cease every seven years so that "it shall be a year of complete rest for the land." Every fifty years God instituted a "jubilee," a year when farming again had to cease and the people eat only what the land spontaneously produced. This was also a year for correcting social and economic imbalances. Alienated property was to be redeemed and returned to its original owners, and slaves were to be freed. Family land was never to be sold or permanently lost, and impoverished family members were not to be enslaved but taken on as hired laborers by their more prosperous kin. Leviticus caps its heap of laws with regulations governing offerings to God and the chilling admonition that: "No human beings who have been devoted to destruction can be ransomed; they shall be put to death" (Leviticus 27:29). This seems to authorize human sacrifice and is consistent with passages in the books of Joshua and Judges where whole communities (man, woman, child, beast, and possessions) of conquered peoples are consecrated as offerings to God and destroyed.

It is uncertain when the various laws that are collected in Leviticus were enacted and if they were all ever enforced. Some ancient law codes were meant to set ideal standards rather than provide statutes punishable by public officials. Hebrew priests were probably not in a position, culturally or intellectually, to draw up elaborate law codes until the era of the monarchy. Both the prophets Amos (5:21-24) and Jeremiah (7:21-23) speak somewhat contemptuously of priestly rituals and sacrifices. Jeremiah, in particular, seems to have regarded these things as recent and unwarranted innovations.

The Book of Numbers advances sacred history by narrating a hodgepodge of events that supposedly occurred during the forty years that the Hebrews spent in the desert. It is called "numbers" because it devotes considerable space to a detailed numbering (census) of the men in Moses' company.[22] This phase in sacred history is characterized by war more than peace, and it reveals God to be an angry, vengeful deity. At one point God even threatened to wipe out the Hebrews and start over again with Moses' family (Numbers 14:11-12). But Moses' family was hardly a model of mutual affection and respect. Moses' brother Aaron and his sister Miriam turn against him, and various rebellious factions challenge his authority. God reacted by destroying the men who opposed Moses, and, for good measure, He obliterated their wives and children and even their possessions. When scouts, whom Moses sent into Canaan, returned to report that the land appeared too strong for the Hebrews to conquer, God was infuriated by their lack of faith. He punished a whole generation by decreeing that no one would be allowed to enter the Promised Land until it had died out. He made only two exceptions: Caleb and Joshua, spies who had disagreed with their colleagues. Into this depressing narrative of tension and dissension Numbers injects a comical folk tale featuring a talking donkey and a befuddled prophet. Numbers' reports of God's pouts and snits are quite similar to the sort of thing found in pagan mythology.

A very different and more theologically sophisticated era dawns with the Torah's last book, Deuteronomy (the Second Law[23]). Deuteronomy proposes a simple explanation for everything that befalls the Chosen People in the books that follow the Torah: Joshua, Judges, I and II Samuel, and I and II Kings. Their narrative, beginning with the acquisition and ending with the loss of the Promised Land, constitutes the Deuteronomistic History.

Deuteronomy (28:1-20) asserts that the people's fortunes rise or fall according to their success or failure in keeping the laws of the covenant:

If you will only obey the Lord your God, by diligently observing all his commandments . . . , the Lord your God will set you high above all the nations of the earth; . . . . All the peoples of the earth shall see that you are called by the name of the Lord and they shall be afraid of you. The Lord will make you abound in prosperity . . . . But if you will not obey the Lord your God by diligently observing all his commandments and decrees . . . , [t]he Lord will send upon you disaster, panic, and frustration in everything you attempt to do, until you are destroyed and perish quickly, on account of the evil of your deeds . . . .

Deuteronomy's position is that no *Problem* of Evil exists; the human condition is neither mysterious nor inexplicable. Justice is entirely rational. God deserves and requires obedience to His laws. When His people fulfill their part of the bargain they have struck in the covenant, they prosper. When they fail in their duty, they are severely punished. All of this takes place here and now; not in some future heavenly state. The reward for fidelity to God is prosperity, security, and respect in this life. The punishment for infidelity is the loss of every good thing — including life. Deuteronomy rejects the idea that good people suffer. People earn the misfortunes that befall them through "the evil of [their] deeds."

This thesis has the virtue of simplicity, but is, fortunately, not the Bible's last word on the subject. The assumption that victims are always responsible for the tragedies that befall them is fundamentally heartless. It lets God off the hook by blaming the victim, but it fails to address an important question: Why would God's righteousness always overwhelm His mercy? Deuteronomy affirms that God is merciful, but his mercy takes the form of giving His people new chances to fail at living by His law. Deuteronomistic history is filled with stories of their failure "to choose life" (Deuteronomy 30:19) by meeting God's expectations.

Deuteronomy is cast in the form of lectures that Moses delivered to the people on the eve of his death and their entrance into Canaan. Allegedly it was an ancient book that was somehow lost and forgotten until it came to light during a renovation of the temple in 621 BCE. This is not likely. Deuteronomy casts Moses in a different role than the one he plays in the other books of the Torah. There he is an intermediary between God and the people. Here he speaks with his own authority, and he prophesies in the sense of predicting the future. He foresees the Exile and promises that if the people — although scattered "among all the nations where the Lord your God has driven you" — return to their covenanted duties, "the Lord your God will gather you, and from there he will bring you back . . . into the land that your ancestors possessed" (Deuteronomy 30:1-5).

The Book of Deuteronomy may have begun as a text used for

covenant renewal services, which was then revised and expanded in response to questions raised by the fall of the kingdom of Israel and the threat that Assyria posed to Judah. Why, worshipers of Yahweh must have asked themselves, would God allow His people to teeter on the brink of extinction? Who was at fault for the seeming breech of the promise of national glory that God had made them in the covenant? The answer, the Deuteronomist claimed, was obvious. It was the people's failure to fulfill the law of the covenant that explained the delay in the delivery of the blessings God promised. If the people wanted to restore their fortunes, they had only to practice rigorous obedience to God's will.

Deuteronomy's theory meshed nicely with the ambitions of Judah's ruler Josiah (r. 640-609 BCE), whose servants supposedly found the book during a restoration of Jerusalem's temple. Josiah's reign corresponded with the decline of the Assyrian empire that had destroyed the Hebrews' northern kingdom of Israel. Assyria's passing created an opportunity for Judah to recover some of the land that had been lost and to emerge as a regional power. The Deuteronomist's theology suggested a plan for a religious revival that would rally the people and build their confidence in God's support for Josiah's program.

The Bible celebrates Josiah as one of the greatest of the Hebrew kings, and it credits him with a reform movement that helped to define orthodox faith. The Deuteronomist argued that it was defection from God that caused the fall of Israel, and the Judean kings who had tolerated idolatry had courted the same fate for their people. If Judah hoped to survive and prosper, it had to commit itself exclusively to Yahweh's cult. The Book of Deuteronomy (4:39) offers the Torah's most explicit endorsement of monotheism: "So acknowledge today and take to heart that the Lord is God in heaven above and on the earth beneath; there is no other." Among the last things that Moses is described as doing in Deuteronomy is exhorting the people and their leaders to renew their covenant with Yahweh and commit themselves solely to Him.

The Bible is clear that the worship of other gods was widespread in both the Hebrew kingdoms. The people flocked to the "high places" sacred to Baal and Asherah, and King Solomon himself installed idols in Jerusalem's temple. To ensure that Yahweh and Yahweh alone was worshiped and worshiped correctly, Josiah brought the practice of religion in Judah under firm government control. He closed all the shrines that were scattered about the countryside and decreed that sacrifices could be offered to God only in Jerusalem's renovated and purified temple. Avoidance of the temptation to worship other gods was so important that Deuteronomy decrees harsh measures to guard against apostasy. It claims that Moses ordered his soldiers to obliterate the Canaanites to avoid being infected by their idolatrous beliefs, and he even instructed the people to inform on one another and alert the authorities if anyone contemplated defecting from Yahweh. Apostates were to be stoned, for they threatened the holiness of God's people.

Deuteronomy's vision of God transcends the primitive anthropomorphism found elsewhere in the Torah. Whereas Exodus represents God as dwelling in the tabernacle and literally traveling with His people,[24] Deuteronomy talks in terms of God's "name," not God Himself, as present on sacred occasions. Just as the book spiritualizes the concept of God, it internalizes God's law. The law is not a matter of specific duties, but of a spiritual attitude pervading all of life. To live according to the law is to live a life totally centered on God.

A transcendent God has no need of sacrifices or of anything His creatures might offer Him. Deuteronomy's God is a deity whose service requires people to serve one another. Deuteronomy dwells on a theme that looms large in the books of the prophets and informs some of the laws in Leviticus: namely, that God cannot be truly honored unless the poor, weak, and defenseless are cared for. It is not idealism that inspires the Bible to elevate the pursuit of social justice to the status of a divine commandment. Its motive, in Deuteronomy's view, is thoroughly practical. The best strategy for strengthening a state (*e.g.*, Josiah's ambitious kingdom) is to encourage acts of justice and charity that minimize internal tensions among its people. The rewards that Deuteronomy promises for fulfilling the spirit of God's laws are the earthly blessings of safety and prosperity provided by a powerful state.

Nation Building

The Deuteronomist claimed that God was in control of the Hebrews' history, and the books of Joshua and Judges depict this as literally true. The Hebrew nation began, they say, as a theocracy. God literally lead His people. His presence is associated with the Ark of the Covenant, which was carried into battle before the Hebrews to guarantee their victory. The Hebrews who enter the Promised Land under Joshua's command are a model of total devotion to God, and therefore, in accordance with the Deuteronomistic theory of history, they sweep aside all obstacles. The river Jordan parts to let them pass, the walls of Jericho fall down before them, the sun stands still when they need time to defeat their opponents, and they overwhelm nearly every Canaanite city. The Promised Land is almost instantly delivered into their hands.

The God described in the Book of Joshua is a fierce warrior deity who shows no mercy to the enemies of His people. The Hebrews are ordered not just to defeat the Canaanites, but to blot them from the face of the earth. Their war is a holy war, and all those whom they conquer are booty consecrated to God. Everything belonging to the enemy — his person, his women, his children, his animals, and all his possessions — all is to be burned as an offering to God. Whenever this rule is not obeyed with absolute strictness, God causes His people to be defeated.

He shows no mercy. The battle for the city of Ai was lost, for instance, because a single soldier (Achan) kept some gold and silver and "a beautiful mantle from Sumer" (Joshua 7:21) for himself. When Joshua discovered what Achan had done, he seized the offender, his spoils, his family, his animals, and even his tent; he then stoned the living, and sacrificed them and their possessions to God. Only on God's specific orders are the Hebrews permitted to keep any of the Canaanites' property.

Theocratic thinking emphasizes God's absolute control and assumes that God is responsible for the defeats as well as the victories of His people. God not only governs the Hebrews, He manipulates other nations and uses them as instruments to punish or reward His people. In the Deuteronomistic tradition the "dominion" that Genesis offered humankind seems limited to the decision to obey God and be rewarded or disobey Him and suffer the consequences. This is not a theology that leaves much room for human initiative or agency. God is all in all.

The Book of Joshua ends with the triumphant conquerors convening at Shechem for a covenant renewal service that acknowledged God's total authority and demand for exclusive loyalty. Joshua divided the spoils of conquest among the tribes, and warned them that they would be able to hold their new lands only if they "put away the foreign gods who are among you, and incline your hearts to the Lord, the God of Israel" (Joshua 24:23). Joshua then erected a stone "in the sanctuary of the Lord" at Shechem to "witness" to the oaths the people had taken. Centuries earlier, Jacob had raised and anointed a pillar in this place. Jerusalem, however, was not among Joshua's conquests. It was still in Canaanite hands and was not yet the Holy City.

The Book of Joshua's description of the conquest of the Holy Lands is inconsistent with the situation depicted in the Book of Judges. In the latter, the Hebrews do not control all of Canaan, and they are far from a dominant, or even a powerful, presence. The book begins with a list of campaigns fought after Joshua's death. The Hebrews take and burn Jerusalem, but apparently do not settle it. Their decision to spare some of those whom they defeat angers God, for God has commanded them to "drive out" all the natives of the land. Because the Israelites "did what was evil in the sight of the Lord" (Judges 3:7), God ceases to guarantee their victory or even their safety. The scattered tribes fight among themselves and suffer repeated sieges by enemies who are stronger than they are.

Archaeological evidence is more consistent with the situation described in Judges than with Joshua's account. In Judges (1:19) the region the Bible describes the Hebrews occupying does not include the coast lands or the fertile Jordan valley. The Hebrews are to be found in the mountainous interior of Palestine. Archaeological evidence suggests that tiny settlements in this previously unpopulated region multiplied after 1200 BCE, and the difficult situation that Judges says the Hebrews found themselves in is consistent with the fate of primitive farming villagers living on the periphery of more advanced, urbanized states. According to I Samuel (13:19-20) the Hebrews, at this stage in their development, lacked basic metal-working skills.

The Book of Judges is less a history than a collection of stories about twelve legendary or semi-mythical deliverers. Most of these "judges" are charismatic leaders whom God empowers to save His people in moments of crisis. The Israelites in the Book of Judges seem incredibly obtuse. Like the people Moses led in the Exodus, they have a remarkable ability to forget their God and an incomprehensible desire to run after other deities. Despite all that Moses and Joshua have told them and all the miracles they have seen, they find "the gods of the land" absolutely irresistible. When they stray, God brings them to their senses by prodding their enemies to rise up against them. A God-fearing judge then appears to recall the people to the service of Yahweh and His law. The people come to their senses, fend off their opponents, and thrive until a relapse into idolatry reignites the cycle.

Judges tells a rather dismal tale of repeatedly plodding over the same ground while, in the long run, things get worse and worse. Many of the Judges are insignificant individuals whom God chooses primarily for their lack of strength, resources, and talents. God even uses women (on no less than four occasions) to bring strong men to ruin! As God explains to Gideon (the least man in the least family in the least clan of the least tribe) that the impossibility of Gideon achieving anything on his own will make it abundantly clear that the hand of God, not man, turns the wheels of history. Gideon, as the obedient subject of a theocracy, knows his place. When his grateful people offer him a crown, he refuses, saying: "I will not rule over you, and my son will not rule over you; the Lord will rule over you" (Judges 8:23).

If the examples provided by the Book of Judges are anything to go by, theocratic government did not work well. The Israelites were unable to remain loyal to God without the discipline imposed by a strong leader, and they learned nothing from their repeated bouts of apostasy. Deborah, a judge and prophetess, lamented the general unwillingness of the tribes to work together. They also fought among themselves, and one occasion the tribe of Benjamin was nearly wiped out by a coalition of the Israelites' other eleven tribes. The Book of Judges closed with a grim assessment of the situation: "In those days there was no king in Israel; all the people did what was right in their own eyes" (Judges 21:25). Theocracy failed to restrain chaos, but monarchy, the only alternative the Hebrews knew, held risks of its own. Not the least of these was a change in the relationship between God and His people.

The Hebrew Scriptures follow Judges with the Book of I Samuel and thus move directly from reign of the judges to the story of the foundation of Israel's monarchy. Christian Bibles, however, follow the pattern of the Septuagint and insert the tiny book of Ruth at this point.[25] The Septuagint's order was probably inspired by the book's setting in the era of the Judges and the information it supplies about the family of King David, the hero of I and II Samuel.

The Book of Ruth may draw on early oral traditions, but it was probably composed after the Exile, perhaps as a defense of Hebrews who were involved in mixed marriages. During the Exile, assimilation became an increasing threat to the survival of the Hebrew people, and the belief developed that they could preserve their identity only by marrying within their own group. The post-Exilic books of Ezra and Nehemiah order Hebrew men with foreign wives to repudiate these women and their children, but the Book of Ruth celebrates just such a marriage and highlights its place in the ancestry of the Davidic dynasty. Ruth tells a romantic tale of the courtship of a widowed Moabite woman (Ruth) by a Judean man (Boaz). Their great-grandson, David, builds the Hebrew kingdom and establishes its ruling house. The Moabites are often described as enemies of the Hebrews (Judges 3:12-14; 11:18; Genesis 19:36-37; Deuteronomy 23:3-4), but the Book of Ruth implies that anyone, even a hereditary enemy, who manifests love, charity, and fidelity can share the blessings of the Chosen People. It understands the religion of Yahweh to be a universal faith open to all.[26]

But with the books of Samuel, the Bible reverts to an earlier point of view and narrowly focuses on God as the God of Israel. I and II Samuel are a single narrative that was divided into two books because the original text was too long to fit conveniently on one scroll. Although a prophet called Samuel plays a key role in the sacred history these books record, they might better have been named for David. Their subject is the rise of David, a young man from the weak tribe of Benjamin, to become the great warrior king who founds the state of Israel. With David God enters into yet another covenant, one that promises that David's descendants will play an eternally significant role in the history of the Chosen People (II Samuel 7:13, 16). The early Christians claimed that Jesus of Nazareth was a descendant of David's who fulfilled this promise in an unexpected way.

Samuel is something of a cross between a judge and a prophet. He is instrumental in founding the Hebrew monarchy and in limiting the power of its kings. Hebrew kings were anointed and consecrated to God. Their authority derived from God, but unlike kings in other ancient societies, they were not regarded as divine or given the right to speak for God or take the place of the priests who mediated, via sacrifices, between the people and God. Each Hebrew king was accompanied by a prophet who served as his conscience. The prophet's role was to explain God's will to the king, but also to hold him accountable by exposing his sins and condemning abuses of royal power.

In the Bible monarchy is not a sacred institution established by God but a form of government the Hebrews demand for themselves. God is described as graciously — if somewhat sadly — yielding to their request. Theocracy (God's personal rule) had sufficed through the period of the Exodus, Joshua, and Judges, but Hebrews finally concluded that it put them at a disadvantage in dealing with other nations, and they prevailed on the curmudgeonly Samuel to ask God to give them a king. Despite warnings about the costs and risks of submitting to a king (I Samuel 8:11-17), the people press the issue, and God yields. Mournfully, He tells Samuel, "They have rejected me from being king over them" (I Samuel 8:7).

The books of Samuel and Kings were written to illustrate the Deuteronomistic thesis that prosperity and suffering are meted out by God as reward and punishment for fidelity and apostasy. This is the key to understanding the successes and failures of each of Israel's kings.

Readers of the story of King Saul need to be aware that the Bible's authors drew on multiple sources and that history is written by the winners. Multiple sources would explain the different versions of stories about Saul and David that the Bible provides (*e.g.*, I Samuel 16:18-19; and 18:2). The harsh judgments passed on Saul's reign would reflect the opinion of the court scholars who worked for the dynasty that was established when David took the crown from Saul's descendants.

Saul faced a formidable task in persuading Israel's unruly tribes to yield to a newly established royal authority. Like Moses, Gideon, and others, he was hesitant to accept the task God assigned him. Like them, he was surprised when Samuel told him that he was God's choice. Echoing Gideon's excuse, he objected, "I am only a Benjaminite, from the least of the tribes of Israel, and my family is the humblest of all the families of the tribe of Benjamin" (I Samuel 9:21). When Samuel presented him to the people, he was so reluctant to accept the crown that he hid himself among the baggage animals. Unlike the judges, however, Saul's fitness for command was obvious. He had a towering build that made him an obvious leader: "There is no one like him among all the people" (I Samuel 10:24).

A fair-minded modern reader of the Bible will probably suspect that Saul got a raw deal. His intentions are good, but he fails the crucial test of trusting entirely to God. This causes God to repudiate him and turn to David. Saul's errors might strike a modern reader as attempts to exercise responsible leadership. On one occasion, a Philistine invasion forced his people "to hid themselves in caves and in holes and in rocks and in tombs and in cisterns" (I Samuel 13:6). The troops that Saul mustered to counter the attack threatened to melt away as the deadline passed for Samuel to appear to make the offering that was required before the army could march. To forestall a delay that promised to cost him men, Saul stepped in and performed the sacrifice himself. Although later kings are sometimes reported doing something similar, Samuel condemned this as royal usurpation of sacred authority. A similar charge was laid against the king when he failed to carry out God's order to obliterate all the Amalekites. Saul wiped out most of them, but he spared the life of their king, Agag, and kept "the best of the sheep and of the cattle and of the fatlings, and the lambs, and all that was valuable" (I Samuel 15:9). This enraged Samuel who took things into his own hands. The prophet "hewed Agag in pieces before the Lord in Gilgal" — a human sacrifice (I Samuel 15:33).

The story of Saul's decline and David's rise resembles secular tales of rebellions and usurpations. David's public career begins with his duel with the Philistine champion, Goliath. Still an immature youth unable to fight in full armor, David slays his opponent with a slingshot. Readers of the story should consider, however, that on ancient battlefields the sling was not a child's toy, but a piece of artillery. Companies of slingers were capable of breaching enemy fortifications.[27]

Much of David 's story could be rewritten as a convincing secular history having no theological dimension. David comes to Saul's court as an appealing and talented young man. He ingratiates himself with the aging and overburdened king. He wins the hand of the king's daughter[28] and entrances the king's son and heir. He becomes an audacious and popular soldier with whom the people unfavorably compare Saul. After Saul finally has enough and drives him from court, David becomes a guerilla fighter and sides with his people's enemies, the Philistines. After the Philistines overwhelm Saul's army and the king and his eldest son die, an Amalekite soldier who escaped the slaughter stumbles into David's camp with the royal crown and armband. Given that Saul had a living heir, Ishbosheth, who was acknowledged as king by the ten northern tribes, it seems strange that the Amalekite would bring the royal insignia to David. A reader's suspicions are further aroused when David orders the execution of his Amalekite benefactor. His offense, David claims, was to lay violent hands on the king, "the Lord's anointed," even though Saul, mortally wounded, ordered the Amalekite to help him end his life. David later meted out the same fate to two men who murdered and brought him the head of his chief remaining rival,

Ishbosheth. Was David, one wonders, covering his tracks by removing henchmen involved in his plots to usurp a throne that belonged to Saul's line? Supporters of Saul's family, denied David's legitimacy, accused him of murder, and continued to plague him until the end of his reign (II Samuel 16:5-7).

Despite David's bloody hands and possibly questionable tactics, he is Yahweh's choice for fulfilling the promises of the covenant. David wins control over all twelve of Israel's tribes. They then push back the Philistines and all the neighboring peoples until Israel's lands extend from the Euphrates to the Egyptian frontier. David takes the Canaanite city of Jerusalem for his capital and launches it on the path to becoming "the Holy City." He builds a palace, assembles a court, and brings the ark to his new town. God refuses to allow him to crown his achievement by building a temple, but God promises him that "your throne shall be established forever" (II Samuel 7:16).

After Jerusalem fell to the Chaldaeans and efforts for its recovery faltered under the rule of the last known Davidic king, Zerubbabel, the Hebrews wondered how this "Davidic covenant" was to be fulfilled. God's promise to David was made without condition or reference to a need for reciprocation. Therefore, it posed something of a challenge to the Deuteronomistic thesis, and it hints at a theological advance beyond Deuteronomy's simplistic view of history. It implied that although God punishes disobedience (as the Deuteronomist insisted), He will not allow His people's sins to force Him to end His relationship with them. This conviction was strengthened by the preaching of Israel's prophets and became a beacon of hope for the Hebrews during the period of their Exile. By the 2nd century BCE, it had blossomed into the belief that God would soon send a "messiah," a being anointed with divine power, to resume David's role and restore his people.

David's career tempers the harsh logic of the Deuteronomist. According to the Deureronomistic thesis David should have been a saint in order to merit the blessings God showered on him. But David was a seriously flawed man. That emerges clearly in the story of his adulterous affair with Bathsheba, wife of his loyal soldier, Uriah the Hittite (II Samuel 11). David impregnates his mistress, and after he fails to make it appear that her husband has sired her child, he clears his way to marry Bathsheba by arranging for Uriah to die in battle. After God reveals this plot to the prophet Nathan, Nathan indicts David. David confesses and repents, but he does not entirely escape punishment. His family breaks down. One of his sons rapes his half-sister and is murdered by a half-brother. Another son tries to overthrow him and temporarily drives him from Jerusalem. Then the northern tribes rebel, and famine descends on the land. Exhausted, the old king's reign ended in a struggle for his throne that hinged on plots involving Bathsheba. The child she conceived in adultery had died, but God gave her a living son by David who was called Solomon. With the help of Zadok, the chief priest, and the prophet Nathan, she elevated him over David's other potential heirs.

If one were strictly to apply the Deuteronomistic formula, there would be little in this soap opera to explain why God did not obliterate the Hebrew monarchy at this point. The Deuteronomist would probably counter that God 's judgment is not always executed promptly, but can play out over a long period. The books of I and II Kings might be read as a long commentary on the failure of David, his successors, and their subjects to make the right use of the opportunities God gives them. The story begins with the glories of Solomon's reign[29] and ends with Israel's king a humiliated exile in Babylon. Along the way some rulers are better than others, but none is sufficiently or consistently loyal to Yahweh.

Solomon, according to sacred history, rivaled the pharaohs in wealth, power, wisdom, and international acclaim. Like them, he was a monumental builder. (Jerusalem's first temple was only one of his undertakings.) And like the pharaohs, he oppressed his people to fund and provide labor for his projects. Despite the glory he allegedly brought his country, he was deeply unpopular with his subjects. After his death, the ten northern tribes repudiated his son and choose their own king.

Much of the Hebrew Bible, in the form in which we now have it, consists of material written, collected, and edited by scholars who served the southern kingdom of Judah. It, therefore, reflects Judah's point of view, which was markedly hostile to the northern kingdom of Israel. The books of I and II Kings devote a lot of space to detailing the sins of the northern kings — particularly Ahab and his wicked wife, Jezebel. But the southern kings also come in for criticism. The worst of them was Manasseh, who offered human sacrifices to idols and false gods. The only real point of light and hope for Judah was the reign of Josiah (640-609 BCE). The Bible heaps immense praise on Josiah: "Before him there was no king like him, who turned to the Lord with all his heart, with all his soul, and with all his might, according to all the law of Moses; nor did any like him arise after him" (II Kings 23:25). Josiah far excelled his ancestor David in fidelity, but he was much less well rewarded. The Bible is vague about the circumstances of his death. It says that he went to meet the pharaoh Necho, who was marching to the aide of Assyria, and Necho killed him (II Kings 23:28-29). The usual assumption is that Josiah died in battle, which is how the later author of II Chronicles (35:20-23) tells the story. But no matter what happened, the virtuous king failed to reverse the course of his people's history. Little more than two decades after his death, Yahweh's harshest punishment fell on them: the Chaldaeans destroyed the temple and carried Judah's leaders into exile. According to the Deuteronomistic historians, the sins that brought on this punishment were those of Josiah's predecessor, Manasseh.

The survey of sacred history provided by the books of Samuel and Kings ends in the thirty-seventh year of the Exile with news of a change in the status of the captive Judean king, Jehoiachin. He was liberated from prison but remained in Babylon as a pensioner of the new Babylonian king E'vil-merodach. The two books that follow this report in the Bible, I and II Chronicles, review and recast the version of sacred history recorded in I and II Kings. Chronicles begins by tracing the descent of the founders of the twelve tribes back to Adam. It lists descendants of each of the twelve sons of Jacob, mentions the Exile, and concludes this preface by shifting attention to the people who were destined to play the major role in the continuation of sacred history: the "Israelites, priests, Levites, and temple servants" who returned from the Exile to begin rebuilding the temple (I Chronicles 9:2).

I Chronicles picks up the thread of Israel's history with a brief recap of Saul's reign and the establishment of the monarchy. The remainder of the book is devoted to David. II Chronicles begins with Solomon's ascension and concludes with the decree of Cyrus the Great, the Persian conqueror of the Chaldaeans, which ended the Exile and ordered the restoration of Jerusalem's temple.

I and II Chronicles cover the same ground as I and II Samuel and I and II Kings, but from a different perspective that produces a much revised interpretation of sacred history. Samuel and Kings reflect the point of view of the Jews who pinned their hopes for the fulfillment of God's covenants on the rise of their kingdom. They believed that the reward God promised them for their faithful service was national glory. Chronicles was written after the Exile as the Israelites struggled to come to terms with a new reality. Israel was now a much humbled, tiny city-state whose only justification for existence was its temple. Its kings were gone — and with them, dreams of wealth, power, and political dominance. The future lay with Israel's temple servants, not its kings, and Chronicles' author rewrote the history of his people to explain this development.

I Chronicles offers the Bible's readers a radically revised

picture of King David. The David previously encountered in the Deuteronomistic history is a much more human figure than the one who appears in Chronicles. The earlier David is ruthlessly ambitious. He schemes, plots, and murders his way to power. He lies, commits adultery, and struggles with a dysfunctional family. Although God promises to uphold David's dynasty, He does not judge the man himself worthy to build the temple. I Chronicles (22:8) admits that David waged many wars and "shed much blood," but it does not dwell on this aspect of his career. It edits out of the record all mention of his schemes, murders, and adulteries. The blood he sheds is a necessary means to a divine end. His wars establish the peace that makes it possible for his son Solomon to build the temple, which is the ultimate goal of the monarchy. Chronicles turns Jerusalem's kings into priestly figures whose chief concern is the temple. It makes much of their gifts to the temple and its staff — a non-too-subtle appeal to the post-Exilic Hebrews for financial support for their impoverished and struggling temple city.

Deuteronomy's theory of history — that suffering is the punishment for infidelity and prosperity the reward for keeping God's law — informs Chronicles. But Chronicles moderates its harshness by noting examples of sinners who recouped their losses after repenting and returning to the strict observance of God's law. The purpose of the monarchy was, the Chronicler implies, not to build a powerful nation as an end in itself, but to create the temple and ensure that all the rules governing its sacrifices and prayers were strictly observed. It was the apostasy of the monarchy that led to the disaster of the Exile. Restoration was not for the purpose of building a kingdom, but for serving a temple.

II Chronicles opens with Solomon's reign, but since its expectations for the future were pinned on Jerusalem's temple, not its kingdom. The book devotes little space to the political history that features prominently in Kings. The Judean kings who receive most attention were those who carried out Deuteronomic reforms: *e.g.*, closing of shrines outside Jerusalem, repudiation of idolatry, devotion to the temple, celebration of Passover, and observation of the law. Chronicles turns Manasseh, the villain of II Kings (23:26-27), into a paradigm of sin and redemption. It says that Manasseh sinned spectacularly by rebuilding the pagan shrines his father had destroyed. Therefore, God punished him by delivering him into the hands of the Assyrians. But as he languished in exile in Babylon, he came to his senses and repented. Yahweh then restored him to power in Jerusalem. The career of the king was recast as a prophecy of the future of his people: Exile, restoration, and faithful service to God.

Exile and Restitution
Although the history of the Hebrew kingdoms reads like an exercise in political futility, the era of the monarchies was of great theological importance. Its challenges inspired the Hebrew Bible's most profound thinkers: the "writing" prophets. The Hebrew Bible groups their works with its books of history in the category called the *Nevi'im*, for it was reflection on history that prompted prophetic insights into God's will.

The Bible bestows the title of *prophet* rather widely. Given that the prophetic task was to mediate God's Word to others, many persons could be called prophets. Abraham, Moses, Moses' sister Miriam, various judges — all of these figures "prophesied." There were also "bands of prophets" who used music, dance, or exertion to induce ecstatic trances. Saul, Israel's first king, was inclined to this kind of activity. This sort of prophet pursued a personal religious experience that had little meaning for others. These prophets rarely preached or taught. The "writing" prophets, however, had encounters with God that were meant not for themselves alone, but as messages for a broader community.

A thin line could separate prophets from the fortune-tellers, mediums, witches, and wizards whom the Bible harshly condemns (Deuteronomy 18:10-12). Consulting a fortune-teller was a capital offense, but one of the functions of the priesthood was to cast lots to determine future courses of action. Perhaps priestly omens were seen as a way of asking God for guidance whereas fortune-telling implied that the future was predetermined. The latter was theologically unacceptable. If the future were predictable, freedom would be an illusion and there would be no basis for moral responsibility.

The Bible's teaching prophets were individuals who were chosen by God to make His will clear to His people. They were not fortune-tellers, for when they predicted future events, their predictions were conditional. They identified probable outcomes that were likely if the people did not come to their senses, repent, and honor their covenant obligations. These prophets resembled political commentators or advisors. They observed what was happening in his world, interpreted it from the perspective of faith, and then suggested what the consequences of various courses of action would be.[30] If their compatriots sinned against God, they usually had no trouble anticipating what God's punishment would be. The kingdoms of Israel and Judah almost always had enemies who were poised to serve as instruments of God's punishment. The fall of Judah, the last of the Hebrew kingdoms, confronted the prophets with their most serious challenge. It forced them to rethink the covenants, God's commitment to His Chosen People, and the future of their prophetic calling. The crisis inspired some of them to transcend the Deuteronomist's simplistic understanding of God's justice and articulate deeper mysteries of faith.

The great age of prophecy dawned with the Hebrew monarchy. Prophets were often paired with kings. Samuel chose and anointed Israel's first two kings; Nathan kept a close rein on David and helped Bathsheba engineer Solomon's ascent to the throne. The prophet Ahijah urged Jeroboam to declare the independence of the ten northern tribes as a separate kingdom to protest Solomon's idolatry (I Kings 11:29-33). But after Jeroboam also embraced idolatry, Ahijah cursed his house (I Kings 14:1-14).

The kingdom of Israel inspired a host of prophets. On one occasion, King Ahab consulted 400 of them. His ally, the king of Judah was skeptical of their advice and urged Ahab to consult yet one more, a man named Micaiah. Ahab was reluctant, for he said, "I hate him, for he never prophesies anything favorable about me, but only disaster" (I Kings 22:8). Ahab was right, and so, as it turned out, was Micaiah!

The most prominent prophetic critics of Israel's kings were Elijah and his student Elisha. They were much given to flamboyant acts to demonstrate Yahweh's superiority to Baal and the other gods worshiped in Israel. The Bible reports that God spared Elijah from death and took him to heaven in a fiery chariot. Elijah's bodily ascension led to speculation that God had reserved him for some future service — perhaps to return as the messenger announcing the world's end. Some of Jesus' contemporaries wondered if he might be the long-awaited Elijah (Matthew 16:14).

Although they are not mentioned in I or II Kings, Amos and Hosea, the first of the "writing" prophets (*i.e.*, those with books bearing their own names), worked in Israel. The first of the three prophets who contributed to the Book of Isaiah[31] served Judah's King Hezekiah (r. 715-687), but curiously little is said about the influence of prophets on some of the decisive reigns that determined the fate of the southern kingdom. No prophet indicted the evil Manasseh, who (in Chronicles' version of his life) managed to repent of his sins entirely on his own. Although Jeremiah was active during Josiah's reign, nothing is said about any role he might have played in the religious reforms of the period. Josiah's reform program was not credited to a prophet, but to an old manuscript found in the temple. At the time of its discovery — according to the account in II Kings (23) — no one in Judah (including, apparently, any prophet) had any knowledge of the practices it prescribed.

It was not long after Josiah's death that Judah joined Israel in the Exile. Jeremiah and the priest Ezekiel, two of the Bible's most important prophets, witnessed the loss of their homeland and lived out the remainder of their lives in foreign countries — the former in Egypt and the latter in Babylon. Exile, however, did not silence the voice of prophecy. Prophets kept alive the hope of a return to Jerusalem, and prophets continued to be active in the period of the Second Temple. Although the Hebrew Bible does not list the Book of Daniel, its youngest item, with the works of the prophets (*i.e.*, in the *Nevi'im*), many people believe it to be, with the New Testament's Book of Revelation, the pinnacle of apocalyptic prophecy.

The prophets clearly distinguished the Bible's God from all other deities. Pagan theology assumed that the gods were fairly self-centered. They demand sacrifices and respect and could be influenced by the "sweet odor of burnt offerings." If they got what they wanted, they might bestow blessings on their favorites. Many cults recognized a high deity who symbolized cosmic justice — the force that keeps the world in balance — but he was too exalted to take much interest in human affairs. A king might be described as presenting his laws to a god for approval, but ordinary people did not presume to approach the great gods. They sought divine patrons among the lesser deities who occupied the inferior ranks of the celestial hierarchy.

The Deuteronomistic History shares aspects of this pagan tradition in that it represents Yahweh as a "jealous" God with a touchy ego. God demands exclusive loyalty, and He is quite specific about the terms of His service. He insists on sacrifices, but will only accept certain things and then only from the altar in Jerusalem. Any deviation from the rules governing His cult could be harshly punished — as King David learned when he brought the ark to Jerusalem. The cart conveying it nearly tipped it into the dirt. When Uzzah, one of the drivers, grabbed hold of it to prevent its fall, Yahweh struck him dead (II Samuel 6:6-7). The rule was that only priests were allowed to touch the ark.

The Deuteronomist insists that so long as the Israelites do exactly what God demands all will go well. But God is nearly driven wild by any whiff of apostasy. When He is angered, He avenges Himself not only on the specific offenders, but on generations of their descendants (Exodus 20:5). There is, however, another side to the story, for some of God's laws in the Torah hint at a more nuanced insight into the divine nature. Many of the Torah's laws reflect God's concern for the well-being of His people. God insists that they care for one another, that they pursue justice and honor, and that they practice charity. He orders His people not only to look after their own weak and needy, but to extend themselves to assist aliens and strangers. They are to treat their slaves with consideration for the humanity they shared, and the rules governing sabbatical and jubilee years extend beyond the human community to compassion for nature itself. Even the fields are entitled to rest. God grants human beings dominion over the earth, but He distinguishes between dominion and abusive domination.

One of the Bible's most important theological advances is the link it establishes between religion and morality. Yahweh is an ethical deity. He is just, but He tempers justice with mercy and love. What He does He expects those who share His image to do. His concern is not only for how His worshipers treat Him, but how they treat one another. In fact, Amos, the first of the "writing" prophets, taught that God was more concerned with how human beings behave toward one another than with how they honor Him. Amos made a clear distinction between religion and faith.

Amos was a Judean who, in the mid-8th century BCE, felt a call to preach to the people of the northern kingdom of Israel. He was what we would now think of as a blue-collar worker, a herdsman and farmer. He makes it perfectly clear that he was not a member of the religious establishment — one of the court's professional prophets. He was a plain man touched by God who had a plain man's empathy for the poor and down trodden. His ministry took place during one of the rare moments in which the Hebrew kingdoms enjoyed peace and prosperity. Israel was by far the richer and more powerful of the Hebrew states, and Amos's anger was kindled by its willful ignorance of Yahweh's true nature. Israel was a land of plenty, but its wealth was concentrated in the hands of the few. The rich and powerful exploited the poor and reveled in luxury. But they felt good about themselves, for they "honored" God with sacrifice and ceremony. Amos had nothing but contempt for them, for they, he argued, were substituting the form of religion for the substance of faith. He insisted that, far from pleasing God, Yahweh was offended by sacrifices that were offered by persons who had no commitment to social justice. God cared for the poor, the weak, and the abused far more than for burnt offerings. Speaking for Yahweh, Amos said:

> I hate, I despise your festivals,
> and I take no delight in your solemn assemblies.
> Even though you offer me your burnt
> offerings and grain offerings,
> I will not accept them;
> and the offerings of well-being of your fatted animals
> I will not look upon.
> Take away from me the noise of your songs;
> I will not listen to the melody of your harps.
> But let justice roll down like waters,
> and righteousness like an ever-flowing stream.
> (Amos 5:21-24)

Amos's great prophetic insight was the realization that Biblical faith was grounded in a passion for social justice. It was impossible, he insisted, to do one's duty to God without doing one's duty to humankind. Worship of God entailed service to humanity.

How we frame our duty to others reflects how we understand God's nature. Hosea, Amos' contemporary, sought to clarify the example that God's conduct set for His creatures. Hosea was a native Israelite who agreed with Amos that his homeland was headed for disaster. Hosea believed that its apostasy and idolatry angered God, but also deeply saddened Him. Amos was nearly blinded by God's righteousness, but Hosea had a deep sense of God's mercy. He was confident that God's covenant would endure despite the transgressions of His people. Unlike the legalistic deity who struck down the well-intentioned Uzzah for presuming to touch His ark, Hosea's God cannot bring Himself to abandon the Chosen People — despite the fact that they repeatedly demonstrate their unworthiness of His love. He feels so deeply that He can rage: "Because of the wickedness of their deeds I will drive them out of my house. I will love them no more" (Hosea 9:15). But He does not yield to this impulse: "My heart recoils within me; my compassion grows warm and tender. I will not execute my fierce anger; I will not again destroy Ephraim; for I am God and no mortal; the Holy One in your midst, and I will not come in wrath" (Hosea 11:8-9). God is beyond manipulation by human beings. No matter how badly they sin and how much punishment justice demands they receive, they cannot compel God to cease loving them.

Justice, love, and mercy are somewhat incompatible ideals, but the prophets labored to reconcile them. The small kingdoms to which they preached struggled with internal and external threats to their survival, and the prophets believed that the survival of those kingdoms was of transcendent importance. Their history was humanity's link with God.

The destruction of the kingdom of Israel by the Assyrians in

721 BCE showed how serious the situation was. Amos and Hosea had warned that this would happen, and the fulfillment of their prediction forced their colleagues to ponder the future of the southern kingdom. The Book of Isaiah contains a collection of oracles by a number of prophets who commented on different periods in the history of the southern kingdom. The book divides into three sections. I Isaiah (1-39) deals with the crises created by Assyria's conquest of Israel and Assyria's demand for tribute from Judah. II Isaiah (40-55) wrote in the environment of the Babylonian Exile, and III Isaiah (the remainder of the book) reflects the concerns of the post-Exilic community that struggled to restore Jerusalem.

Biblical prophecy is premised on the assumption that the future is not predetermined or fated. Prophets sometimes almost sound as if they anticipate no escape from God's wrath, but this is a function of their hard-nosed recognition that even when the risk is obvious, people do not do what they know to be right. Punishment is virtually inevitable, but the possibility of repentance and recovery always remains. If there were no hope for the people's conversion and no ability for them to change course, there would be no point to prophecy. The prophet's task is not to reconcile people to a fated doom, but to persuade them to come to their senses and merit a better future.

Isaiah, like Amos, warned that Yahweh is a moral deity who holds His people accountable to the highest standards. Isaiah also pointed out that Yahweh is the universal deity who uses all nations to further His ends. If Assyria overruns Judah, it does so as an instrument of God's will. Foreign threats are punishments for internal injustices. A society that allows abuse and exploitation of any of its members makes itself vulnerable to its enemies.

The Bible's various major and minor prophets differed on some points. Some emphasized the importance of loyalty to the Davidic monarchy and the temple. Others were critical of these political and religious institutions and claimed that the core issue for Yahweh was the practice of justice and charity. Isaiah's contemporary, the prophet Micah, famously swept aside religious rituals, temples, offerings, and laws, and expressed the duties of faith in a single sentence: "What does the Lord require of you but to do justice, and to love kindness, and to walk humbly with your God?" (Micah 6:8).

The prophets who were alarmed by their rulers' willful flirtations with disaster could be moved to extremes. Jeremiah was attacked for appearing to urge Judah to submit to foreign domination. Zephaniah (1:2) went so far as to predict that God would break the promises He made to Noah and David and "utterly sweep away everything from the face of the earth." But most prophets, including Zephaniah, held out some hope for forgiveness and deliverance. Once the various axes had fallen and the Hebrews had been driven from their homeland, prophecies promised that the chastened exiles would eventually be allowed to return to Jerusalem and resume their mission as a holy nation.

The chief prophet from the period of the Exile was Ezekiel. His sermons recounted elaborate visions and employed colorful symbols and metaphors. Although it might seem that a deity who lost his temple and allowed his worshipers to be dispersed had failed and revealed a fatal weakness, this was not Ezekiel's view. He imagined God rising in glory, vacating the ill-fated temple, but continuing to exercise dominion over the universe and His scattered people. God's power was such that He could restore life to dead bones — a metaphor for His ability to resurrect a vanished nation that the people could never rebuild on their own. Ezekiel's confidence in God led him to promise that Jerusalem would be reborn as a paradise on earth. The twelve tribes of the Chosen People would be restored. God would return to a fabulous new temple that, like Eden, would send forth a river to nurture trees whose "leaves will not wither nor their fruit fail, but they will bear fresh fruit every month . . . their fruit will be for food, and their leaves for healing" (Ezekiel 47:12). The path of return to the Promised Land was the road to an earthly paradise.

Ezekiel believed that a forgiven and restored Israel would be a magical land of self-generating plenty, but II Isaiah, another prophetic voice from the Exile, envisioned a different situation for those who returned to Jerusalem. He was the first prophet whose references to God are unambiguously monotheistic. For him, Yahweh is sole master of the universe and God for all peoples. The Chosen People's role in the divine plan is to reveal Him to all nations. Isaiah believed that they would do so not by triumphing over the world but by their persistent survival as a faithful remnant of suffering servants.

In 539 BCE, when Cyrus the Great authorized Babylon's exiles to return to Jerusalem, the Hebrews' initial hope was that the Davidic monarchy would be restored. That dream quickly faded. Zerubbabel, the king who returned with the exiles, was soon removed by his Persian overlords, and the temple's chief priest assumed responsibility for Jerusalem. Life was difficult for the returnees. A few prophets assured the people that God's blessings would flow once the temple was fully restored. But others concluded that their tiny state had little hope of survival unless God intervened to save it. Their speculations introduced a new theme to sacred history, the anticipation of an apocalypse.

Apocalyptic prophecies imagined history culminating in a final showdown between the forces of good and evil. God would finally assert Himself to bring life's struggles to an end. On a day of judgment He would vindicate the faithful and defeat their opponents. After a period of upheaval, He would "create a new heaven and a new earth." Strife would cease as people united in the worship of Jerusalem's God. The Problem of Evil would dissipate like a bad dream, for the poor would finally be fed, the needy cared for, and justice would cover the earth. The world would become the paradise that it was meant to be.

The fact that Jerusalem's restoration did not, in a timely fashion, herald the glorious future that many prophets promised may explain why prophecy declined during the post-Exilic era. The Book of Jonah, which the Hebrew Bible includes among the books of the prophets, even seems to poke fun at prophets. The other prophetic books all comment on real historical circumstances, but Jonah is a somewhat ridiculous fable. After fleeing to avoid preaching salvation to the people of Nineveh — and ending up inside the belly of a fish (where he is somehow supplied with oxygen and shielded from digestive juices), Jonah does as God orders. The unwilling prophet is then infuriated by his own success. The people to whom he preaches actually heed his warnings and turn from their evil ways. This makes him so angry with God that he says he wants to die.

Although the hero of the Book of Daniel prophesies, has visions, and interprets dreams, the Hebrew Bible does not catalogue the book with the *Nevi'im*. Daniel belongs to the *Kethuvim*, the Bible's catch-all collection of assorted "Writings." Other sections of the Bible are integrated by shared themes. Deuteronomy's claim that the Israelites' fate is a simple function of their fidelity (or lack therefore) to God's law weaves a thread through the Torah and the historical books. The books of the prophets delve into the struggle between God's justice and mercy that seems to lie at the heart of sacred history. That history suggests that the covenant between God and His people is more complicated than a simple *quid pro quo*. The people cannot annul it by violating its terms, and God refuses to give up on them. Therefore, no simple explanation for the human condition and the Problem of Evil is to be found. But faith holds that God will resolve the moral complexities that confound understanding and realize the goodness of creation.

No single theme runs through the Writings, but some of the Bible's most popular and influential books are found in this category. The variety of opinions, theories, and attitudes documented in the Writings should give pause to anyone who assumes that the Bible must represent only one point of view. The Writings are an archive of diverse materials, some of which (*e.g.*, Song of Solomon, Esther) seem to have little or nothing to do with God or faith.

A diversity of outlooks is an obvious characteristic of the Book of Psalms, which takes its title from the Septuagint's Greek term for instrumentally accompanied singing. The common assumption is that the psalms were written for the temple's liturgy, but some may have had other uses. The book contains 150 poems written over a period of centuries and is distinguished from the Bible's other texts in that it focuses less on understanding God's Word than on addressing words to God. The psalms explore the full range of religious feelings. Some rejoice and exalt in gratitude for God's love. Others are cries of discouragement and disillusionment — desperate appeals from the brink of loss of faith. Some articulate the concerns of a community, and others speak to intimate, individual, and personal needs. The psalms are among the most popular texts in the Bible and have shaped public worship and private prayer for countless generations of Jews and Christians.

For some readers the Bible's books of "Wisdom Literature" (Proverbs, Ecclesiastes, and Job) are its most puzzling elements. "Wisdom Literature" was a popular genre in the ancient world. It consists of collections of (usually pithy) sayings that offer advice on how to live successfully and deal with life's challenges. What shocks many of the Bible's readers is the degree of skepticism or overt disillusionment with tenets of faith expressed in some Wisdom teachings. Wisdom's observations are not credited to God as prophecies sometimes are. They are the lessons that wise people have learned from the experience of living.

The lifestyle that the Book of Proverbs recommends might be regarded by some as hopelessly bourgeois. Proverbs promises that prosperity and contentment will come to those who keep their noses to the grindstone, avoid bad influences, respect God and their elders, honor their promises (including fidelity to mates), speak truth, embrace discipline, act with caution and discretion, avoid impulsive emotions and ill-considered words, stay away from strong drink, guard their reputations, are charitable to their neighbors, cherish humility, keep a tight reign on their children, and content themselves with the common pleasures of food and family — but without indulging in excess! Proverbs is comfortable with the Deuteronomist's thesis that virtue is rewarded and vice punished.

The Book of Ecclesiastes, on the other hand, doubts — almost ridicules — Proverbs' simple faith in the universe's moral logic. Indeed, the book claims that trying to make sense out of life is vain. Things simply have to be accepted as what they are. The wise man is reconciled to the random nature of reality and protects himself from hurt by maintaining a degree of stoic detachment. The inevitability of death robs life of meaning. Human achievement is an illusion, for everything is ultimately swept away as the universe cycles through endless repetitions of integration and disintegration:

> For everything there is a season, and a time for every matter under heaven: a time to be born, and a time to die . . . . For the fate of humans and the fate of animals is the same; as one dies, so dies the other. They all have the same breath, and humans have no advantage over the animals; for all is vanity. All go to one place; all are from the dust and all turn to dust again. Who knows whether the human spirit goes upward and the spirit of animals goes downward to the earth? (Ecclesiastes 3:1-2, 19-21)

Given that God does not appear to enforce justice in this world — a place where "the race is not to the swift nor the battle to the strong, nor bread to the wise, nor riches to the intelligent, nor favor to the skillful; but time and chance happen to them all" (Ecclesiastes 9:11) — life has little value. The dead are more fortunate than those who must endure life's burdens, and the most fortunate of all are those who are never born (Ecclesiastes 4:2-3). If we are given life, however, Ecclesiastes advises us to make the most of its fleeting pleasures. But it warns against becoming caught up in our affairs and imputing to them more significance than they merit, for the world is subject to random chance. Either God is not acting in it or, as the Book of Job, argues His ways are so far above us that we have no hope of grasping their logic or justice.

The Book of Job overtly challenges the Deuteronomist's claim that suffering is a punishment for sin and prosperity a reward for fidelity. The Bible's version of Job's story was probably written sometime after the Exile, but the book has very ancient precedents. A thousand years before the Bible's author pondered the mystery of unmerited suffering, a Sumerian author explored the theme.[32] Even he was probably not the first. Human beings may have begun to puzzle over the Problem of Evil as soon as they acquired moral consciousness.

Job is not the story of a specific historical individual but a philosophical model for a test case: how to make sense of the moral conundrum created when bad things happen to good people. No less a being than God testifies to Job's righteousness, saying: "There is no one like him on the earth, a blameless and upright man who fears God and turns away from evil" (Job 1:8). When Satan ("challenger") suggests that Job is faithful only because his virtue has been lavishly rewarded with wealth, family, and health, God agrees to a test. Job is stripped of his possessions, his family is killed, and his body afflicted with loathsome sores. Three friends then appear and try an odd tactic to comfort him. They insist that he must be a sinner who deserves his fate, for otherwise if God permitted unmerited suffering, He would not be just. Even if Job had committed no particular sin, his human nature might be so far beneath God's perfection that it offends His majesty. Job dismisses all such facile attempts to excuse God and calls on God to account for Himself. God's response is not an explanation, but a display of majesty. He asks Job a series of questions about mundane things for which Job has no answers. If human beings are ignorant even of the processes of nature and the behavior of animals, how, God asks, can they be morally indignant about their inability to comprehend Him? It should be expected that God's ways are well beyond human understanding.

Having learned that thinking about God is quite different from experiencing Him, Job confesses, "I have uttered what I did not understand, things too wonderful for me, which I did not know" (Job 42:3). The book's lesson seems to be that people have no grounds for demanding that God account for Himself as if God were one of us. The Problem of Evil is created by the application of human standards of justice to God, but what grounds could exist for insisting that God be confined within such limits?

It seems never to have occurred to the Deuteronomist, the prophets, and the wisdom authors that the Problem of Evil could be solved by assuming the existence of a life beyond this one in which the moral balance is struck. The reward Job receives for submitting to God was not the promise of eternal life in heaven but restoration of his former comfortable life on Earth. His health returns, his wealth increases, and he has a new stable of children — presumably quite adequate replacements for those whom God had killed.

Not until the mid-2nd century, when the Bible's last book (Daniel) was written, do the Hebrew Scriptures assert that at least some of the dead will be resurrected and subjected to a final moral accounting. Even then (Daniel 12:2) the idea receives only a brief, passing reference. The understanding of death that informs the rest of the *Tanakh* is the one that was common throughout the ancient Mesopotamian world. The spirits of the dead were believed to descend into the earth, into the "pit" of Sheol, a place of darkness and no return that was the antithesis of life[33]. Kings and slaves, virtuous people and heinous sinners — all had the same fate: death.

The Hebrew Bible's indifference to life after death comes as a shock to many Christians for whom the pursuit of eternal life has become the chief motive for faith. But the Hebrews did not begin to pin their hopes on heavenly rewards until well after the Exile. The idea appealed as post-Exilic circumstances undercut confidence in the Deuteronomist's thesis. The Deuteronomist had argued that suffering was the punishment for transgressing God's law. But in the Exile and thereafter Jews began to be persecuted because they refused to violate God's laws. When they resisted pressure to assimilate (*e.g.*, by eating forbidden foods, by ceasing to circumcise their sons, or by tolerating idolatry), gentile governments sometimes threatened them with torture and death. The result was the appearance of something new: Hebrew martyrs — people whose suffering was caused not by sin, but by their courageous refusal to sin. Their faith made no sense if this was the end of their story. Justice required that the death of the faithful not be the end of their role in sacred history but only a transition to a new phase. As this idea spread, interest shifted from the rewards virtue might earn in this life to the vindication it would receive in a life to come.

At this point, canonical reflections on the implications of God's justice for human destiny came to an end, but speculation continued. It bore abundant fruit in the books of the Apocrypha that set the stage for sacred history's next anticipated event: the appearance of the Messiah, God's final agent. When Christians claimed that Jesus of Nazareth was the Messiah, a split developed within the biblical tradition. Jesus' followers created Gospels and letters to explain the "new covenant" (*i.e.* New Testament) with God they believed that he represented, but they clung tenaciously to the Word of God mediated by the Hebrews' sacred history.

NOTES

1   Finkelstein and Silberman, *The Bible Unearthed*, p. 318.

2   Barack Obama, *Dreams From My Father* (NY: Times Books, 1995), p. 294.

3   Kugel, *How to Read the Bible*, p. 102.

4   Finkelstein and Silberman, *The Bible Unearthed*, p. 43.

5   The lands that Genesis 15:18-21 claims that God promised Abram reflect the specific territorial ambitions of Judah with respect to its 7th century BCE neighbors:
    On that day the Lord made a covenant with Abram, saying, "To your descendants I give this land, from the river of Egypt to the great river, the river Euphrates, the land of the Kenites, the Kenizzites, the Kadmonites, the Hittites, the Perizzites, the Rephaim, the Amorites, the Canaanites, the Girgashites and the Jubusites."

6   Various explanations have been offered for circumcision. The Hebrews may have adopted it from the Egyptians, among whom it was a common practice. The Bible associates the rite with the birth of Isaac and the beginning of God's fulfillment of His promise to create a populous Hebrew nation. It may, therefore, have begun as a sacrificial ritual. Ancient peoples offered harvests, animals, and even children to their gods in the expectation that the gods would return these things many times over. The sacrifice of a portion of the male organ of generation may have been intended as an offering

to enhance its potency — making circumcision a fit symbol for the covenant's promise to multiply and preserve the people.

7   His name was a rebuke to his aged mother who "laughed" (Genesis 18:12) in disbelief when God's messengers predicted his birth.

8   The Danish philosopher, Søren Kierkegaard, intriguingly explored its implications for faith and ethics in a book entitled *Fear and Trembling* (NY: Penguin Classics, 1986).

9   Such sacrifices do continue, however. They are made by parents whose faith leads them to deny their children medical treatment in order to demonstrate their total reliance on God.

10   Child sacrifice is not simply a legend. Abundant archaeological evidence exists for it at sites associated with the ancient Phoenicians, neighbors of the Canaanites. Roman law gave a father the right to put even an adult son to death.

11   Jesus' parents offered two birds in the temple as a substitute for him, for as Luke 2:23 explains: the law stated that "every firstborn male shall be designated as holy to the Lord" (*i.e.*, consecrated as an offering.). A veritable flood of blood flowed from the altar of Jerusalem's temple right down to the day of its destruction by the Romans. Hyper-conservative Jews and Christians, who believe that the temple must be reconstructed and all of the rites decreed in biblical law resumed before prophecies of the end times are fulfilled, are currently attempting to breed animals that meet biblical qualifications for sacrifice.

12   The prophet Jeremiah (49:17-22) predicted that God would harshly punish the Edomites for their opposition to Judah as did one of the Isaiah prophets.

13   With the Joseph stories, the Bible begins to draw more on Egyptian than Mesopotamian sources. The attempt of Potiphar's wife to seduce Joseph when he was her husband's slave is an adaptation of an Egyptian folk tale. The story of how Joseph obtained "ownership" of all Egypt's land and people for the pharaoh was a fanciful explanation for the absolute authority of Egypt's god-king.

14   Trees are important symbols in the religious iconography of the ancient world.

15   Even more miraculous was the fact that the manna bred worms if it was kept overnight — except on Fridays, when it would stay fresh so that the Hebrews would not have to labor on the following Sabbath!

16   The early medieval monastery of St. Catherine was supposedly founded on the mountain from which God issued the law, but no evidence substantiates this or even identifies which of the mountains in the region the Bible might be referencing. When the Bible is unclear about something we would like to know, that may be a sign that we are searching it for answers to the wrong kinds of questions. For purposes of sacred history, what is important is to understand what the Sinai event means, not where, when, or if it happened.

17   A stickler for literal reading might argue that there are really eleven commandments. The second commandment is actually two. It forbids making idols and bowing down to

idols, which are separate acts.

18   This was particularly important for ancient societies. Their
      basic units were family organizations headed by elders. The
      state provided no "social safety net" outside the family, and
      family unity forged by respect for the authority of elders
      was important for the maintenance of civic order.

19   Because women in the ancient Middle East were considered
      to be dependents of males for their entire lives, all of the Ten
      Commandments should probably be understood as having
      originally been addressed only to men.

20   The Bible does, however, mention priests who came from
      other tribes. Later in sacred history the line of men
      descended from Zadok, Solomon's high priest, acquired
      elevated priestly status.

21   "In Leviticus 11, there's a list of birds that are abominations:
      the eagle, the vulture, the osprey, the pelican, and so on.
      Problem is, those birds are just our best guesses. The true
      identity of the birds has been lost in the haze of time."
      Jacobs, *The Year of Living Biblically*, p. 307.

22   The Bible is of two minds about census taking. In some
      places (*e.g.*, I Chronicles 21) it is regarded as a heinous sin,
      for it implies that a leader is relying on his own strength of
      arms rather than on God for victory.

23   "Second Law" or "reiteration of the law" derives from the
      Greek title the Septuagint gives the book. It suggests that the
      book is a review of the history of some of the events of the
      Exodus and of the laws that express God's will in the
      covenant.

239

24   II Samuel (7:6) goes so far as to quote God saying to David, when David proposed building a temple, "I have not lived in a house since the day I brought up the people of Israel from Egypt to this day, but I have been moving about in a tent and a tabernacle."

25   In the Hebrew Bible, Ruth is one of the "festival rolls" found in the *Kethuvim* (Writings). It was associated with a spring harvest celebration.

26   The most misused text in the Bible may be Ruth 1:16-17. Many a bride and groom have included in their wedding ceremony the lines: "Where you go, I will go; where you lodge, I will lodge; your people shall be my people, and your God my God." Although this may sound like a pledge of love between a man and a woman, it is widowed Ruth's promise to her widowed mother-in-law! Brides might reconsider the use of this text if they realized that it was making devotion to the groom's mother central to their special day.

27   The Bible (I Samuel 17) makes things difficult for literalists by later reporting that Goliath, the Philistine, was not killed by a youthful David, but by a soldier (Elhanan) who served the king in his old age (II Samuel 21:19).

28   Michal, his royal bride, is reported later to have "despised him in her heart" (II Samuel 6:16). She may not have done so because she saw him "leaping and dancing before the Lord." Her father had been prone to even more excessive "prophetic frenzy" (I Samuel 10:10). Her anger was more likely kindled by his treatment of her family after David assumed (usurped?) her father's throne.

29 Sacred history may here make its most extreme divergence

from secular history. Although archaeological evidence for
the existence of a Davidic dynasty has been found, none
supports the territorial or political claims the Bible makes for
its kings David and Solomon. "Judah remained relatively
empty of permanent population, quite isolated, and very
marginal right up to and past the present time of David and
Solomon, with no major urban centers and with no
pronounced hierarchy of hamlets, villages, and towns. . . .
tenth century Jerusalem was rather limited in extent,
perhaps not more than a typical hill country village"
(Finkelstein and Silberman, *The Bible Unearthed*, p. 132-133).

30 Like modern political observers, prophets' predictions could
be wrong. Ezekiel claimed that God would use the
Babylonians to destroy the city of Tyre (26:2-14) and that he
would devastate Egypt and drive its people into exile (29:8-
12). Neither thing happened.

31 The current Book of Isaiah is a compilation of material
dating from three different periods. For convenience, one
can speak of it as the work of three prophets, but how many
people contributed to it is uncertain.

32 Samuel Noah Kramer, *History Begins at Sumer* (Garden City,
NY: Doubleday Anchor, 1959), p. 115: "The main thesis of
our poet is that in cases of suffering and adversity, no matter
how seemingly unjustified, the victim has but one valid and
effective recourse, and that is to glorify his god continually,
and keep wailing and lamenting before him until he turns a
favorable ear to his prayers."

33 The Book of Psalms contains a collection of hymns written
over many centuries. Therefore, they reflect the evolution of
Hebrew theology. Some Psalms mention God's power to

"ransom" or "deliver" their souls from "the power of Sheol" or "the depths of Sheol," but they may not imply a belief in resurrection. Psalm 86 speaks of this delivery as something God has already done. In this text Sheol serves as a metaphor for deep depression, for the Psalm is a prayer in which the author rejoices in his faith that God will defend him against the "ruffians" who seek his life and hate him. Psalm 49, however, reflects the influence of the wisdom tradition ("my mouth shall speak wisdom"). It warns that wealth is ultimately impotent and insignificant, for "no ransom avails for one's life." Death is inescapable, for "mortals cannot abide in their pomp; they are like the animals that perish." But the psalmist claims that "God will ransom my soul from the power of Sheol." The Psalmist admits that the wise die, but his belief is that while the memory of the wealthy quickly fades as others inherit their fortunes, the wise are not forgotten. James Kugel (*How to Read the Bible*, p. 472) warns that mistranslations, influenced by Christian theology, have led to erroneous assumptions about popular psalms — particularly Psalm 23. The verses that the King James Version renders as promises of delivery from "the valley of the shadow of death" and the ability to dwell in God's house "forever" should actually be rendered, as they are in the New Revised Standard Version: "Even though I walk through the darkest valley, I fear no evil" and "I shall dwell in the house of the Lord [*i.e.*, the temple] my whole life long."

7

The Christian Phase: Part I

The God of the Bible is not a normally absent God who sometimes inter-venes. This God is always present and active, often surprisingly so.[1]
— N. T. Wright

Jesus is not the revelation of 'all' of God, but of what can be seen of God in a human life. Some of God's traditional attributes or qualities cannot be seen in a human life. . . . But — and this is what matters — what can be seen is the character and passion of God.[2]
— Marcus J. Borg

Christ's Context

A span of about two centuries separates the last book written for the "Old Testament" from the first thing (a letter) written for the "New Testament."[3] Fortunately, this gap, unlike the one that sacred history posits between the patriarchs and the Exodus, is documented. During this period, Hebrew religious thought continued to evolve as Jews engaged gentile cultures. Changing political situations also affected their thinking about their covenant relationship with God. All of this had implications for the life of a first-century Jew from Galilee, a man named Jesus through whom Christians believe that God most fully revealed Himself. Most modern scholars, conservative as well as liberals, agree that Jesus — even if he is the incarnation of transcendent deity — must first be understood as a man of a particular time and place.

The preoccupations of the religious environment into which Jesus was born can be traced back at least to the era in which the Book of Daniel was written (*ca.* 165 BCE). In some respects Daniel resembles the books of the Apocrypha more than those of the Hebrew canon — particularly in its endorsement of ideas not found in the older books of the Bible (*e.g.*, resurrection) and its preoccupation with the apocalypse. Speculation about the *eschaton* ("end times") and life beyond death increased greatly in the years between the formation of the Hebrew and Christian canons, and Jesus is reported as having much to say on both topics.

The fourteen books of the Apocrypha, which include some works purporting to be additions to the Book of Daniel, are not included in the Hebrew canon today. Only the Torah and the Prophets had achieved canonical status for Jews of Jesus' generation. The section of the Hebrew Bible known as the Writings was still in a state of flux. Not surprisingly, therefore, given that the gate was still open, many of the Apocrypha's books were included in the Septuagint, the Greek version of the Hebrew Scriptures that was used by many early Christians and by many Christian translators of the Bible. The books of the Apocrypha document the environment in which the Christian religion appeared.

"Apocrypha" derives from a Greek verb, *apokryptein*, which means "to hide." Although no one is quite sure why that label was applied to them, it fits.[4] Like the Book of Daniel many of the books of the Apocrypha used symbols and strange images that purported to hide secret meanings and prophecies. Their true messages were not on the surface, but concealed from common view. This, of course, was part of their appeal. People like puzzles and are excited by the challenge of cracking a code that promises to yield secret information.

Many items in the Apocrypha are modeled on books from the Hebrew canon. Of special interest to historians is I Maccabees, which continues the narrative found in Kings, Chronicles, Ezra, and Nehemiah. It provides a straightforward account of events that are only alluded to in the Book of Daniel. Both books focus on the Jews' struggle to resist pressure from their gentile ruler,

Antiochus IV (r. 175-163 BCE), to adopt Greek customs. When resistance developed to his program of assimilation, Antiochus ordered his army to do whatever was necessary to obliterate Judaism. Matthias, an elderly member of a priestly family (the Hasmoneans) from a village called Modin, refused a soldier's orders to preside at a pagan sacrifice, and a fight broke out. Matthias and his five sons took to the hills and raised a guerilla army. Under the leadership of Matthias's son Judas "Maccabeus" ("the Hammer"), the rebellion became a revolution. In 165 BCE Judas drove the Greeks from Jerusalem, and after his death, command passed to his brother Jonathan. Jonathan came to terms with the Greeks, restored Israel's independence, and ruled as a kind of royal high priest. The Maccabean dynasty his family founded was forced to accept Roman overlordship in 63 BCE, and in 40 BCE the Romans replaced the Maccabees with a half-Jewish client king, Herod the Great. Jesus was born one of Herod's subjects.

The Maccabean uprising is commemorated in the Jewish festival of Chanukah, the Feast of Lights. Because the Greeks had profaned Jerusalem's temple with pagan sacrifices, the Maccabees had to purify it. I Maccabees says that an eight-day-long festival was then decreed to celebrate its restoration. According to the Talmud, this was the occasion for a miracle. Rituals of purification took time, and there was not enough consecrated oil to supply one of the temple's sacred objects — the menorah (a seven-branched oil lamp whose eternal flame symbolized the burning bush from which God first spoke to Moses). A miracle enabled a single day's supply of oil to suffice until new oil could be prepared.

In addition to the Apocypha there is another major source of information on the development of Judaism in the inter-testamental period, the works of an aristocratic Jew of priestly descent who took the Roman name Flavianus Josephus (*ca.* 37 — 101 CE). He was caught up in the war with Rome that led to the destruction of Jerusalem and the temple in 70 CE. Although at the outset of the war he had commanded soldiers fighting Rome, he was pardoned and granted Roman citizenship. He wrote a multi-volume work (*Jewish Antiquities*) to help the Romans understand the history of his people and their religious customs. It provides modern readers with an insider's view of developments in Palestine that had consequences for Jesus' life, the rise of the Church, and the writing of the New Testament.

Although II Maccabees does not add much to our knowledge of the political history of the period, it documents important theological developments. The book recaps I Maccabees and adds detailed descriptions of the excruciating tortures that Antiochus inflicted on Jews who refused his orders to violate their sacred laws. II Maccabees argues that their suffering was redemptive. It was, despite what one might assume, part of God's just and merciful plan. It would earn the Jews leniency at the Last Judgment, and by allowing their enemies to multiply their sins, it would increase the gentiles' punishments. The Greeks who perse-cuted the Jews would suffer extinction, but the Jewish martyrs would be bodily resurrected and restored to the lives of which they had been unjustly deprived.[5]

In the interim II Maccabees promised — on the basis of a dream vision God granted to Judas Maccabeus — the great prophets and holy men of Hebrew history would pray "fervently for the people and the holy city."[6] The novel concepts of resur-rection and of saints interceding with God for people on Earth, which were embraced by some Jews during the inter-testamental period, flourished in the Christian community. II Maccabees also endorsed prayers and offerings for the dead, to make "atonement for the dead, so that they might be set free from their sin."[7]

Although the books of Ezra, Nehemiah, and Daniel, warned against the dangers of assimilation, the Apocrypha makes it clear that the Jews of the 2nd and 1st centuries BCE were absorbing many ideas from other cultures. Persian influence is apparent in the angels and demons that loom large in its stories, and these supernatural beings meshed neatly with the dualistic worldview that some Jews were adopting from Persian and Greek sources. Dualism — the belief that world events are guided by the interaction of two cosmic principles — offered a rational explanation for the upheavals of history. It argued that faithful people suffered in this world because they were caught in a war between God (and His angels) and Satan (and his demons). This struggle would culminate in the Apocalypse and a final confrontation on the battlefield at Armageddon.[8]

Belief in personal contacts with angels and demons was consistent with an increasing tendency toward the individualization and privatization of the practice of religion in the intertestamental period. In the Hebrew Bible God deals with the people as a whole. They are punished or rewarded as a group. But once the Jews were scattered in the Exile and lost their homeland, the concept of "the people" became something of an abstraction. The individual's struggle to be faithful to the Torah and to preserve a Jewish identity in an alien land was the new reality. Reliance on private prayer to beseech God's help in dealing with the myriad personal challenges this entailed emerged naturally.

Some of the authors of the Apocrypha's books attempted to reconcile Hebrew beliefs with Greek philosophy. This promoted another kind of dualistic thinking that was to have a major influence on Christianity. As well as imagining the cosmos as a realm where two quite different realities engaged, it taught that the individual was a composite of two kinds of being: a mortal body and an immortal soul. Traditional Hebrew faith maintained the unity of the human being. People were "dust" into which God had breathed life. They were living bodies, not self-subsisting souls temporarily encased in flesh. Major Greek philosophers held that the soul was eternal and existed before birth and incarnation. This belief encouraged asceticism in both pagan and Christian circles, for it denigrated the body, its needs and appetites, as sources of temptation leading to the sinful corruption of the soul.

Dualistic beliefs of various kinds also featured in the gradual transformation of the ancient concept of Sheol (Hades) into Hell. Sheol was not a place of reward or punishment. It was simply death — the grave, the subterranean darkness from which there was no return. The Bible's concern was for life lived on Earth. But concepts of the underworld changed as belief in resurrection spread. The Deuteronomist had claimed that people got their just desserts — that they were rewarded or punished according to their ability to keep God's laws. But the author II Maccabees, whose martyrs had been punished with death because they were true to their faith, concluded that God's justice required their resurrection to enjoy the good lives their faith merited. Furthermore, the apocalyptic vision of God's faithful pitted in battle with the allies of Satan suggested that God, like a human general, would punish His defeated opponents. Thus there was a need for a Hell, a place of eternal damnation, and a heaven, an abode for the blessed.

The ancient Hebrew belief in the unity of the human being led to the assumption that resurrection would involve the restoration of a body, but what kind of body this would be was difficult to imagine. Paul talked of a "spiritual body" (I Corinthians 15:44) that had no "flesh and blood" (15:50). Likewise, the concept of heaven was ambiguous. Sometimes it was a spiritual realm for souls and sometimes a perfected Earth.

The finality of a Hell raised new questions about God's character. Permanently denying sinners a chance to repent seemed unduly harsh. Therefore, this (and the ancient and widespread practice of praying for the dead) prompted belief in Purgatory, a separate realm where the chastened dead could do penance and ultimately achieve salvation. Christians also believed that it would be patently unfair if people who had died before God revealed Himself in Christ had no chance to be saved. A custom of being baptized "on behalf of the dead" had already developed in Paul's day as a way to bring the departed into the Kingdom of God (I Corinthians 15:29). The author of I Peter went further. He claimed that "the gospel was proclaimed even to the dead" to prepare them as well as the living for the final judgment (I Peter 4:6).

All the new ideas (and the new questions they raised) swirling around the Roman Empire increased the complexity of the religious environment into which Jesus was born. Despite the variety of practices and beliefs that characterize modern Judaism and Christianity, we can meaningfully talk about them as two fairly coherent faith traditions. This is the outcome of centuries of weeding, culling, and conflict outcomes, and reorganization within the two communities of faith. If now, after all that, Judaism and Christianity must still be thought of as plural concepts — as schools of "Judaisms" and "Christianities" — the situation in the ancient world was even more complex.

As a consequence, the fact that Jesus was born to a Jewish family does not do much to clarify our understanding of his religious beliefs. It only raises the issue of what kind of Jew Jesus might have been. There were distinctly different "denominations" of Judaism in his world, but most Jews probably did not strongly identify with any of them. Given the humble circumstances of Jesus' birth (despite Matthew's and Luke's claim that he was of royal descent), he would not have had much in common with the Sadducees. They were the party of the aristocratic and priestly upper classes whose Judaism centered on temple worship and literal Torah interpretation. Jesus did, however, participate in temple rituals and affirm that the Torah would be fulfilled to the last "jot" and "tittle" (Matthew 5:18). Despite some speculation, no evidence suggests that Jesus had any ties with the monastic Essenes. He shared their sense of the imminent approach of the Apocalypse, but he did not follow their ascetic practices. He also did not behave like a typical Zealot, a militant Jewish nationalist. But he must have looked enough like one for a Roman court to execute him for what it took to be his resistance to imperial authority. The Gospels often represent the Pharisees, as his opponents. He did not share their enthusiasm for the rigorous pursuit of ritual purity, but he did embrace some of the new ideas (*e.g.*, resurrection, angels, *etc.*) they introduced into Judaism.

We cannot even be certain what form the Hebrew Scriptures took for Jesus. The current canon had not been defined in his day. We do not know how many of its books he might have been familiar with. The Gospels characterize the Scriptures as "the Law and the Prophets." This omits the third category of the modern canon, the Writings. Given that Jesus was a Galilean peasant from a very small and insignificant village, he may have known the Scriptures primarily as an oral tradition. His father was a *tekton* and according to one Gospel he also took up this occupation. A *tekton* was a manual laborer, a kind of builder-handyman combination. Such vocations were often the only resort for peasants who had lost their lands and had to take whatever jobs they could find in order to survive.[9] No archaeological evidence for a synagogue building has been found in Nazareth, but its men might have thought of themselves as a synagogue when they gathered together for religious or communal purposes.[10] They could hardly have afforded expensive Torah scrolls or been able to support a school where villagers could learn how to read them. Jesus may have been illiterate, and he may have known the Scriptures as an Aramaic oral tradition recited by a local *meturgeman*.[11]

The Gospels

When readers approach the New Testament today, they need to remind themselves that most of the authors of its Gospels and Epistles did not write with the expectation that their work would be read in conjunction with that of the others. Some letter writers knew Paul's work and wrote either to expand on (*e.g.*, the Pastoral Epistles) or challenge (*e.g.* James, perhaps) his point of view. Although Paul's letters are the earliest extant Christian documents, they were not collected and circulated until the end of the 1st century CE. Nothing suggests that the authors of the Gospels consulted them or knew of their existence.[12] The authors of Matthew and Luke certainly knew Mark's Gospel, for they made extensive use of it when composing their own Gospels. Given that they included most of Mark[13] (sometimes nearly verbatim) in their works, they obviously did not expect people to read Mark with their texts.[14] The author of John may have known the other Gospels, but he had no interest in meshing his work with theirs. His account of what Jesus said and did is strikingly different from theirs. The fact that Matthew and Luke based their work on Mark means that these three Gospels can be coordinated to produce a fairly coherent sketch of Jesus' life. But the contradictory information John provides seriously complicates (perhaps defeats) the search for the "Jesus of history" (which is discussed in the following chapter).

The Gospels were not intended to be biographies of Jesus or works of history. They are, as their Greek title (*evangelion*) signifies, proclamations of "good news" — testimonies to faith in Jesus from people who found redemption through him. Each one presents Jesus in a different way. The result is four different pictures that cannot (with any honesty) be melded into one. As in the case of the Hebrew Scriptures, readers who respect the Bible will take the New Testament's contradictions and conflicts seriously. If these features are ignored or rationalized, the Bible loses its power to prod the progress of faith. Its message is distorted to bring it in line with some preconceived doctrine or supposition. The result is usually a flat, platitudinous substitute for God's Word. To read the Gospels as their authors intended, each needs to be interpreted without importing ideas from the others. For Christians familiar with the Bible, this is difficult, but eye-opening.

It seems clear from their contents that all of the Gospels were written after Rome's sack of Jerusalem and destruction of the temple in 70 CE. The dangerous context created by the war between Rome and the Jews gave Christians an urgent motive to establish an identity of their own. Elaine Pagels cautions: "We cannot fully understand the New Testament Gospels until we recognize that they are . . . wartime literature."[15] Christians who wanted to avoid being mistaken for Jews and targeted as enemies of Rome were eager to court Rome while distancing themselves from the Jews. For their part, by the end of the 1st century CE, the Jews had come to regard Christians as blasphemers who were spreading a perverted form of the Hebrew faith, and Christian sympathizers were being driven out of synagogues. All of this conspired to create a volatile situation to which each of the Gospel writers responded in a different way.

Mark's Apocalyptic Messenger

No one knows who wrote the Gospels or even where or for which communities they were written. Traditions about authorship began to develop at an early period, but they are not reliable.[16] A 4th century source says that a mid-2nd century source claimed that Mark was a young companion of Peter's who, after Peter died, based his Gospel on what he remembered of Peter's preaching. The source also cautioned that Mark had no personal knowledge of Jesus and that his account was somewhat jumbled. If, as some scholars believe, Mark's Gospel was written in Rome, that might explain its presumed association with St. Peter, who, according to tradition, was the city's first bishop. The Gospel, however, does not paint a very flattering picture of Peter or of any of the Apostles.

The kind of Christian faith that inspired Mark's Gospel had no need for stories of virgin births, divine parentage, and descent from David to support its belief that Jesus was the Messiah. It had little interest in the first thirty years of his life. Because the Gospel makes no mention of Bethlehem, its readers would assume that Jesus was born as well as raised in Nazareth. It says that he was a carpenter (Mark 6:3). It names his mother (Mary) and his brothers (James, Joses, Judas, and Simon) and notes that he also had sisters. Surprisingly, it does not mention his father, for it was the custom in the ancient world to identify a man by naming his father even if his father was deceased.

Mark's Gospel implies that Jesus lived most of his life as an ordinary man and in ignorance of the role he was to play. It was at his baptism that he first became aware of his divine calling. Mark does not explain why Jesus sought what the Gospel describes as "a baptism of repentance for the forgiveness of sins" (Mark 1:4). Jesus simply appears, is baptized, and immediately has a vision in which God tells him that he is God's beloved Son. At that point, the Holy Spirit took charge of Jesus' life and "drove him out into the wilderness" (Mark 1:12). Mark only mentions Jesus' retreat into the desert. He says that Jesus was tempted by Satan and "waited on" by angels, but he does not mention fasting or the nature of the temptations.

Jesus' ministry begins after John the Baptist is arrested, and the first words that Jesus speaks in the Gospel succinctly state his understanding of his mission. He is to proclaim: "The time is fulfilled and the kingdom of God has come near; repent, and believe in the good news" (Mark 1:15). The "good news" (*i.e.*, gospel) is not the coming of Jesus himself, but the imminence of the long awaited Apocalypse. God is on the verge of bringing history to its culmination.

Mark's Gospel is full of urgency and haste. Jesus insists that little time remains in which to prepare for God's coming in power. Jesus repeatedly promises that some of his contemporaries will live to witness the end times and the establishment of God's Kingdom (Mark 9:1; 13:30). One of the reasons why the

Gospel ends without reporting any sightings of the resurrected Jesus may be that its author anticipated Jesus' return (fully manifested as the Christ, the Greek equivalent for *messiah*) as the event that would trigger the Apocalypse. The empty grave, with which the Gospel ends, testified to Jesus' resurrection, but Mark may have believed that Jesus' resurrection would not become part of human experience until Christ brought in God's kingdom.

Mark's Jesus is a man of action more than words. He sets examples for his followers by what he does, but he is not focused on giving them instructions for living their lives and passing on their faith to future generations. Because the end times are presumably at hand, such instruction is unnecessary. Jesus' acts serve primarily to indicate that God has begun to intervene in human affairs to overthrow demonic forces and bring about the end of the world. Jesus' chief opponents are Satan's[17] demons, the evil powers that cause illness, sin, madness, and "hardness of heart." Demons immediately recognize who and what he is, and he casts them out by "legions." His exorcisms are the beginning of God's promised correction of all that has gone wrong with the world.

The divine power that Jesus uses to exorcize demons also gives him authority over the Torah. In light of the imminence of the end times, the religious law that preserved the separate identity of the Chosen People loses its importance. The crucial distinction now is not between Jew and gentile, but between those who believe in Jesus' message and those who do not. Jesus, therefore, freely revises laws governing Sabbath observations. He boldly sweeps aside distinctions between clean and unclean foods, saying, "There is nothing outside a person that by going in can defile, but the things that come out are what defile" (Mark 7:14). He shocks his disciples by claiming that Moses erred when he authorized divorce, and he insists that anyone who divorces and remarries commits adultery (Mark 2–11). In light of Mark's conviction that the end times were about to erupt, however, he may not have understood this to be a new marriage law. Like St. Paul (I Corinthians 7:6-7), he may have thought that the time for such things as remarriage had passed. The evils associated with divorce were about to be expunged.

God's power enables Jesus to manipulate the world of nature: quieting storms, multiplying loaves and fishes, walking on water, withering trees with curses, and raising the dead. Three of his disciples are even permitted to see him transformed in God-like fashion and conversing with Moses and Elijah.

The odd thing about all of the various manifestations of Jesus' messianic identity that Mark reports is that they make little or no impression on those who witness them. Jesus' family was embarrassed by him and tried to "restrain" him because people were saying that he was insane (Mark 3:21). His fellow villagers in Nazareth were so hostile to him that he could do few "deeds of power" in their presence. But dimmest of all the witnesses were his twelve disciples. They saw everything that he did and comprehended almost nothing of what it meant. They missed the points of his parables, and the three occasions on which he foretold his persecution, death, and resurrection made no lasting impression on them. When the end came, they fled. The women who sought out the tomb where his body was laid came not expecting his resurrection but intending to anoint him for burial The empty tomb startled them so much that they fled in terror and refused to talk about what they had seen and heard from the mysterious "young man, dressed in a white robe" (Mark 16:5) whom they found in the tomb.

Throughout the Gospel Jesus refused to proclaim his messianic identity. His true nature was first recognized by the demons he exorcized. Some of the people he healed realized who he was, but he ordered them to say nothing. After witnessing him walking on water and feeding 9,000 people, Peter confessed faith in him as the Messiah, but Jesus responded by "sternly" ordering his disciples "not to tell anyone about him [Jesus]"

(Mark 8:30). At Jesus' trial when the high priest bluntly asks, "Are you the Messiah, the son of the Blessed One?" Jesus answers simply, "I am" (Mark 14:61-62). But Marcus Borg points out that Mark might not have understood this to be as direct a statement as it appears in English translations. He writes: "The Greek behind the English 'I am' is ambiguous. It can be translated either as an affirmative ('I am') or as an interrogative ('Am I?'). Matthew and Luke both understand it to be ambiguous. Matthew has: 'You have said so' (26.64). Luke has: 'You say that I am (22.70).'"[18] Later in Mark's Gospel, when Pilate asks Jesus if he is the "King of the Jews," Jesus gives him an indirect answer: "You say so" (Mark 15:2).

Scholars have speculated about the purpose of Mark's "Messianic Secret," his claim that Jesus suppressed confessions of faith in his messianic identity. The "secret," coupled with the Gospel's lack of references to resurrection appearances, might imply that the Gospel's author believed that no one could correctly comprehend Jesus' messiahship until his death and resurrection had completed his mission. Premature "recognitions" could only have encouraged erroneous expectations, for Jesus did not fulfill any of the standard messianic roles.

The Jews of Jesus' generation had many theories about the Messiah whom they awaited. The title of messiah was not new or reserved for a single individual. There had been many messiahs in Hebrew history. The word was a Greek approximation for a Hebrew term meaning "anointed." Anointing was a ritual for inducting kings, priests, and some prophets into their offices. It signified a commission from God. Some Jews thought that *the* Messiah they expected to appear at the end of history would be a human being — either a king from the long vanished house of David or a prophet (most likely Elijah, for he had been bodily translated to heaven). Others expected a supernatural being who would suddenly appear at the head of an army of angels. No one anticipated a messiah who died on a cross and left the world seemingly unchanged. Early Christian missionaries faced a great challenge when trying to explain the grounds for their faith in Jesus. Mark's view was that the signs of the coming of God's Kingdom that Jesus performed were sufficient evidence for faith in his messiahship until he returned in glory, resurrected as the Son of God.

Jesus' mission follows a sad trajectory in Mark's Gospel. Jesus begins by boldly and freely performing "works of power." But those who witness the wonders he performs not only fail to understand him; they are often actively hostile. They criticize him, resist him, and ultimately torture and kill him. His disciples betray, deny, and abandon him. No one seems to respond with much faith, and Jesus finally gives up trying to get through to them. After the apparent resignation to the hopelessness of his situation that is implied by his half-hearted response to Pilate's question about his kingship, he falls silent. He has nothing more to say until his agonized final cry from the cross: "My God, my God, why have you forsaken me?" (Mark 15:34) As Mark represents them, Jesus' last words were not a shout of personal triumph, but they might be understood as an appeal to God to turn his apparent defeat into victory. Jesus chose as his final statement to quote the first line in Psalm 22 — and to allude to all that follows in the psalm's hymn to God's omnipotence, mercy, and concern for all peoples.

If Mark's were your only Gospel, what would your Christianity be like? Your community would be Greek-speaking (the Gospel's language), and you would probably be a gentile convert. You would have had no access to the temple, and your attachment to Jewish religious law would not be strong. You would share Jesus' easy-going attitude toward traditional Jewish institutions (e.g., "The sabbath was made for humankind, and not humankind for the sabbath," Mark 2:27). You might be more encouraged than dismayed by the destruction of the temple. Mark claimed that the temple's curtain, which concealed the

Holy of Holies, was violently ripped apart at the moment of Jesus' death (Mark 15:38). This was a sign that God no longer wished to be concealed from gentiles within a temple to which they had no access. By allowing His temple to be destroyed, God had terminated His exclusive relationship with the Jews and passed judgment on them for spurning His Son. According to Mark', Jesus' Hebrew kin and neighbors had rejected him. His disciples (all Jews) had failed him,[19] and the leaders, who represented the Jewish people as a whole, were more responsible for his death than the Romans who had carried out his crucifixion. Mark says that Jesus himself denied the importance of blood descent from the Chosen People and established a new kind of family in their place: "Whoever does the will of God is my brother and sister and mother" (Mark 3:35).

In the ancient world people drew close to their gods by sharing food with them. Part of the animal they offered up on a temple altar was returned to them as meat for a sacred feast. At the final meal Jesus shared with his disciples he declared that his body and blood, which he was about to sacrifice on the cross, sealed a "covenant, which is poured out for many" (Mark 14:24). Only Jews had access to reconciliation with God at the temple's altar, but Jesus' body and blood were effective for everyone everywhere. Your Gospel, however, said nothing about Jesus ordering his followers to establish a ritual meal of bread and wine. The imminent expectation of the end times, which was central to your faith, would have diverted you from making long-range plans for the future. You and your companions were not founding a church or a religion with commemorative rituals. You knew that the need for such things would soon end.

Your conviction that the end of history was at hand was strengthened by the increasing threats you saw to your community. The apocalyptic tradition maintained that deteriorating circumstances on Earth were a sign that the end times were near. What you saw transpiring around you suggested that demons were massing for the final conflict. In your Gospel Jesus repeatedly warns his followers that they must anticipate suffering. Just as he had experienced rejection, dismissal, criticism, and ultimately torture and death, so would you. Jesus' messianic role was, as Isaiah had predicted, the role of God's "suffering servant." Jesus had allowed evil free reign and then emerged triumphant over death, the worst of evil's threats. Through him, God revealed the power of good over evil and life over death — not by pitting force against force, but by demonstrating the impotence of evil. Jesus' example implied that true discipleship lay in enduring, not overwhelming, evil: "If any want to become my followers, let them deny themselves and take up their cross and follow me. For those who want to save their life will lose it, and those who lose their life for my sake, and for the sake of the gospel, will save it" (Mark 8:34-35).

Jesus' example encouraged your community to trust that your weakness and vulnerability were truly sources of strength. Demonic powers, whose exorcism was a major part of Jesus' work, were raging about you. The world was hastening to destruction. Rome, like Babylon 600 years earlier, was crushing God's people. And, as in the era of the Exile, it was necessary to trust in God's purposes at a time when evil seemed to make a mockery of faith.

Unlike the Jews of old, however, you do not dream of returning to Jerusalem, reconstructing the temple, and resuming the burdens of sacred history. The promised end is near at hand. The future lies with the new covenant community that Jesus' self-sacrifice has established. Your challenge is to follow Jesus' example and cling to your faith through the time of trial. The "good news" of your Gospel is that even in the depths of despair, when you feel abandoned by God, God is hastening your salvation.

Matthew's New Moses

Matthew's Gospel opens the New Testament, but that was not its author's plan. Matthew did not intend his work to be followed by Mark's for he includes over 90% of Mark's Gospel in his own. Plainly he expected his Gospel to stand alone as a more complete account. Several things about Matthew's Gospel might explain how it came to assume its prominent place in the New Testament canon. It is well suited to serve as a link between the Old and the New Testaments, for it makes extensive use of the Hebrew Scriptures (in Greek translation). It justifies faith in Jesus as the Messiah by pointing again and again to ways in which he fulfilled Hebrew prophecy. It is also the only Gospel to claim that Jesus instituted the Church.

The author of Matthew's Gospel is unknown. Tradition credits it to the disciple Matthew (a tax collector), but this is unlikely. One of Jesus' companions would not have based his memoire on the work of a man like Mark, who got his information second-hand. The contents of the Gospel suggest that its author might have been a Hebrew Christian convert who was thoroughly at home in the Greek language. It may be that the Gospel was written for the church in Antioch, a city that, according to the Book of Acts, had a thriving congregation of Christianized Jews. The apostle Peter is said to have worked in Antioch, and Matthew's Gospel (16:18) claims that Jesus associated Peter with the foundation of the Church.

In Mark's Gospel Jesus is relatively indifferent to the Hebrews' religious law. Matthew, however, reports Jesus saying that he did not come to abolish the law but to fulfill it and that anyone who broke the least of its commandments would suffer punishment (Matthew 5:17-19). Matthew also claimed that Jesus warned that those who teach others to break the law will "be called least in the kingdom of heaven." These reminders sounds like criticism directed at missionaries to gentile churches, who, like Paul, taught that the era of the law ended with the appearance of the

Messiah. Matthew's quotations read like a warning from a Christian Jew who wanted to emphasize continuity between faith in Torah and faith in Christ.[20] On the other hand, Matthew is harshly critical of the legalistic Pharisees, for he is not a champion of the law for its own sake. His concern is that his readers understand how the law and prophecy were fulfilled in Jesus.

Matthew would have agreed with Paul on at least one thing. They both believed that faith in Jesus brought a new covenant community into being — that Christians were to replace Jews as the Chosen People. For Paul this implied Christian freedom from the law, but for Matthew it meant that Christians embraced the law as revealed in Christ.

The obvious way to depict Jesus as the founder of a new Chosen People was to associate him as closely as possible with Moses, the leader of the Exodus and the lawgiver who launched the nation of Israel. Matthew's desire to associate Jesus as closely as possible with Moses explains one of the major additions he made to Mark's Gospel. Mark began his story with Jesus' baptism, but Matthew started with an account of Jesus' ancestry and birth.[21] These verses form a preface to his Gospel — an introduction to its theme: the transition from the old covenant community to the new one.

Matthew's genealogy traces Jesus' descent back to Abraham. As was customary, his ancestry is tracked through the male line — through "Joseph the husband of Mary, of whom Jesus was born" (Matthew 1:16). Given that Matthew immediately follows this with the story of Jesus' virgin birth (an implicit denial of Joseph's fatherhood), he could hardly have intended his genealogy to be read as history. To assume otherwise is to infer that Matthew was so sloppy or intellectually deficient that he failed to spot the obvious incongruity in what he had written.

Matthew's account of Jesus' ancestry and birth do not make sense as history but as theology their meaning is clear. They establish Jesus as heir to the covenant God made with Abraham, but his authority exceeds that of his Hebrew ancestry. He is conceived by the Holy Spirit so that through him God's covenant promises to the Chosen People can be fulfilled and a new covenant established.

Although Jesus was known to be from Nazareth, Matthew assumed that as the Messiah he must have been born, as prophecy decreed, in Bethlehem. He had, therefore, to explain how Jesus came to be raised in Nazareth. His solution was to assume that the Messiah who would fulfill sacred history would have a life that recapitulated that history. Like Moses, who escaped a slaughter of Hebrew children ordered by a pharaoh, Jesus escaped a massacre of Bethlehem's children ordered by King Herod by being carried into Egypt. After sojourning there for some time, the new Moses, like his ancestors, embarked on an Exodus that took him to the Promised Land. Instead of returning to their home in Bethlehem, God directed his parents to settle in Nazareth.

Matthew's stories about Jesus' origin root him firmly within Hebrew sacred history, but they forecast a broader mission for him. Matthew claims that the first people to acknowledge Jesus' messianic identity were not Jews, but gentiles ("wise men from the East," Matthew 2:1). Herod and his Hebrew astrologers do not grasp the significance of a new star that the "wise men" say is the sign that a "king of the Jews" had been born. Not only do these prescient gentiles announce the king's birth, they seek him out and worship him with gifts.

Matthew's Gospel argues that Jesus' earthly mission was only to the Jews. He quotes Jesus giving his disciples explicit instructions: "Go nowhere among the Gentiles, and enter no town of the Samaritans, but go rather to the lost sheep of the house of Israel" (Matthew 10:5-6). God's promise was to the house of Israel, and the Messiah was to be the savior of the Jews. But, like their king Herod, the Jews not only failed to recognize their Messiah, they killed him. They thus forfeited their role in sacred history to gentiles who respond with faith. The child Jesus' sagacious gentile visitors foretell the outcome of his adult life.

Having stated the thesis of his Gospel in stories about Jesus' birth and infancy, Matthew skips over most of Jesus' life and begins where Mark begins: with Jesus' baptism. From there to the empty grave he follows the trail blazed by Mark, but adds much new information. Mark's Jesus did not do much teaching, but teaching is a major concern of Matthew's Jesus. Matthew groups Jesus' teachings in five great sermons to emphasize his role as successor to Moses, the author of the five books of Torah. Matthew's Jesus is less human and more divine than Mark's. Mark's Jesus seems to discover his messianic identity after his baptism "for the forgiveness of sins." But Matthew's Jesus approaches baptism in full knowledge of who he is. John the Baptist also knows who Jesus is. He is reluctant to baptize him and claims that Jesus should baptize the baptizer. Jesus insists, however, on being baptized — explaining (obscurely) that "it is proper for us in this way to fulfill all righteousness" (Matthew 3:15). Nothing is said about repentance and forgiveness of sins. The implication seems to be that the baptism was needed for *pro forma* fulfillment of some law or prophecy.

Throughout Matthew's Gospel Jesus is always in charge. Although he has the power to call "more than twelve legions of angels" (Matthew 26:53) to his aide, he eschews such histrionics in order to do what must be done to fulfill the Scriptures. Matthew makes this point at the start of Jesus' mission. Where Mark merely says that Jesus retreated to the desert after his baptism and wrestled with temptation, Matthew expands the story by cataloguing Jesus' temptations. This gives him an opportunity to counter one of the major objections to the claim that Jesus was the Messiah — namely, Jesus' failure to fulfill any traditional messianic expectations. Matthew insists that this was precisely what Satan tempted Jesus to do:, *i.e.*, to triumph as a supernatural being — bringing on the anticipated earthly paradise by turning stones to bread, or floating down from heaven in a crowd of angels, or by reigning as a Davidic king over the world's empires. Matthew's point is that Jesus could have done what was anticipated, but he chose instead to be faithful to the difficult role forecast for him by the God-inspired prophets.

After Jesus emerged from the desert, Matthew says that he called the first of his disciples and preached the first of his five sermons. Jesus astounded those who heard him, for he did not teach like a man, but with "authority." That is, the words of Jesus, like those of Moses, carried the weight of a divine mandate.

Jesus' first sermon, like Moses' law, was delivered from a mountain. It contained novelties such as the famous Beatitudes (a list of the types of people who are close to God's heart) and the Lord's Prayer. It affirmed the continuing relevance of "the law and the prophets," but Jesus interpreted the law in a way that revealed its "higher righteousness." He warned that if people did not rise to this spiritual level — superior to the letter-of-the-law example "scribes and Pharisees" set — they "will never enter the kingdom of heaven" (Matthew 5:20). Matthew's Jesus endorsed a standard of perfection for human conduct that cannot be reduced to a list of codified laws. "Be perfect," Jesus say, "as your heavenly Father is perfect." Jesus reminds his followers of God's generosity (God's willingness to bestow blessings on both the deserving and the undeserving), and he urges them to guide their actions by always doing whatever is necessary to preserve peace and foster love: Be generous; never respond in anger; never retaliate — even when retaliation is justified.

If Matthew's Jesus does much more teaching than Mark's, Jesus' disciples are also much more responsive to his instruction. He sends them out as apostles[22] to spread his words — forecasting their future mission. By the time Matthew took his pen in hand, Christians had begun to rethink their situation. The

Apocalypse was still expected as an event that could suddenly erupt at any moment (like lightening, Matthew says), but its delay meant that it was important to heed Jesus' instructions on how to live a God-oriented life in the interim. Matthew's Gospel is the only one that says that Jesus predicted the rise of the Church after his death. This documents a major departure for some Christians from Mark's apocalyptic faith. If, as Mark reported, Jesus preached the imminent end of history, would he also have prophesied the development of a new religious institution?

The brief passage in which Matthew quotes Jesus saying the only thing the Bible reports Jesus ever saying about the Church has had tremendous influence on the history of Christianity. Although there has never been a time when all Christians have recognized the authority of single leader (such as Rome's pope), Roman Catholics believe that Jesus clearly intended his Church to be ruled by a papal dynasty. Their case rests on Matthew's account (16:13-19) of a conversation between Jesus and his disciples that is confirmed by none of the other Gospels.

As Matthew describes it, the episode took place after Jesus' disciples had been traveling with him for some time. They had watched him teach and heal, but they had not yet said what they thought all of this might mean. Jesus broached the topic indirectly by asking them privately what people were saying about him. They reported that some thought that he was Elijah, or a resurrected John the Baptist, Jeremiah, or another prophet. Jesus said nothing in response to this, but followed up with the question to which he really wanted an answer: "But who do you say that I am?" Peter then spoke up and made the first[23] profession of faith: "You are the Messiah, the Son of the living God." Jesus then declared that Peter's insight had been inspired by God, for the testimony of "flesh and blood" (i.e., ordinary experience) was not enough to justify such a conviction. Jesus then prophesied: "you are Peter [Petros], and on this rock [petra]

I will build my church . . . I will give you the keys of the kingdom of heaven, and whatever you bind on earth will be bound in heaven, and whatever you loose on earth will be loosed in heaven" (Matthew 16:18-19).

Catholics believe that at this moment Jesus appointed Peter the founder and leader of the Church and gave him authority to act for God. Although the Bible says nothing about it, tradition holds that Peter pioneered the community of Christians in Rome, served as its first bishop, and died in the persecution ordered by the emperor Nero. His sacred office and the unique authority Jesus had given him then passed to his episcopal successor in Rome and down the line of popes to the present day.

Protestants have interpreted Matthew 16 differently. They believe that Jesus' remarks should be understood as addressed not to Peter as an individual, but to Peter as a symbol — a representative of all people who profess faith in Christ. Metaphorically speaking, Peter was "the first Christian," the first to declare the faith on which the Church is founded. The power he is promised is granted to all Christians — the power to open the gates of heaven by spreading the message of Christ.

If Matthew was a Jew who fervently believed that Jesus was his people's long-awaited Messiah, the refusal of his former faith community to accept the Christian claims for Jesus must have been a bitter experience. Matthew says that Jesus called the scribes and Pharisees "snakes" and "a brood of vipers," and condemned them to Hell for killing the prophets and persecuting the righteous. Matthew rejoiced in the destruction of Jerusalem, for he saw this as God's judgment on a recalcitrant Israel. He quotes Jesus calling Jerusalem "the city that kills the prophets and stones those who are sent to it," and he says that Jesus, like a mother hen, tried to bring Jerusalem's people [the Jews] under the protection of his wing, but they were unwilling. Therefore, they were delivered into the hands of the Romans and their "house" (i.e. temple) was rendered "desolate" (Matthew 23:1-37).

Bad as this punishment was, Matthew believed that the Jews would suffer even more for their treatment of Jesus. Matthew is the only Gospel author who claims that at Jesus' trial, the Jews took on themselves *and* their descendants full responsibility for Jesus' execution. When Pilate professed belief in Jesus' innocence, Matthew claims that "the people as a whole answered, 'His blood be on us and our children!'" (Matthew 27:25). This passage has been cited for centuries as a justification for anti-Semitism and persecution of Jews.

Mark devotes only six verses to the story of Judas's betrayal of Jesus, but Matthew expounds extensively on Judas's villainy. Scholars have speculated that Judas (which means "Jew") may not have been a historical individual but a symbol for the Hebrew people. The story of Judas may have arisen in the context of the early Church's campaign to minimize Roman responsibility for Jesus' crucifixion by blaming it on the Jews.

Matthew agreed with Mark that Jesus' message was apocalyptic, but how Matthew understood this is unclear. The sources he drew on for his Gospel reflected the early Christian belief that the arrival of the Messiah implied that the Apocalypse was at hand. Matthew's Gospel quotes Jesus speaking of the Apocalypse as imminent. He says that Jesus told his apostles on one occasion that they would not complete a preaching circuit of "the towns of Israel before the Son of Man comes" (Matthew 10:23). Later Jesus promised them: "Truly, there are some standing here who will not taste death before they see the Son of Man coming in his kingdom" (Matthew 16:28).

But what did Matthew make of these predictions? He wrote his Gospel at least a half century after Jesus' death, and he was the only evangelist to claim that Jesus predicted the rise of the Church. There would have been no role for such an institution if the Apocalypse were at hand. Matthew's solution to this problem may have been to assume that Jesus envisioned the Apocalypse not as a single dramatic event, but as an extended period of war, famine, false prophecy, and persecution. Matthew claimed that Jesus predicted that his followers "will be hated by all nations because of my name" (Matthew 24:9). Given that Matthew believed that during Jesus' lifetime Jesus dealt only with Jews, this makes sense only if sufficient time was to pass for Christians to separate from Jews, be recognized as a distinct group defined by loyalty to Christ, and become numerous enough to be known to and declared enemies "by all nations."

Jews and Christians were going separate ways by Matthew's day, but he was convinced that it was the Christians who were truly fulfilling the Hebrew law and destined to receive its rewards. When the Son of Man arrives, Matthew's Gospel says that he will separate "the sheep from the goats." The sheep will enter his kingdom and the goats will be dispatched to "the eternal fire prepared for the devil and his angels" (Matthew 25:32-41). In the parable, the sheep are surprised by their reward, for they were not aware of the significance of what they were doing when they fed the hungry, clothed the naked, and visited the sick and imprisoned. They had not recognized God in the faces of the poor and needy. They had simply acted out of the divine law that was written on their hearts, and in obeying the impulse to serve others they had served God. This, Matthew implies, was the point of the Hebrew law and the reason why Jesus upheld it. It was why he condemned the legalistic Pharisees — they persisted in misunderstanding the nature of true obedience. The law, despite its seeming complexity, was fundamentally simple. All that the law and the prophets decreed boiled down to two principles: "You shall love the Lord your God with all your heart, and with all your soul, and with all your mind. . . . You shall love your neighbor as yourself" (Matthew 22:37-39). The Apocalypse might be imminent, but that did not justify quietism or toleration of suffering and injustice. So long as time remained, it was crucial that Christians use it well to prepare for God's judgment.

Matthew follows Mark's account of the Passion, but, unlike Mark, whose Jesus seems to resign to his fate, Matthew represents Jesus as remaining in charge right to the end. When Judas shows up to betray him, Jesus says: "Friend, do what you are here to do" (Matthew 26:50). Mark says that the disciples abandoned Jesus and fled when he was arrested.[24] But Matthew claims that at least one of them, came armed, drew a sword, and tried to defend Jesus. Jesus, however, rebuked him and reminded him that if Jesus wanted to escape, he could call a legion of angels to his aid. What was happening had to happen so that the Scriptures could be fulfilled. Only then — and with his implied permission — did the disciples leave him to the destiny he had willingly accepted.

Matthew follows Mark in claiming that Jesus said little during the Passion. He responds to Pilate's question about his kingship ("You say so.") and then falls silent. Matthew emphasizes the point, saying that Jesus refused to answer "a single charge" brought against him or react to those who taunted him while he hung on the cross. Jesus keeps quiet, Matthew's context implies, because events are unfolding as he knows they must. His last words are, as in Mark: "My God, my God why have you forsaken me." But in Matthew's Gospel this sounds more like an anticipated conclusion than a sigh of surrender.

Mark's Gospel ended with the report of an empty tomb and a promise of a future encounter with the risen Christ in Galilee. Just as Matthew prefaced Mark's account with stories about Jesus' birth, he added a postscript to bring the narrative to a more complete conclusion. Matthew claims that Jesus' female friends not only discovered his empty tomb, they witnessed the resurrected Christ. Rather than then saying "nothing to anyone" (Mark 16:8), they did as ordered and told the Apostles that Jesus would reveal himself to them in Galilee. Matthew says that they were (somehow) directed to "a mountain" (recalling Moses' encounter with God on Sinai) where they saw Christ and worshiped him. But Matthew adds the curious detail that "some doubted" (Matthew 28:17). Perhaps he was countering the complaint of a later generation — heard now as well as then — that it would have been easier for the first Christians to believe in Jesus because they saw him in person.[25]

Jesus' last act in Matthew's Gospel was to issue "the Great Commission," a challenge to his followers "to make disciples of all nations, baptizing them in the name of the Father and of the Son and of the Holy Spirit, and teaching them to obey everything that I have commanded you" (Matthew 28:19:20). This was Matthew's explanation for the delay in Christ's return and the rise of the Church. There was work to be done.

If Matthew's Gospel were your only Gospel, what would your Christian faith be like? You would be a student of the Hebrew Scriptures (probably in the Septuagint edition). You might be a converted Jew, or might have been one of the many gentiles of the period who had affiliated with a synagogue.[26] Your Gospel implies that Christians are the "true" Jews, for it quotes Jesus decreeing that if a member of the church sins and does not repent, the church should regard him as a "Gentile and a tax collector" (Matthew 18:17). You would search the Hebrew Scriptures for verses that could be read as prophecies of Christ, for this is how your Gospel filled in many details about Jesus' life (e.g., his virgin birth, his entry into Jerusalem, etc.). You would treasure those Scriptures because you thought of the Church as the New Israel, and you would assume the continuing validity of Mosaic law — at least in principle.

Despite your respect for the Hebrew Scriptures, you would be hostile to Jews who did not join you in allegiance to Christ. Your Gospel taught that Jesus opposed the equation of justice with vengeance (i.e., "An eye for an eye and a tooth for a tooth," Matthew 5:38), but you are tempted to forget this when you contemplate the guilt of your Hebrew opponents.

Your Gospel tells you that Jesus came, as promised, to the

Jews and devoted his entire earthly ministry exclusively to them. However, not only did they spurn his offer of salvation, they literally forced Rome to execute him. Your Gospel says that the Roman procurator, Pilate, went to great lengths to spare Jesus' life. He tried to persuade the Jews to free Jesus as an act of mercy, but they insisted instead on liberating "a notorious prisoner, called Barabbas" (Matthew 27:16). Dreams prompted Pilate's wife to testify to Jesus' innocence. Pilate agreed that he was innocent, but "he [Pilate] could do nothing." The agent vested with the power of the Roman Empire was compelled to yield to the demand of Jerusalem's "crowd" that Jesus be crucified. Before Pilate gave the order for Jesus' execution, he washed his hands to signify his innocence "of this man's blood." But even this testimony to the travesty of justice that was about to take place did not diminish the Jews' bloodlust. They eagerly claimed responsibility for whatever consequences might result from Jesus' death — not only for themselves but for their descendants forever.

After Jesus' burial, the Jewish authorities were still not content. They set a guard over his tomb, for they feared that his disciples might steal his body and claim that he had been resurrected. When an angel appeared to open the tomb, the guards fainted from fright. After they recovered and reported this miracle to the priests and elders, the leaders of the Jews remained as obstinately obdurate as Moses' pharaoh. They bribed the guards to say that Jesus' disciples had taken the body while they slept. The Jews, Jesus' own people, had hounded him to the grave and beyond.

Your hostility to the Jews is probably matched by theirs to you. They would not have responded well to your claim that they had forfeited their legacy as God's chosen. You anticipate persecution by "all nations" because you call yourself a Christian (i.e., by "the name" of Christ). In your Gospel Jesus warns that your allegiance to him will set people — even members of your family — against you.[27] He declares: "I have not come to bring peace, but a sword . . . and one's foes will be members of one's own household" (Matthew 10:35). You have turned your back on Judaism and now understanding yourself to be the member of a separate community with "the name" of Christ, but the world is still unclear on the distinction between your faith and that of the Hebrews. You are eager to make sure that the Romans understand that you take their side in their struggle with the Jews. But you know that both parties are likely to turn on you for simply being a Christian. You have no choice, however, but to profess your faith. Your Gospel's prime directive is a commission from Christ to "make disciples of all nations."

You expect suffering, for you believe that the end of the world is approaching. Speculation about the end times is all around you, but you are not quite so confident in its immediacy as the first Christian generation was. Your Gospel warns you against all the false prophets who try to predict the date of the Apocalypse. You believe that you have to be prepared for the sudden return of the Son of God at any moment, but your Gospel cautions that even the Son does not know the date God has set for this (Matthew 24:36).

Your Gospel does not authorize your retreat from the world in expectation of Christ's speedy return. In fact it suggests that history still has a course to run. The last line in your Gospel is a promise from Christ: "And remember, I am[28] with you always, to the end of the age." This implies that you can expect his help, but no quick deliverance from life's struggle. This is why Jesus foresaw the Church, why many of his parables stressed the importance of being a productive servant, and why he commissioned you to convert the world. None of this would make sense if there were no time to attempt it.

Rather than focusing on imminent death and resurrection, your Gospel has much to say about living a Christian life in the world as currently constituted. Its message is the message of

Moses and the prophets. Like them, it affirms that God's concern is how you treat other people. What you do to them, you do to Him. To guide your conduct your Gospel gives you a mountain of advice: You are to be meek and humble. You must show mercy and strive to make peace. You must resign yourself to persecution in defense of the truth. You should never react in anger or seek vengeance. You should not concern yourself with material wealth, but with acts of charity and generosity. You should not presume to judge others or yield to hate even for your enemies. You should freely forgive those who stray, and you should seek to return lost sheep to the Church's fold. You should be honest and faithful to your oaths. You must guard your tongue and avoid saying or doing anything that would cause another to sin. You should rise above lust and greed. You must find the courage to overcome fear of torture and death. You must remember that the kingdom of heaven that you hope to win is a treasure that is worth the sacrifice of all that you have. You must "take up your cross," and above all you must pray and pursue "the higher righteousness" that inspires the law. You must "be perfect . . . as your heavenly father is perfect." Failure is not an option, for angels stand ready to cast sinners into the "lake of fire."

Your Gospel tells you to expect a final judgement in which justice will be done. You will be dealt with according to how you have conducted yourself in this life. No grey area exists between good and evil. You must cope with the world's (and the Church's) moral ambiguity in the knowledge that ultimately only God can sort things out. The seeds for a good harvest are freely scattered, but wheat and weeds spring up together.[29]

Luke's Universal Savior

With the Gospel of Luke the Bible's readers enter a different world than they met in Mark's and Matthew's texts. Luke was written by someone who had an excellent Greek education and knew the conventions of Greek history writing. The Gospel is addressed to a certain Theophilus and opens with a formal dedication and preface. No one knows if Theophilus was a real person or simply Luke's way of characterizing his audience. (The name translates as "Lover of God.") The Gospel's author had Christian readers in mind, for he says that his intention was to establish "the truth concerning the things about which you have been instructed" (Luke 1:4). He represents himself as writing well after Jesus' lifetime, for he says that many attempts had already been made to "set down an orderly account of the events that have been fulfilled among us" (Luke 1:1). These drew on things that had been "handed on to us" by eyewitnesses and "servants of the word." The Gospel's author claimed no apostolic authority or personal acquaintance with Jesus.

Luke's stated desire (to sift through the earlier attempts to create "orderly" accounts of Jesus' mission) suggests that he found significant confusion in those accounts. This is more than probable, for it appears that early Christian authors had only fragments of information at hand (e.g., lists of Jesus' sayings and parables, and stories about his "works of power," etc.).[30] They had to invent a context for these things, for no outline of Jesus' life had been passed down to them. Scholars have long noted that the Gospels contain large numbers of *pericopes*, episodes or narratives that stand on their own. Each evangelist grouped and ordered these separate bits of information about Jesus in the way that made most sense to him, given his vision of Jesus.

The first Christians were missionaries who believed that the end of the world was at hand and that they only had a short time in which to make as many converts as possible. Their sermons would not have surveyed the whole of Jesus' life and instruction, but would have focused on only a few specific teachings or episodes at a time. These sermons created the pericopes. The earliest Christians had no need for a narrative to preserve the story of Jesus for future generations. They did not think beyond their own generation, for it was commonly believed that people who had known Jesus would still be alive when he came again. So long as there were eyewitnesses, there was no need for a Gospel. But as time passed and the early preachers died off, Christians began to gather up and record whatever information they could find. And by the last quarter of the 1st century CE, the Gospel writers took pen in hand to make sense out of what had, as Luke says, been "handed on."

Matthew and Luke based their Gospels on Mark. The three Gospels have similar outlines, therefore, not because they confirm a story from three independent witnesses, but because two of them copy the third one. They are called the Synoptic Gospels because of the similar overview they share.

Matthew and Luke have more than Mark in common. They also have similar versions of over 200 verses that are not found in Mark. Given that these are often nearly identically in both Gospels, they probably came from one of the lists of pericopes that are assumed to have preceded composition of the Gospels. No copy of this alleged document has been found, but the German scholars who have tried to recreate it have named it "Q" (from *Quelle*, "source").[31]

In addition to material from Mark and Q, the Gospels of Matthew and Luke each have some unique material not found elsewhere. This accounts for almost a third of Luke's Gospel, which is the largest of the three. Luke omitted more Markan material than Matthew did, probably to make space[32] for more of Jesus' teachings (again, from unknown sources). Luke highlights Jesus' work as a teacher and describes him as a kind of wisdom instructor or philosopher. This doubtless made Jesus more intelligible to the Greek gentiles to whom Luke directed his Gospel.

Internal evidence suggests that Luke's Gospel was written sometime after Rome's destruction of Jerusalem (Luke 21:20-24) in 70 CE and possibly well after the conclusion of that war in 73 CE. Who Luke was is unknown. Tradition affixed the name "Luke" to the Gospel because of its author's second volume, the

Book of Acts. Acts deals with the foundation of the Church, which it credits to Jesus' Apostles. But Acts quickly shifts its attention to the work of the missionary Paul, who was not one of the Twelve. The interest Acts takes in Paul suggests that it (and the Gospel) might have been written by one of Paul's companions, an impression that is strengthened when, at Acts 16:10, the narrative suddenly switches into the first person. Paul's letters name some of the men who traveled with him, and Luke is mentioned in three of them (Colossians 4:14, II Timothy 4:11, and Philemon 24). Luke was a Greek gentile convert whose education would have equipped him to write something as sophisticated as Luke-Acts, but the author of Luke-Acts was not likely to have been one of Paul's acolytes. Paul's letters and Luke-Acts differ theologically, and the bits of information about Paul's career found in Paul's letters do not mesh with what Acts says about him. About all that can safely be inferred about the author of Luke-Acts is that he wrote for a gentile audience and wrote very well.

Although Luke relied on Mark's Gospel, his interests were not those of his source. Writing from a later period, he was less concerned with the imminence of the now much delayed Apocalypse. He was also less preoccupied with the Jews and much more interested in the Church's mission to the gentile world. Mark and Matthew hint at the role gentiles were to play in the Church after Jesus' resurrection. They both say that the first person to confess faith in Jesus was a gentile, a Roman centurion who at the cross cried, "Truly this man was God's Son" (Matthew 27:54; Mark 15:39). But Luke's Gospel is the only one of the three to claim (what Matthew denies) that Jesus himself set a precedent for (and thus authorized) the mission to the Gentiles.

Like Matthew's Gospel, Luke's begins with stories about Jesus' birth. The two narratives are quite different, but both have the same function. Each introduces its readers to the interpretation of Jesus the Gospel will develop. Luke starts with an angelic annunciation — not of Jesus' birth, but the birth of John the Baptist, who is said to be his cousin. John, like Abram's Isaac, is the only offspring of elderly parents, and his father, Zechariah, is incredulous when the angel Gabriel tells him that his wife Elizabeth will conceive. Gabriel's second mission (*the* Annunciation) is to inform Mary that she will conceive by the Holy Spirit and bear the Son of God. Mary greets the news with a song, *The Magnificat*, which introduces the major theme of Luke's Gospel. The Messiah's mission is to bring about God's kingdom on Earth — to establish a realm of universal justice that exalts the lowly and humbles the mighty. Jesus' messianic identity is decreed before conception and acknowledged before birth. When Mary visits Elizabeth, the child Elizabeth is carrying (the future John the Baptist) leaps "for joy" in her womb at the Messiah's approach.

Matthew solved the problem of Jesus' life in Nazareth and the tradition of the Messiah's origin in Bethlehem by claiming that Mary and Joseph were natives of Bethlehem who relocated to Nazareth after Jesus' birth. Luke opts for the alternative explanation. He claims that Jesus' parents were natives of Nazareth who went to Bethlehem to register for a tax and were in the City of David only long enough for Mary to give birth to Jesus. The circumstances of his birth forecast the nature of his mission. As the ultimate champion of the poor, he is born in a stable in their circumstances. And the first to know of his appearance are the poorest of the poor, humble shepherds to whom angels bring the news.

As Hebrew law prescribed, Luke says that Jesus was circumcised at the age of eight days and given the name[33] by which Gabriel said he was to be called. The infant was also presented in the temple, and because he was a first-born son (a "first fruit"), a substitutionary sacrifice of two doves was offered for him. The Holy Spirit, whose agency runs through Luke-Acts, then prompted an elder named Simeon to testify to the infant's identity as the Messiah and, like Mary, he broke into song (the

Nunc Dimittis). Luke included a number of hymns in his Gospel to highlight its themes. In this case, the claim is made that the Messiah will do more than fulfill God's promise to the Jews. He is to be humanity's universal savior, "a light for revelation to the Gentiles, and for glory to your people Israel" (Luke 2:32).

Luke says that Jesus' parents raised him in Nazareth, but each year they went to Jerusalem to celebrate Passover. In the twelfth year of their son's life something remarkable happened. Jesus was left behind, and his parents had to return to look for him. They "found him in the temple, sitting among the teachers, listening to them and asking them questions." Luke says that they were all "amazed at his understanding and his answers" (Luke 2:46-47). This is another tale that makes poor history and good theology. Twelve was the age of maturity for a Hebrew male, the point at which the boy ought to begin to assume his role as an adult. In light of all the angelic and human testimony Mary and Joseph had received to their son's messianic identity, why would they have been "amazed at his understanding and his answers"?

Luke's fabulous stories about Jesus' infancy and youth are not history, but a mythic introduction for his Gospel. Like Mark and Matthew (and John), Luke skips over virtually all of Jesus' life and begins his story of the Messiah with Jesus' baptism. Luke follows ancient convention and dates the initial event in his narrative by associating it with a year in the reign of a public official. He says John the Baptist inaugurated his "baptism of repentance for the forgiveness of sins" in the fifteenth year of the reign of the Roman emperor Tiberius. Luke does not explain Jesus' motive for seeking baptism from John. He simply reports that Jesus was baptized, and at that moment "the Holy Spirit descended upon him" and a heavenly voice proclaimed him the Son of God.

Between Luke's accounts of Jesus' baptism and the first phase in his mission, Luke interposes the Messiah's genealogy. Matthew had traced Jesus' lineage back to Abraham to symbolize how his life recapitulated the sacred history of the Chosen People, but Luke tracked Jesus' ancestry (through a different male line) the whole way back to Adam. Luke's Messiah does not come to the Chosen People and only pass to the gentiles when they reject him. He is born the savior of the whole human race.

Luke was aware that two of his claims about Jesus' birth were contradictory. Like Matthew, he asserted that Jesus was born of a virgin mother, but he traced Jesus' ancestry through her husband Joseph. Luke's method of dealing with this inconsistency was simply to acknowledge it. He said that Jesus "was the son (as was thought) of Joseph" (Luke 3:23). What Luke expected his readers to think can be debated, but historical accuracy was plainly not his primary concern.

After his temptation in the desert, Luke says that Jesus began his mission by preaching in the synagogues of Galilee. Despite what Luke has previously claimed about Jesus' role as universal savior, this implies that his first concern was for the Jews. Jesus "was praised by everyone" (Luke 4:15) until he reached his hometown of Nazareth, where his declaration of his messianic calling was met with murderous hostility. His rejection by the Jews who knew him best forecasts the general response of the Chosen People to the news that their Messiah had been sent "to proclaim good news to the poor, . . . release to the captives, and recovery of sight to the blind.[34]"

After his escape from the Nazarenes, who tried to throw him off a cliff, Luke says that Jesus resumed preaching, began to perform exorcisms and healings (fevers, leprosy, paralysis, withered hands, *etc.*), and chose twelve men to receive special instruction as his apostles.[35] Having demonstrated his authority by his power to heal and having assembled his inner circle, Jesus turned to teaching. Where Matthew has a great "Sermon on the Mount," Luke has a shorter sermon "on a level place" (Luke 6:20-49). Matthew's version of the "Beatitudes" spiritualizes them (Matthew 3 — 12). He says that Jesus blessed "the poor *in spirit*" and "those who hunger and thirst *for righteousness.*"[36] Luke, however, took the blessings literally. He says that Jesus blessed "the poor" and promised to fill the bellies of those "who are hungry now." Luke's Jesus preached social justice in practical terms.

Mark's Gospel devotes so much of its space to Jesus' arrest and crucifixion that it might be thought of as an extended Passion Narrative[37] rather than an account of Jesus' ministry. Luke, on the other hand, devotes only two chapters (22 and 23) to the Passion. His concern is much more for Jesus' teaching — both by word and example. Mark's Gospel was written for Christians who believed that the end of the world was literally at hand. But Luke wrote for Christians who were beginning to accept that it might be some time before the Son of God returned. In the interim, they needed to know how to live in obedience to God. The Jews had their laws, but the gentiles needed Jesus' instruction.

Luke's Jesus is a fount of advice for a young religious movement that was dealing with internal tensions and external threats. He says that Jesus ordered his followers to love their enemies, not to judge one another, not to be critical of one another, and not to rebel against their spiritual masters. They were not to divorce and remarry. They were to indict sinners for their transgressions, but freely and repeatedly forgive them if they repented. They were not simply to wait for the kingdom to arrive. They were to be trees bearing good fruit. If they did not do so in a reasonable amount of time, he warned that they could expect to be cut down. They were to avoid hypocrisy, for Jesus cautioned that double-dealing eventually comes to light. They were to try to settle all their disputes out of court. They were to pay their taxes. They were to give all that they could to charity. They were not to heap up riches, for wealth would not serve them in death. They were to live according to the law, but not to mistake its letter for its spirit. They were not to be so distracted by the "worries of this life" that they neglected preparing for the

Kingdom of Heaven. They were to avoid drunkenness and dissipation. They were to anticipate their faith causing divisions within their families. They were not to despair if their efforts on behalf of the kingdom seemed to have little impact, for from small things (such as mustard seeds and yeast spores) great things grow. They were continually to call on God. They were to live prepared for the end times, but to pay no attention to those who claimed to see signs of their approach: "The kingdom of God is not coming with things that can be observed" (Luke 17:20).

Along the way, Luke claims that Jesus set many precedents for a mission to gentiles. When a centurion approached Jesus for help in curing a servant, he confessed that he was "unworthy" to ask Jesus into his home, but that he believed that if Jesus would only speak the word, his servant would be healed. Jesus granted his wish and told his followers that "not even in Israel have I found such faith" (Luke 7:9). Jesus' famous parable of the "Good Samaritan," which appears only in Luke's Gospel, taught that even a Samaritan (who as a follower of perverted form of Judaism was worse than a gentile) could have an understanding of God's will that surpassed that of Israel's priests. A second parable, the Great Dinner, told the story of a man who planned a banquet for his friends (a symbol of God's promises to His Chosen People). When they all refused their invitations (as the Jews did their Messiah), he broke with them and threw open his house to everyone (to the gentiles).

Luke departs from Mark and Matthew by claiming that Jesus himself actually began the mission to the gentiles. He says that Jesus dispatched two groups of apostles to preach on his behalf. The Twelve Apostles were sent to the twelve tribes of Israel (Luke 9:1-6), and another "seventy"[38] were commissioned to preach to everyone else (Luke 10:1-12).

If Luke's Gospel were your only Gospel, what would your Christian faith be like? You would probably be a gentile, perhaps one of the many who were intrigued by the antiquity of the Hebrew religious tradition. You probably would not know much about the Hebrew Scriptures, but you would be confident that the savior whom God promised to send to the "children of Abraham" had invited you to enter the company of His Chosen People. You would fault the Jews for failing to recognize their Messiah. You would believe that they were primarily responsible for his arrest and condemnation, but you would not be as harsh in your condemnation of the Jews as some Christians were. You believe that Jesus' fate was necessary in order to fulfill prophecies. You would be a great believer in prophecy, for your Gospel taught you that Jesus repeatedly warned his disciples that "everything written about me in the law of Moses, the prophets, and the psalms must be fulfilled" (Luke 24:44).

You would believe that you have a major duty to undertake missionary work. In your Gospel Jesus' last charge to his followers, before he ascended to heaven, was to use the power of the Spirit to call "all nations" to repentance and offer them forgiveness of sins in Jesus' name. Missionaries did not just try to argue and persuade others into faith. They could expect to exercise the power of the Holy Spirit in Jesus' name. They were, in some sense, extensions of Jesus.

You would honor the laws found in the Scriptures as having come from God, but not be bound by them as the Jews had been. Jesus had said that "not one stroke of a letter in the law" could ever be dropped (Luke 16:17). This was true, but because Jesus, by his mission, had fulfilled the law and opened the way for the proclamation of a new dispensation: "The law and the prophets were in effect until John came; since then the good news of the kingdom of God is proclaimed" (Luke 16:16-17). The old covenant of the law has been fulfilled, and the new covenant of the kingdom has begun. This is what Jesus implied by the advice he gave the wealthy ruler who had asked him what he should do to be saved (Luke 19-25). When the man claimed always to have obeyed the law, Jesus told him to give his fortune to the poor. This was not a new law, but a warning that life in God's kingdom was a life of concern for others that had no limit. Your Gospel repeatedly warned the rich of the spiritual danger they were in if they hoarded their wealth so long as others were in need.

As a Christian, you believe that you are called to live in God's kingdom here and now. Of course, you still expect the Apocalypse and the end of history, but it is no longer as significant an issue for you as it was for earlier Christians. You do not have to wait for the end times for the good times of the Kingdom to begin. Your Gospel does not really end with reports of experiences of the resurrected Christ. It continues into a second volume that describes your Church as the first sign of the Kingdom's breaking into history. You have been warned not to pay attention to prophets of the end times, but to live as if the Kingdom had already come. Your Gospel is filled with advice on how to do this. You believe that there will be a final judgment and that there is a heaven and a hell. But you also believe that God is as merciful, loving, and freely forgiving as the father in the parable of the prodigal son. On the brink of death Jesus even promised salvation to a criminal crucified beside him.

The kingdom you expect to build requires a social revolution, for it reverses the current order of society. It exalts the weak and condemns the powerful. It is a realm of perfect justice in which no one is exploited or abused — a place of charity and good will where everyone is provided for and no one is persecuted. It requires you not to stand on your rights, but to sacrifice yourself and "go the extra mile" to preserve peace. It obligates you freely to forgive others — again and again, so long as any hope survives for their salvation. Those who fall from the faith are to be welcomed back into the family of Christ, a family not based on kin but on hearing the word of God — and on doing it (Luke 8:21).

Simply believing is not enough; you must also do good

works. Your Gospel is a practical document. It orders you to feed the hungry with solid food, not just promises of redemption. It insists that you honor the least people in your world as the ones who are most important to God. Your deeds are to be a "leaven" that spreads justice and charity throughout the world. But you are a realist. Some of Jesus' parables caution you to prepare for failure. Only some of those who hear the word of God will respond to it, and some of those will drop away (Luke 8:4-8).

Your faith requires you to challenge the conventions of society. In some of Jesus' parables people are punished not for a specific sin but for accepting the world as they found it — for not doing anything about its injustices. No castes or classes exist in God's kingdom, and there can be none in your Church. The distinction between Jew and gentile should be meaningless for you. You must reach out, as your Gospel says Jesus often did, to "untouchables" — to society's outcasts.

You must accord women more respect than they usually get in your world, for women are prominent figures in your Gospel. Jesus often enjoyed their company and relied on them for support and comfort. He even taught women and treated some of them like disciples. When he visited the sisters Mary and Martha, Martha played the traditional female role of preparing food and drink while her sister Mary sat listening to Jesus' conversation. When Martha complained about being left to do all the work, Jesus told her that Mary had "chosen the better part" and that it would "not be taken away from her" (Luke 10:42). Your Church, therefore, cannot stand in the way of any woman who also wants to choose "the better part," even if that part has traditionally been reserved for males.

Challenging conventions that are important to others is dangerous. It is likely to make you a target for persecution.[39] But your Gospel's description of Jesus' Passion offers you encouragement and hope. Unlike Mark's Gospel, where Jesus appears to die in some anxiety, in your Gospel Jesus faces martyrdom calmly and confidently. His last words do not, as Mark records them, reflect fear of abandonment. They express confidence in God's approval: "Father, into your hands I commend my spirit" (Luke 23:46). If your service to God's Kingdom proves to be personally costly, as Jesus' was, so be it. Suffering is part of a divine plan in which all turns out well in the end.

Because you may be more steeped in gentile culture than Judaism, you may not find it difficult to believe that God was present in a man like Jesus. You are familiar with the divine savior cults of the pagans; you know your mythology. Your Gospel says that an entity called the Holy Spirit descended on Jesus at his baptism. It seemed to "inhabit" Jesus and be the source of his healing power and his ability to teach with divine authority. In your Gospel people are often healed simply by touching Jesus and feeling the power that flows from him. Just how the Spirit is related to God is not explained in your Gospel, but the Spirit is what enables things to be done on Earth with God's power.

The Spirit is very important to you, for your faith has a strong charismatic element. You believe that the Spirit that was in Christ descended on his followers after his ascension to heaven and that it lives in your Church. Jesus promised that anyone who had true faith could perform the wonders he performed, and the Book of Acts, which continued the story told in your Gospel, is full of evidence for that. The ultimate confirmation of your faith and your Church is the manifestation of the "gifts of the Spirit" — the power to prophesy, to heal, and even to raise the dead. For you, faith is less a matter of doctrine and fidelity to codes of conduct than a transforming experience that occasionally overwhelms you and sends you forth to do good works.

John's Incarnate Deity
John's Gospel begins Jesus' story with something far grander than a birth narrative. It celebrates Jesus as an eternal divine

being, as the Word that God spoke to effect the creation. John's preface equates Jesus with God: "the Word was with God, and the Word was God" (John 1:1). Not surprisingly, therefore, the Jesus readers meet in John's Gospel is a less human and far more magisterial figure than the anointed Son of Man they find in the other Gospels.[40]

Five items in the New Testament are credited to a man named John: the Gospel, the Book of Revelation, and three letters. Their contents and styles suggest that they were not all the work of the same person. The Gospel's author does not claim to have been one of Jesus' companions, but he does imply that his work is based on the testimony of an especially well informed disciple. For some reason, however, he never names the disciple. He simply describes him as "the disciple whom Jesus loved" (John 21:7) and with whom Jesus had shared a dining couch at the Last Supper (John 21:20).

John's Gospel has much in common with the Gnostic literature that circulated widely in the ancient world. The Gnostics (i.e., "knowers") claimed to have secret knowledge that saved souls by awakening them to their true identity. The claim that Jesus did some secret teaching that was known only to the Apostles crops up in Luke's Gospel as an explanation for why Jesus taught using parables. Luke quotes Jesus saying: "To you [the Apostles] has been given to know the secrets of the kingdom of God; but to others, I speak in parables, so that 'looking they may not perceive, and listening they may not understand'" (Luke 8:10). John's professed reliance on an anonymous Beloved Disciple may be his way of asserting that he had access to insider information not found elsewhere — information that might even be more accurate than the knowledge Jesus shared with his other disciples. If John knew the other Gospels, he was certainly not reluctant to part company with them.

As with the other Gospels, nothing is known about the origin of the Gospel of John. There are no references to it until late in the

2nd century CE, but fragments from a copy of it that date to the mid-2nd century have been discovered in Egypt. They are the oldest extant remnants of a document from the Christian canon. This and John's extreme hostility to Judaism suggests that the Gospel was written during the period when the synagogue and Church were decisively parting company (*i.e.*, the end of the 1st century or very early in the 2nd).

The long period of upheaval and war in 1st-century Palestine had discredited Judaism in the eyes of Roman authorities. Christians were, therefore, eager to distinguish themselves from Jews for political reasons, and Jews, for their part, were in no mood to tolerate what they regarded as a spreading Christian heresy. Having lost their temple and homeland, they were again in exile fighting for the survival of their identity. They sensed a serious threat from a Christian religion that consciously blurred the boundaries between the Jewish and gentile worlds. John claims that the Jews of Jesus' day already had a policy of expelling Christian converts from their synagogues: "the Jews had already agreed that anyone who confessed Jesus to be the Messiah would be put out of the synagogue" (John 9:22).

John's Gospel may have troubled some early Christians because of its apparent flirtation with Gnosticism. Gnosticism, as was previously noted, was a pre-Christian phenomenon that had roots in religion and philosophy. It endorsed dualism, the view of the world as a contest between spirit and matter. Human beings were souls that had somehow been captured in flesh, and their salvation lay in escaping this blinding imprisonment and returning to the spirit realm. To do that, they needed enlightenment — knowledge that awoke them to their true condition and taught them the disciplines they needed to break the bonds of the flesh. Gnostic religious myths often featured a deity who came to Earth to bring *gnosis*, saving knowledge and rituals. Salvation lay not in redeeming, but in escaping, the body.

Many modern Christians endorse beliefs that perpetuate a

form of Gnosticism. They equate sin with the "appetites of the flesh," and they imagine that at death their souls will be freed to go to heaven. Their true identity is not a physical self, but a spirit-being that temporarily inhabits the body's shell. These Christians would be branded heretics by the Christians who wrote the New Testament. The early Church vigorously opposed Gnosticism by grounding itself in the Hebrew Scriptures and by asserting the resurrection *of the body*. The Hebrew Creation stories affirmed that human beings were living bodies, not pre-existent souls wrapped in flesh. Meaningful resurrection required that they be raised as what they truly were. They would get their bodies back.

John's affirmation of this doctrine testifies to his orthodoxy. His claim that Jesus was the eternal Word of God sounds gnostic, and the way Jesus identifies himself with God in John's Gospel suggests parallels with one of the savior deities from the gnostic myths. But John insists that "the Word became flesh and lived among us" (John 1:14). It did not simply assume a fleshy disguise. It became flesh just like we are. John also agreed with the authors of the Synoptics that Jesus was resurrected in the flesh and not as a spirit. Mark does not report a resurrection appearance, but his emphasis on the empty tomb implies his belief in a physical resurrection. The women who in Matthew's Gospel met the resurrected Christ after viewing his empty tomb "took hold of his feet" (Matthew 28:9). In Luke's Gospel, the resurrected Christ invited his disciples to touch him to confirm for themselves that he had "flesh and bones." He further demonstrated his corporeal nature by eating a piece of boiled fish (Luke 24:39-43). In John's Gospel the body of the resurrected Christ still carries the wounds of Jesus' crucifixion, and Christ invites Thomas, who had doubted reports of the resurrection, to poke his fingers and hands into the holes that had been made by nails and spear.

Although they hold important beliefs in common, John's Gospel diverges in tone and detail from the Synoptic Gospels.

John's emphasis on Jesus' god-like nature and John's hostility to Judaism help to explain some the major differences. His Jesus is endowed with God's knowledge and guided by God's will from the moment of creation. His human origins are unimportant. John has no use for a birth narrative, for a baptism, or a period of temptation in the desert. His Jesus has no need to wrestle with himself, to come to terms with his destiny, or to struggle with temptation. He appears in maturity fully aware of who he is and how his mission will play out. The Gospel mentions John the Baptist, but says nothing about him baptizing Jesus. John's only function in the Gospel is to deny that he is the Messiah and to declare that Jesus is (John 1:19-34).

In John's Gospel the Baptist's testimony inspires two of his own followers to switch their allegiance to Jesus and become his first disciples. One of these, Andrew, brought his brother Simon Peter to Jesus; Jesus himself then called Philip and Nathaniel. With his new disciples in tow, Jesus embarked on the first public act of his ministry. At a wedding in a place called Cana he performed the first of seven miracles — or "signs" as John calls them. Supernatural signs were of great importance for the author of John's Gospel, both as demonstrations of Jesus' power and as symbols. At Cana Jesus turned six "twenty or thirty" gallon jars of water into wine of the highest quality. Jesus' career thus began with an extraordinarily festive banquet. 180 gallons of wine would have made for a merry time for a gathering of Galilean villagers. It signaled the glorious heavenly feast that Jesus' work on Earth prepared for his followers.

Jesus' next recorded act suggested the purpose of his mission. Whereas the Synoptics say that the "cleansing of the temple" was one of the last things that Jesus did and that it was the event that caused the Jews to plot his death, John claims that Jesus began his career by attacking the temple. John describes the event in much more vivid detail than the Synoptics. The other Gospels mention Jesus turning over some tables and driving people out.

John adds the detail that he attacked them with "a whip of cords," chased sheep and cattle from the precinct, "poured out the coins of the money changers," and told the dove sellers to take their birds and get out (John 2:15-16). According to John, when the Jews asked Jesus what authority he had to object to established temple practices, he responded with a coded prophecy. He said that if they tore down the temple, he would "raise it up" in three days. John's Gospel implied that the Romans had been the agents God used to punish the Jews for their failure to embrace their Messiah. Rome's destruction of Jerusalem's temple was God's judgment on the old dispensation. It cleared the way for a new mode of mediation between God and humankind. Faith in the resurrected Christ replaced the law and opened the way to salvation for all who believed.

John's Jesus is little concerned with Hebrew law and religious taboos, and the Gospel is addressed to gentiles more than to Jews. John says that the Jews wanted to kill Jesus "because he was not only breaking the sabbath, but was also . . . making himself equal to God" (John 5:18). Because John's readers were likely to be gentiles raised on anthropomorphic religious myths, he found it necessary to explain why the staunchly monotheistic Jews, who did not even presume to speak God's name, were offended by Jesus. They objected "because you [Jesus], though only a human being, are making yourself God" (John 10:33).

Although John claims that Jesus said that "the Father is greater than I" (John 14:28), John's description of Jesus' sermons makes it clear why his opponents thought that he was equating himself with God. As a teacher, Jesus focuses on himself more than on sacred law or prophecy. His interest is in explaining his nature, his relationship with God, and how God is acting through him and seen in Him. He claims the greatest possible intimacy with God: "Whoever has seen me has seen the Father" (14:9). When he refers to the law, his purpose is to point out how his Jewish opponents break it (John 7:19-23) or how they ought to break it (John 8:5-11). Sometimes John seems to forget that Jesus was a Jew, and he disassociates Jesus from his own people. John has Jesus refer to "their" law and accuse "them" (the Jews) of fulfilling its prophecies by hating him and his "Father" (John 15:25).

The Synoptic tradition stresses Jesus' message of love for God and for one's neighbor. But John's Jesus asserts that belief in him is the key to salvation. To believe in him is to believe in God, and to reject him is to reject God: "No one comes to the Father except through me" (John 14:6). John's Jesus dismisses the law as an instrument of salvation and claims that salvation comes only through belief in him: "God did not send the Son into the world to condemn the world [as the law does], but in order that the world might be saved through him. Those who believe in him are not condemned; but those who do not believe are condemned already, because they have not believed in the name of the only Son of God" (John 3:17-18). The law was given through Moses, but "grace and truth came through Jesus Christ" (1:17). Only those who claim Christ's name (i.e., call themselves Christians) will be saved. Those who reject him do so because something perverse in them makes them love darkness more than light.

Faith seems more important than works to John. Nowhere in his Gospel is much said about the importance of loving one's neighbor. Nor does John have the kind of passionate concern for social justice that characterizes the Synoptic tradition.

John agrees with the Synoptics that Jesus showed unusual openness to women, but gender in John's stories is sometimes less important than the female's usefulness as a symbol for the "other." For instance, the story of the Samaritan woman with whom Jesus has an extended exchange by a well (John 4) is intended to indicate Jesus' openness not just to women, but to everyone. Jesus' conversation with her leads to a two-day meeting with her neighbors and their conversion. The Samaritans, unlike the Jews who despised them, become confessors: "we believe, for we have heard for ourselves, and we know that this is truly the Savior of the world" (John 4:42). For John, Jesus did not simply predict or dispatch a mission to non-Jews. He actually conducted one.

While Jesus was in Jerusalem, John says that he was secretly visited by a learned Pharisee named Nicodemus who treated him with respect and deference. Nicodemus was, however, mystified when Jesus told him that he would have to be born again in order to enter the kingdom of God. Nicodemus' birth as one of the Chosen People was, Jesus taught, irrelevant. Such birth was only flesh born of flesh. What counted was to be "born of water and spirit" (John 3:5). Jesus then wondered at Nicodemus' ignorance: "Are you a teacher of Israel, and yet you do not understand these things?" (John 3:10) John's tale implies that the Jews, even their scholars, fail to grasp what is obvious in their sacred texts. John represents Jesus as scorning the Jews' claim to privileges as Abraham's children and telling them that if they were truly Abraham's descendants they, like Abraham, would recognize the word of God. By refusing to do so, they revealed their true parentage: "You are from your father the devil, and you choose to do your father's desires" (8:44). The only meaningful distinction among peoples is between those who believe in Jesus and those who do not.

Although Jesus claimed that his purpose was not to judge the world but to save it, he warned that those who rejected him would be judged "on the last day" (12:47-48). However, unlike the Synoptic Gospels, John's Gospel is not much concerned with the approach (imminent or otherwise) of the end times. John's congregation did not burn with apocalyptic fervor. It was more preoccupied with the expectation that the Holy Spirit would continue Jesus' work on Earth. The new age was not to dawn when Jesus came again. It dawned with Jesus' crucifixion and resurrection.

In Luke's Gospel (22:42), Jesus, showing understandably

human trepidation, asks God if he might avoid crucifixion, but in John's Gospel Jesus coolly embraces crucifixion as the goal of his life. He says that it will be the moment of divine reckoning when Satan will be defeated: "Now is the judgment of this world; now the ruler of this world will be driven out. And I, when I am lifted up from the earth, will draw all people to myself" (John:12:27-32).

John believes that the reality of God that Jesus represented never really departs from Earth. The Messiah's appearance did not mark history's end; it inaugurated a new phase in its development. As Jesus approached the end of his mission, John says that he promised his disciples that he would "ask the Father, and he will give you another Advocate, to be with you forever" (John 14:16). Later, he assured them: "I will not leave you orphaned; I am coming to you. In a little while the world will no longer see me, but you will see me; because I live, you also will live" (John 14:18-19). Those who abide in love for him, Jesus said, could be confident that he and the Father "will love them, and we will come to them and make our home with them" (John14:23).

What other Christians hoped for in the future, John's people believed they were already enjoying. Jesus, John says, promised that "anyone who hears my word and believes him who sent me has eternal life, and does not come under judgement, but has passed from death to life" (John 5:24). Judgment became irrelevant once one passed the only crucial test — profession of faith in Christ. A believer was assured of continuing access to the power manifested in Christ, for after the resurrection the Father sent "the Advocate, the Holy Spirit" to provide whatever guidance was needed and to ensure that all that Jesus had taught was remembered (John 14:26).

If John's Gospel were your only Gospel, what would your Christian faith be like? You would most likely be a Greek-speaking gentile. The author of your Gospel thought that it was necessary to define some terms for you that would be familiar to

Jews (*e.g.*, rabbi, messiah, and *rabbouni*; John 1:38; 20:16). He also thought that you might not understand some customs — such as the significance of Jesus asking a Samaritan woman for a cup of water. As an aside, he explained: "Jews do not share things in common with Samaritans" (John 4:9).

You would believe that the God you worship is the same deity the Jews worship, and you would assume that the Hebrew Scriptures were a valid, if not indispensable, means of salvation. In your Gospel Jesus says to the Jews, "If you believed Moses, you would believe me" (John 5:46). If the Jews truly understood their law, therefore, they would recognize Jesus as their Messiah. The fact that they do not is not the fault of the text but of its readers. The Jews, Jesus says, have the law, but do not keep it (John 7:19). If they did, they would see Jesus as Christians see him. The law is not necessary, however, if by other means one recognizes God in Christ

You and your fellows have broken decisively with the Jews. This does not concern you, for in your Gospel Jesus several times predicted that "they will put you out of the synagogues" (John 16:2). Jesus also promised that "anyone who comes to me I will never drive away" (John 6:37), and he told the Jews, "I have other sheep that do not belong to this fold [Israel]. I must bring them also . . . So there will be one flock, one shepherd" (John 10:16). Although Jesus warned Jews who did not accept his claim to be the Messiah that "you do not belong to my sheep" (John 10:26), he said that his death was "for the nation [Israel], and not for the nation only, but to gather into one the dispersed children of God" (John 11:52).

Although other Gospels call for Christians to convert the world, you may not believe that your faith is intended to be universal. The children of God are the elect. They are literally a Chosen People, for Jesus said that "no one can come to me unless it is granted by the Father" (John 6:65). This explains, you believe, why some people see the many "signs" of who Jesus is and believe while others see those signs and do not believe. Jesus did not equivocate (as he seems to in other Gospels). He plainly said that he was the Messiah (John 4:26), and your Gospel is filled with examples of the miraculous "signs" that make his case (John 2:23). The evidence is so abundant that your Gospel claims that if everything that Jesus did "were written down, I suppose that the world itself could not contain the books that would be written" (John 21:25).

Jesus' "signs" are crucial, for he explained that he "came into the world for judgment" (John 9:39). That is, he is the test. In him people are given a chance to recognize God. Those who do are those who were destined for the "resurrection of life," and those who do not were fated to the "resurrection of condemnation" (John 5:29).

Other Gospels are filled with Jesus' teaching and his directions for how to live, but yours contributes little to these topics. Its single-minded concern is to stress the importance of belief in Jesus as savior. Jesus responded simply when asked, "What must we do to perform the works of God?" He did not at that point take the opportunity to lay down a law of love or urge the pursuit of justice and charity. Instead he said: "This is the work of God, that you believe in him whom he sent" (6:28-29). Faith is the means of salvation. Works of love follow knowledge of salvation.

In your Gospel Jesus issues only one specific commandment. He says, "I give you a new commandment, that you love one another" (John 13:34). This is hardly a new mandate in the sense of an original idea. You know that similar admonitions appear in other ancient religious and philosophical texts. It is new to your Gospel in the sense of "additional." The prime requirement is to believe in God through Jesus. Then comes the duty to love.

It may well be that you follow other rules as well, for your evangelist sometimes quotes Jesus referring to commandments in the plural: "If you love me, you will keep my commandments"

(John 14:15). He also says that those who "have" his commandments and keep them will be loved by him (John 14:21). Perhaps,
like a gnostic sect, your church cherished some secret teachings
that were not published in your Gospel. One of its passages hints
at this when a disciple asks Jesus, "Lord, how is it that you will
reveal yourself to us, and not to the world?" (14:22) There may
also have been a distinction within your community between
those who were fully and those who were only partially
instructed in its teachings. Your Gospel implies that Jesus gave
his disciples information that he did not share with other
followers: "I do not call you servants any longer . . ., but I have
called you friends, because I have made known to you everything
that I have heard from my Father" (John 15:14-15).

Your Gospel says nothing about Jesus instituting a meal of
bread and wine, but you must have practiced this ritual, for your
Gospel quotes Jesus saying, "unless you eat the flesh of the Son
of Man and drink his blood, you have no life in you" (John 6:53).
You also insist on baptism. Your Gospel says that Jesus himself
did not perform the rite but accompanied his disciples while they
baptized. This might have been to forestall claims that some
baptisms, such as those traced back to Jesus, were superior to
others. The one ritual that your Gospel overtly commands
Christians to perform is mutual foot washing. It says that after
Jesus washed the feet of his disciples, he said, "I have set you an
example, that you also should do as I have done to you" (John
13:15).

Again and again your Gospel hammers home the importance
of believing that God is revealed in Jesus, for this is what brings
salvation. You believe that Jesus was so close to God that he knew
the plan for his life from the start and intervened from time to
time to keep its progress on track. His goal was always the cross,
and his death was necessary so that he could rise again. All of this
was part of God's plan as laid out in the Hebrew Scriptures — but
it was Scripture that "they did not understand" until it had been

fulfilled (John 20:9). Your Gospel explains Jesus' death as a sacrifice, a sin offering. It opens with John the Baptist's proclamation that Jesus is the "Lamb of God who takes away the sins of the world" (John 1:36). Unlike the other Gospels, which claim that Jesus was crucified on the day after he celebrated the Passover, your Gospel closes with the assertion that Jesus was slaughtered at the same time as the lambs being offered up for Passover.

You believe that Jesus' resurrection prepares the way for him to raise you up "on the last day" (John 6:54). But your Gospel says almost nothing about the "last day." It does not propose any signs for the approach of the end times or caution you to prepare for the final judgment. Nothing need concern you so long as you remain firm in your faith that Jesus is the Son of God.[41]

In the meantime your Gospel assures you that you can rely on guidance by the Holy Spirit that played a major role in Jesus' life. Jesus time on Earth was limited, but he promised his disciples that the Spirit would descend and serve them as a source of revelation after he was gone. As the end of his earthly life neared, he told his disciples: "I have much to say, but not now. When the Spirit of truth comes, he will guide you into all the truth" (John 16:13). A Gospel whose subject was Jesus' earthly ministry was not wide enough in scope to encompass all that has been revealed to your community. But you recognize dangers for a congregation that is Spirit-guided. Disputes can easily arise about what is and is not a legitimate manifestation of the Spirit, and these can lead to divisions. The final prayer that your Gospel says that Jesus made for his disciples was a prophetic request that they be kept from fighting among themselves "so that they may be as one" (John 17:11, 22-23).

Your Gospel only hints at some of what your community was inspired by the Spirit to believe. Some of you may have embraced ascetic disciplines, for your Gospel quotes Jesus saying, "Those who love their life lose it, and those who hate their life in this world will keep it for eternal life" (John 12:25).

Your Gospel certainly led you to expect suffering and self-sacrifice: "If they persecuted me, they will persecute you" (John 15:20).

You may face threats from a variety of sources, but you reserve your greatest enmity for the Jews. Jesus' career, as described in your Gospel, was an endless struggle with the Jews. Some of them see the "signs" that testify to his identity and profess faith, but most of them — particularly the Pharisees and chief priests — seem determined to do all they can to neutralize the effects of Jesus' miracles. They even plotted to murder poor Lazarus and send him back to his grave to halt the spreading wonderment at his resurrection. You are firmly convinced that it was the Jews and not the Romans who are responsible for murdering Jesus. Your Gospel quotes Jesus himself making that charge. It describes Pontius Pilate desperately attempting to persuade the Jews to allow him to release Jesus. The Roman governor even shed his dignity and condescended to run back and forth to negotiate with "the Jews" in a futile attempt to dissuade them from forcing Jesus' crucifixion. Jesus seems almost to try to comfort Pilate by telling him that he is only a pawn in the divine plan, the point of which was to give the Jews plenty of rope with which to hang themselves. Jesus said, "the one [Judaism] who handed me over to you is guilty of a greater sin" (John19:11).

The most surprising thing about your Gospel is its seeming indifference to the pursuit of social justice and the cultivation of human community. It does not emphasize the importance of showing concern for the poor — except for Judas's peevish and allegedly insincere grumble that an expensive ointment poured over Jesus' feet should have been sold and the money given to the poor (John 12:5). The only disciple to propose charity as the higher priority is the one who betrayed Jesus, and the Gospel brands him as insincere.

Perhaps this is why at some early point someone added a new

chapter to your Gospel. It originally ended with its author's explanation of why he took pen in hand: "These [things] are written so that you may come to believe that Jesus is the Messiah, the Son of God, and that through believing you may have life in his name" (John 20:31). But your Gospel, as we have it now, concludes with another chapter in which the Jesus of the resurrection commands Peter to feed his sheep. The leaders of your community are at least urged to care for their own.

NOTES

1 Borg and Wright, *The Meaning of Jesus*, p. 171.

2 Marcus J. Borg, *Jesus: Uncovering the Life, Teachings, and Relevance of a Religious Revolutionary* (NY: HarperCollins, 2006), p. 7.

3 This excludes the books of the Apocrypha — which, although they appear in some Bibles, many Christians do not regard as part of the canon.

4 *Apocrypha* is the plural of the Greek noun *apocryphon*, implying a secret document or a text with a "hidden" meaning. St. Jerome, the translator of the Latin vulgate, used (possibly, coined) the term to describe the books that are found in the Septuagint but not in the Hebrew Scriptures.

5 Dying martyrs sometimes predicted that the hands or other parts of their bodies that torturers had cut off would be restored to them. And Razis, an "elder" of Jerusalem "pulled out his bowels with both hands and hurled them at the crowd, and so expired, calling upon him who is lord of life and spirit, to give these back to him again" (II Maccabees 14:46, tr. Edgar J. Goodspeed).

6   *Ibid.*, 15:12-14.

7   *Ibid.*, 12:45.

8   *Armageddon* is a corruption of the Hebrew for "Mountain of Megiddo." The plain of Megiddo lay west of the Sea of Galilee and was the site of several significant ancient battles. Its prominence in biblical circles may derive from its identification as the place where Josiah, the great Judean king, was killed. The Bible's only use of the term is found in Revelation 16:16, where "Harmagedon" is identified as the location "for battle on the great day of God the Almighty."

9   Borg, *Jesus*, p. 92.

10   "in the Jewish homeland at the time of Jesus, the term synagogue referred primarily to a gathering, and less so to a building with an accompanying, well-defined liturgy." John Dominic Crossan and Jonathan L. Reed, *Excavating Jesus: Beneath the Stones, Behind the Texts* (NY: HarperSanFrancisco, 2001), p. 26.

11   The people of Nazareth's "understanding of the covenant came not from the written Torah and Prophets in Hebrew, which few could read, but from their oral *targum* (Aramaic for 'translation'). A *targum* was more than a verbatim translation of the Hebrew text; whole paragraphs were added and long sections loosely paraphrased by the *meturgeman,* a 'translator' who handed on the local tradition of rendering Scripture. (Just as a local rabbi designed ethical norms for living the Torah, a *meturgeman* memorized and recited the oral Scripture)." Bruce Chilton, *Rabbi Jesus: An Intimate Biography* (NY: Image Doubleday, 2000), p. 4-5.

12   Although the Book of Acts, which was written by the author
      of Luke's Gospel, devotes a lot of space to Paul's career, it
      does not mention him writing influential letters.

13   In the case of Matthew, nearly 15/16th of Mark. Luke used
      less Markan material, probably to make room on his scroll
      for other things he wished to record.

14   Most scholars believe that Mark's Gospel was the first, but a
      few argue that Mark condensed Matthew's work. This
      theory, however, raises needless and unanswerable
      questions. Unlike Matthew's Gospel, Mark's Gospel has no
      account of Jesus' birth and no sightings of the resurrected
      Christ. Why would Mark have omitted Jesus' birth, and —
      more puzzling — why would he have deleted all the reports
      of those who witnessed the most crucial event in the
      Gospels, Christ's resurrection?

15   Elaine Pagels, *The Origin of Satan* (NY: Vintage Books, 1995),
      p. 8.

16   Names do not begin to be mentioned for the Gospels until
      about 180 CE. "It is unlikely that Christians knew the names
      of the authors of the Gospels for a period of a hundred years
      or so but did not mention them in any of the surviving liter-
      ature (which is quite substantial)." E. P. Sanders, *The
      Historical Figure of Jesus* (NY: Penguin, 1993), p. 65.

17   Satan's role changes as the biblical tradition evolves. Initially
      he is God's servant, not His opponent. He does not lead
      forces of his own, but carries out missions from God, who
      sometimes orders him to oppose or test the faithful (*e.g.*, Job
      1-2). But gradually Satan began to be used to explain the sins
      and blunders of Israel's kings and people. He inspired the

people to do things that displeased God. (*e.g.*, I Chronicles 21:1). In the Apocrypha Satan became a fallen angel, God's rebellious opponent. As dualistic thinking infiltrated the Judeo-Christian tradition and history came to be understood as a struggle between forces of good and evil, Satan became the leader of a mighty army marching toward a final battle with God and His angelic legions. Those who believe in Satan face a "satanic" temptation, for they easily slip into the error of regarding their opponents as evil beings who must be destroyed.

18 Borg, *Jesus*, p. 263.

19 If Mark's Gospel were the only one we had, the disciples would never have become the apostles. The job of a disciple is to learn and prepare for an independent mission as an apostle. Jesus' disciples in Mark's Gospel never graduate. They consistently fail to understand him. Their chief interest seems to be in promoting themselves to positions of power in his coming kingdom (Mark10:35-45). When the final tests come, they flee and abandon him. Only a few of their women witness the crucifixion and try to conduct funeral rights for him. Nothing is said about the disciples coming to faith in the resurrection or playing an important role in founding the Church.

20 Paul, in his letter to the Galatians (2:11-14) mentions a quarrel he had with Peter at Antioch over the issue of imposing dietary laws on gentile converts.

21 Matthew and Luke's birth narratives are analyzed in greater detail in chapter 8.

22 A disciple is someone who is taught; an apostle is some one

sent on a mission — usually to spread the teachings of the master.

23　The first, that is, in sacred history — as opposed to the mythic story of the eastern kings who worshiped Jesus in early childhood.

24　Mark adds a detail that has long puzzled scholars: "A certain young man was following him, wearing nothing but a linen cloth. They caught hold of him, but he left the linen cloth and ran off naked." (Mark14:51)

25　This is the point of the story of "doubting Thomas" at the end of John's Gospel: "Blessed are those who have not seen and yet have come to believe" (John 20:29).

26　Such people were so common that synagogues evolved rules of conduct (modified Torah) for them and called them: "God-followers."

27　This may have been particularly true if Matthew was writing for a congregation of Jewish converts, who likely had extended families whose members did not all share their new faith.

28　"I am" is an evocative phrase in the Bible, for it recalls the "name" of God (Exodus 3:14). This association seems quite intentional in John's Gospel, which quotes Jesus as delivering a number of "I am Sayings" — claims for his close association with the divine Father.

29　It would not have been possible, however, to hold a church together unless discipline was imposed on its members. Therefore, the Gospel establishes an elaborate procedure for giving up on someone and expelling him from the community. The only reference to the Church in the Gospels apart from Matthew's 16th chapter is found in Matthew 18:15-19, which explains how a kind of trial should be conducted. Matthew was a realist who knew that sometimes weeds had to be plucked out.

30   "The earliest Christians did not write a narrative of Jesus' life, but rather made use of, and thus preserved, individual units — short passages about his words and deeds. These units were later moved and arranged by editors and authors. This means that we can never be sure of the immediate context of Jesus' sayings and actions." Sanders, *The Historical Figure of Jesus*, p. 57.

31   Some of the verses in the Q source also appear in the *Didache* (*The Teachings of the Twelve Apostles*), a manual of advice for early Christian congregations that was written in the last half of the 1st century CE. Much Q material is also similar to passages found in the non-canonical Gospel of Thomas.

32   Space limits for ancient texts were dictated by the length of the scrolls on which they were written. If a scroll became too long, it was difficult to unroll for purposes of finding passages that its reader needed to consult.

33   Jesus is not a unique or unusual name. It is the Hellenized version of Joshua and means "Yahweh is Salvation." If Jesus were an invention of fiction, he probably would not have been given a common name.

34   Luke 4:18. Later in the Gospel Luke presents a similar list of the signs that were to indicate that Jesus was the Messiah (Luke 7:18-22). When John the Baptist sends messengers to

ask Jesus if he is "the one who is to come" (*i.e.*, the Messiah), Jesus says: "Go and tell John what you have seen and heard: the blind receive their sight, the lame walk, the lepers are cleansed, the deaf hear, the dead are raised, the poor have good new brought to them."

35 Four lists of the names of the Apostles appear in the New Testament: Mark 3; Matthew 10, Luke 6 and Acts 1. There are some discrepancies among them. A Thadaeus appears on Mark's and Matthew's lists, but not in Luke-Acts. There we find a "Judas son of James," who does not appear on the other lists.

36 Italics added.

37 Mark devotes about 40 percent of his text to the last week in Jesus' life.

38 Seventy was the traditional number of gentile nations.

39 Ehrman, *Misquoting Jesus*, p. 141: "Luke's Passion narrative, as has long been recognized, is a story of Jesus' martyrdom, a martyrdom that functions, as do many others, to set an example to the faithful of how to remain firm in the face of death."

40 Determining how much, if anything, John might have known about the other canonical Gospels is difficult. Burton L. Mack, *Who Wrote the New Testament: The Making of the Christian Myth* (NY: Harper Collins, 1995), pp. 177-178, sees significant parallelism between the outline of Jesus' story in Mark and in John. He notes that John's description of Jesus' trial and crucifixion "follows Mark so closely that some form of textual dependence is probable. . . . The passion plot was

a postwar Markan creation, and it is impossible that John would have come up with the same plot independently."

41 "What matters for John's Gospel is not the future of the world. What matters is eternal life in heaven, which comes to those who believe in Jesus . . . . Jesus' message in John is not a call to repentance because the kingdom of God is near at hand, it is a call for people to believe in him as the one who opens the way to heaven." Bart Ehrman, *God's Problem* (NY: HarperCollins, 2008), p. 257.

8

The Christian Phase: Part II

The Bible is the inerrant . . . word of the living God. It is absolutely infallible, without error in all matters pertaining to faith and practice, as well as in areas such as geography, science, history, etc.[1]
— Jerry Falwell

Reading a text necessarily involves interpreting a text. . . . [T]exts do not speak for themselves.[2]
— Bart D. Ehrman

Religion, like other experience, is to be tested not by its origin but by its fruits[3]
— Daniel J. Boorstin

History's Jesus

If we did not have the Gospel of John, we might be deluded into thinking that we could easily write a biography of Jesus. All we would need to do is follow the outline and combine the information that we find in the Synoptic Gospels. John, however, makes that impossible, for he contradicts the Synoptics both theologically and with respect to details of Jesus' life. Close examination also reveals that the Synoptic Gospels are not three sources that independently confirm the same story of Jesus. Two of them (Matthew and Luke) simply rely on the third (Mark) for their outline and much of their material. And Mark, the "original" Gospel, did not intend to offer an objective account of Jesus' life. A gospel is "good news," a proclamation of the *kerygma*: "Jesus is the Christ." Its purpose is to explain what its author thought that phrase meant.

The differences among the canonical sources have spawned an enterprise called the "search for the historical Jesus."[4] Scholars have expended vast quantities of ink arguing about how much, if any, reliable historical information can be recovered about Jesus. Given the influence his life has had on the course of western and world civilization, it might seem incredible that the historical records of his era do not mention him. No extant Roman documents testify to his existence, and not until well after his death do the ancient world's historians begin to take note of his followers and what they said about him. But the fact that Jesus of Nazareth was unnoticed by most of his contemporaries is to be expected. He was a peasant who spent his life in a rural backwater. It was not his history as a man that made him significant and memorable. It was faith in his resurrection (a supernatural event for which there can be testimony but no historical evidence) that launched the movement that made his life one of the hinges of history.

Given Jesus' ethnic identity and region of activity, Jewish sources would logically be the first to search for information about him. The Talmud (a collection of rabbinical commentaries), however, makes no mention of him until a generation after his death. It simply condemns as absurd the claims his followers made about him, but it may be significant that it does not suggest that he never even existed. The Jewish historian Josephus, who was active at the end of the 1st century CE, and who wrote to explain his people's customs and history to the Romans, mentions Jesus twice. He notes the existence of a man named James who was active in Jerusalem prior to the Roman war, and he says that this James was the brother of Jesus, "who is called the Messiah." His second reference is longer, but both are historically questionable. Josephus' books were preserved and copied by generations of medieval Christian scribes who appear to have inserted explanatory passages into them. Some of these are easy to identify, for they make Josephus sound like a Christian —

which the body of his work makes clear that he was not. When these interpolated passages are removed, little of significance remains. Josephus says that Jesus was a wise man who did amazing things and attracted a following among both Jews and gentiles. When Jewish leaders indicted him, Pilate crucified him. But this did not discourage his followers, for "up until this very day the tribe of Christians, named after him has not died out."[5]

Roman sources are devoid of references to Christians for over a century after Jesus' birth. About the year 110 a Roman provincial governor named Pliny the Younger wrote a letter to the emperor Trajan asking for advice on the empire's policy toward Christians. In case his superior was unsure who the Christians were, Pliny explained that they met and sang hymns to Christ as if he were a god. A little later, a historian named Suetonius recorded that the emperor Claudius drove the Jews from Rome because they were prompted to riot by a certain "Chrestus." Suetonius did not distinguish Jews from Christians, and he assumed that Christ was an agitator active in Rome during Claudius's reign (r. 41-54 CE). Later still, Tacitus (c. 56-c.117), an excellent Roman historian, explained to his readers that Christians were followers of a man named Christ whom Pontius Pilate executed during Tiberius's reign. Nothing in these sources adds much to our knowledge of Jesus.

Archaeology has also been of little help. In 1962 an inscription came to light that commemorated a building erected in Caesarea Maritima by Pontius Pilate, prefect of Judea.[6] In 1990 an ossuary (a box for burying bones) was discovered in a cave in Jerusalem with the name of the high priest, Caiaphas, scratched into its side. The cave appears to be the family tomb of the official whom the Gospels claim led the plot to destroy Jesus.[7] Given Jesus' humble origins and peripatetic lifestyle, his activities would not have left behind identifiable physical traces. Nazareth, in his day, was an impoverished village with between 200 and 400 inhabitants. Apart from the Gospels, no reference to its existence appears in any text before the 4th century.[8]

Little survives from the world that Jesus knew. The remains of a 1st century house that may have belonged to the family of St. Peter have been excavated beneath a church in the town of Capernaum. An argument can be made that Peter's tomb survives in a Roman cemetery beneath the Vatican.[9] The places in the Holy Land associated with events in Jesus' life were not commemorated with great churches until the middle of the 4th century CE. No one knows on what evidence their sites were identified. A 4th-century Christian bishop and historian, Eusebius, mentions the last traces of Jesus' family. He says that two of Jesus' great nephews, grandsons of his brother Judas, were hauled before the emperor Domitian (r. 81-96 CE). They claimed to be descendants of King David. But when the emperor discovered that they were only manual laborers scraping by on a tiny farm, he released them.[10]

Given the available options, historians have no alternative but to rely almost exclusively on the Bible for information about Jesus. The oldest portions of the New Testament, the ones closest to Jesus' lifetime, are letters attributed to St. Paul.[11] The first of these is I Thessalonians, which was composed about 50 CE (about 20 years after the traditional date for Jesus' death). Unfortunately for historians, Paul never met the historical Jesus and was not much interested in his earthly life. Paul's devotion was to Jesus the Christ, the resurrected lord Paul encountered in a vision. Only in passing does Paul make any reference to the circumstances of Jesus' life.

Paul says that Jesus was "born of a woman, born under the law to redeem those who were under the law" (Galatians 4:4-5). (In other words, Jesus was a Jew whose concern was only for Jews.) Paul notes that Jesus had brothers who, like all his Apostles, were married men (Romans 9:5). Paul encountered one of Jesus' brothers (James) in Jerusalem (Galatians 1:19), and he confirms that Jesus had twelve Apostles (I Corinthians 15:5). Paul believed that Jesus instituted a ritual meal of bread and wine that was to be celebrated in his memory (I Corinthians 11:22-26). He claims that Jesus prohibited divorce (I Corinthians 7:10-11), and he says that Jesus "commanded that those who proclaim the gospel should get their living by the gospel" (I Corinthians 9:14). Of course, Paul had no doubt that Jesus had been betrayed, crucified, and resurrected "by the power of God" (II Corinthians 13:4), for he preached "Christ crucified, a stumbling block to Jews and foolishness to Gentiles" (I Corinthians 1:23).

Paul is the only one of the people called "apostles" in the New Testament who is reported to have written anything. The letters ascribed to Peter come from an era after his death. The various materials ascribed to a John — including, as previously noted, the Gospel of John — also are post-Apostolic. This absence of documents from people who were members of Jesus' circle should be expected. Few if any of them were likely literate,[12] and their faith was ardently apocalyptic. It is doubtful that they had the ability to create formal records and clear that they had no motivation to do so. They believed that the need for such things would shortly be at an end. Even Paul did not write with the future in mind. His letters, with the exception of the letter he wrote to introduce himself to the Christians in Rome, were attempts to exercise a kind of pastoral supervision from a distance. He hoped by means of his correspondence to keep his current converts in line until "we who are alive, who are left, will be caught up in the clouds" to meet Christ as he descends (I Thessalonians 4:17).

Given that nothing is known about the authors of the Gospels or about the accuracy of the sources of information they drew on, and given that their intention was to write about the Christ of faith, not the Jesus of history, major obstacles lie in the way of attempts to discern objective information about the man from Nazareth. Some highly probable details can, however, be recovered.

First of all, Jesus was a man from Nazareth. The most dependable information the Gospels provide about him are aspects of his story that were obstacles to faith and challenges to messianic expectations. These are details that Christians had to struggle to explain and which they certainly had no motive to invent. Ranking high among these was Jesus' origin in Nazareth. The Gospel of John acknowledges the kind of reaction with which this news was met: "Can anything good come out of Nazareth?" (John 1:46). Nazareth was an unknown Galilean village. As the Pharisees pointed out, "Search and you will see that no prophet is to arise from Galilee" (John 7:52). There were no biblical prophecies relating to Nazareth. As "the crowds" of Jews scoffed: "Has not the scripture said that the Messiah is descended from David and comes from Bethlehem, the village where David lived?" (John 7:42). John's Gospel never attempts to explain away this troubling fact or to argue for Jesus' birth somewhere other than Nazareth. It simply notes the surprise and moves on.

Mark calls Jesus, "Jesus of Nazareth." He says nothing about any doubts this raised about Jesus' messianic identity, but then Mark implies that Jesus never publically claimed to be the Messiah. Matthew and Luke, however, both develop elaborate tales to explain how Jesus of Nazareth could also have been Jesus of Bethlehem. Their case rested less on historical evidence than on their conviction that Jesus was the Messiah and, therefore, must have fulfilled all prophecies — including those referencing Bethlehem.

Matthew simply assumed that Jesus' parents, Mary and Joseph, were natives of Bethlehem,[13] that they were living there when Jesus was born, and that they remained there until he was almost two years old.[14] Bethlehem was where the "wise men from the East" found Jesus, who was by then living in a "house," not lying in a manger (Matthew 2:11). Jesus' family left Bethlehem and sought refuge in Egypt, Matthew says, because a dream warned Joseph that Herod was scheming to kill the boy. After Herod's death another dream inspired Joseph not to return to his home in Bethlehem but to travel north to Galilee and settle in Nazareth. Matthew claims that this was in fulfillment of a prophecy: "He will be called a Nazorean" (Matthew 2:23). The author of John's Gospel was obviously not aware of any such prophecy, and it does not appear in any of the current canonical books. Some scholars have tried to explain it by claiming that Nazareth derived from a word meaning "flower" or "set apart." Therefore, any reference to an individual maturing or being consecrated for a holy purpose would serve as the prophecy Matthew had in mind. The other possibility, of course, is that Matthew simply assumed that because it was the truth there must have been a prophecy predicting it.

Luke, as mentioned in the previous chapter, develops a much more elaborate story to link Jesus with Bethlehem. He assumes that Jesus' parents were residents of Nazareth who traveled to Bethlehem in time for Jesus to be born and then went back to Nazareth for the rest of their lives. The reason for Joseph dragging his wife on an arduous and risky journey[15] to Bethlehem late in her pregnancy was to register for a tax.[16] Many things suggest that this tale owes more to legend than to history.

First, there is the issue of dates. Luke agrees with Matthew that Jesus was born while Herod the Great was still alive. Herod died in 4 BCE.[17] Luke says that the taxation edict was issued while Quirinius was governor of Syria, but it was not until 6 CE that Rome assumed direct control over Syria and ordered a census to compile its tax roles. (Josephus confirms that Quirinius was appointed to govern the region in 6 CE[18]). Luke adds yet a third date to the story. He says that John the Baptist appeared in the fifteenth year of the reign of the emperor Tiberius (*i.e.*, 28 CE) and at the time Jesus was about thirty years old (Luke 3:23). If so, 4 BCE becomes a more plausible date for his birth than 6 CE.[19]

Second, if, as Luke claims, Joseph and Mary were permanent

residents of Nazareth,[20] they would not have registered to pay taxes in Bethlehem. People pay taxes where they live and work, not where they or their ancestors came from.[21] And even if Joseph made such a journey, why would he have taken his heavily pregnant wife along? Husbands in the ancient world had full fiscal responsibility for their wives. Mary would not have been called upon to register as a separate taxpayer.

The other information Luke provides about Jesus' infancy and youth is simply inference from the fact that he was born a Jew. Jewish law decreed the circumcision of all male infants eight days after birth. Offerings were also to be made in the temple for first-born sons, and it was plausible that Jesus' family might have journeyed to Jerusalem to celebrate Passover — particularly on the occasion of their son's coming of age. Luke reports nothing about Jesus' upbringing that might not have safely been assumed for any of his male contemporaries.

As previously noted, the genealogies and birth stories that Matthew and Luke created for Jesus cannot be taken seriously as history. Their function is theological. The evangelists assumed that because Jesus was the Messiah, he was a descendant of King David. But they had difficulty reconciling this with another of the claims they based on prophecy. They both traced Jesus' ancestry through the male line — through Mary's husband Joseph. But they both denied that Joseph was his father. Each insisted that Jesus' mother was a virgin and that his conception was an act of God's.

Matthew, as noted in chapter 4, believed that the virgin birth was the fulfillment of a prophecy found in Isaiah 7:14. But he may have been misled because he read Isaiah in the Septuagint's Greek translation, not in Hebrew. Matthew believed that Isaiah had written "the *parthenos* (virgin) shall conceive and bear a son" (Matthew 1:23). But Isaiah's original Hebrew text spoke of an *almah* (young woman) who had conceived. In Greek *parthenos* meant "virgin" (also usually a young woman). But *almah* referred only to a woman's youth, not her sexual condition.

Luke does not mention Isaiah's prophecy. But for his gentile readers, who were steeped in the mythology of the pagan world, the claim that Jesus was the Son of God implied that he was literally God's son. The same claim was made not only for legendary figures like the heroes of Homer's *Iliad*, but for historical individuals like Alexander the Great and a number of Rome's emperors.[22]

Matthew and Luke agree about Jesus' virgin birth, but disagree about the ancestry they trace for him through his non-father, Joseph. Luke names 41 men in the line from David to Joseph whereas Matthew says there were only 25. Luke tracks his descent through David's son Nathan while Matthew claims that Solomon was his ancestor. The point of noting this is not to discredit the evangelists, but to remind ourselves of the kind of stories they wanted to tell. Neither was concerned with writing history. Each wanted to make a case for his faith in Jesus as the Christ and to explain what he believed that meant. Matthew's birth story and genealogy root Jesus in the Hebrew tradition as the fulfillment of God's covenanted relationship with Abraham. Therefore, Matthew begins Jesus' line with Abraham. Luke, however, traced Jesus' family back to the first man, Adam. This signaled his conviction that Jesus was the savior of all humankind. The opening chapters of the Gospels of Matthew and Luke should be read as elaborate parables that were invented to illustrate the kind of savior each evangelist believed Jesus to be.

Mark gives us our only hint about how Jesus spent most of his adult life. Mark (6:3) says that he was a carpenter. Matthew (13:55) says that his father was a carpenter. It was common in the ancient world for men to take up their father's occupations. There were few opportunities for education, and men trained their sons in what they knew. By mentioning Joseph, but not Jesus, Matthew might have been trying to put a little distance between him and his father's humble station. The Greek word translated as "carpenter" did not imply a sophisticated craftsman's trade. It signified a man who worked with his hands, usually in construction of some kind. Given that Mark (6:3) says that Jesus had four brothers (James, Joses, Judas, and Simon) and an unspecified number of sisters, his family was doubtless land poor, and its men were required to take what work they could get.

Average life expectancy for a man of Jesus' station in the ancient Middle East was only about 30 years. Luke says that was approximately Jesus' age at the time of his baptism (3:23) — John (8:57) implies that he might have been significantly older.[23] At any rate, Jesus was on the brink of transition to elder status[24] when he began his mission. From this something about his past might be inferred. It would have been unusual for a man (particularly a Jew) of his age and class not to have taken a wife. Marriage was an economic necessity for peasants who lived in virtually self-sufficient households, and for Jews it was a requirement of sacred law.[25] Paul claims that all of Jesus' Apostles (including Peter, the first "pope") were married (I Corinthians 9:5), and Matthew's Gospel mentions Jesus healing Peter's mother-in-law of a fever (Matthew 8:14-15). Jesus may have been a widower, or the Church may have suppressed the fact of his marriage.[26] The dualistic tendency to pit the spirit against the flesh, which thrived in early Christian and pagan communities, encouraged the feeling that it was unseemly for a religious leader to marry and engage in sex.

All of this is speculation, for the Bible says nothing about how Jesus spent most of his life. Everything that the Synoptics mention could have transpired in less than one year, Jesus' last year.[27] John's Gospel mentions three Passover seasons. One fact that seems totally trustworthy, however, is the event that marked Jesus' emergence as a public figure: his baptism by John the Baptist.

Jesus' baptism was clearly the turning point in his life — the start (possibly the beginning of his awareness) of his earthly mission. This was an inconvenient truth for those who believed him to be the Messiah. Baptism was a purification ritual — a form of the washing that was required before a Jew approached the temple to make a sacrifice. The baptism John offered was a sign of repentance. What, therefore, did Jesus' baptism mean? And why should the Son of God submit to baptism at the hand of a human inferior? Doing so made Jesus look like John's disciple. This was particularly problematic for the evangelists, for there were people who believed that John, not Jesus, was the Messiah.

The Gospel of John handled the problem posed by Jesus' baptism by utterly ignoring it and having John vigorously assert his subordination to Jesus. It says that the Baptist predicted the coming of one whose sandal he was unworthy to untie, and that he referred to Jesus obliquely, saying: "After me comes a man who ranks ahead of me because he was before me" (John 1:30). It claims that when John saw Jesus, he hailed him as "the Lamb of God who takes away the sin of the world," that he reported seeing the Spirit of God descending on Jesus from heaven, and that he said his baptizing with water was inferior to the baptism with the Holy Spirit that Jesus offered. Then to make things perfectly clear and nail down the case, the Gospel of John claims that the Baptist swore an oath: "I myself have seen and have testified that this is the Son of God" (John 1:29-34). Although nothing is said about Jesus submitting to John's baptism, the Gospel's defensiveness on the subject of the relationship between Jesus and John suggests the kinds of issues that the story of the baptism would have raised.

For the Synoptic Gospels the tradition of Jesus' respect for John was so strong that it could not be ignored.[28] Matthew and Luke both quoted Jesus saying: "Truly I tell you, among those born of women no one has arisen greater than John the Baptist"

(Matthew 11:11; Luke 7:28[29]). Did this mean that Jesus' respect for John exceeded his reverence for Abraham and Moses? Did it mean that John was a more important figure than King David or any of the prophets? Did it mean that John was greater than Jesus? Mark (1:14) says that Jesus only began preaching after John was arrested. The Gospel of John (1:37-42) assumes that the Baptist was still active when Jesus began his mission, but it claims that Jesus' first two followers were disciples who defected from John's camp. These reports create the impression that Jesus began his career as one of John's disciples and then stepped into the vacuum of leadership created by John's arrest and execution. This interpretation would not have been consistent with the evangelists' conviction that Jesus was the Messiah, and they were at pains to propose alternative explanations for his relationship with John.

The Gospel of John, as noted above, omits any reference to Jesus' baptism, and repeatedly describes John the Baptist as testifying to Jesus' superior status. Mark represents Jesus' baptism as a private affair — John and Jesus say nothing to each other, and only Jesus witnesses the vision that followed. Mark says that Jesus saw the heavens opened, the Spirit descending, and heard a voice that was directed only to him: "You are my Son, the Beloved; with you I am well pleased" (Mark 1:10-11). The private nature of the experience is consistent with Mark's claim that Jesus' kept his messianic identity a secret. If God had publically and dramatically proclaimed Jesus His Son at his baptism, that would not have been possible.

Luke follows Mark's lead and says as little as possible about the baptism. He notes that Jesus was baptized and that afterward, *while he "was praying*, the heaven was opened, the Holy Spirit descended upon him" (Luke 3:21-22, italics added), and God spoke only to him: "You are my Son . . ." (Luke 3:22). Matthew, however, develops a more elaborate tale to make it clear that John the Baptist was Jesus' inferior. Matthew claims that John and Jesus conferred before Jesus' baptism and that John "would have prevented him" from seeking baptism. John told Jesus, "I need to be baptized by you" (Matthew 3:14), but Jesus ordered him to proceed, "for it is proper for us in this way to fulfill all right-eousness" (Matthew 3:15). Matthew's description of what happened following the baptism straddles the line between a public and a private event. Matthew says that "the heavens were open to him [Jesus] and he saw the Spirit of God descending," but the voice of God then introduced Jesus to those who were standing by: "This is my Son, the Beloved, with whom I am well pleased" (Matthew16-17). Later, however, Matthew claims that John sent some of his disciples to Jesus to ask him if he was the Messiah (11:2-6). This seems odd given Matthew's claim that John had previously acknowledged Jesus' identity and heard it confirmed by the voice of God at his baptism. It also does not fit with the role into which Matthew casts John in Jesus' story — as "the voice of one crying out in the wilderness" who comes to "prepare the way of the Lord" (Matthew 3:1-11). When something that Jesus did (*e.g.*, submitting to baptism) was so inconvenient for the evangelists' claim that he was the Messiah, the likelihood is that they recorded the memory of an actual event.

Jesus' retreat after his baptism to meditate in isolation is not improbable. People often step back after a profound, life-altering experience to give themselves time to think it through. John makes no mention of this, either because he did not know it or found it inconsistent with his belief that Jesus was a manifes-tation of the omniscient deity. Mark (1:12-13) mentions it very briefly. He says that Jesus spent forty days in the desert and was tempted, but he says nothing about the nature of Jesus' tempta-tions. Matthew (4:1-11), however, expands the story considerably and uses it to explain why Jesus was the kind of messiah he was and not the kind that the Jews had expected. Satan's temptation is to urge Jesus to conform to traditional expectations, but Jesus chooses instead to follow the path that God ordained for him. Luke's (4:1-13) account resembles Matthew's and has a similar purpose.

The accuracy of the claim that Jesus traveled with twelve special companions — the disciples who became his Apostles[30] — is difficult to evaluate. The Twelve Apostles symbolize Jesus' mission to the twelve tribes of Israel. But the Gospels mention many more than twelve apostles, and the Book of Acts (1:21-26) claims that some of these people were with Jesus as long as the Twelve. The tradition that Jesus had an inner circle of twelve special companions is very early, for it was known to St. Paul (I Corinthians 15:5). But surprisingly little is said about them. The New Testament provides four lists of their names (Mark 3, Matthew 10, Luke 6, and Acts 1). Mark and Matthew's lists agree, but differ in some respects from Luke's list (found both in his Gospel and repeated in Acts). Peter, James, and John are the disciples most often mentioned by name. And although the Book of Acts begins by saying the Apostles gathered in Jerusalem after the resurrection and reconstituted their number by choosing a certain Matthias to replace Judas, the Twelve quickly disappear from the story. Peter is the only one of them whose contribution to the rise of the Church is recorded. Acts devotes most of its attention to men like Paul, James, Philip, and Stephen who were not members of the Twelve. The disappearance of most of *the* Apostles from the Bible prompted the growth of legends about their adventures, but no historical evidence substantiates any of these.

No itinerary can be constructed for Jesus' travels. John claims that Jesus moved back and forth between Galilee and Jerusalem for a period of three years. But the Synoptics limit him to Galilee and represent his single journey to Jerusalem as a unique, decisive event.

The audience Jesus targeted during his wanderings might

come as a surprise to attentive readers of the Gospels. Despite the evangelists desire to hint at precedents for a gentile mission, both Mark and Matthew agree that Jesus' ministry was only to the Jews. Matthew reports Jesus telling the Twelve, as he sent them out on a preaching mission: "Go nowhere among the Gentiles, and enter no town of the Samaritans, but go rather to the lost sheep of Israel" (Matthew 10:6). Both Mark and Matthew suggest that Jesus could even be verbally abusive in his dealings with gentiles. When a Canaanite woman approached him to ask for healing for her daughter, he spurned her saying, "Let the children [the Jews] be fed first, for it is not fair to take the children's food and throw it to the dogs [the gentiles]" (Mark 7:27). They add, however, that he yielded to her appeal when she cleverly used his insulting image to make a case for her request. She reminded him that "even the dogs under the table eat the children's crumbs." Matthew (15:24 - 28), when retelling the story, claims that Jesus very explicitly explained to the woman, why he refused her request: "I was sent only to the lost sheep of the house of Israel."

Although both Mark and Matthew use this exchange between Jesus and a gentile woman to suggest that Jesus could at least be persuaded to make exceptions for some gentiles, Paul believed that Jesus took a harder line. Paul was the strongest advocate for a mission to the gentile world. If he had believed that Jesus had set any precedent for such a thing, he would have seized on it eagerly. But, instead, he confessed "that Christ has become a servant of the circumcised [the Jews] on behalf of the truth of God in order that he might confirm the promises given to the patriarchs" (Romans 15:8). Paul accepted that Jesus' mission was only to the Jews, but this did nothing to diminish Paul's belief that Jesus' work was part of a greater divine plan for universal salvation.

All the Gospels agree that Jesus combined teaching and preaching with the performance of wondrous deeds. They do not all agree, however, on what he did and said. Given the different perspectives found in the Gospels, generalizing about Jesus' teaching is difficult. The only one of Jesus' pronouncements that Paul mentions was Jesus' firm opposition to divorce. The Synoptics' Jesus taught using parables, but John's does not. Mark's Jesus does little teaching, but Luke's Jesus is an instructor in the principles of social justice. Luke's Jesus is much given to homey analogies drawn from ordinary life, but John's Jesus delivers elevated theological discourses. Mark's Jesus is primarily a prophet of the Apocalypse. Matthew and Luke confirm this as one of Jesus' themes, but apocalyptic predictions loom less large in their versions of his message and disappear almost entirely in John's Gospel.

What Jesus taught about himself is debatable. Mark implies that he did not openly claim to be the Messiah, but John insists that right from the beginning he did so in the most explicit terms. Jesus was apparently accused by some who knew him of making overt or implied messianic claims, but what these might have been is unclear. Many different kinds of messiahs were looked for in Jesus' day, but his career did not fit any of the anticipated models. If Jesus encouraged the belief that he was the Messiah, what sorts of expectations would he have intended to encourage? The nature of his messiahship only became clear from the perspective of his death and resurrection.[31]

All the Gospels agree that Jesus worked wonders, but their descriptions of these do not entirely agree. Mark's Jesus, for instance, is an exorcist, but John's is not. The miracles that the Gospels credit to Jesus — particularly those in which he commands the forces of nature — are viewed skeptically by many of the Bible's readers (even its faithful believers). Many modern folk are willing to entertain the possibility that Jesus' acts of healing were successful treatments for psychosomatic illnesses. But reports of his ability to calm storms, walk on water, turn water into wine, and feed thousands with a few loaves of bread are, for them, simply beyond belief.[32]

When contemplating the theological significance of the Gospels' miracle stories, it is important to reflect on how the context for reading the Bible has changed since the 1st century. In the 1st century CE, a *lack* of stories about Jesus' miracles would have incited doubts about his messianic identity. The sorts of things that confirmed faith in the 1st century tend to challenge it in the 21st. The significant issue for the Bible's readers today is not to determine whether such things actually happened, but to discern what message they are meant to convey.

The most important portions of Jesus' story for Christian faith are the accounts of his death and resurrection. Nothing that Jesus did up until the time of his death was unprecedented. There were many other figures in both sacred and secular literature who urged people to prepare for the Apocalypse and divine judgment, who fought for social justice, who healed the sick, and who performed miracles. None of these things made Jesus the Messiah — which is why John's Gospel can so casually accept the fact, as it says, that only a small portion of what Jesus did and said is recorded. It is why Mark's Gospel gives so much less attention to Jesus' career than it does to the last few days of his life. Despite (or maybe because of) the importance of the circumstances of Jesus' death for the faith of the Church, what actually happened is difficult to determine.

All of the Gospels describe Jesus' entrance into Jerusalem at the beginning of the last week of his life as a triumphant procession. But their reports rely heavily on the assumption that this was the fulfillment of a prophecy (Zechariah 9:9): "Lo, your king comes to you; triumphant and victorious is he, humble and riding on an ass, on a colt the foal of an ass."[33] Suspicion that descriptions of Jesus "Palm Sunday" procession owe more to prophetic expectation than to eyewitness observation are raised by the way in which Matthew tells the story. Matthew's desire to be literally faithful to Zechariah's text unintentionally illustrates the hazards of reading documents before punctuation was invented. Matthew's misreading conjures an absurd scene. Zechariah meant to make it clear that the animal he spoke of, "an ass," was young, "a colt the foal of an ass." Matthew mistook Zechariah's words in apposition as a reference to two separate animals, so that was how he described Jesus' mount as he rode into Jerusalem: "they brought the donkey and the colt . . . and he sat on *them*" (Matthew 21:7, italics added). The thought of Jesus simultaneously sprawled across the backs of two animals, or hopping back and forth from one to the other, should be enough to convince most people that this is something other than a description of what actually happened that day.

John's Gospel places Jesus' assault on the temple at the beginning of his mission — long before Palm Sunday. The Synoptics associate it with the Palm Sunday procession at the end of his life, but they disagree on the sequence of events. Mark says that Jesus merely visited the temple on Palm Sunday. He then spent the night at the village of Bethany and returned the next day to "cleanse" the temple. Matthew and Luke, however, heighten the drama by implying that the Palm Sunday procession ended at the temple with Jesus' assault on its moneychangers.

All of the Gospels mention an evening meal that Jesus shared with his followers on the eve of his death, but they disagree about what kind of meal this was. The Synoptics claim that it was the Passover feast, but John insists that it took place earlier. He says that Jesus died on the cross on the "Day of Preparation" (*i.e.*, the day on which the lambs were slaughtered for the Passover meal). Given John's characterization of Jesus as "the Lamb of God that takes away the sin of the world" (John 1:29), we might suspect that he has altered the date for theological purposes. But his account is actually more probable than the one found in the Synoptics. The Roman and Jewish authorities would hardly have risked riling the people by profaning Passover with a trial and execution. Their concern for a holy day that was approaching at sundown led them to break the legs of the men crucified with Jesus to hasten their deaths and burials.

Following the "Last Supper," the Gospels describe Jesus and his companions leaving the city to spend the night at a place called Gethsemane (*i.e.*, "oil press" — perhaps an olive orchard) by Matthew and Mark and "the Mount of Olives" by Luke. This is probable. Jerusalem would have been crowded at Passover season, and poor people, like Jesus and his disciples, would have camped out rather than paid the inflated prices for accommodation in town. Jews were only required to hold the feast within the city, which the Synoptics say that Jesus did by renting a room specifically for that purpose.

Much of the story of what took place that evening must owe more to imagination than observation. The prayers and private thoughts that the Gospels ascribe to Jesus on this occasion are suppositions, for the Gospels say that Jesus went off by himself to pray and that his disciples fell asleep.[34] They did not hear or witness his prayers. He woke them just as Judas and an armed crowd appeared to arrest him. Events moved quickly from that point on. Mark (14:47-48) says that there was a little swordplay, which Jesus quickly ended. But Jesus had no time then, or opportunity later, to tell any of his followers what had been going through his mind while they slept and he prayed.

The Synoptic Gospels describe Jesus as having a normal human reaction to his situation. They say that he knew the danger that he was in, that he beseeched God for an alternative, but that he was prepared (like any martyr) to accept God's will. Luke highly dramatizes the situation. He claims that Jesus' "sweat became like great drops of blood falling down on the ground," but that an angel appeared from heaven to strengthen him (Luke 22:43-44). There were, however, no witnesses to any of this.

The motives of Judas, the Apostle who betrays Jesus, are unclear. John's Gospel accuses Judas of taking an unhealthy interest in money that made him vulnerable to bribery. Judas, John says, was the treasurer of Jesus' group — that he "had the common purse" (John 13:29), made purchases for Jesus, and stole some of the money. John relates an ugly incident in which Judas attacked Mary of Bethany for wasting money on perfume with which she anointed Jesus. It should, Judas said, have been sold and the money given to the poor. John opines, however, that Judas had no interest in the poor but merely resented being deprived of the opportunity to skim some of the profits from the sale for himself (John12:1-8). In John's Gospel, Judas needs no motive. He is possessed by Satan (John 13:27) and has been given a role to play that he cannot escape. John's Gospel describes Jesus as being totally in control of the events leading to his arrest and crucifixion — so much so that he seizes the initiative and, hastening forth, identifies himself to the men who accompany Judas. Judas does not need to point him out by any means, let alone a traitorous kiss.

The Synoptic tradition relating to Judas is briefer than John's. Mark says that it was Judas's idea to approach the chief priest and offer to betray Jesus, and the priests then proffered him a reward. This leaves Judas's motive vague. Did he decide to betray Jesus for some private reason and then receive an offer of money? Or did he ask for payment in exchange?

Matthew, too, offers no explanation for Judas's treachery, and he and Luke follow Mark in magnifying its depravity by claiming that Judas betrayed Jesus with a kiss. This is not entirely credible. If what the Gospels say Jesus had done just a day or so earlier is accurate, he would have been a public figure known to some in the "large crowd" that came to seize him. There would have been no need for Judas to finger him. Matthew says that when Judas was offered his payment of thirty pieces of silver, he was filled with remorse, threw the money on the ground, and went out to hang himself. His priestly employers then decided to use the morally contaminated money for an unclean purpose. They purchased a burial ground.

Luke offers an explanation for Judas's actions. He says that "Satan entered into Judas" (Luke 22:3) and inspired him to plot Jesus' capture with the priests and scribes. Luke also implies that Judas negotiated a fee for his services and that the money was used to buy land. But in Luke's Gospel, Judas used his ill-gotten wealth to buy a piece of property (a field) for himself. He did not, however, live to enjoy it, for he fell down, "burst open in the middle and all his bowels gushed out" (Acts 1:18). All three of the Synoptics maintain that Jesus knew that one of his intimates would betray him but that Jesus did not name the individual.

Judas has puzzled scholars. No one knows what the word "Iscariot," which is sometimes joined with his name, means. It may be that Judas was not a historical individual, but a symbol for the Jewish people and their betrayal of their own Messiah. "Judas" means someone from Judea: a Jew.

The Gospels are not clear on who took Jesus captive. Mark and Matthew say that it was an armed mob sent by "the chief priests, the scribes, and the elders." Luke, however, claims that "the chief priests, the officers of the temple, police, and the elders" (Luke 22:52) came in person to do the deed. And John adds "a detachment of [Roman] soldiers" to the "police from the chief priests and Pharisees" (John 18:3). The Gospels all suggest that Jesus rebuked one of his followers for drawing a sword to defend him, and Mark reports that "all of them deserted him and fled" (Mark 14:50). The Gospels agree that Jesus was the only one captured, but Mark suggests that others would have been taken if they had not succeeded in running away. He says that a "certain young man was following him [Jesus], wearing nothing but a linen cloth. They caught hold of him, but he left the linen cloth and ran off naked" (Mark 14:51).

From this point on the sources from which the evangelists might have drawn information about Jesus' fate are unknown. The Apostles appear to have gone into hiding. Only a few of their women (who, as females, were of no interest to the authorities) surfaced later to witness Jesus' crucifixion. Where Jesus' Apostles went following his arrest, the Bible does not say. The Synoptics claim that Peter joined the crowd that took Jesus to the high priest's residence and infiltrated a group that gathered in its courtyard. Given that the courtyard was "below" (Mark 14:66) the chamber where Jesus was being interrogated, Peter would not have witnessed what was taking place. He would also have kept his distance, for he was afraid of being recognized. When a servant girl accused him of being one of Jesus' followers, he thrice denied that he knew Jesus.

The author of John's Gospel may have spotted the problem posed by the absence of a witness in the Synoptic tradition. He says that "another disciple," whom he does not name, accompanied Peter, and because "he was known to the high priest" (John 18:15), he was allowed into the courtyard and permitted to bring Peter with him. Peter, however, feared being recognized as a disciple and denied being one. John's story may be meant to suggest that there was a secret disciple who infiltrated the high priest's court and provided information about what transpired at Jesus' trial.

Much scholarly debate swirls around the subject of Jesus' alleged trial. Mark claims that Jesus was immediately taken (in the middle of the night) to an assembly of "all the chief priests, the elders, and the scribes" (Mark 14:53). This would constitute a meeting of the Sanhedrin, the Jews' governing council. If so, it was illegal. The Sanhedrin was not to hold trials at night or to convict an accused and pass sentence at the same meeting. Matthew says that Jesus was taken to the high priest Caiaphas's house where "the scribes and the elders had gathered" (Matthew 26:57). Luke's account accords better with the legal procedure. Luke says that Jesus was beaten during the night by the men who had taken him prisoner, and it was the next morning that he was brought before the Jews' "council" (Luke 22:66). John's Gospel claims that Jesus was taken not to Caiaphas's residence, but to that of Caiaphas's father-in-law, Annas. It was Annas who interrogated him and then sent him to Caiaphas, who forwarded him to Pontius Pilate.

The nature of the crime of which Jesus was accused is unclear. Mark and Matthew say that it was blasphemy. Luke seems to agree without specifically saying so. The problem with this is that claiming to be the Messiah or even the Son of God would not have been a blasphemy for Jews of Jesus' generation. Most of them expected an entirely human messiah — a prophet or a Davidic king. A man who claimed to be the Messiah might be deluded, but he would not be a blasphemer. It would not even have been blasphemous to claim to be the "Son of God." The title did not imply an assertion of personal divinity. Psalm 2:7 quotes God telling one of Israel's newly anointed kings: "You are my son; today I have begotten you." The Sanhedrin would have regarded messianic claims for Jesus as blasphemy only if its members thought of messiahship as Christians reinterpreted it *after* Jesus' resurrection — as a claim that Jesus was the incarnation of God.

John's Gospel does not mention blasphemy. It says that the high priest[35] "questioned Jesus about his disciples and about his teaching" (18:19), but it does not say what he concluded. Caiaphas also makes no specific charge against Jesus when he takes him to Pilate. When Pilate asks about Jesus' crime, he is only told that if Jesus were not a criminal, Caiaphas would not have urged his execution. Pilate at first assumes that Jesus is charged with some violation of religious law and orders Caiaphas to try Jesus himself. The Jews, however, consider Jesus' unstated offense to be a capital crime, and they claim that they are "not permitted to put anyone to death" (John 18:31). If so, the rules must soon have changed, for the Book of Acts reports that not long after Jesus' resurrection the Sanhedrin convicted Stephen, a first-generation Christian preacher of blasphemy. The

Jews then dragged him out of the city and stoned him to death (Acts 7:1-60).

Rome had no interest in enforcing Jewish religious law or shielding non-citizens from crucifixion. Pilate's concern was solely for secular offenses. Therefore, he asked Jesus if he was a revolutionary — a claimant to the kingship of the Jews. Jesus did not defend himself, but Pilate, finding "no case" (John 18:38) against him, simply yielded to the Jews' demands for Jesus' crucifixion. Following Roman custom, he posted a sign at the cross to identify the victim's crime and to deter any who might be tempted to follow his example: "Jesus of Nazareth, the King of the Jews" (John 19:19).

Unlike some Jews, Jesus did not have Roman citizenship. Roman law forbade the crucifixion of citizens. Crucifixion was a torturous punishment designed to prolong the dying process, and it was reserved for slaves and outsiders. It was the posture the cross imposed on the body rather than the wounds of crucifixion that resulted in death. The crucified individual was suspended by his arms with nothing to stand on. In order to provide room for his diaphragm to operate, he had to pull himself up and arch his back. As his strength declined, so did his ability to breath. Death was by asphyxiation.

Jesus' crucifixion was unusual in that he died quickly. Mark says that he was raised on the cross at 9:00 in the morning (Mark 15:25). John, however, says that it was not until "about noon" that Pilate passed judgment on him. The Synoptic tradition says that he died at 3:00 in the afternoon (Mark 15:33), and it provides no explanation for Jesus' rapid demise other than to imply that he was weakened by the beating he received while he was in captivity. Condemned men were forced to cooperate in their executions by carrying their crosses to the killing field, but the Synoptics say that Jesus was unable to do so. The soldiers who had been charged with his execution forced a certain Simon from Cyrene (North Africa) to carry his cross for him. The author of

John's Gospel apparently knew of this tradition and dismissed it. He specifically states that Jesus went forth "carrying the cross by himself" (John 19:17). John's image of a divine Christ admitted no implication of weakness. John, however, agrees with the Synoptics that Jesus died sooner than expected. The Synoptics claim that Jesus was arrested on the evening after he ate the Passover meal, but John said that Passover was to begin on the evening of the day Jesus was crucified. Because executions would have polluted the sacred day (which began at sundown), he says that two soldiers were ordered to hasten the deaths of Jesus and the two men crucified with him by breaking their legs. When they came to Jesus, however, they found that this was unnecessary. He had already died.

Conflicting reports within the Gospels are not the only things that complicate efforts to uncover the historical facts behind the Passion narratives. The sources from which the evangelists' information might have come must be evaluated. To what extent were the evangelists relying on eyewitness information, and to what extent were they creating scenes by inferring what must have happened to fulfill scriptural passages that they thought were prophecies?

The Synoptics admit that none of the Apostles or any of Jesus' male followers witnessed his crucifixion. They were all in hiding lest they involuntarily join him on crosses of their own. The only acquaintances who could risk observing Jesus' execution were some women. Mark (15:40) says that even they kept their distance and only looked on from afar. Mark names three of them: Mary Magdalene, Mary the mother of James the younger and Joses, and a certain Salome. Matthew agrees that the only witnesses were women. He insists that there were many of them, but he names only three: Mary Magdalene, Mary the mother of James and Joseph, and Zebedee's wife. Luke, unlike Matthew, was apparently reluctant to follow Mark and rely solely on female testimony to back up his account. He claims that "all his

[Jesus'] acquaintances, including the women who had followed him from Galilee stood at a distance, watching these things" (Luke 23:49). He provides no names. John's Gospel does not appeal to an anonymous crowd of distant witnesses. It claims that four of Jesus' friends and relatives were able to stand at the foot of the cross and talk with him. Three of these were women (Jesus' mother, his aunt, and Mary Magdalene) and the fourth was the mysterious "Beloved Disciple" whose name John never provides. This scenario is not very likely for both practical and political reasons.

Another witness might be identified: the Simon of Cyrene who, the Synoptics say, carried Jesus' cross. None of the Gospels says anything about Simon other than that he carried the cross. But if he existed, he might have stayed to watch Jesus' execution. Mark's Gospel assumes that his sons were known to its readers, for it identifies him as the father of a certain Alexander and Rufus. In addition to Simon, Mark (15:39) and Matthew (27:54) claim that one of the centurions who crucified Jesus was converted by Jesus' death and would, therefore, have been a source of information for other Christians. They quote him saying, "Truly this man was God's Son!" But Luke reports the man making something less than a profession of faith: "Certainly this man was innocent." John's Gospel does not mention any testimony from a Roman soldier.

The only common factor in all the Gospel reports is a tradition that identified Mary Magdalene as a source of first-hand information about Jesus' death and resurrection. Given that women were not regarded as reliable witnesses in the courts of the ancient world, this did not provide the strongest support for the Church's message. Therefore, it is unlikely that her role was invented. John's "Beloved Disciple" is a much less well substantiated figure.

Most of the details in the description of the crucifixion — the claim that none of Jesus' bones were broken, the piercing of his side, the casting of lots for his clothing, and the words he is reported saying — are references to prophecy or quotations from the Hebrew Scriptures. The Gospel of John's pointed observation, for instance, that none of Jesus' bones (legs or otherwise) was broken derives from its author's belief that Jesus was the ultimate Paschal Lamb. Given that Exodus (12:46) decreed that none of the bones of the Passover lamb were to be broken, Jesus' bones had to have remained unfractured. People could be crucified by having their arms tied to the beam of a cross, but John's Gospel claims that Jesus was nailed to his cross. To avoid the implication that this would have broken some of his bones, the Gospel notes that nails were driven through Jesus' hands (John 20:27). This, however, is unlikely. Nails through the soft tissues of his palms would not have secured the weight of his body to the cross.[36]

John's Gospel says that Jesus was crucified at Golgotha, a Hebrew word that John translates as "Place of the Skull" (John 19:17). Any place associated with executions or burials could have earned this name. Romans left corpses hanging on crosses until they decayed or were destroyed by carrion birds and animals. This may not have been the custom near Jerusalem, given Hebrew concerns for ritual purity. Common burial practices interred corpses until they decayed. Their bones were then retrieved and placed in ossuary boxes.

Given that none of Jesus' relatives or friends dared come forward to claim his body or had the influence to persuade the Roman authorities to release it, Mark says that a member of the Sanhedrin, Joseph of Arimathea, assumed responsibility for it. Mark implies, but does not explicitly state, that Joseph was a secret convert. He says only that Joseph "was waiting expectantly for the kingdom of God" (Mark 15:43). The same could, of course, be said of any pious Jew no matter what his attitude toward Jesus. Matthew mentions no connection with the Sanhedrin, but he goes beyond Mark, his source, by asserting that Joseph was a rich man who "was also a disciple of Jesus" (Matthew 27:57) and who placed Jesus' body in his own family's tomb. Luke stayed closer to Mark's original account. He says that Joseph was a member of the Sanhedrin, but he had objected to its action against Jesus. Luke does not call him a Christian and, like Mark, does not imply more than that Joseph was a pious Jew (*i.e.,* "he was waiting expectantly for the kingdom of God," Luke 23:50). Luke adds that the tomb Joseph used was a new one. He was not giving Jesus honored burial with members of his family, and the Synoptics are clear that this entombment was not meant to be Jesus' final burial. Because a holy day was approaching his body had to be concealed from sight, but the women who came to the tomb after the Sabbath had passed came intending to anoint the corpse for burial. As a Hebrew official, Joseph's motive for concealing Jesus' body may simply have been to fulfill his duty to guarantee that the approaching Sabbath not be polluted. There would be time later for another arrangement to be made for the disposal of the corpse.

John, not surprisingly, tells a different story. He says that Joseph was a Christian who hid his faith "because of his fear of the Jews" (John 19:38). Apparently that fear did not prevent him from risking exposure by claiming Jesus' body from Pilate and joining Nicodemus, another secret Christian, in preparing the body for burial with "a hundred pounds" of myrrh and aloes (John 19:39). John also says that the "new" tomb was in "a garden in the place where he was crucified" (John 19:41). If a hundred pounds of expensive spices were combined to embalm the body for burial, funeral arrangements must have been completed in record time. The body had to be buried before sundown on the day of the crucifixion.

John's story is the least credible. The reason for John's claim that Jesus' body was elaborately embalmed was to counter the charge that Jesus (who had not received a mortal wound) had only passed out and not really died on the cross. Skeptics must often have posed this possibility to preachers of the resurrection. The Synoptic tradition handled doubts about Jesus' death in other ways. Mark says that Pilate himself asked for confirmation of Jesus' death (Mark 15:44-45). Matthew says that the priests and Pharisees interrupted their Passover celebration to go to Pilate and request that a guard be put on the tomb. They told Pilate that Jesus had promised that after three days he would rise from the dead, and that his disciples would probably try to steal his body to make it appear that this had happened. The Roman guards then "sealed" the stone that closed the tomb. Luke was content simply to state that Jesus was buried in a tomb sealed by a stone.

Matthew's claim that Jesus' disciples had heard him predict his resurrection and planned to steal his body makes no sense on several grounds. If they were true disciples who had faith in their master, they would not have thought it would be necessary to fake his resurrection. They would have awaited it with eager anticipation. The way the disciples behaved, however, suggests that they were not waiting for Jesus' resurrection. They fled and greeted the news, when first they heard it, with skepticism. The two disciples who failed to recognize the resurrected Christ as their companion on the road to Emmaus confessed their disappointment in him (Luke 24:21). Although several Gospel passages claim that Jesus told his disciples that he had to suffer and die and would rise again in three days (e.g., Mark 8:31), they also say that "they [his Apostles] did not understand what he was saying" (Mark 9:31). When the moment came, none of them seemed to remember what he had allegedly taught them. The Gospels also insist that before the crucifixion and resurrection took place, no one had recognized the prophecies predicting these events. It was only when the resurrected Christ "beginning with Moses and all the prophets" explained to his disciples "the things about himself in all the scriptures" (Luke 24:27) that they grasped the true nature of the Messiah God had promised through the prophets. John's Gospel maintains that no one had spotted predictions of the events in Jesus' life until after he was resurrected. At the time of Jesus' death his disciples "did not understand the scripture, that he must rise from the dead" (John 20:9). The scriptural passage to which John probably refers is Hosea 6:2:[37] "After two days he will revive us; on the third day he will raise us up, that we may live before him."[38] The story of Jesus was written backwards from the perspective of faith in his messiahship. This faith and the knowledge of what had happened to Jesus is what caused some previously insignificant scriptural passages suddenly to look like prophecies.

Resurrection is by definition a supernatural occurrence and, therefore, beyond the possibility of historical verification. All that historians can do is to trace the history of the witness to faith in the resurrection — to try to discover who had what sort of experience and what they said about it. Once again the Bible does not provide us with a single, coherent account.

Mark's Gospel directs its readers' attention to the other side of the line that divides the Jesus of history from the Christ of faith, but it does not cross that line. It claims that the three women who witnessed the crucifixion came to the tomb after the Sabbath had passed bringing spices to anoint the body. The fact that they expected to care for a corpse and their shocked reaction at finding the tomb empty suggests that they knew nothing about Jesus predicting his resurrection. This is puzzling given that Mark claims that on three occasions (Mark 8:31-33; 9:30-32; 10:32-34) Jesus privately informed his disciples that he would be crucified and resurrected. He forbade them to tell anyone, but it seems unlikely that they would have ensured their obedience by blotting it out of their memories. The women found the tomb unsealed and a "young man, dressed in a white robe" (Mark 16:5) sitting inside it. He told them that Jesus had been "raised" and had gone to Galilee, where they would see him "just as he told you" (Mark 16:7). The women whom the "you" addresses appear not to have recalled Jesus saying any such thing, and they were so terrified by the experience that they fled and "said nothing to anyone" (Mark 16:8). Mark does not describe anyone's experience of the resurrected Christ, but he does claim that such experiences took place — in Galilee, not Jerusalem.

Matthew follows, but augments, Mark's outline. Matthew insists that a prediction of his resurrection featured in Jesus' public preaching, which is why the Romans guarded his tomb. He does not suggest, however, that it was anticipation of this event that brought two, not three, of Jesus' followers to the tomb ("Mary Magdalene and the other Mary," Matthew 28:1). Their only motive appears to be a desire to see it. They found the tomb sealed and guarded by soldiers. But as they approached, there was an earthquake and an angel appeared to roll back the stone that covered its entrance. The soldiers, but not the women, fainted dead away. The angel (an upgrade of Mark's "young man") told them that Jesus had "been raised, as he said" (Matthew 28:6), and had gone to Galilee where he would appear to them. As the frightened but overjoyed women ran off to tell the disciples, Jesus, who had apparently not yet left for Galilee, "met them." He was no ghost or spirit, for they "took hold of his feet." He repeated the angel's instructions that they should tell his disciples to go to Galilee, and unlike the women in Mark's Gospel, Matthew's women delivered the message. Matthew then added an important detail to Mark's account. He said that the disciples saw Jesus on "the mountain to which Jesus had directed them" (Matthew 28:16). Matthew does not say when Jesus gave them those directions, but he clearly implies that the resurrection should not have surprised them if they had any faith in their master. Even the priests and Pharisees had been told that Jesus had predicted it, which was why they set guards over his tomb. Apparently, however, earthquakes, angels, predictions, and even resurrection appearances were not enough. Matthew says that when the disciples did encounter the risen Christ on a Galilean mountain, "some doubted" (Matthew 28:17).

Luke's Gospel represents a crowd of women (all those "who had come with him from Galilee," Luke 23:55) involved in preparations for Jesus' burial. They tracked Joseph of Arimathea to find out where Jesus was buried; then they went away to prepare "spices and ointments," and on the morning of "the first day of the week" they came to the tomb to care for the body. They found the tomb already open. Going in, they discovered that the body was gone. Then "two men in dazzling clothes" appeared to them and reminded them of something they had somehow forgotten: "Remember how he told you, while he was still in Galilee, that the Son of Man must be handed over to sinners, and be crucified, and on the third day rise again" (Luke 24:6-7). The women suddenly "remembered" and went off to inform the disciples. Luke names three female witness to the empty tomb: Mary Magdalene, Mary the mother of James, and Joanna. The disciples, whose memories were not jogged by the news, dismissed the women's report as "an idle tale." Peter, however, finally went to the tomb to check it out, and he (a reliable male witness) then confirmed that it was indeed empty.

At this point Luke made a small change in Mark and Matthew's report that had major consequences. His fellow evangelists said that Jesus had promised to appear in Galilee. But Luke's belief was that the appropriate place for the Christian Church to be founded (by the first confessions of resurrection faith) was Jerusalem. Therefore, Luke said that Jesus had merely predicted his resurrection when he was preaching in Galilee, but the actual event took place in Jerusalem. Oddly, however, Luke did not describe Jesus' first appearance in the city. He turned instead to the story of two disciples[39] who meet the Christ on the road to Emmaus. Once they finally recognized him, they hasten back to Jerusalem where they learned that Christ had already appeared to Simon Peter. Peter's encounter is not recorded, but Luke says that while this conversation was taking place Jesus appeared again — this time to all of the Apostles. To dispel their fear that he was only a ghost, he invited them to touch him and he ate "a piece of broiled fish" to prove that he still had normal human functions.

John's Gospel, like Luke's, sets the resurrection in Jerusalem. He dismisses the motive that the Synoptic tradition says brought Jesus' female followers to his tomb by insisting that Jesus' body had already been buried with "a hundred pounds" of spices and ointments by Joseph of Arimathea and Nicodemus. He also reduces the number of women to one: Mary Magdalene. He does not explain why Mary came to the tomb, but it was evidently not in anticipation of a resurrection. When she found the tomb open and empty, she returned to tell Peter and the Beloved Disciple that Jesus' body had been stolen. John claims that no one knew that Jesus' resurrection had been prophesied until after the event had occurred (John 20:9). Peter and the unnamed disciple ran to the tomb, confirmed that it was empty of all but the grave wrappings, and then returned "to their homes" (John 20:10).[40] Mary Magdalene, however, remained at the tomb, and when she looked into it, it was no longer empty. She saw "two angels" who asked her why she was weeping. She said that she was distressed because she did not know where Jesus' body had been taken. At that moment a man whom she took to be a gardener asked her the same question. When he spoke her name, she recognized him as Jesus, but here, unlike in the Synoptic tradition, Jesus ordered her not to touch him. Mary then hastened to the disciples to report the first resurrection experience. More soon followed in John's Gospel.

That evening Jesus mysteriously appeared inside a locked room to which ten of his Apostles had retreated for safety. He showed them the wounds of crucifixion on his body, "breathed on them and said to them 'receive the Holy Spirit'" (John 20:22). The Apostle Thomas was absent on this occasion, and he insisted that he would not believe their testimony unless he could personally confirm Jesus' resurrection by sticking his fingers in the nail holes in Jesus' hands. A week later Jesus again appeared in a room whose doors had been shut and offered Thomas his chance. This episode served John as a kind of parable, a story with an encouraging message for his Gospel's readers. They, like Thomas, had to believe on the testimony of others. John promised that if they would do so, they would find themselves exalted even above the Apostles. Jesus final words to Thomas were an exhortation for all Christians to come: "Have you believed because you have seen me? Blessed are those who have not seen and yet have come to believe" (John 20:29).

At this point John's Gospel seems to come to an end. It wraps up with the claim that Jesus did more things than could be recorded, but it has provided enough information to enable its readers to "have life" by believing (without seeing) "that Jesus is the Messiah" (John 20:31). But the Gospel has yet another chapter. Many scholars believe that this 21st chapter was a latter addition to John's original text, for it does not fit with what transpired in the previous chapter. In chapter 20 the Apostles have all had experiences of their resurrected lord, and they have received the Holy Spirit. But in chapter 21 none of this seems to have made any difference. Seven of the Apostles have gone back to Galilee and resumed their profession as fishermen. After a night in which they caught nothing, Jesus called to them from the beach, but they did not recognize him. After he directed them to a spot where they made a large haul of fish, the Beloved Disciple recognized him and told Peter, "It is the Lord!" (John 21:7) Peter then leapt overboard and raced the others to shore where he found that Jesus had begun a fire over which to cook some of the 153 fish that they had snared in their net. John rather oddly says that none of them dared to ask him who he was because they knew who he was. After breakfast Jesus delivered his final orders and appointed Peter shepherd of Jesus' "flock."

Some scholars think that this last chapter of John's Gospel

may be an account of the missing resurrection appearance that brought Peter to faith. If so, it may also account for Peter's prominent role among the disciples in the Gospels. If Peter and the others had believed that Jesus' story ended with his crucifixion, they would have returned disappointed to Galilee and resumed their former way of life. This would explain why, according to Mark, the first resurrection appearance occurred there and not in Jerusalem. If Peter was the first of Jesus' followers to have such an experience and the one who brought the others to faith, tradition would quickly have made him the man Jesus designated to be their leader.

Luke's Ideal Church

With reports of resurrection experiences, the story of Jesus ends and the story of the Church begins. The evangelist Luke provides the bridge between the two. As he explained in a second dedicatory note to Theophilus, his Gospel recorded what "Jesus did and taught from the beginning until the day when he was taken up to heaven" (Acts 1:1-2), and the purpose of its companion volume, The Book of the Acts of the Apostles, was to explain what happened after Jesus' Ascension — i.e., the birth of the Church, an institution empowered by a new manifestation of God by the Holy Spirit.

The Church that Luke describes in Acts is an idealized model that bears little resemblance to reality. Luke believed that all Christians should be members of a single, unified community founded on a common set of Apostolic teachings. Therefore, he imagined the Church beginning from a single congregation organized and lead by the Apostles in Jerusalem and then moving by stages from its origin within Judaism into the wider gentile world. Reality was doubtless considerably messier. The differences in the traditions that inspired the Gospels suggest that the Church had many parents who understood the Christ event in different ways. Independent clusters of Christians doubtless sprang up in a variety of places, and few of the named Apostles seem to have had anything to do with organizing or supervising them.

Despite the fact that Jesus did most of his teaching in, and drew his followers from, Galilee — and the tradition that the resurrected Christ was first experienced in Galilee, Luke believed that the appropriate place for Christianity to begin was Jerusalem, God's Holy City. Christianity was, Luke claimed, the fulfillment of God's promise to restore Israel. Therefore, as prophesied, the Messiah had come first to the Jews. They forfeited their birthright by rejecting him, but his crucifixion and resurrection had revealed the full nature of God and the deepest meaning of the Scriptures. Jesus had prepared for what would transpire after his earthly career ended by training a group of disciples to carry on his work as his apostles. God endowed them with gifts of the Holy Spirit that enabled them to build a new Israel encompassing all peoples: the Church.

The Church, Luke says, began as a single congregation of 120 people (including Jesus' mother and brothers) permanently settled in Jerusalem. Its first act was to restore leadership by twelve men bearing the title of Apostle. This equated the Church with the twelve tribes of Israel and stated its claim to be heir to the Hebrews' covenant with God. A certain Matthias was chosen to replace Judas. He was fully qualified to become one of the Twelve, for Peter testified that Matthias had been among Jesus' companions "from the baptism of John until the day when he [Jesus] was taken up from us" (Acts 1:22). Those were better credentials than many of the other Apostles could claim, except for the fact that Matthias would not have been privy to what Jesus said on the occasions when he had taken the Twelve aside for private instruction. Speculations about Matthias's identity and qualifications are beside the point, for Luke's concern is with theological imagery, not history. The only use Luke makes of the Twelve is as a symbol for the authority of the Christian message, for they began to fade from view shortly after their number is restored. Acts devotes most of its attention to leaders who were not members of the Twelve.

Luke says that the resurrected Christ appeared to his disciples for forty[41] days after his resurrection. He ordered them to remain in Jerusalem until God "baptized" them with the Holy Spirit. This occurred ten days after Christ's Ascension into heaven on Pentecost, a Jewish holiday celebrating the creation of God's people and marking the fiftieth day after Passover. Tongues of flame appeared over the heads of the Apostles, and they instantly acquired the miraculous fluency in multiple languages the Church needed to fulfill its mission to preach the message of Christ to all nations.

Given that ancient historians seldom had any records, transcriptions, or published sources to consult, it was their practice to invent the speeches they believed that their subjects ought to have delivered. Luke records texts for a number of sermons in Acts, but it is impossible to know how accurately they reflect the kind of thing that might have been said by the men who allegedly preached them. In only one case is it possible to compare Luke's recreation of a man's message with that individual's own words — and the comparison is not reassuring. Luke describes Paul taking positions that do not mesh well with what Paul says in his extant letters.

Pentecost's gifts of the Holy Spirit included the power to heal and perform wonders. Simply having Peter's shadow fall on the afflicted sufficed to cure their ailments (Acts 5:15). Such "signs of power" were effective missionary tools, and "day by day the Lord added to their number those who were being saved" (Acts 2:47). There was, however, also continuing persecution. The Apostles were arrested and flogged by the High Priest and the Sadducees. But the Pharisees seem to have changed sides. In the Gospels they are often depicted as hostile challengers who try to trap Jesus into saying things that would get him in trouble, but in Acts Pharisees appear more open-minded. Luke claims that Gamaliel, a Pharisee and one of Judaism's most respected teachers, saved the Christians from execution[42] by persuading the Sanhedrin that if the Christian movement was of human origin, it would fade away as similar ones had. If, however, it was from God, nothing they did would be able to stop it. The Pharisees were the Jewish faction that embraced ideas (e.g., the resurrection of the dead) that were rejected by more conservative Jews and preached by Christians. The Church, which apparently did much of its early missionary work in synagogues, may have found Pharisees more willing than other kinds of Jews to at least listen to its message.

Because a missionary's work is not economically productive, a missionary organization has to find a way to support itself. Luke claims that the Church got its start by pooling the possessions of its converts and organizing a kind of pre-Marxian commune: "All who believed were together and had all things in common; as they would sell their possessions and goods and distribute the proceeds to all, as any had need" (Acts 2:44-45) — "no one claimed private ownership of any possessions, but everything they owned was held in common" (Acts 4:32).[43] Luke tells a story to illustrate how seriously this rule was taken. When two converts, Ananias and his wife Sapphira, held back some of their wealth, God struck them dead.

If the congregations described in Paul's letters are an indication of what early Christian communities were really like, Luke's description of the Apostolic Church as a gathering of radical equals owes little to history and much to his desire to depict the first Christian community as the representative of God's Kingdom on Earth. As such, the Church would have to have been a society characterized by justice and love. It would have been ruled by consensus, for no one would have dominated anyone else. It would have cared for the poor and needy, and all its members would have eagerly supported its mission and shared its spiritual gifts.

But Luke did not totally idealize the first Christian community. He admitted that it had internal problems. In particular, he described a split that developed between its "Hellenist" and its Hebrew members.[44] The Hellenists believed that their poor were not receiving their fair share of food distributions. The problem, Luke claims, was simply the result of poor organization, and the solution was establishment of an administrative hierarchy for the Church. The Apostles told the congregation: "It is not right that we should neglect the word of God in order to wait on tables" (Acts 6:2). Luke imagined the Church, at its birth, as a community of radical equality that made no distinctions among its members. Everyone shared every task as well as all property. Luke explained the real, more highly organized churches of his own day as the products of experience. Without formal leadership, Christians had discovered that important duties might be overlooked and people's special gifts not be used to best advantage. Acts' Apostles decided that they had better uses for their time than pitching in on the kitchen detail. Therefore, they suggested that the community choose seven men to handle practical matters (i.e., food distribution) while they devoted themselves to "prayer and serving the word" (Acts 6:4). The Apostles then assumed the authority of priests and laid their hands on the newly elected servers to ordain them as deacons. Acts lists the names of the new junior officers. All of them were Greek.

Despite the theoretical division of labor between Apostles and deacons, the deacons did not just handle the internal affairs of the community while the Apostles devoted themselves to preaching and outreach. The crucial public sermon that forced the Jerusalem congregation to flee and scatter its members throughout rural Judea and Samaria was preached by the deacon Stephen. Stephen got into a debate in a synagogue and was dragged before the Sanhedrin and charged with blasphemy. The long sermon Luke reports him preaching to the members of the council enraged them to the point where they ordered his execution by stoning — earning Stephen the honor of becoming the first Christian martyr. A general persecution of the Church followed, and its members fled — "all except the apostles" (Acts 8:1). If such an event had actually transpired, surely the Apostles, the leaders of the community, would have been most endangered. But Luke left them in Jerusalem to provide an anchor for the Church as it began to spread into the wider world.

Stephen's execution was the occasion, Acts says, when Paul (still bearing his Hebrew name, Saul) entered the Christian story. Paul not only approved of Stephen's execution, he enthusiastically joined a campaign to root out other Christians. He broke into "house after house" and dragged both men and women off to prison. This, however, proved counterproductive, for it only served to spread the Christian "infection."

The faith spread because the Christians who carried the news of Christ abroad (none of whom was an Apostle) began to make converts. Luke depicted this as the first time Christianity intentionally reached beyond Judaism. Philip, one of the recently ordained deacons, took the lead. He preached to and baptized many of the hated Samaritans. But they were not fully inducted into the Church until the Apostles sent Peter and John to lay hands on them. At that point, the Samaritans received the Holy Spirit — the proof of their acceptability to God. The story emphasizes Luke's vision of the Church as a unified community held together by apostolic authority. One of Philip's converts dramatically asserted Luke's claim that the Church was intended for everyone, no matter what their rank and condition. Philip baptized an Ethiopian Eunuch. The ancients regarded Ethiopia as the end of the world,[45] and eunuchs were universally despised as creatures who were less than men.

Opening up to the gentile world was not easy for Jesus' Jewish followers, but Luke says that God forced the issue. An angel appeared to a righteous centurion named Cornelius and instructed him to send for Peter, who was then in Joppa. Peter was reluctant to pollute himself by entering a gentile's home, but God sent him a vision, the import of which was that all God's creatures were henceforth to be regarded as clean. Peter agreed to preach to Cornelius and his household, and when he did, the Holy Spirit descended on them — much to the amazement of the Jewish Christians who were standing by. In this case baptism with water followed baptism by the Spirit.

Acts claims that Jerusalem's scattered Christians still "spoke the word to no one except Jews" (Acts 11:19). That is, they only sought out Jewish converts. But in Antioch so many gentiles heard the Word and sought admission to the Church that they could not be refused. The Christian leadership in Jerusalem sent a man named Barnabas to check out what was happening in Antioch, where Luke says, "the disciples were first called 'Christians'" (Acts 11:26). Barnabas traveled on to Tarsus to recruit Paul's help for the mission field. Paul (the former Saul) had previously been brought to faith by a vision of Christ, and the church in Antioch charged Barnabas and Paul with a missionary journey to Cyprus and Asia Minor. Meanwhile, a second wave of persecution (launched this time by King Herod Agrippa I) erupted in Jerusalem. The Apostle James, John's brother, was put to the sword, and Peter[46] was imprisoned. He escaped with the aid of an angel, and Herod got his just deserts: "the Lord struck him down and he was eaten by worms and died" (Acts 12:23). From this point on, Acts focuses almost exclusively on the career of Paul, the self-designated Apostle to the Gentiles.

Acts credits Paul with missionary journeys to Cyprus, Asia Minor, and Greece, but it does not mention the field in which Paul himself says he first worked: Nabataean Arabia. A visit to Jerusalem put a temporary end to Paul's travels. Jews who knew him from his work in Asia Minor accused him of smuggling

gentiles into the inner court of the temple. A riot broke out, and
Paul had to be rescued by Roman soldiers. He escaped flogging
by informing a centurion that he was a Roman citizen. Suspicion
of a Jewish plot to assassinate him prompted the Roman authorities to send him under guard to Caesarea and to Felix, the
region's Roman governor. Hoping for a bribe that never materi-
alized, Felix kept Paul in limbo for two years. He was still in
prison when a new governor, Festus, took charge. When Festus
made preparations to bring him to trial, Paul exercised his rights
as a citizen and appealed to the emperor's court in Rome. Acts
closes with Paul's journey to Rome and the claim that he
preached unhindered there for "two whole years" (Acts 28:30).

Luke's account ignores much that is known about the history
of the early Church. He says nothing, for instance, about
Christianity's spread to Egypt and North Africa, where it thrived
earlier and more vigorously than in the western Mediterranean
and Rome's European provinces. He also does not complete
Paul's story. Writing as Luke did in the closing years of the 1st
century, he surely knew that Paul had been executed in Rome.[47]
But he leaves his readers under the impression that Paul was
welcomed in the empire's capital: "He lived there two whole
years . . . proclaiming the kingdom of God and teaching about the
Lord Jesus Christ with all boldness and without hindrance" (Acts
28 30-31).

Luke's two volumes were designed to appeal to gentiles and to
make a case for Christianity as a universal faith acceptable to
Rome. Luke's model for Acts, therefore, traces the spread of the
news of Christ from its origin among Jerusalem's Jews, into the
gentile community, and finally to the whole world through the
city of Rome and its empire. The faith that was first preached
among Galilean and Hellenized Jews becomes a universal
message of salvation, and the man most responsible for its spread
is Paul, a Roman citizen. This story of growing welcome within
the empire would have been spoiled if Luke had closed his

account by acknowledging Rome's preference for Christian martyrs over Christian converts.

Paul's Perspective

Paul plays so prominent a role in the history of the early Church that he has sometimes been called the real founder of Christianity.

> Next to Jesus, it is Paul who dominates the pages of the New Testament. Of the twenty-seven books in the New Testament, fully thirteen claim to be written by Paul; one other book, the Book of Acts, is largely written about Paul; and another, the Letter to the Hebrews, was accepted into the canon because it was believed (wrongly) to have been written by him. That makes fifteen of the New Testament books directly or indirectly related to Paul.[48]

Most scholars agree that not all the letters in the New Testament credited to Paul were actually written by him, but that is where consensus ends. Seven letters seem certain to be authentic: Romans, I and II Corinthians, I Thessalonians, Galatians, Philippians, and Philemon. Three letters, the "Pastoral Epistles" (I and II Timothy and Titus), are usually dated on the basis of their contents to a period well after Paul's death. Less certain is the status of the three remaining letters: Ephesians, Colossians, and II Thessalonians. More scholars doubt that they are Paul's than believe that he wrote them, but arguments continue to be advanced for both sides.

Marcus Borg and John Dominic Crossan make a convincing case for viewing the three categories (*i.e.,* authentic, questionable, unlikely) in which the letters attributed to Paul are divided as three stages in the development of a Pauline tradition.[49] The universally accepted letters are the work of the *"radical Paul,"* whom they describe as a "Jewish Christ mystic" who, like Jesus, challenged the injustices and inequalities that were inherent in the ancient world's established order. The disputed letters, which represent a *"conservative Paul,"* mark the first step in the Church's backing away from Paul's original positions, and the letters that few accept as his suggest a *"reactionary Paul,"* who endorses principles that the Paul of history opposed.

As time passed, the early Church came to terms with the world by downplaying aspects of its earlier message. The apocalyptic fervor of Mark's Gospel was, for instance, a blunt condemnation of the world order and an expression of an ardent desire for its destruction. By the time John's Gospel was written, however, Christian apocalypticism envisioned the gradual reformation of society more than its sudden and violent obliteration. In similar fashion the Paul who had preached gender equality, who had taken it for granted that women, like men, could "prophesy" (I Corinthians 11:5), and who had called a woman an "apostle" (Romans 16:7), became the Pseudo-Paul who ordered women to submit in silence and not presume to "teach" any man (I Timothy 2:11). As the early Christians' confidence that the world was destined to imminent destruction faded, they had to work out ways to live in the world. This involved a degree of conforming to the world's standards and expectations.

Exactly what Paul thought is difficult to determine, for in addition to the three "Pauls" represented in the letters attributed to him, a fourth Paul appears in the Book of Acts. This Paul serves as the lens through which many Bible students read the Paul of the letters. Luke's Paul was, however, very much a Christian of Luke's generation, not Paul's own. Much had changed for the Church in the decades that transpired between Paul's last letters and Luke's literary activity. The major event was, of course, the great Roman-Jewish war. Luke's Paul was much more concerned to court Rome's favor than the Paul of the letters seems to have been. Luke claims Roman citizenship for him, but the beatings

Paul himself reports having received call that into question. Roman law might have protected citizens from such treatment. Luke's model of the Church as a unified organization under centralized Apostolic leadership also lead him to subordinate Paul to the Twelve Apostles and assert that all disagreements among Christians were settled by generous compromises. But in Paul's letters Paul bluntly insists on his independence of the Apostles, and he claims equal (sometimes superior) "apostolic" authority. His hearty condemnation of "false apostles" who preach a gospel other than his does not suggest that the early Christian community was a warm fellowship of universal brotherly love and doctrinal conformity.

If Paul's story is begun in Acts, continued in Paul's letters, and finished in the Pseudo-Pauline epistles, Paul's preaching dissolves into a cloud of confusion and self-contradiction. Understanding Paul is made even more difficult by the fact that Paul was not a systematic thinker.[50] Most of his letters were written in response to particular situations involving members of the churches he had founded. The fact that his converts had so many questions and disagreements about what they thought he had taught them might indicate that his teaching was not always entirely clear. One New Testament letter documents the fact that even early Christians found "some things in them [Paul's letters] hard to understand" (II Peter 3:16) and open to dangerous misinterpretation. That is as true today as it was in the 1st century CE.

Experts are at odds over something as basic as the issue of Paul's fidelity to Jesus. Did Paul preach a message that was consistent with, or a continuation of, what Jesus taught? Or did Paul turn Jesus into something that Jesus would not have recognized? Borg and Crossan see continuity between Jesus and Paul: "His genuine letters generate an understanding of Paul and his message that is remarkably consistent with the message of Jesus . . . | — | the radical Paul, we are convinced, was a faithful follower of the radical Jesus."[51] But New Testament authority

Brad Ehrman disagrees: "Jesus taught his followers to keep the law as God had commanded in order to enter the kingdom. Paul taught that keeping the law had nothing to do with entering the kingdom. For Paul, only the death and resurrection of Jesus mattered. The historical Jesus taught the law. Paul taught Jesus."[52]

The historical Jesus and Paul obviously viewed events from different perspectives. Jesus looked forward to the crucifixion and resurrection, and Paul looked back at those key events. The Gospels make it clear that Jesus' followers did not understand him (or the Scripture's prophecies) until after his death and resurrection. Jesus, therefore, could not say things about himself that Paul could say, for Jesus' revelatory work was not complete until he rose from the grave. Paul's letters make it clear that he did not believe that his proclamation of Jesus as the Christ (the Messiah) was beginning a new religion or altering Paul's own status as a Jew. No one, however, will ever know how the conversation would have gone if the historical Jesus and Paul had been able to meet for lunch.

Some of the confusion about Paul's teaching derives from a tendency to forget that Paul was not writing for us. Paul never imagined that we would exist. He would be profoundly shaken if he returned to find that his words were still being read almost 2,000 years after he wrote them, for Paul was convinced that the Parousia (*i.e.*, Second Coming of Christ) was near at hand. His concern, therefore, was not to leave directions for constructing a new society or founding a new religion. He wrote to advise the congregations of his era on how to conduct themselves in the short time left before God transformed the world. The time for worrying about family, politics, and institutions (such as slavery) had passed, as far as he was concerned. The important thing was to remember to act from the conviction that all Christians were equal in Christ and called to guide their conduct by the love of Christ. That would be enough to advance their mission and bring in converts until God took charge and remade the world as His Kingdom. To be fair to Paul he should be read in the context of the first half of the 1st century, not the first half of the 21st.

Paul was probably about twelve or fifteen years younger than Jesus. Although both men were Jews, they came from very different backgrounds. Jesus was a rural peasant who had little experience of the wider gentile world and who was probably illiterate. Paul was a city boy of the *diaspora* — born and raised in Tarsus, one of the Roman Empire's intellectual centers. He was fluent in Greek and a gifted writer. Acts claims that Paul studied in Jerusalem under Gamaliel, a famous rabbi. Paul himself never mentions this, but he was certainly well educated.

Luke's model of history centers all important events in Jerusalem, but both Luke and Paul agree that the crucial event in Paul's life took place in or near Damascus. It was there that Paul had the vision that brought him to faith in Jesus as the Christ and there that he received baptism.

At that point Acts' story about Paul and Paul's own story begin to diverge in major ways. Acts claims that after his baptism Paul went to Jerusalem and submitted to the authority of the Twelve Apostles, but Paul adamantly denies this. Paul insists that his knowledge of Christ and his authority to teach derived not from the Apostles, but directly from his experience of the resurrected Jesus. In his opinion he was, therefore, an Apostle and the equal of the Twelve. Indeed, Paul was not at all reluctant to criticize the Apostle Peter and other leaders of the Church and to claim that his grasp of the faith was superior to theirs.

Paul says that after his baptism he began missionary work among the Nabatean Arabs in the region of modern Jordan. Acts says nothing about this, and Paul's letters report no lasting fruits from this venture. A war that broke out between Aretas, king of the Nabateans, and Herod Antipas probably forced Paul to terminate this venture, flee from Damascus, and return to his hometown, Tarsus. It was there that Acts says Barnabas, an early

Jewish convert from Cyprus, found him and recruited him for a second missionary journey. Barnabas brought him to Antioch and vouched for him to the Christians in Jerusalem who, given his background, were understandably suspicious of him. Barnabas and Paul traveled through Syria and Cilicia. Paul's letters mention this venture, but say nothing about its results. It ended with a trip to Jerusalem for a conference with other leaders of the Church. Paul claims that on this occasion an agreement was reached to divide up the mission field. Peter, John, and James would work among the Jews, and Barnabas and Paul would attend to gentiles. But if there was amity at this meeting, it quickly broke down when a quarrel erupted among Christians in Antioch. The issue was the status of Jewish law. Jewish Christians, who still respected the Torah, refused to share meals or associate with gentile Christians who did not meet the Torah's standards of purity. Some Christians believed that the law remained binding. Others thought that it had been fulfilled and was no longer important. Some believed that male gentile converts had to be circumcised, and others did not. Paul stood with the latter group and accused Peter and James of hypocrisy in supporting the former. The result was a break in relations, and Paul struck out on his own.

The work that Paul then undertook in the region of the Aegean is documented by his extant letters — all of which may have been written during the decade of the 50s. Paul wrote more letters than have survived, and some of his canonical letters (*e.g.*, II Corinthians) may really be made up of pieces taken from a number of different letters. Only one of his letters (Philemon) was addressed to an individual, and even that one was intended to be read to the congregation to which its recipient belonged.

Modern Christians should not imagine Paul's churches as bearing much resemblance to their own. Paul concentrated on major cities and on the urban working class.[53] Roman cities were densely inhabited[54] places where uprooted, diverse populations congregated. The Roman Empire was in the early stages of consolidation in Paul's day, and its evolving economy was destroying traditional self-sufficient peasant farms and encouraging the development of large commercial plantations. Many of the poor were losing their land and being forced into the teaming, unhealthy urban clusters. In the process, they lost the support of extended families and were forced to make their way among strangers from a wide variety of backgrounds. One important thing that Christian faith offered them was a basis for creating a new kind of family. Whereas many modern Christians think of evangelism in terms of individual conversions, Paul was concerned with forming communities. These would have been quite small. Paul's converts gathered in their homes or shops, and the urban poor did not have much space in which to conduct their lives. By the time of Paul's death (*ca.* 64 CE) there may only have been about 2,000 Christians in the whole Roman Empire.[55]

The extensive allusions to the Hebrew Scriptures and to Hebrew history in Paul's letters suggest that his converts must have had some knowledge of Judaism before he began to instruct them. They are not likely to have been Jews, for Paul claimed that his mission was to gentiles and he was adamant in opposing the efforts of Jewish Christians to impose circumcision or other aspects of Jewish law on gentile converts. The most likely targets for his attentions were the gentiles ("God-fearers") who associated themselves with synagogues. There appear to have been large numbers of these. Josephus, the Jewish historian, claimed that Jews "were constantly attracting to their religious ceremonies multitudes of Greeks, and these they had in some measure incorporated with themselves."[56] Paul doubtless found this a fertile field in which to work. He could offer these gentiles much of what attracted them to Judaism without requiring them to accept the full burden of Jewish law. For adult males contemplating the prospect of circumcision in an age that had no anesthetics, this would have been no mean advantage. Paul's inroads into this gentile community, which was an important source of support and protection for Jews, may be what stirred up so much Jewish hostility to his missionary work.

Paul was a mystic given to visions, ecstatic trances, bouts of glossolalia, and other "gifts of the Spirit." His faith was also apocalyptic. Questions about Christ's Second Coming inspired I Thessalonians — his first extant letter and the earliest Christian document (*ca.* 50 CE). Paul, building on Hebrew tradition, thought of Jesus' resurrection not as a unique individual event, but as the beginning of the general resurrection of all humanity. Jesus was, Paul said, "the first fruits" of what would be a universal harvest "of those who have died" (I Corinthians 15:20). Given that Jesus had begun the process, Paul expected it to play out rapidly during Paul's generation. Paul had stressed this so strongly that his Thessalonian correspondents had concluded that all Christian converts would live to witness Christ's return. When some died, their friends worried about what this implied for their salvation. Paul wrote to reassure them that the dead would be raised to welcome their Lord. Paul urged the Thessalonians to continue their efforts to live sober, virtuous lives, to avoid idolatry and sexual transgressions, and to cling to what Paul had taught them. He pointed to the spiritual gifts that were active among them as evidence that the Parousia was near at hand, but he was well aware of the problems that charismatics could cause. He cautioned against new prophecies that might undermine their faith, and he condemned efforts to predict the date of Christ's appearance.

Paul's two letters to the Corinthians dealt with a multitude of issues that arose in what might have been his largest congregation. Corinth's church was an unruly community. Its wealthier members claimed the privileges of their rank, and factions following different leaders fought among themselves. One of Paul's strongest principles was his insistence on equality among Christians. They were all, he said, members of one body, the body of Christ (I Corinthians 12:12-27). But Paul walked a fine line when explaining what this meant. On the one hand, he pointed out to his converts that they were all equal because none of them could take any credit for his or her own salvation. No one deserved salvation more than anyone else. It was a free gift of God's grace, which all should receive with due humility. They should give thanks for the way it liberated them from concern for themselves and freed them to serve others. On the other hand, however, Paul insisted that the gift of unmerited grace and freedom in Christ did not mean rules and standards no longer applied. He had much to say to the Corinthians about sexual transgressions, marriage, acceptable foods, modes of dress, conduct of the Lord's Supper, use of Spiritual gifts, charitable obligations, dealing with sinners (repentant and otherwise), maintenance of a good public image, and avoiding "false apostles."

This latter issue plagued Paul throughout his career, for his understanding of Christianity was by no means universally shared. Other missionaries taught a different faith and sometimes caused his converts to question what he had taught them. Nothing seems to have angered Paul more than this. His temper is displayed most vividly in the letter he wrote to the Galatians. He goes so far as to call them fools and to wish that his circumcising opponents would complete the job and castrate themselves (Galatians 3:1, 5:12)! The issue between Paul and the "false apostles" seems always to be the long-standing quarrel over the status of Jewish religious law. Paul pointed out to the Galatians that they had begun to receive the gifts of the Spirit as soon as they believed the message of faith. "Works of law" had not contributed to their salvation. Paul insisted that Christians were "called to freedom" and that all that was required of them was: "You shall love your neighbor as yourself" (Galatians 5: 13-14). But Paul's experience had taught him that this message of "good news" was open to misinterpretation. He cautioned: "Do not use your freedom as an opportunity for self-indulgence" (Galatians 5:13).

Paradox lies at the root of profound religious insights, and the great paradox at the heart of Paul's gospel is the relationship between faith and works. Paul believed firmly that salvation comes through Christ — the product of what God accomplishes through Jesus' crucifixion and resurrection. Salvation is not something that people can achieve, earn, or win for themselves. It is a free gift, not payment or reward for an individual's deeds. But this raises all kinds of questions. Is not faith itself a work — a decision one must take, a leap one has to make, or something that one must embrace? Faith may be freely offered, but a gift is not a gift until the receiver accepts it. Is the power to believe, to accept God's gift, itself a gift from God? If so, does that mean that God has predestined those who will receive it and those who will not? If that is the case, does that imply that God intends salvation for everyone or that God intentionally creates some persons expressly for eternal punishment? If so, what does that imply about God?

Paul's most ambitious attempt to explain his understanding of faith and salvation is the letter that he wrote to introduce himself to the Christians living in the city of Rome. These Christians were not, like the recipients of his other letters, people whom he had taught in person and who, therefore, could be presumed to know the general outline of his belief system. They were strangers whom he hoped to persuade to welcome him to work among them.

The letter to the Romans has probably received more scholarly attention than any of Paul's other works, and it has had a major influence on the history of the Church through its impact on theologians such as Augustine of Hippo and Martin Luther. The letter's reputation as a dense and difficult text might cause amateur readers to approach it with fear and trembling. But Marcus Borg and John Crossan point out something reassuring that is often overlooked. They write:

> Small libraries could be filled with discussions and commen-
> taries on Romans whose cumulative results have rendered it
> almost incomprehensible to ordinary modern readers. Yet, no
> matter how profound its theology may be, it had to be
> comprehensible to the artisan communities and shop
> churches in Rome to whom it was written.[57]

Paul did not write for people trained in philosophy and theology.
He wrote for the ordinary men and women of his day — people
who might be assumed to have far less literary education than is
common in Western societies today. Most modern readers
should, therefore, be able to penetrate his prose, but only if they
remember that he wrote with the questions, disputes, and
assumptions of 1st-century Christians in mind. If he is lifted out
of that context, essential clues to his thought can be lost.

Modern Christians, for instance, are often fixated on the
individual's pursuit of heaven. The whole point of faith, they
assume, is to win translation from this world to a perfect,
spiritual realm. This is not how Paul and other early Christians
thought. Their hope was for the redemption and perfection of
this world, not its destruction and their removal to a different
place. When they spoke of "eternal life" they had in mind life in
the world as God intended it to be — the perfect life of the new
age that had begun to dawn with the Christ event. Their hope
was not for the separation of their souls from their bodies, but for
new bodies that Paul struggled to describe as the products of a
transformation as dramatic as the comparison between a mature
plant and its seed. Their dream was not of a heaven of endless
idleness, but of a world of peace, justice, and plenty.

Paul, like Jesus, lived and died a Jew. He believed that the
Torah's laws were essential preparation for the Christ event.
Their purpose was to awaken humanity to its true condition and

thereby stimulate an appetite for salvation. No one can know that they are offending their Creator and diminishing their own humanity until they grasp the fullness of their human potential. The law sets the standard that God envisions for those creatures who share His image — particularly the Bible's summaries of the law as a call to a life of perfect self-giving love. The problem with the law, however, is its inability to engender salvation, for knowledge of the law does not create the will to do what the law commands. Paul argues that the histories of both Jews and gentiles demonstrate the law's power to condemn, but not to save. The Jews had the advantage of the Mosaic law, and the gentiles had the knowledge of the law God embedded in nature. But neither people has been able to live according to what both know perfect humaneness requires.

Human fallibility, which Paul refers to as Adam's sin, is corrected by what God achieves in Jesus, the "second Adam." Paul's point in pairing Jesus with Adam is to make clear that Jesus' death on the cross is as universally effective an event as humanity's creation in Adam. What all people once were all people can now become. Attempts to take Paul's metaphorical images literally and turn them into explanations rather than proclamations have led to bizarre and unwarranted assumptions about genetics and human origins. The same can be said for his characterization of Jesus' saving work as a sacrifice. Paul talks about Jesus taking humanity's sins on himself, and this leads some people to think of Jesus as a scapegoat — an innocent being whose death satisfied God's demand for the punishment of sinners. Other Christians are troubled about what this implies about the character of God. The "Jesus-as-scapegoat" explanation for why Jesus had to die makes God out to be a vengeful monster who can be appeased by nothing less than the torture and death of His own blameless son. Given that modern Christians have no experience of the kinds of religious sacrifices that were at the heart of religion in the ancient world, they need to reflect on

Paul's understanding of what was taking place on Hebrew and pagan altars in his day. Some sacrifices were "substitutionary" — that is, an animal took the place of a human offering. But these sacrifices were not punishments. They were giving to God the "first fruits" that were rightfully His. Routine sacrifices, however, were the means for bringing the sacred and secular realms together, for connecting God and humankind. To sacrifice something, was literally to make it sacred and then to share it with God and commune with Him. The animals slaughtered on altars were not being executed to pay the penalty for the crimes of those who offered them; they were being butchered for a sacred feast of reconciliation or reunion. This is why the Gospels do not treat the execution of Jesus as an end in itself, but an act that is completed by his followers sharing in his body and blood.

The Christian life for Paul, was a life of gratitude to God for the gift of freedom from anxiety for the self — a gift that freed Christians to serve others. In light of all the advice he gave his converts on how to conduct their lives, Paul obviously did not understand a life of faith to be a dispensation from the duty to do good works. If that had been Paul's belief, he would not likely have pursued the arduous career of a self-supporting missionary. Paul's objection was to "good" works that were devoid of faith. He knew that good deeds can contribute to the preservation and strengthening of bad systems. People can do "good" to advance their own interests and exalt themselves over others. They can do "good" to forestall essential reforms. They can participate in evil in order to amass the resources with which to "do good." Paul's conviction was that "works" could only be good if they proceeded from authentic faith.

Paul was also a charismatic and a mystic who understood faith to be a tangible experience, the perceived activity of the Holy Spirit within a believer. Faith was not determined adherence to a set of doctrines or a willful decision to "believe." It was a transforming experience that marked entrance into the

Christ event through which the world was being redeemed. It was a condition of life that simple people could comprehend and embrace with joy.

Epistles and Apocalypse

The New Testament's newest items document the evolution of the Church from spontaneous, charismatic clusters of believers to a formal organization with hierarchical leadership and a concern for orthodoxy — from a community improvising beliefs and practices for the short term (in expectation of an imminent Apocalypse) to an established institution enforcing codes of conduct and theological conformity. This biblical material is difficult to categorize. Epistles compose much of it, but some of these might more accurately be described as sermons or theological treatises. The Book of Revelation is entirely unique, the only work by a Christian prophet.

Respect for Paul's epistles led some early Christians to compose letters in his name and in the names of other founders of the faith (*e.g.*, Peter, James, and John). The issues these documents address make it clear, however, that they are not products of the Apostolic generation. Today, forgery is a crime that earns its perpetrators stiff punishment. Some people in the ancient world also objected to it, but the ancients had no copyright laws or registered trademarks. If the source of a document was unknown, tradition might attribute it to a prominent individual. Authors might also, for a variety of reasons, intentionally credit their writing to someone else. Pseudonymous authorship could be used to identify a work with a particular school of thought. It might be used to update the teachings of a venerable master and apply them to new circumstances. Or it could be used to court support for a controversial position by crediting it to a trusted authority.

No first generation Christian author had as much influence as Paul. Others collected Jesus' sayings and stories about him, but

Paul was the Church's first theologian. As early as the 90s a collection of his letters was in circulation and beginning to be thought of as Scripture. The temptation was strong, therefore, for later generations of Christians to invoke Paul's authority for the positions they wanted to defend. This seems to be the explanation for the Pastoral Epistles, I and II Timothy and Titus.

The Pastoral Epistles earned their name because they are cast in the form of advice to pastors (congregational leaders). They clearly reflect a much more advanced ecclesiastical organization than existed in Paul's day. They spell out qualifications for offices in the Church, such as bishop (*episkopos*, a Greek word for "overseer"), deacon (*diakonos*, "server"), and elder (senior Christians, some of whom preached, taught, and "ruled," I Timothy 5:17). Pseudo-Paul, author of I Timothy (3:1-7), sets a high standard for would-be bishops. He assumes that they will be male and says that such a man "must be above reproach, married only once, temperate, sensible, respectable, hospitable, an apt teacher, not a drunkard, not violent but gentle, not quarrelsome, and not a lover of money. He must manage his own household well, keeping his children submissive and respectful in every way . . . not a recent convert . . . [and] well thought of by outsiders." The qualifications for deacons are almost as high: they "must be serious, not double-tongued, not indulging in much wine,[58] not greedy for money; they must hold fast to the mystery of the faith with a clear conscience . . . [be] tested . . . married only once, and let them manage their children and their households well" (I Timothy 3:8-12). The issue of a woman's right to this office is not specifically addressed — but because it was taken for granted or because it was assumed to be out of the question?

The leaders of Timothy's congregation faced a number of practical problems. They were obliged to support "widows," but to limit the financial burden[59] Pseudo-Paul narrowed the definition of the kind of widow who qualified. The widows who were to be aided were women over sixty who had been married only once, who had raised children, and had a reputation for good works — which included having "washed the saints' feet" (I Timothy 5:9-10). Church leaders also needed procedures for enforcing justice. Accusations against elders, for instance, were not to be trusted unless backed up by two or three witnesses. Leaders were cautioned against hastily ordaining anyone — a ceremony Pseudo Paul describes as "the laying on of hands by the council of elders" (I Timothy 4:14). Timothy's job as pastor was to "give attention to the public reading of scripture, to exhorting, [and] to teaching" (I Timothy 4:13). He was also to expect a salary: "The laborer deserves to be paid." (I Timothy 5:18)

Timothy's congregation was eager to make its peace with the world and not be seen by the authorities as suspect or seditious. Timothy was instructed to offer "supplications, prayers, intercessions, and thanksgivings . . . for everyone, for kings and all who are in high positions, so that we may lead a quiet and peaceable life in all godliness and dignity" (I Timothy 2:1-2). The women in his congregation were ordered to be submissive, silent, and obedient. They were to dress modestly, eschew elaborate hairdos and jewelry, not to presume to exercise any authority over men, and to seek their salvation "through childbearing" (I Timothy 2:9-15). Christian slaves were not to aspire to equality with their masters, but to serve them all the more faithfully for "those who benefit by their service are believers and beloved" (I Timothy 6:1-2).[60] Although Timothy was warned that "the love of money is a root of all kinds of evil" (I Timothy 6:10), he was not advised to criticize the rich,[61] but only to caution them against haughtiness and to encourage them to use their wealth to support good works.

Concerning doctrine, Timothy was to beware of "certain people" who "preoccupy themselves with myths and endless genealogies that promote speculations" (I Timothy 1:3-4). He was to oppose those who "forbid marriage and demand abstinence from foods, which God created to be received with thanksgiving" (I Timothy 4:3). He was to avoid those who had "a morbid craving for controversy and for disputes about words" (I Timothy 6:4-5), particularly if they tried to gain financial advantage by winning a reputation for superior knowledge and holiness.

The concerns of the Pastoral Epistles do not reflect the environment in which Paul lived. His generation of Christians anticipated being the last generation of Christians. They had no need for a formal organization, officers, ordinations, and financial regulations. Paul was proud of supporting himself, but thankful for occasional gifts. The opponents whose messages he was concerned to counter were not Timothy's ascetic Gnostics (Christian dualists), but "Judaizers" ("circumcisers"), Christians who insisted that gentiles observe the Torah's regulations. And Paul had a much higher opinion of women than Pseudo-Paul appears to have had. Timothy's advisor assumed that women were given to slandering others, "gadding about" gossiping, "saying what they should not say," and prone to "sensual desires" (I Timothy 5:9-13). Paul himself would not have met the qualifications that I Timothy set for a church leader. Paul had never married and demonstrated his fitness to supervise a church by managing a household and raising well disciplined children. For his part, I Timothy's author would probably have been eager to quash the free-wheeling behavior that appears to have been a feature of life in Paul's charismatic congregations. II Timothy issues from the same environment that produced I Timothy, and the letter to Titus recapitulates I Timothy's qualifications for ecclesiastical offices, its concern for demonstrating support for governmental authorities, and its advice to avoid theological controversies.

The letters that may or may not be Paul's raise questions of a different sort. II Thessalonians repeats a lot of what is found in I

Thessalonians, but it contradicts the first letter in an important detail. In I Thessalonians Paul writes to clear up misconceptions about the Parousia, and he condemns those who speculate about the date for Christ's return. "The Lord," he says, "will come like a thief in the night" (I Thessalonians 5:2). But II Thessalonians chastises people who were so confident in Christ's imminent return that they had given up working and preparing for the future (II Thessalonians 3:6-15). The letter warns that the Last Days are not imminent, for it lists a number of things that will have to occur before Christ comes again. It mentions a rebellion and the appearance of "the lawless one" who will take "his seat in the temple of God, declaring himself to be God" (II Thessalonians 2:1-12). Whereas I Thessalonians says that there will be no signs, II Thessalonians explains what the signs will be.

The letter to the Colossians has strong similarities to the Gospel of John, which was written long after Paul's death. Like the preface to John's Gospel, it describes Christ as the divine agent through which the cosmos was made, and it claims that "he is the image of the invisible God,[62] the firstborn of all creation" (Colossians 1:15). Despite seemingly Gnostic imagery, it warns against Gnostics who are preoccupied with "the elemental spirits of the universe" (Colossians 2:20) and who urge "severe treatment of the body" as a means to salvation (Colossians 2:23). It says that salvation comes to those who are inducted into Christ's body by baptism. They are incorporated into his life — into his crucifixion, death, and resurrection. This means that they are free of the law and united as equals. But the letter warns its readers not to abuse their freedom or presume on their equality. Wives are to be subject to their husbands. Husbands are never to treat their wives harshly. Children are to obey their parents. Fathers need to take care not to break the spirits of their offspring. Slaves must obey their masters (and look for their reward in heaven). Their masters must treat them fairly. As the author of Colossians saw it, Christian faith was not an excuse for challenging or upsetting the established order.

The author of the letter to the Ephesians seems to have relied heavily on Colossians. He may have been a student of Paul's letters who wrote well after Paul's lifetime. His letter affirms Pauline themes. It speaks of Christians having been saved by grace through faith — not by their works but by God's gift (Ephesians 2:8-9). It affirms their unity in Christ and the status of gentiles as "fellow heirs" with Jews to the mysteries that have been revealed to the Apostles and prophets. But, unlike Paul, the letter's author seems to have been profoundly influenced by gnostic dualism — by a vision of life lived in the midst of an endless conflict between the forces of light and darkness. He understands the Christian struggle to be against "the cosmic powers of this present darkness, against the spiritual forces of evil in heavenly places" (Ephesians 6:12).

The letter to the Hebrews is not a letter, but a sophisticated theological tract written by someone who was well schooled in Greek philosophy. It ascribes to the Platonic theory that the world of sight and sense is an inferior imitation of a spiritual realm. It views Christ as both the ultimate priest-mediator and the fully sufficient sacrifice reconciling God with humanity. The earthly practices of the Hebrews and their temples are interpreted as allegories for the spiritual realities of heaven. Just as the old covenant was sealed with blood sacrifices so the blood shed by Christ has established a new covenant promising redemption to all humanity.

The remaining New Testament letters are called the Catholic (*i.e.*, universal) Epistles because they are addressed to a general audience, not to a specific person or congregation. On linguistic grounds alone (*i.e.*, its excellent command of Greek) the letter of James is not likely to have been written by Jesus' brother. Its emphasis on the importance of good works for salvation might have been a reaction to extreme interpretations of Paul's message of salvation by faith: "What good is it, my brothers and sisters, if you say you have faith but do not have works? Can faith save you?" (James 2:14). The letter is, for whatever motive, deeply concerned with the practical application of faith in the traditional sense of caring for the poor and needy: "be doers of the word, and not merely hearers" (James 1:22). Associated with this is the usual caution to the rich to be aware of the spiritual dangers inherent in wealth.

I Peter was not written by the Galilean blue collar Apostle of that name, but by an author skilled in the composition of polished, literary Greek. It was addressed to Christians who were threatened by an organized campaign of persecution — described as a "fiery ordeal" (I Peter 4:12). This would suggest that it was written at the end of the 1st century or even in the 2nd. Despite a relatively late date, its author was still confident that the Last Days were at hand, and he urged those who faced martyrdom to find encouragement in Christ's suffering and ultimate vindication: "After you have suffered for a little while, the God of all grace, who has called you to his eternal glory in Christ, will himself restore, support, strengthen, and establish you" (I Peter 5:10).

II Peter appears to be from the pen of a different author, and it may be the last of the canonical texts to be written — dating to some time in the first half of the 2nd century. It derived much of its material from another of the Catholic Epistles, the letter of Jude. Jude's preoccupation with fighting heresy and the letter's assumption that there was an established body of orthodox Christian doctrine marks it as a late text. The church to which Jude was written was evidently divided by theological disputes that excited Jude's passionate concern. He urged "his side" to have mercy on "some" who were wavering, to snatch others from the fire, and "have mercy on still others with fear, hating even the tunic defiled by their bodies" (Jude 23)! II Peter sets out to revive belief in the imminence of Christ's Second Coming as a motive for combating false doctrine. It notes that "scoffers" have ridiculed belief in the Parousia because it has been so long delayed, but the delay, it claims, is evidence of God's patience and mercy. God, "not wanting any to perish, but all to come to repentance" (II Peter 3:9) has provided ample, but not infinite, time for the world to be saved. Meanwhile, the faithful should beware of "ignorant and unstable" people who twist obscure passages from Paul's letters — "as they do the *other* scriptures" (II Peter 3:16, italics added). If the Apostle Peter had read Paul's letters, he would not likely, like the author of this letter, have placed them on the same level as the Hebrew Scriptures — the only Scriptures known to St. Peter.

The three letters (two of which are quite short) that are ascribed to a certain John may have been written by the same person. He was not the author of John's Gospel but a Christian who was strongly influenced by the evangelist's ideas. A late date for these epistles is suggested by their opposition to a fully developed heresy, a form of Christian Gnosticism. The insistence in John's Gospel that Jesus is the pre-existent Word of God and God incarnate led Christians, who accepted the Gnostic belief that spirit and matter were opposed to each other, to conclude that Jesus was either a spirit who only appeared to have flesh or was a physical being separate from God. The letter's author rejected both of these theses: "No one who denies the Son has the Father; everyone who confesses the Son has the Father also" (I John 2:23), and "every spirit that confesses that Jesus Christ has come in the flesh is from God, and every spirit that does not confess Jesus is not from God . . . [but] of the Antichrist . . . [who] is already in the world" (I John 4:2-3). John's second letter briefly repeats the warning of his first: the end times are at hand, for the Antichrist has come. It warns that the Antichrist's strategy is to dissuade Christians from the belief that "Jesus has come in the flesh" (II John, verse 7). John's third letter was an appeal for help from a friend who John hoped would intervene in a power struggle between John and a certain Diotrephes. Diotrephes was driving John's partisans from his church and refusing to receive a man whom John had sent to him. It has very little, if any, theological content, but it witnesses to the presence in the canon of frail humanity (the medium through which the Bible mediates the Word of God).

The Christian Bible ends with a mysterious book that draws on imagery from both its testaments and ends with the promise of a new heaven and earth that will mirror the perfection of Genesis's first creation. The Book of Revelation releases a flood of vivid symbols that call to mind multiple associations and stimulate (perhaps overstimulate) the imagination. As a result, it is easily open to the abuse to which all Scripture is vulnerable — the temptation to impose on it ideas of one's own. The safest approach to studying the text is to remind oneself that it was not written for us but for its author's own place and age. If it had been meant to speak to the 21st century rather than the 1st, it would never have been preserved for inclusion in the canon. It, of course, also has a timeless aspect — an affirmation of the Bible's fundamental promise that we can trust life, that God is supreme, and all will be well in the end. But the Book of Revelation is by no means a complete summary of the Bible's teachings. Glaringly absent from it is the message of divine and human love that threads its way though most of Scripture. The God of Revelation is a merciless judge and its Christ an avenging warrior. The book's thirst for justice overwhelms any appeal to love.

Revelation's author identifies himself as a man named John who had been confined on the island of Patmos "because of the word of God and the testimony of Jesus" (Revelation 1:9). Scholars conclude from the way he wrote Greek that his first language was a Semitic tongue.[63] He was certainly fully at home in the Hebrew Scriptures — to which he made hundreds of allusions. The Book of Revelation itself appears to have been modeled on the books of the Hebrew prophets. John calls himself a prophet, and his book is a long, detailed description of a vision he claims to have had on a certain "Lord's day."

John directs his prophecy to a specific audience — to the congregations of churches in seven towns in western Asia Minor, which he names. The advice he gives them makes it clear that the Christians of this region were experiencing persecution and in need of encouragement to persevere in their faith. An early tradition claims that John wrote during the reign of the emperor Domitian (r. 81-96 CE). There was at that time no empire-wide attempt to stamp out Christianity, but spontaneous local uprisings against Christians were common. Whenever a famine, earthquake, or other disaster occurred, blame was likely to fall on a region's resident Christians. Their neighbors sometimes leapt to the conclusion that Christian denial of the pagan gods had roused those deities to vengeful action.

Like the Book of Daniel (to which it sometimes alludes) Revelation is filled with mysterious, evocative images that cry out for interpretation. It develops an elaborate scheme for an Apocalypse that begins in heaven, unfolds in stages, and involves numerous battles between opposing supernatural forces. Satan (the Dragon, the Beast) is conquered, confined, and released to be battled again. Afflictions of all kinds descend upon the Earth. Resurrections take place for different kinds of people at different times. At one stage angels mark 144,000 people for salvation, and "the Beast" imprints his mysterious number (666) on others. In the end the damned are condemned to eternal punishment in a lake of fire and left beyond all hope of repentance and forgiveness, the heavenly Jerusalem descends to Earth, Eden is restored, and those who are saved find themselves in the company of God. What one makes of all of this often reveals more about the reader than about the text.

NOTES

[1]   Jerry Falwell, *Finding Inner Peace and Strength* (NY: Doubleday, 1982), p. 26.

[2]   Ehrman, *Misquoting Jesus*, p. 216.

[3]   Boorstin, *The Seekers*, p. 261.

[4]   The fact that Matthew and Luke saw fit to change and modify Mark — and John may purposefully have set out to contradict parts of the Synoptic tradition — makes it quite clear that these authors did not believe that they were dealing in the Gospels with divinely dictated, inerrant accounts of God's words.

[5]   Bart Ehrman, *Jesus Interrupted: Revealing the Hidden Contradictions in the Bible (and Why We Don't Know about Them)* (NY: HarperOne, 2009), pp. 149-150, quoting: Josephus, *Antiquities* 18.3.3.

[6]   Crossan and Reed, *Excavating Jesus*, pp. 59-62.

[7]   *Ibid.*, pp. 237-244. Another ossuary that recently came on the antiquities market with the claim that it was made for the burial of Jesus' brother, James, has proven to be a forgery.

[8]   The village may not have existed early enough to have been mentioned in the Hebrew Scriptures. It may have been a settlement created in response to a colonization program sponsored by the Hasmoneans after they established Jerusalem's independence of Greek rule in the 2nd century BCE. See: Crossan and Reed, *Excavating Jesus*, pp. 18-36.

9   The Vatican has recently submitted what are said to be the bones of St. Paul to archaeological investigation. Nicole Winfield, "Pope: Scientific Analysis Done on St. Paul's Bones," Associated Press Release, 6/28/2009.

10   Crossan and Reed, *Excavating Jesus*, p. 21, quoting Eusebius, *Ecclesiastical History* 3.20.

11   It was common practice in the ancient world to attribute anonymous documents to famous authors or actually to compose new work in their name. On the basis of style and content, most scholars agree that Paul did not write some of the letters attributed to him in the New Testament (*e.g.*, I and II Timothy, Titus, Ephesians). Those that appear to be indisputably authentic are: I Thessalonians, I and II Corinthians, Philippians, Philemon, Galatians, and Romans.

12   "Luke, himself a learned scholar, takes it utterly for granted, as do many modern scholars, that Jesus was literate and learned. This is very unlikely. The best general work on ancient literacy in the Mediterranean basin concludes about a 5 percent literacy rate. The best specific work on ancient literacy in the Jewish homeland concludes about a 3 percent literacy rate." Crossan and Reed, *Excavating Jesus*, p. 30.

13   Matthew's story of Jesus' nativity draws not only on canonical sources, but on popular folk tale additions to the Bible's story of Moses' birth. See: *Ibid.*, pp. 45-48.

14   Herod's order to kill all children in Bethlehem "who were two years old or under" (Matthew 2:16) suggests that Matthew did not picture Jesus as a newborn when his family fled into Egypt.

15 a distance of well over seventy miles

16 It would have taken five days of hard travel for a Galilean to get as far as Jerusalem, let alone Bethlehem. The trip would have exposed Mary to considerable risk.

17 It was not until the European Middle Ages that the custom of dating years from the birth of Christ was established. The scholars who calculated the date made an error. As a consequence, modern people maintain, absurdly, that Jesus was born in 4 BC (*i.e.*, born four years "Before [the birth of] Christ").

18 Some scholars try to resolve this conflict by claiming that Quirinius was active in the region of Armenia and elsewhere as early as Herod's era and that there were probably more censuses than are documented in our records. This, however, is an attempt to argue away the evidence the Bible gives us by an argument from lack of evidence.

19 The Bible says nothing about the day on which Jesus was born. It may not have been until the 4th century that his natal day was celebrated as a religious festival. The Church designated December 25 as the appropriate day for commemorating his birth. In the earlier versions of our calendar, it was the date of the winter solstice, the turning of the year or the point when the sun ceased to decline and began to grow stronger. Because Jesus was "the light of the world," the day when the sun was reborn was the fit day for celebrating his incarnation.

20 which Luke calls "their own town of Nazareth" (Luke 2:39)

21 Some scholars may have misunderstood extant Roman

decrees that ordered men to return to their homes for a census. The reference is not to people permanently living elsewhere, but to those who were traveling or temporarily residing abroad. Given the mobility of populations even in the ancient world, the Roman government would have caused chaos if it ordered everyone to return to the places where their ancestors were born. If it had, there would then have been the problem of deciding which ancestor's birthplace should take precedence.

22 The virgin birth story also exalts Jesus over John the Baptist. John's birth follows the Hebrew tradition of stories about divine intervention enabling infertile, aged couples to have a child. But Jesus' birth from a virgin is a more miraculous event, and in line with tales familiar to gentiles from pagan sources. Justin Martyr, an early Christian apologist, pointed out to his pagan readers that the Christian message was similar to what they already professed to believe: "When we say also that the Word, who is the first-birth of God, was produced without sexual union, and that He, Jesus Christ, our teacher, was crucified and died, and rose again, and ascended into heaven, we propound nothing different from what you believe regarding those whom you esteem sons of Jupiter." (Justin Martyr, *First Apology*, quoted in: Crossan and Reed, *Excavating Jesus*, pp. 268-269.)

23 "Then the Jews said to him, 'You are not yet fifty years old, and have you seen Abraham?'"

24 "life expectancy, for the luckier half [of the peasantry] who survived childhood, was somewhere in the thirties. Those reaching fifty or sixty were rare." (Crossan and Reed, *Excavating Jesus*, p. 20.)

25   God's first commandment in Genesis was: "Be fruitful and multiply," and Adam's union with Eve set the pattern.

26   A circumstantial case can be made for Mary Magdalene as Jesus' wife. The possibility has intrigued fiction writers.

27   Bart Ehreman (*Jesus Interrupted*, p. 42) raises the possibility that the period of Jesus' activity may have been only a few months. He notes that at the start of Jesus' travels with his disciples in Mark's Gospel, he is attacked for allowing his followers to pick and eat grains of wheat on the Sabbath. This suggests the fall harvest season. The action then moves rapidly to the spring's Passover festival when Jesus was crucified.

28   Marcus Borg (*Jesus*, p. 120) writes: "From a post-Easter perspective, John was the forerunner of Jesus who proclaimed Jesus' coming. But in a pre-Easter context, he was the teacher of Jesus, and Jesus was his disciple. And it was during his time with John that Jesus had his first reported experience of God."

29   "I tell you, among those born of women no one is greater than John"

30   Bart Ehrman (*Jesus Interrupted*, p. 163) writes: "There can be little doubt that Jesus chose twelve followers to be a kind of inner circle around him. The twelve are attested to in various Gospel sources as well as by Paul and Acts." Ehrman also notes that Matthew (19:28) and Luke (22:28-30) quote Jesus promising the Twelve that they would some day sit on thrones and judge the twelve tribes of Israel. Because at the time this included Judas, this must be one of Jesus' authentic sayings. Ehrman does not believe that tradition would have

invented the promise of such an honor to Judas (p. 159). John Dominic Crossan (*Jesus: A Revolutionary Biography*, NY: HarperSanFrancisco, 1994, pp. 108-109) questions the historical existence of the Twelve. On practical grounds he believes that a group of thirteen men traveling together through the tiny villages of Galilee would have stirred up fear and alarm. He notes also that although Paul mentions the Twelve, he never refers to them as a group exercising any authority. They are also not mentioned in early sources such as the Q Document, The Gospel of Thomas, or the *Didache*. (Crossan believes that the *Didache's* title, *The Teaching of the Twelves Apostles*, is a late addition to the text that is unsupported by its contents.)

31 Bart Ehrman (*Jesus Interrupted*, pp. 169-171) argues that Jesus did identify himself as the Messiah but only in private to his disciples. His intention was not to identify himself with God, but to claim that God would rule His coming Kingdom through Jesus and his Apostles. Ehrman suggests that Judas' real betrayal of Jesus was to reveal these private teachings to the temple authorities.

32 "The miracles attributed to Jesus are not greatly different from those attributed to other Jews in the same period." "The most curious aspect of the nature miracles is the lack of impact that, according to the Gospels, these events had." Sanders, *The Historical Figure of Jesus*, p. 163 and 156.

33 I Maccabees (13:51) might have suggested some of the additional details found in the Gospel stories: *e.g.*, waving palm branches and cheering crowds.

34 Luke proposes an odd excuse for their apparent lack of sympathy for Jesus' suffering. He says that they were

"sleeping because of grief" (Luke 22:45). Grief for many of us would lead to insomnia.

35   John makes no mention of the Sanhedrin or any assembly.

36   The remains of only one crucified individual have been found. His arms appear to have been tied to the crossbeam of the cross. His feet were nailed through their heels to both sides of the upright of the cross, and the nails were driven through pieces of olive wood to clamp the heels to the cross and prevent them being torn free.

37   Psalm 22 and Isaiah 53 were also cited as sources of prophetic information justifying faith in Jesus as the Messiah.

38   There is a chronological problem with accounts of the resurrection. Matthew (12:40) reports Jesus saying: "For just as Jonah was three days and three nights in the belly of the sea monster, so for three days and three nights the Son of Man will be in the heart of the earth." But only about 35 hours passed from Friday evening (the beginning of the Sabbath), when Jesus was taken down from the cross, and "early" on the morning of the day after the Sabbath, when the tomb was discovered empty. This means that Jesus could have spent only one full day and two nights in the tomb.

39   These were not members of the Twelve. Luke names only one of them: Cleopas — a contraction for a Greek name.

40   Did John mean to imply that they were living in Jerusalem?

41   This chronological detail, which is found only in Luke, is probably meant to associate Jesus' mission with other major

biblical events: *e.g.,* Noah's flood and the rebirth of the world, Moses' sojourn on Mount Sinai to receive the world of God, Jesus' own retreat to the desert to decide on the course he would take for carrying out his mission.

42 Later in the story Pharisees also help Paul escape condemnation by the Sadducees (Acts 23:6-8). Paul breaks up a meeting of the council by sowing dissent between its two parties. He tells the Pharisees that he is being condemned for preaching what they believe and what the Sadducees deny: "the hope of the resurrection of the dead" (Acts 23:6).

43 "From each according to his ability, to each according to his needs!" a slogan popularized by Karl Marx, *Gotha Program* (1875).

44 The "Hellenists" Luke had in mind would have been Hellenized Jews from the Diaspora, not gentiles. The Book of Acts explains how later the gentile mission came to be established and accepted. The tension here was between acculturated Jews and the more conservative Palestinian community.

45 Homer describes it as a place where the gods went for vacations!

46 At this point references to Peter cease in the Book of Acts. Paul describes Peter as active in Jerusalem and mentions him visiting Antioch (Galatians 2:11), but the Bible says nothing about Peter in Rome. If Peter did found the church in Rome, as tradition maintains, it seems odd that Paul does not list him among the acquaintances he mentions in his Letter to the Romans.

47   Sometime in the mid-60s, during the reign of the emperor Nero.

48   Ehreman, *God's Problem*, p. 236.

49   Marcus J. Borg and John Dominic Crossan, *The First Paul: Reclaiming the Radical Visionary Behind the Church's Conservative Icon* (NY: HarperOne, 2009).

50   His only attempt to create an overview of his faith is the letter he wrote to the Romans. The church in Rome was not one of his foundations, and he wrote to introduce himself to its members in advance of his arrival.

51   Borg and Crossan, *The First Paul*, p. 19.

52   Ehrman, *Jesus Interrupted*, p. 239.

53   Paul considered himself a member of the working class. He boasted of paying his own way by practicing a trade as a tent or awning maker.

54   The island of Manhattan today has a population density of about 100 people per acre. Ancient cities could have twice that — and without the option of skyscrapers to provide room for people to live and work. See: Borg and Crossan, *The First Paul*, p. 83.

55   *Ibid.*, p. 90.

56   *Jewish War* 7.45. Quoted in: John Dominic Crossan and Jonathan L. Reed, *In Search of Paul: How Jesus's Apostle Opposed Rome's Empire with God's Kingdom* (NY: HarperSanFrancisco, 2004), p. 35. For a fuller treatment of

the "God-fearer" phenomenon see pp. 23-37.

57 Borg and Crossan, *The First Paul*, p. 157.

58 Although Pseudo-Paul did advise Timothy to "take a little wine for the sake of your stomach and your frequent ailments." (I Timothy 5:23)

59 "If any believing woman has relatives who are really widows, let her assist them; let the church not be burdened so that it can assist those who are real widows." (I Timothy 5:16)

60 Curiously, although the letter accepts slavery as a legitimate institution, it lists "slave traders" in its catalogue of sinners (I Timothy 1:9-10).

61 as the evangelists occasionally represent Jesus doing (*e.g.* Matthew 19:24; Mark 10:25; Luke 18:25)

62 "Whoever has seen me has seen the Father" (John 14:9).

63 This is strong evidence that Revelation was not written by the same man who wrote John's Gospel. The latter wrote a more fluent and polished Greek. Despite the fact that Revelation uses a number of terms common to the Gospel of John (*e.g.*, Lamb of God), it makes no use of the Gospel's major theme: the love of God.

9

The Dark Glass

the best theology is always a game of playing *with language until it becomes an image of the Word beyond words*[1]
— Robert Farrar Capon

Disquieting as it may be, one is left with the conclusion that most of what makes the Bible biblical *is not inherent in its texts, but emerges only when one reads them in a certain way*[2]
— James L. Kugel

He spoke the word to them, as they were able to hear it
— Gospel of Mark 4:33

Faith and Knowledge

The King James Bible translates I Corinthians 13:12 as: "For now we see through a glass darkly." The New Revised Standard rephrases this as: "For now we see in a mirror dimly." The two versions do not have quite the same meaning. Looking through something is different from seeing something (ourselves?) reflected back at us. But taken together, both translations may come closer to the truth than either one alone. In the right light a dark glass yields both a dimly-mirrored reflection of the viewer (the subject) and a shadowy vision of its object. This is a suggestive metaphor for how the Bible functions. We try to look through its texts to a transcendent reality, but what we see is always in some sense a reflection of what we are. This, of course, should come as no surprise to creatures who have been told that they are made in the "image of God." When we look for God, we invariably encounter a reflection of some aspect of ourselves.

If we are in God's image, to know ourselves is to know God — and to know God is to know ourselves. This does not imply that human beings are divine, for an image is not equal to the reality it reflects. It can be a very pale and inadequate — even a distorted and misleading — representation of its original. Human beings do have some traits that mirror the divine. For instance, they share a weak version of transcendence. They can stand apart from themselves, make themselves objects to themselves, and view themselves with a degree of detachment. But they can never step entirely outside themselves and achieve pure objectively. They see through human eyes that are the "mirrors of the soul." The vision they see is *their* vision. Its truth is truth as truth appears to them. The absolute objectivity that eludes them in the field of knowledge is like the perfect love that eludes them in life. The divine command to love one another as we love ourselves is always more an aspiration than an achievement.

The "image" the divine shares with the human explains why the Bible teaches that God reveals Himself through history. History is the realm of humanity. Only human beings have histories and make histories. History is the arena in which people act, and by acting seek and give meaning to the process of living. History is where they realize their potentials, cope with their failures, and pioneer newness. When viewed from the perspective of faith, the human record of unique experiences (*i.e.,* history) takes on deeper dimensions of meaning. As the creature comes to understand itself, it begins to intuit more about its origin and the context for its existence. This produces a kind of knowledge of God that is distantly analogous to the kind of knowledge human beings have of one another. Such knowledge can only be conceptualized by paradoxes and metaphors. The more profound the experience one person has of another, the more complex and contradictory the attempt to describe it in words. Love, for instance, is both an intensely selfish and selfless form of knowledge. It feeds urgent appetites for personal fulfillment and motivates the ultimate self-sacrifice. If we struggle to understand the relationship of one person with another, how much greater must the challenge be to intuit something about the relationship of a human being to the source of humanity itself?

To acknowledge the gulf that yawns between God and His human images is not to give up hope of finding secure anchors and dependable guideposts for life's journeys. It is not, on one hand, to be driven to relativism and skepticism or, on the other, to surrender to blind and irrational faith. It is, however, a reminder to be conscious of limits and be careful not to overstep bounds. We need as accurate as possible an understanding of what is real (*i.e.*, "true") to guide our actions. But it is supremely dangerous to presume to more knowledge than we can legitimately claim. If we forget that our perception of truth is never absolute, we are at risk of crossing the line between the human and the divine and mistaking a human image for the divine reality. When we quote the Bible's words, 1) as if they were God's own words, and 2) claim that they can mean only what we say they mean, the distinction between ourselves and God disappears. To speak as God is to claim to be God.

Muslims should be in greater danger of misappropriating the authority of God than Jews and Christians, for *Qur'an*, the title of their sacred text, means "recitation." The order God's messenger, the angel Gabriel, gave Muhammad to establish him as *the* Prophet was to recite the words God inspired. For a modern person to read the Qur'an is literally to read God's words. Hence, accurate reading requires knowledge of the Qur'an's original Arabic text. Many conservative Christians have a similar understanding of the Bible (although they are less skeptical of the authority of translations).

As the vast majority of Muslims demonstrate, belief in literal inspiration of a sacred text does not inevitably lead to theological fundamentalism. When believers respect the crucial distinction between the words God speaks and the ways in which human beings hear those words, they avoid the fundamentalist error.

Christians who insist that their understanding of the Bible's words is literally God's meaning for those words shatter the dark glass that Paul said is our only valid instrument for viewing God. Although they humbly profess to be obedient to God's words, their practice is more presumptuous. By claiming that the words they speak are God's, they take His place, speaking for Him, and drown out His voice.

Rational arguments alone seldom seem to succeed in persuading fundamentalists and extreme literalists to rethink their position and consider its dangers. Their determination to ignore all challenges to their position may owe something to the fear that if they acknowledge the Bible's human origins, contradictions, and evolving perspectives, they will lose confidence in the assurances of faith. But the effort required to deny, rationalize, and ignore the issues raised by the Bible's complicated history of compilation and transmission is a heavy burden. Monumental feats of denial are needed to block out, or compartmentalize, a great deal of inconvenient material from and about the Bible. Doing so then leads to a kind of voluntary schizophrenia. Rather than strive to distinguish the essentials of faith from the time-bound scriptural vehicle that conveys them, these people assert the modern equivalent of the medieval "doctrine of the two truths": one standard for faith and another for everything else. The unintended effect of this misguided attempt to respect the Bible is for its readers to see more of themselves and less of God reflected in its dark mirror.

Christians who are inclined to literal interpretation are sometimes shocked when the implications of what they profess to believe are made clear to them. The contrast between what they intend and what their action proclaims can appall them. Art history provides an example. Michelangelo Merisi da

Caravaggio (1573-1610) produced dramatic paintings remarkable for their vivid realism and striking contrasts of light. He was often audacious in his choice of models and his treatment of subjects — and he was not above mocking his patrons. One of his earlier commissions was an altar piece for the Contarelli Chapel in Rome's Church of San Luigi dei Francesi. Its subject was to be St. Matthew writing his Gospel. The painting that Caravaggio first submitted was rejected as unseemly, for the painter had too literally illustrated his patrons' professed belief that Matthew's Gospel literally contained God's words.

Caravaggio depicted Matthew as an old man with the sturdy, but worn, body of an aged peasant. The evangelist wears a tattered tunic, and his legs and feet are bare. He sits hunched over an open book that is precariously perched on his crossed legs, and the clumsy way he grasps his pen suggests that he is illiterate. A bored, somewhat effete angel leans over Matthew's shoulder and moves his hand as he laborious scrawls letters on a page. There could be no more literal description of literal inspiration than the one Caravaggio painted, and it was too literal for the literal-minded patrons who commissioned it. Caravaggio was ordered to replace it with a more conventionally pious design. The first version was bought by a private collector and eventually made its way to Berlin, where it became a casualty of World War II. Only copies of the spurned *Matthew* survive today to remind us how uncomfortable it can be to think through the implications of what we think we think. Caravaggio's painting bluntly illustrates the threat that literalistic readings pose to the dignity of the Scriptures.

Literal readings, which are meant to defend the Bible, often serve only to expose it to ridicule, and this has the unfortunate effect of persuading some people who might otherwise read the Bible to dismiss it as unworthy of serious consideration. This is not a new concern, but an issue that has confronted the Church almost from the beginning.

As briefly noted in chapter 2, Literalists delude themselves if they believe that theirs is the traditional way to read the Bible — the way in which Christians have "always" read it. Fundamentalism (the doctrinaire form of literalism) is a fairly modern development, a reaction to the rationalism of an 18th century movement called the Enlightenment.[3] Literalism, however, is nothing new, and far from representing the practice of the early Church, it was spurned by many of the most influential of the Church Fathers as an obstacle to faith. These pioneer theologians were highly educated men deeply schooled in Classical Greek and Latin literature. They found the language of the Bible inelegant in comparison to the works of the ancient pagan poets, and they regarded some of the Bible's stories as beneath the dignity of a sacred text.[4]

Jerome (*ca.* 347-420), author of the Latin Vulgate, was so enthralled by the beauty of secular literature that he had a nightmare in which Heaven accused him of being a "Ciceronian," not a Christian — that is, of loving pagan literature more than Scripture. Augustine of Hippo (354-430), the most important of the early Latin theologians, came late to Christianity for a similar reason. His pious mother introduced him to Christianity in childhood, but he was so put off by the presumed literary shortcomings of the Scriptures that he could not bring himself to convert. He was unable to make a profession of faith until St. Ambrose of Milan introduced him to an alternative to literal interpretation. In Augustine's autobiographical account of his slow, tortured progress toward faith, he claimed that it was Ambrose's technique of reading biblical texts as allegories that enabled him to find God's Word in the Bible's words:

at last I had been shown how to interpret the ancient Scriptures of the law and the prophets in a different light from that which had previously made them seem absurd . . .

I was pleased to hear that in his sermons to the people Ambrose often repeated the text: *The written law inflicts death, whereas the spiritual law brings life,* as though this were a rule upon which he wished to insist most carefully. And when he lifted the veil of mystery and disclosed the spiritual meaning of texts which, taken literally, appeared to contain the most unlikely doctrines, I was not aggrieved by what he said, although I did not yet know whether it was true.[5]

There is no telling how many people, like Augustine, have found that biblical literalism poses an insurmountable obstacle to faith (and therefore, in Ambrose's words, "inflicts death").

Literalists would probably argue in defense of their position that their method of reading is the only one that guarantees the authority of the Bible's text. Gleason Archer succinctly summarized the grounds for their belief: "If the biblical record can be proved fallible in areas of fact that can be verified, then it is hardly to be trusted in areas where it cannot be tested."[6] Archer's position implies that if we find the authors of the Bible to be poor natural scientists, we must assume that they were also poor theologians. If we doubt their claim that God caused the sun literally to stand still to give the Israelites an extra long day to win a battle,[7] then we must also doubt everything else that the Bible says about God. Any error anywhere condemns the whole book in all its aspects. This claim is unconvincing, for it depends on a somewhat circular argument:

God is infallible.
God has inspired the Bible.
Therefore, the Bible contains no errors.

Anyone who wishes to defend this position has to resort to elaborate feats of sophistry to reason away the numerous passages in the Bible that are obvious errors (*e.g.,* the claim that the Euphrates and the Nile rivers have a common source: Genesis 2:10-14) or verses that are in plain contradiction (*e.g.*, the point at which human beings began to address God as Yahweh: Exodus 3:15 versus 6:3). Most seriously, apologists for literal inspiration have to perform mental gymnastics to reconcile the Bible's conflicting claims about God's character and what God wants from those who serve Him. For example: A prayer for God to wreck vengeance on an enemy is one of the most common petitions in Psalms.

> Rise up, O Lord! Deliver me, O my God! For you strike all my enemies on the cheek; you break the teeth of the wicked. (Psalm 2:7)

> The righteous will rejoice when they see vengeance done; they will bathe their feet in the blood of the wicked. (Psalm 58:10)

> O daughter Babylon, you devastator!
> Happy shall they be who pay you back what you have done to us! Happy shall they be who take your little ones and dash them against the rock! (Psalm 137:8-9)

But Leviticus 19:18 forbids the lust for vengeance or even holding grudges:

> You shall not take vengeance or bear a grudge against any of your people, but you shall love your neighbor as yourself.

If it is argued that Leviticus was meant to apply only to members of the Hebrew community, what can be made of the praise God heaped on young King Solomon? When God asked Solomon what gifts he would like, God was pleased that Solomon did not ask for vengeance on his enemies:

Because you have . . . not asked for yourself long life or riches, or for the life of your enemies, but have asked for yourself understanding to discern what is right, I now do according to your word. (I Kings 3:11-12)[8]

Does God want readers of these texts to follow the example of the Psalmist or of Jerusalem's wise king? What are God's core values? What does He expect His "image" to reflect?

Some literalists might stand with Tertullian, the early Christian preacher who swept all the Bible's challenges to rationality aside by claiming that he believed because faith frustrated reason. But most literalists would probably deny that their reading of the Bible requires willful ignorance — i.e., the determination to believe no matter what reason and common sense say. Hence the many convoluted and speculative arguments they propose to explain away difficulties with troublesome texts. Despite such attempts to rationalize the Bible's contents, all forms of literalism, however, leave faith defenseless. They play into the hands of the critics of religion who dismiss faith as willful self-delusion. They offer nothing with which to counter the arguments of atheists who dismiss religion as a superstition that the human species should long since have outgrown.

Even worse perhaps is the fact that a faith that rests on willful ignorance fosters the kind of religion that discredits faith. It feeds the sort of piety that is comfortable with prejudice, hostility, irrationality, and abuse — the piety that characterizes terrorists, persecutors, and tyrants. Literalism is not a sign, as is often claimed, of a strong faith that has overcome doubt. It is instead an anxious defensive position desperately fighting a rearguard action. It is driven by the fear that faith cannot withstand critical examination. Its core conviction is that rational analysis will raise doubts about the Bible and doubts of any kind will bring down faith's fragile edifice.

No one should lightly dismiss the literalists' fear that critical

thinking might threaten belief. Many college sophomores have
been turned into skeptics by taking courses that pressed them to
defend religious assumptions that they had never seriously
analyzed. But fearful literalists are wrong in assuming that the
choice is between clinging to a set of beliefs by denial or determination and abandoning belief entirely. It is not a matter of
rejecting critical thinking or giving up the claim to be a Christian,
of believing that the world was created in six days or rejecting
the whole Bible as a lie, or of trusting in the theory of evolution
or abandoning the Scriptures.

Reason does not simply tear down; it builds up — and on
firmer foundations. After all, most intelligent sophomores who
care enough to make the effort eventually work through their
doubts and come out the better for their struggle. And the insistence that Christianity requires affirmation of absurdities may do
more to turn people away from faith than any amount of critical
analysis of the Bible's text.

Literalism demands a kind of dualistic and absolutist
thinking that rests on a set of unwarranted assumptions: 1) that
there is only one way in which something can be true; 2) that
there are no degrees of truth; and 3) that the choice is always
between total veracity and total falsehood — that to doubt
anything the Bible says invalidates the whole book. This is far
too easy a stand to take (which may explain some of its appeal).

If the Bible is to be read seriously as a sacred book, it must be
read with the expectation that it will be a source of revelation.
Revelation implies the discovery of something new. This may be
a new insight that challenges old assumptions and preconceptions. Or it may be a new sense of conviction that motivates new
commitments to action. As the Bible documents (and common
experience confirms), revelation is often accompanied by shock
and surprise. It does not always succeed in engendering faith.
Sometimes it causes dismay and is successfully countered by
resistance. These were the reactions, the Bible reports, of many

who heard Jesus himself teach. Some believed; some doubted. A living faith is a journey to an uncertain destination, not a flight to a refuge from challenges that are fundamental to the human condition.

A journey does not always end happily or at its planned location. There is risk in opening oneself to the surprise of revelation and in struggling to reconcile old principles with new knowledge. Danger is inherent in the fact that faith and knowledge may not develop in tandem and that faith will remain unreformed while knowledge moves on. This was the fate of one of the giants of biblical scholarship, the Julius Wellhausen (1844-1918) whose JEDP theory of the Torah's origin was discussed in chapter 5. Wellhausen began his academic career as a theologian training clergy, but in 1882 he resigned that post to become a professor of oriental languages. It was, he explained, a decision of conscience to which he was forced by his own discoveries about how the Torah came to be rewritten and repeatedly rewritten:

> I became a theologian because I was interested in the scientific study of the Bible. It has only gradually dawned on me that a professor of theology also has the practical task of preparing his students to serve in the Evangelical Church, and that I was not performing this practical task, but rather, in spite of all restraint on my part, I was actually incapacitating my listeners for their position.[9]

Wellhausen apparently feared that if he taught his students what he had come to believe about the origin and history of the Bible, he would make it more difficult for them, as clergy, to preach the Bible as God's word. Instead of equipping his students for their professional roles, his discoveries would undermine their faith and unfit them for their future positions. Wellhausen had arrived at a new understanding of the Bible, but he was not, at the time, able to conceive of a new understanding of faith. His effort to do what he assumed was the "responsible thing" was charitable but condescending. He assumed that the Church could survive only if it was protected from the truth and its leaders kept in ignorance.

Pioneers in all fields take risks and sometimes suffer for the consequences of their contributions to progress. The alternative, however, is not to shy away from new discoveries by trying to shove "the genie back into the bottle," but to find the courage to reorganize and revise what we think we know to accommodate new information. Explorers wield two-edged swords. The world would undoubtedly be better off, for instance, without atomic weapons, but without the knowledge that led to the bombs it would not have the medical and energy-generating resources to which the study of atomic physics also led. New knowledge brings risks as well as opportunities.

Bart E. Ehrman, one of America's foremost biblical scholars, has written movingly about his life-long struggle with the Scriptures and the consequences for his faith. The event that launched Dr. Ehrman on his life's work might have been predicted to send him down quite a different path than the one he has trod. As an adolescent, he had a "born-again" experience that confirmed his desire to study the Bible. He began his education at Chicago's hyper-conservative Moody Bible Institute because he wanted to be taught what he already believed — namely, that "the Bible is the inerrant word of God . . . [containing] no mistakes . . . inspired completely and in its very words . . . ."[10] After a stint at the Moody Institute, he completed his undergraduate degree at Wheaton College, an intellectually creditable, but religiously conservative, institution. From there he went to Princeton University's theological seminary to study under one of America's leading biblical scholars. His determination to take the words of the Bible with absolute seriousness convinced him that he had to master the ancient languages in which they had been composed. Linguistic studies confronted him with the difficulties of translation and the challenge of unraveling the history of the Bible's manuscript tradition. The result was to deepen and widen his approach to interpreting the Bible. He came to understand that the Bible had many authors who wrote in many different contexts and whose words have been passed on by a process of transmission that has altered or confused some of the Bible's passages. These discoveries were revelations that led him to formulate a new basis for his work: "It is important to know what the words of these authors were, so that we can see what they had to say and judge, then, for ourselves what to think and how to live in light of those words."[11]

Professor Ehrman's determination to take the words of the Bible with utmost seriousness lead him to transcend the simplistic literalism of his youth and brought him a much more profound and nuanced understanding of their import. He discovered that "the Bible makes *better* sense if you acknowledge its inconsistencies instead of staunchly insisting that there aren't any, even when they are staring you in the face."[12] Taking the Bible seriously (as opposed to literally) liberated him from the arbitrary, irrational, and inhumane constraints of fundamentalism. It revealed a Bible that was a dynamic, living Word of God rather than a dead collection of legalistic edicts.

But that was not the end of his journey. Dr. Ehrman ultimately severed his ties with the Church and now considers himself an agnostic, not a Christian.[13] He is clear about what did, and what did not, undercut his earlier religious convictions. He says, "I decidedly do *not* think that historical criticism necessarily leads to a loss of faith."[14] There are many scholars trained in biblical criticism who are sincere Christians, and their work has guided the reflections of some of the modern era's most influential theologians. The obstacle that Professor Ehrman could not surmount is one that the Bible confronts in the opening chapters of Genesis (and in many other places as well). He writes: "There is so much senseless pain and misery in the world that I came to find it impossible to believe that there is a good and loving God who is in control . . . ."[15] The rock on which Ehrman's faith foundered was the Problem of Evil: If God is the good and all-powerful Creator, why is there so much evil and suffering in His world? The Bible offers a number of different explanations for this puzzle. But the fact that it proposes several is in itself a sign that none is entirely convincing.

Evil's challenge to faith persists, but the Problem of Evil is not a product of the historical-critical approach to reading the Bible. It poses difficulties for the conservative fundamentalist as much as it does for the liberal text critic — but often for different reasons. The fundamentalist must reconcile literal under-standings of the many biblical passages that represent God as violent and vengeful and those that describe Him as loving and forgiving. The liberal has to surmount the confines of human reason — the inability to imagine how God's power and goodness could be reconciled with His willingness to leave His creatures in misery. If for Wellhausen new scientific knowledge caused him to move beyond old paradigms of faith, perhaps for people struggling with Professor Ehrman's quandary old paradigms of reason handicap progress toward new conceptual-izations of faith.

It is very difficult, even for sophisticated scholars, to avoid lapsing back into pre-modern ways of thinking about God and faith. For instance, as Dr. Ehrman, writes: "No one any longer thinks that above the clouds is a place where God and Jesus live. . . . [W]hat does one do with that idea in a universe such as ours where there is, literally no up and down, except in relation to where you happen to be standing at the moment?"[16] But it is all too easy to slip into the error of thinking about God as if He were a "person," a thing among things, rather than the Bible's "I am that I am." The Problem of Evil becomes more of a problem the more God is thought of as "a good and loving God who is in control."[17] By speaking of "a" God ("good and loving" or not) we inevitably begin to diminish God in our imaginations to the stature of a person — a "being" like those we ordinarily experience. But such a God would be the kind of deity that inhabits the sort of place above the clouds that, as Ehrman notes, is no longer creditable in the 21st century. This is a deity whom principles of morality would seem to obligate, like any decent person, to come to our aide and do what he can to set things right. But maybe this is the wrong way to think about God, particularly the God revealed as incarnate in Jesus of Nazareth — a God who participates in the world's suffering and whose participation is said to open the way for evil's ultimate defeat.

Pre-modern ways of thinking about God and faith cannot be allowed to set the standard by which to decide what is and is not a legitimate interpretation of the Bible. Every generation of Christians has faced the challenge of reconciling its reading of the Bible with the current state of its knowledge of the world. From time to time traditional interpretations of the Bible have lagged behind and fallen out of sync with advances in the way people conceive of truth and knowledge. Old concerns and questions lose their relevance, fade away, and are replaced by new perspectives. This equips fresh eyes to see new things in old texts, and it occasionally causes seismic shifts in the Bible's interpretation (*e.g.*, the Protestant Reformation). The Bible seems to resist being pinned down in any specific historical era or cultural context, for it refuses to be reduced to a consistent set of principles or concepts. It is not the product of a single prophet or teacher, but a record of a millennial long process of reflection, discovery, revision, and moral development. It inspires wrestling with enduring mysteries (*e.g.*, the origin of the cosmos, the Problem of Evil, the challenge of death, *etc.*) more than it decrees answers to perennial questions. Its complexity and contrasting points of view defeat attempts to read it as if it were the secret answer key to life's test — a cheat sheet that the cosmic principal slips to a few of his favored pupils.

The Bible serves less to provide solutions for life's puzzles than inspiration for those who want to undertake the search for the principles of a well lived life. The Bible documents an eons-long pursuit of strategies to guide a meaningful human existence. But there is no reason to assume that the pursuit was assumed to end at the book's back cover. The faith the Bible describes is a living, evolving perspective, not the application of a final formula. Faith calls for continuing reflection and action in pursuit of a world characterized by love and justice (*i.e.*, God's Kingdom). The Bible's stories, images, symbols, disciplines, prayers, and hymns encourage and guide the hard work of thinking about life's meaning and purpose — but only *if* they are not mistaken for edicts that end the quest and dispel the mystery.

The Bible is the product of a religious tradition that claims that history provides the insights of revelation. Nature is the realm where fixed laws function, but history is the arena of both random and purposeful change. It is the dimension of life that can have meaning. The Bible is a record of sacred history, but that history is sacred because it is the vehicle for the newness of revelation. Therefore, the intended function of the Bible is not to confine the faithful to the limited horizons of past generations, but to urge them to grow in wisdom and charity.

Only a few gifted individuals have the ability and the opportunity to become ground-breaking scholars, but, fortunately, not everyone needs to. In every field of intellectual endeavor, the few blaze the way for the many. The process of inquiring into the Bible's origin, transmission, and translation has been lengthy and complex. It entails sophisticated analyses of arcane languages, obscure cultural practices, and fragmentary manuscripts. Like all scientific inquiries, it remains open-ended and subject to revision by new insights and textual and archeological discoveries. Its conclusions lack the comfort of absolute certainty. But none of this diminishes the duty all Christians have to come to terms (as best they can) with what it has to teach. To that end they need to engage in serious study and seek help from knowledgeable sources. Above all, they must try to look past their assumptions about the text and read what is really on the Bible's pages. And if they are to see what is there, they need to cultivate openness to the unexpected.

The alternative is to lapse into idolatry — to worship a thing, the Bible as an end in itself rather than as an instrument of revelation. To view the Bible simply as a directive from God is to reduce it to the status of a relic or idol, a dead thing with which it is impossible to have a living relationship. Faith then becomes nothing more than submission to something less than oneself, to an object (a code of laws and dogmas). But a living faith is a relationship with something at least as "alive" as the self, and living relationships are built through interactions that promote growth in understanding. The Bible must be engaged, questioned, and wrestled with, for the alternative is literally deadly. It leads to a blind faith that demands the sacrifice of humanity and moral accountability.

The degree of an individual's inclination to sacrifice his or her moral autonomy depends on how much he or she trusts an authority greater than conscience. This is why religion is so dangerous. Religious people profess allegiance to an ultimate authority which, as ultimate, takes precedence over their own judgment. It is extremely important, therefore, that they think carefully about what they believe represents the authority to which they owe absolute allegiance. If a book is vested with that authority, idolatry looms. Faithful readers who believe that a book literally tells them what a higher power (the only thing to which they are ultimately accountable) wants them to do find it all too easy to sacrifice reason, morality, conscience, and humanity. Divine words, which are said to be beyond dispute, lift responsibility for believers' actions from their shoulders. This is how religion produces suicide bombers, torturers, tyrants, and practitioners of genocide. An idolized sacred text is an instrument of death that turns a religion of peace and love into a cult of apocalyptic hate. A great deal depends on how a sacred text is believed to function as "the Word of God".

The Future of a Faith

Everyone learns to speak and to read in a cultural context. In the process of learning their skill, readers internalize principles fundamental to the culture that has spawned their language. Therefore, people come to any text, but particularly to religious texts, with sets of assumptions, some of which are so deeply ingrained that they do not rise to a level of awareness.

Since the 16th century, Western cultures have increasingly privileged the kinds of "sense-making methods" that are utilized in science and technology — specifically, categorization and quantification. The modern West places its confidence in the sort of thinking that relies on measuring, defining, classifying, and sequencing causes and effects. As a result, Westerners have become extremely adept at explaining how things work. They have invented instruments that enable them to examine nature on both infinitesimally small and inconceivably large scales. They have peeked into the inner workings of atoms, peered at the outer rim of the universe, and (thanks to a new "super collider" or "particle accelerator") soon may be able to look back almost to the moment of the universe's creation. They have accumulated mountains of data and have inferred logical chains of interrelated events that have given them unprecedented understanding of, and control over, the processes of nature. Physicists may even be closing in on a "unified" theory that will provide a single coherent explanation for the attributes of existence itself. Modern scientists know more about how the world works then any human beings have ever known. But knowing *how* things function is not the only thing that people need to know.

Human beings have an unrelenting hunger for an understanding of *why* things are as they are. This appetite is not
satisfied by explanations of the laws of nature, theories about the
dynamics of economic and social systems, or the coordination of
thoughts and emotions with signs of excitation in different
regions of the brain. Once we discover how things operate, we
want to know why things should be as they are. This is the root
of the moral awareness that is fundamental to human nature.

The most human of all questions, the kind that we presume
only human beings are capable of framing, concern the search for
meaning. These are the perennial questions that have traditionally been associated less with the sciences and more with
philosophy and religion: Why is there something rather than
nothing? What are the bases for moral and aesthetic judgments?
What is the relationship between good and evil? What is the
purpose of existence? Some people dismiss such questions are
unanswerable. They argue that these are not real questions about
the world but simply reflections of human psychology, the
byproducts of a self-conscious mind. There is no way, they insist,
to test whether or not existence has a purpose. To do so would be
like using logic to prove that logic is logical — the mental equivalent of lifting oneself by one's bootstraps. All that rational beings
can do is to take the world as they find it. The belief that there is
meaning beyond an understanding of the laws of physics is, they
maintain, a fantasy inspired by our tendency as self-aware
animals to put ourselves at the center of existence. Our superior
moral and intellectual capacities convince us that our lives must
have special significance and greater value than the life of a plant
or animal. Because our lives are of immense importance to us, we
want to believe that our existence has greater dignity than all
other kinds of existence — that we are integral to a grand
transcendent scheme. But, skeptics ask, why should we have any
more importance to the universal order than its single-celled
creatures or inanimate objects? Why should the universe be more

than a machine that has neither awareness of, nor concern for, its parts?

The belief that life has no purpose beyond its own perpetuation holds some appeal. It frees us from wrestling with difficult metaphysical and ethical questions, and it sets limits to our search for understanding. If all that we can know is what we can measure mathematically and experience empirically, our intellectual challenges become much simpler. We need only devote ourselves to gathering data points and searching for patterns among them. We can abandon our inclination to look up and out and turn our gazes down and in. Science is, in some sense, an easy pursuit, for scientists study things that are less than themselves. Even astronomers who map the universe treat their subject as an object. It is a thing — an extraordinary thing of mind boggling proportions — but only a thing.

People who claim that life has no purpose hold to a position that is as much a matter of faith as the ancient and enduring religious conviction that there is meaning to existence. There is no way to demonstrate the necessity of life not having meaning. Logicians advise against trying to prove a negative. The world religions also counter the nihilist's claim by insisting that there is evidence of life's meaning. The difficulty, of course, lies in the nature of what religions regard as evidence.

Modern people, particularly in the West, tend to have a narrow understanding of evidence. They assume that "real" or convincing evidence is the kind that answers *how* questions. It derives from measurable, repeatable experiences. Sincerely religious people sometimes buy into this. They assume that their faith must be founded on evidence of this kind, and they go looking for it in their sacred texts. However, those texts are products of an ancient quest for understanding that was based on presuppositions quite different from modern assumptions. Readers who turn to the Bible for answers to "how" questions discover two frustrating things: 1) the Bible's authors were not very interested in those questions, and 2) when they proposed answers, they were often wrong.

People who search the Bible for an explanation for how the world came into existence, how it functions, and how it will end find plenty of verses to inflame their imaginations and distract them with unprofitable speculations. All this does is to divert them from exploring the Bible's key question: What does it mean if creation has a Creator?

Religious texts do not prove their contentions by offering evidence of the kind found in a report by a scientist or an article by a historian. Instead, they invite their readers to view the world from a perspective that reveals a kind of significance that otherwise would be missed. Revelation does not add to the total of facts known about the universe so much as it discloses a new dimension of meaning for those facts. Faith is like the transformation that takes place when we view the metaphorical glass as half full rather than half empty. We do not learn anything new, but discover new significance in what we already know. That is of great importance, for it can alter our behavior every bit as much as the discovery of a new fact. When we stand outside on a beautiful summer evening to watch the "sun go down," we know that it is Earth and not the sun that is moving. Yet were we to abandon the poetic metaphor of a "sun set" and remind ourselves that we are really enjoying a fine "Earth turning," the experience would seem quite different. Accurate but different ways of describing the same thing have consequences for how we think, feel, and act. A poetic description of a sunset would probably do more, for instance, to promote a romantic evening than a coolly clinical reference to planetary rotation.

The primary purpose of the Bible is not to add to our knowledge of the world. It does, of course, provide reliable information about some real people and historical events. But this information is a means to a greater end — a demonstration of how the world of ordinary experience might be seen to have transcendent significance. The Bible offers examples (*e.g.*, from the teachings of the prophets, Jesus, and Paul) that illustrate how we might develop faith perspectives on our generation's evolving understanding of the world of nature and history. The Bible does not require us to conform our minds to the ancient worldviews of those who wrote the Scriptures; it only illustrates how their experience of their world meshed with awe at its mysteries to heighten their aspirations for humanity.

Not everything in every book is meaningful to everyone at all times. What we connect with in a text (what we are ready to notice) depends to a great deal on what our preparation has been for reading it. If we read *War and Peace* at age 16 and again at age 50, we may find that in the interim the book has changed a great deal. This is as true of the Bible as of any other volume. The gifts of insight that we receive from our reading and reflection are those that our lives equip us to receive. The answers we find are determined by the questions we are able to ask. Portions of the Old Testament (*e.g.*, the Genesis genealogies) may mean far less to modern Christians than they did to the ancient Hebrews at some points in their history. The Gospel of Matthew might seem more meaningful and accessible to some Christians than the Gospel of John. And as Marcus Borg and John Crossan point out, some people find St. Paul "appealing" and others "appalling."[18]

The 21st century is, in this respect, no different from any other. It has its own particular needs, and the faith that thrives in this century will be the faith that correctly intuits what those needs are and courageously addresses them. Not everything in the Bible will be relevant. It never has been — as the Bible itself testifies. Some of its authors, for example, were preoccupied by prophecies of the Apocalypse, but others were largely indifferent to the subject. The challenge for modern readers of the Bible is to clear away their assumptions about what it must say in order to open themselves to being surprised by what it does say — by what it says that is of relevance to them.

One thing that might startle modern Christians and stir them to new insights is how little the Bible says about individuals and how much it says about groups. American Christians are particularly conditioned to assume that the individual is always primary, but many of the Bible's authors had a corporate mentality. They thought in terms of communities more than separate selves. They assumed that people rose and fell together, that personal salvation (however that was understood) was bound up with creating a community of love and justice. This biblical focus comes as something of a shock (or annoyance) to Christians imbued with American individualism and competitive capitalism, but it also speaks to a deep need. The most successful American churches are those that engineer new forms of community for their members. Americans hunger for connectedness. Communication technologies may have turned the world into a Global Village, but it is a village whose inhabitants often do not know each other's names or meet face-to-face.

The Bible's focus on "the people" rather than "the person" is linked with another one of its themes. Many American Christians, whose faith is tinted by 19th century revivalism, assume that Christianity is less concerned with this world than it is with another. The goal of life "here below," they believe, is the pursuit of personal salvation.[19] The salvation they imagine involves an individual transition from this world to a heavenly realm, and they value this world only as a stepping stone to the other. But this is an attitude alien to much of the Bible. It is this world that God creates and declares good. It is dominion over this world that God gives to His human creatures. It is failure to promote justice and share resources in this world that earns God's condemnation. It is this world that God redeems. Even the Bible's prophets of the Apocalypse yearned for the restoration of this world to a state of perfection.

In truth, no one knows what, if anything, lies beyond death. Indeed, from the Bible's point of view we have no need for such knowledge. The responsibility given to us here and now is plenty for us to handle. If we truly believe that earning a reward in death is the only thing that gives life value, we miss the opportunity to live life and we fail to serve the God who created it. Should that happen, a death might be a lesser tragedy than a squandered life.

Truly faithful Christians will have the humility to live on God's terms, not their own. Among other things, that means that they will be content to live within human limits. People have an infinite appetite for knowledge, but a limited capacity to acquire it. Not all the questions they want answered can be answered. Absolute certainty is beyond reach. This is why faith is important. Without the guidance of a faith tradition, the only logical options are to refuse to act, to act blindly or randomly, or to rely solely on reason. A number of moral philosophers have explored the last option, but with only limited success.[20] The Bible calls its readers to act while warning them that they are accountable for their actions. It, therefore, advises a middle way (a course of action guided by its long tradition of reflection on the motives, deeds, and consequences of the decisions that shaped sacred history).

There is, however, more to faith than acting in responsible ways. Too often "liberal" Christians seem to reduce Christianity to nothing more than a political, economic, and social agenda. There seems, in their view, to be little difference between their concept of a life of faith and the vocation of a conscientious social worker. This reduces religion to something so pale and bloodless that it might as well be dispensed with. After all, many a secular social worker does more to realize the Bible's ideal of a just, caring community than many a pious Christian. The fallacy of the caricatured liberal version of biblical faith is its excessive emphasis on some of the Bible's fundamental teachings at the expense of others. The Bible's guideposts are all paradoxes — "this, but also this." The Bible sums up its message in the famous command to love God and love one another. But this is not as simple as it at first might appear. There can be no love of God without love of neighbor, but this does not mean that love of God is only love of neighbor. There is a deeper experiential dimension to faith than this, and psychologists warn that to love others people must first learn to love and accept themselves.

In several places the Bible points out that there is a difference between knowing what should be done and finding the will to do it. Reason alone is a weak motivator, for reason, in the form of rationalization, is its own enemy. It is often possible to reason oneself out of fulfilling an inconvenient obligation or performing a costly act of self-sacrifice. (Reason is less effective at soothing the uneasy conscience that follows.) Faith, on the other hand, has a better potential to keep conscience raw — to fuel the impulse to self-criticism, self-restraint, and the desire to reform.

Christianity's critics sometimes claim that it is nothing more than a system for inducing guilt. There is a degree of truth in this slander, for Christianity adds the dimension of sin to a crime. It gives transcendent significance to what would otherwise be merely human offenses. But if that were all there were to Christianity, it would long since have faded away.

The reality of life is that we are condemned to live in the gap between what we know we should do and what we actually bring ourselves to do. Biblical faith makes it possible to live confidently, but not comfortably, within this confluence of inclinations. It condemns failure without destroying the motivation to struggle against failure. It forgives without allowing forgiveness to lower the standards the faithful demand from themselves. Faith teaches that love lies at the source of life itself and that God's love will, through the agency of his human "images," ultimately bring things right.

The mind cannot think beyond itself, but it may — for some people at some times — take a leap toward a deeper kind of understanding than can be conceptualized. This experience is not given to everyone. Only gifted mystics may directly sense an all-encompassing divine reality that transcends separateness and immanence. Those who have written about these experiences usually claim that what they experience cannot be described. Mystics can testify to the reality of their contacts, but they cannot share them with others. It appears, therefore, that religious life, like ordinary life, is not fair. Everyone is not given the same experience from which to work toward the gift of faith. Therefore, a willingness to live in humble acceptance of what one is given is the most appropriate stance for those who are open to the hope of an encounter with the Bible's God.

Readers who search the Bible for knowledge of God need to remember that although God may speak through the words of the Bible, the Bible does not contain Him. He cannot be extracted from its text as if He were some bit of encoded information. This is a reality of biblical faith that the New Testament describes as "grace." The Bible does not speak on its own. It speaks the Word only when God condescends to illuminate readers of its words. If God is the omnipotent Creator, He is contained by nothing and limited by nothing but His own will. As the medieval philosopher and logician William of Ockham pointed out, that means that God is not governed by reason in the way that human beings are. Reason is not some kind of overarching order that contains God. God may have created a world governed by rational principles, but that does not mean that these principles apply to God Himself. This is not to say that God is irrational. If His human partners are to have any understanding of Him, His revelation must be grounded in reason. But, as Thomas Aquinas warned over half a millennium ago, reason can penetrate only so far into the mystery of the divine. Faith cannot be reduced to reason, but neither is faith totally divorced from reason. Every attempt to separate the two has resulted in actions that are destructive of humanity. Reason without faith risks the loss of a moral grounding, and faith without reason can unleash demonic passions.

Just as our languages force us to speak of God in gendered terms, which we have to remind ourselves not to take literally, our languages also make it impossible for us to conceive of the kind of "consciousness" God might have. We can understand a consciousness that is rational or irrational, but we have no way of conceiving of a consciousness that is more than rational. The Bible, however, assures us that we, at our moral and ethical best, are a window into the nature and character of God. We are His image. An image may be imperfect, but it must convey something of what it represents.

Modern Christians might, therefore, profit from focusing attention more closely on the first of Genesis' Creation stories. Many people appear to believe that the second Creation story cancels out the first, that the world whose creation is described in the first is obliterated by Adam and Eve's sin and replaced by something else. If that were the case, the Bible could well have dispensed with the first Creation story. But since it does not, it behooves faithful readers to take both stories seriously as descriptions of the context for their lives. As is so often the case in the Bible, similar stories offer two perspectives from which to view one thing. The second Creation story might be thought of as a lens laid over the first. It, too, begins in the beginning, but traces a different course to a different ending. Holding two different accounts of the same thing in mind at the same time is difficult, and our tendency is to favor one over the other. For long periods in the history of Christian consciousness the rebellious human sinner has loomed far larger than the faithful human mirror of God's image. The second Creation story has often, therefore, been read as the important one. However, it is neglect (or misreading) of the first story that has nurtured the excessive fixation with sin and guilt for which Christians have at times legitimately been indicted[21]. Each story is, however, of equal authority, and both together work to undermine dangerously simplistic views of the

Bible's insights into the ways of God. Genesis represents life as a struggle to realize humanity's divine potential in the midst of its abysmal failures — life lived with the pessimistic optimism and the optimistic pessimism of knowing that the glass is both half empty and half full. The Bible's most profound and complex word is *grace*, the word that may come closest to expressing the Word.

Religious people seem to cause the most trouble for themselves and others when they lose their humility and presume to knowledge they do not have. The key to reading the Bible to our benefit rather than our detriment is to cultivate that humility by accepting the Bible on its own terms, restricting the temptation to rewrite it to bring it in line with our expectations and desires, and thinking seriously about its paradoxes, metaphors, and symbols.

The history of religion suggests that knowledge of God comes most clearly to people who are most adept at cultivating quiet minds. A good reader is also a good listener. It takes practice and discipline to become a good listener. As Christian mystics warn, it is particularly difficult to wait patiently for a divine Word that may or may not condescend to be spoken. This, however, is the task the Bible's readers are given. Their mission is to listen for the voice of God whenever it sounds through the babel of the Bible's many human voices.

Jesus, according to the Gospel of John (16:12-13), warned that the Bible's stories are not yet fully told: "I have many more things to say to you, but you cannot bear them now. However, when the Spirit of truth comes, the Spirit will draw from what is mine, and reveal it to you." The biblical drama, therefore, is not yet finished. New challenges and experiences prepare new generations "to bear" the new things it is the Spirit's mission to reveal. Faith is not a determined adherence to a relic from the past — to something finished and complete. It is an ongoing adventure of exploration — sometimes an Exodus, or an Exile, or a journey to

Jerusalem, or a climb to a mountain top. Such expeditions are usually difficult. They entail the sacrifice of former securities and the risk of errors in judgment, but the Bible urges its readers onward with the assuring promise that "mercy triumphs over judgment" (James 2:13).

NOTES

1 Robert Farrar Capon, *Genesis, The Movie* (Grand Rapids, Michigan: Wm. B. Eerdmans, 2003), p. xvi.

2 Kugel, *How to Read the Bible*, p. 668.

3 "[Fundamentalism] is not so much a return to a pre-modern worldview but precisely to one form of modernism (reading the Bible within the grid of a quasi- or pseudoscientific quest for 'objective truth')." N. T. Wright, *The Last Word: Beyond the Bible Wars to a New Understanding of the Authority of Scripture* (NY: HarperSanFrancisco, 2005), pp. 9-10.

4 For example: In Genesis 34:13-25, the sons of Jacob plot a strategy that exploits the sacred rite of circumcision to avenge the rape of Dinah; in I Samuel 18:25, King Saul orders David to obtain 100 Philistine foreskins as a brideprice for his daughter Michal.

5 Augustine, *Confessions*, pp. 115-116.

6 Archer, *Encyclopedia of Bible Difficulties*, p. 23.

7 Actually, it would have been the Earth that stood still — with drastic consequences for gravity.

8 Solomon, according to the Bible, actually did avenge himself

on, and take the lives of, many of his opponents in the process of securing his throne (I Kings 2:1-46).

9   Quoted in: Kugel, *How to Read the Bible*, p. 300.

10   Ehrman, *Misquoting Jesus*, p. 4.

11   *Ibid.*, p. 14.

12   Ehrman, *Jesus Interrupted*, p. 6.

13   *Ibid.*, p. 273.

14   *Ibid.*, p. 17.

15   *Ibid.*

16   *Ibid.*, p. 281.

17   *Ibid.*, p. 17.

18   Borg and Crossan, *The First Paul*, pp. 1-27.

19   "[The Bible] that people think is the story of otherworldly salvation, is in fact a story about power — real earthly power — power that could change lives, disrupt traditions, overturn customs . . . . [S]alvation is to make life whole and free . . . . In this attitude I find a clue to the understanding of the Bible. It focuses on the here and now, it calls us to step out and embrace the future by affirming the present." John Shelby Spong, *This Hebrew Lord: A Bishop's Search for the Authentic Jesus* (NY: HarperSanFrancisco, 1993), pp. 25-28.

20   Moral philosophers often seem to acknowledge the wisdom

of the kind of conduct the Bible endorses and then struggle to find ways to ground selflessness in rational self-interest rather than faith.

21 There was a brief moment during the era of the Italian Renaissance when the first Creation story pulled ahead in popularity. It coordinated well with humanism's discovery of what it believed to be previously under-realized human potentials.

RESOURCES

Anthony, Susan B., Speech, the National American Women's Suffrage Association, Jaunary, 1896; quoted in: Jack Huberman, *The Quotable Atheist* (NY: Nation Books, 2007).

Apocrypha, trans. by Edgar J. Goodspeed (NY: Random House, 1959).

Archer, Gleason, *Encyclopedia of Biblical Difficulties* (Grand Rapids: MI: Zonderan,1982).

Aristotle, *The Generation of Animals*, 737a 25–28.

Armstrong, Karen, *Buddha* (NY: Penguin Group, 2001).

Augustine, *Confessions*, trans. by R. S. Pine-Coffin (NY: Penguin Books, 1961).

Bachofen, J. J., *Das Mutterrecht* (Stuttgart: Krais and Hoffman, 1861).

Balmer, Randall, *God in the White House: A History* (HarperCollins, e-books).

Blumenthal, Sidney, "Apocalyptic President," *The Guardian* (March 23, 2006).

Boorstin, Daniel J., *The Seekers, The Story of Man's Continuing Quest to Understand His World* (NY: Vintage Books, 1999).

Borg, Marcus J., *Jesus: Uncovering the Life, Teachings, and Relevance of a Religious Revolutionary* (NY: HarperCollins, 2006).

———, and John Dominic Crossan, *The First Paul: Reclaiming the Radical Visionary Behind the Church's Conservative Icon* (NY: HarperOne, 2009).

———, and N. T. Wright, *The Meaning of Jesus: Two Visions* (NY: HarperCollins, 2007).

Boston, Rob, *Pat Robertson: The Most Dangerous Man in America* (NY: Prometheus Books, 1996).

Cameron, Averil, and Amélie Kuhrt, *Images of Women in Antiquity* (Detroit, MI: Wayne State University Press, 1983).

Capon, Robert Farrar, *Genesis, The Movie* (Grand Rapids, MI:

Wm. B. Eerdmans, 2003).

Chilton, Bruce, *Rabbi Jesus: An Intimate Biography* (NY: Image Doubelday, 2000).

Crossan, John Dominic, *Jesus: A Revolutionary Biography* (NY: HarperSanFrancisco, 1994).

_____, *In Search of Paul: How Jesus's Apostle Opposed Rome's Empire with God's Kingdom* (NY: HarperSanFrancisco, 2004).

_____, and Jonathan L. Reed, *Excavating Jesus: Beneath the Stones, Behind the Texts* (NY: HarperSanFrancisco, 2001).

Didache, trans. by J. B. Lightfoot, http://www.earlychristian-writings.com/didache.html

Doctorow, E. L., *Creationists: Selected Essays, 1993 – 2006* (NY: Random House, 2007).

Dodd, C. H., *The Bible Today* (Cambridge, England: Cambridge University Press, 1946/1960).

Dover, Kenneth, *Greek Homosexuality: Updated and with a New Postscript* (Cambridge, MA: Harvard University Press, 1978/1989).

Doyle, Roger, "Sizing Up Evangelicals," *Scientific American* (March, 2003).

Ehrman, Bart D., *Jesus Interrupted: Revealing the Hidden Contradictions in the Bible (and Why We Don't Know about Them)* (NY: HarperOne, 2009).

_____, *Misquoting Jesus: The Story Behind Who Changed the Bible and Why* (NY: Harper Collins, 2005).

_____, *God's Problem* (NY: HarperCollins, 2008).

Eusebius, *Ecclesiastical History*, trans. by C. F. Cruse (Peabody, MA: Hendrickson Publishers, 1998).

Exposito, John L. and Dallia Mogahed, *Who Speaks for Islam? What a Billion Muslims Really Think* (NY: Gallup Press, 2007).

Falwell, Jerry, *Finding Inner Peace and Strength* (NY: Doubleday, 1982).

Finkelstein, Israel, and Neil Asher Silberman, *The Bible Unearthed: Archaeology's New Vision of Ancient Israel and the Origin of Its*

Sacred Texts (NY: Simon and Schuster, Touchstone, 2002).

Financial Times/Harris Poll (December 20, 2006), "Religious Views and Beliefs Vary Greatly by Country."

Fundamentals, The, vol. 1 (CA: The Bible Institute of Los Angeles, 1917).

Gilgamesh, The Epic of, trans. by Andrew George (Harmondsworth, England: Penguin Books, 1999).

Greeley, Andrew, and Michael Hout, *The Truth about Conservative Christians: What They Think and What They Believe* (Chicago, IL: University of Chicago Press, 2006).

Gospel of Thomas, trans. by Thomas O. Lambdin, http://www.gnosis.org/naghamm/gthlamb.html

Greenberg, Steven, *Wrestling with God and Men: Homosexuality in the Jewish Tradition* (Madison, WI: University of Wisconsin Press, 2004).

Groopman, Jerome, *How Doctors Think* (NY: Houghton Mifflin Co., 2007).

Hamilton, Marci A.. *God vs. Gavel: Religion and the Rule of Law* (NY: Cambridge University Press, 2005).

Hardisty, Jean, *Mobilizing Resentment: Conservative Resurgence from the John Birch Society to the Promise Keepers* (Boston, MA: Beacon Press, 1999).

Harris, Sam, *The End of Faith: Religion, Terror, and the Future of Reason* (NY: W. W. Norton, 2005).

Harris, Stephen L., *Understanding the Bible*, 7th ed. (NY: McGrawHill, 2006).

Haught, John F., *God and the New Atheism: A Critical Response to Dawkins, Harris, and Hitchens* (Louisville, KY: Westminster/John Knox, 2008).

Horowitz, Michael, "War on Christians," *Time* (April 10, 2006).

Jacobs, A. J., *The Year of Living Biblically: One Man's Humble Quest to Follow the Bible as Literally as Possible* (NY: Simon and Schuster, 2007).

Jaspers, Karl, *Way to Wisdom*, 2nd ed., trans. by Ralph Manheim

(New Haven, CN: Yale University Press, 1954).

Jenkins, Philip, "The Next Christianity," *The Atlantic* (October 7, 2003).

John of Salisbury, *Metalogicon* (1159).

Josephus, *The Works of Josephus*, trans. by William Whiston (Peabody, MA: Hendrickson Publishers, 1980).

Juergensmeyer, *Terror in the Mind of God* (Berkeley and Los Angeles, CA: University of California Press, 2000).

Justin Martyr, *First and Second Apologies*, trans. by Leslie William Barnard (NY: Paulist Press, 1996).

Kierkegaard, Søren, *Fear and Trembling* trans. by Alastair Hannay (NY: Penguin Classics, 1985).

Kirsch, Jonathan, *God Against the Gods: The History of the War between Monotheism and Polytheism* (NY: Penguin Group, 2004).

Kramer, Samuel Noah, *History Begins at Sumer* (Garden City, NY: Doubleday Anchor, 1959).

Kugel, James L., *How to Read the Bible: A Guide to Scripture, Then and Now* (NY: Free Press, 2007).

LaHaye, Tim, and Jerry B. Jenkins, *The Left Behind Series*, 13 vols. (Tyndall House republication, 1995).

Lester, Toby, "What is the Koran?" *The Atlantic* (January 1999) http://www.theatlantic.com/doc/199901Koran

Lincoln, Abraham, Address to Congress (December 1, 1862).

Mack, Burton L., *Who Wrote the New Testament: The Making of the Christian Myth* (NY: Harper Collins, 1995).

Marsden, George M., *Fundamentalism and American Culture: The Shaping of 20th-Century Evangelism, 1870-1925* (NY: Oxford, 1980).

Marus, Robert, and Greg Warner, "Ronald Reagan's Assent to Office Paralleled in the Rise of Religious Right" (http://www.abpnews.com/2034.article).

Miles, Jack, *God: A Biography* (NY: Vintage Books, 1995).

Mohler, R. Albert. "America's Vanishing Protestant Majority — What Does it Mean?" www.albertmohler.com/commentary_

read.php?cdate=2006-06-23

Newmark, Elle, *The Book of Unholy Mischief* (NY: Atria Books, 2008).

Niebuhr, Reinhold, *Christianity and Power Politics* (NY: Archon Books, 1940).

Obama, Barack, *Dreams From My Father* (NY: Times Books, 1995).

O'Brien, David, *Animal Sacrifice and Religious Freedom* (Lawrence, KS: University Press of Kansas, 2004).

Oldfield, Duane Murray, *The Right and the Righteous: The Christian Right Confronts the Republican Party* (NY: Rowan and Littlefield, 1996).

Oliver, Anne Marie, and Paul F. Steinberg, *The Road to Martyrs' Square: A Journey into the World of the Suicide Bomber* (NY: Oxford University Press, 2005).

Pagels, Elaine, *The Origin of Satan* (NY: Vintage Books, 1995).

Pew Forum on Religion and Public Life, "U.S. Religious Landscape Survey" (June 23, 2008).

Reeves, Thomas C., *The Empty Church, the Suicide of Liberal Christianity* (NY: Simon and Schuster, Free Press, 1996).

Robertson, Pat, Interview with Molly Ivins (1993), www.geocities.com/capitolhill/7027/quotes.html

"Ronnie Floyd, on Fox News, Discusses Pulpits and Politics," (August 2, 2004), http://www.bpnews.net/bpnews).

Sanders, Lauren, *Righteous: Dispatches from the Evangelical Youth Movement* (London: Viking/Penguin, 2006).

Sanders, E. P., *The Historical Figure of Jesus* (NY: Penguin, 1993).

Sanders, Scott Russell, *A Private History of Awe* (NY: North Point Press, 2006).

Smith, Huston, *Why Religion Matters: The Fate of the Human Spirit in an Age of Disbelief* (NY: HarperCollins, 2000).

Southern Baptist Convention, "The Baptist Faith and Message," http://www.sbc.net/brm/bfm2000.asp

Spong, John Shelby, *The Sins of Scripture: Exposing the Bible's Texts of Hate to Reveal the God of Love* (CA: HarperSanFrancisco,

2005).

_____, *This Hebrew Lord: A Bishop's Search for the Authentic Jesus* (NY: HarperSanFrancisco, 1993).

Sullivan, Andrew, "My Problem with Christianism: A Believer Spells out the Difference Between Faith and a Political Agenda," *Time* (May 15, 2006, P. 74); Martyn Whittaker, Letter to the Editor in Reply (June 5, 2006, P. 12).

Terry, Randall, interview, *The News Sentinel* (Fort Wayne, Indiana; August 16, 1993): www.geocities.com/capitolhill7027/quotes.html

Tertullian, *De Carne Christi*, V, 4.

_____, "On the Apparel of Women," trans. by S. Thelwall, http://www.newadvent.org/fathers0402

Torjesen, Karen, *When Women Were Priests* (San Francisco, CA: HarperSanFrancisco,1993).

Utter, Glenn H., and James L. True, *Conservative Christians and Political Participation* (Santa Barbara, CA: ABC Clio, 2004).

Waldman, Stephen, "The Power of Prayer," *The Wall Street Journal* (January 17-18, 2009).

Winthrop, John, "A Model for Christian Charity" in: Alan Heimert and Andrew Delbaco, eds., *The Puritans in America: A Narrative Anthology* (Cambridge, MA: Harvard University Press, 1985, pp. 89-92).

Wogaman, J. Phillip, "It's Time for You to Tell the Truth", *The Circuit Rider* (April, 1994).

Wright, N. T., *The Last Word: Beyond the Bible Wars to a New Understanding of the Authority of Scripture* (NY: HarperSanFrancisco, 2005).

Index

Evangelicals, 33ff
evangelion, 251
Eve, 85ff, 111ff, 175ff, 408
evolution, 22, 35, 37, 391
Exile, 94, 96, 123, 124, 142, 149,
 154ff, 171, 193, 198, 204, 211,
 215 — 220, 223, 227ff, 233,
 235, 241, 247, 259, 287, 409
Exodus, 149, 152ff, 163, 189,
 195ff, 200, 209, 212, 243, 261,
 262, 409
Exodus, Book of, 195, 206, 333
Ezekiel, 95, 187, 223, 228ff
Ezra, 123, 155, 158
Ezra, Book of, 123, 211, 244, 246

faith and works, 291, 358, 361
Falwell, Jerry, 41, 67, 307
Feast of Lights, see Chanukah
Federal Period, 33
Felix, 348
Feminist Movement, 38
Festus, 348
Finkelstein, Israel, 160ff, 187
Floyd, Ronnie, 42
Focus on the Family, 41
Foot Washing, 296
Foundry United Methodist
 Church, 54
fundamentalism, Christian, 4,
 6, 11, 13, 18, 19, 35 — 41, 54,
 59, 77, 385 — 394; Muslim,
 38, 59; see literalism
Fundamentals, The, 35ff

Gabriel, 277, 384
Galatians, 127, 349, 357
Galilee, 128, 133, 136, 243, 250,
 269, 279, 289, 312, 320, 332,
 336ff, 338, 340, 341ff
Gamaliel, 344, 353
gay-rights movement, 38
Genesis, Book of, 167ff, 195; see
 Creation Stories
gentile, 94ff, 137, 142, 155, 235,
 243 — 246, 254, 257 — 263,
 270, 275 — 287, 290, 293, 309,
 311, 315, 341, 346ff, 353 —
 356, 360, 365, 367, 375
Gethsemane, 325
Gideon, 210, 213
Gifts of the Spirit, 285, 356, 357
Gilgal, 214
Gilgamesh of Uruk, 174
Gilgamesh, The Epic of, 167ff,
 173, 179
glossolalia, 356
gnosis, 287
Gnostic, 99, 129, 286, 296, 366;
 Christian, 287ff, 365, 367, 369
God Is Not Great, 6
God Delusion, 6
God-fearer, 355
Golgotha, 333
Goliath, 187, 214
Good Samaritan (parable), 281
Goshen, 151ff
gospel (message), 10, 43, 44, 48,
 49, 57, 91, 127, 138, 235, 249,

Hout, Michael, 49ff
humanism, 38, 139
Hyksos, 151ff

idolatry, 25, 84, 113, 115ff, 161,
    197ff, 200, 205ff, 209, 217,
    220, 222, 226, 235, 356, 398ff
Idumea, 193; see Edom
Iliad, 80, 315
Immaculate Conception, 8
Internal Revenue Service, 42
Isaac, 16ff, 125ff, 151, 191ff, 277
Isaiah, Book of, 222, 227ff; I, 95,
    138, 227, 314, 315; II, 227,
    229, 259; III, 227
Iscariot, 327, see Judas
Ishbosheth, 214ff
Ishmael, 193
Islam, 17, 38, 47, 67, 136
Israel, 17, 68, 84, 94ff, 98, 123ff,
    138, 148, 151, 153ff, 156, 158,
    160 — 165, 187ff, 193ff, 205,
    208, 210 — 229, 245, 261ff,
    266ff, 270, 278, 281, 292, 294,
    320ff, 329, 342
Israelites, 80, 163, 165, 209ff,
    218, 224, 230, 288; see
    Hebrews, see Jews

Jacob, 60, 95, 151, 161, 187,
    193ff, 208, 218
Jahweh, 157ff, 190; see Yahweh
James (apostle), 320, 347
James (brother Jesus), 253, 308,

310, 316, 354, 362, 367
James (deacon), 320
James, Gospel of, 131
James, Letter of, 134, 251, 367ff
Japheth, 181
JEDP, 392; see Documentary
    Hypothesis
Jehoiachin, 218
Jenkins, Jerry B., 100
Jeremiah, 202, 222ff, 228, 265
Jericho, 156, 207
Jeroboam, 221ff
Jerome, 138, 387
Jerusalem, 94ff, 102, 123ff, 128,
    130, 132, 154ff, 158, 162, 188,
    192, 206, 208ff, 215, 220, 223,
    227, 228, 229ff, 245ff, 252,
    259, 266, 270ff, 275, 278, 290,
    292, 310, 314, 320, 323ff, 325,
    333, 337, 338ff, 341, 342ff,
    345 — 348, 353ff, 371, 390,
    409
Jesus, 10, 22, 34, 36, 41, 67ff, 74,
    77, 83, 90ff, 94, 96 — 98, 101,
    119ff, 124, 128 — 134, 136 —
    138,165, 192, 197, 199, 212,
    222, 235, 243 — 343, 346, 348
    — 353, 356, 358 — 362, 367,
    369ff, 392, 395ff, 403, 409;
    search for historical, 307ff,
    311ff, 352
Jews, 25,60, 70,76,83ff, 84, 87,
    93 — 102, 116, 119, 122ff,
    137, 154ff, 160, 189, 191, 218,

Judge, 153, 209ff
Judges, Book of, 161, 202, 203, 207ff

kadesh, kadeshah, kadeshim, 82, 135
Kentucky, 23
Kerry, John, 41, 42
Kerygma, 207
Kethuvim, 123, 124, 130, 230, 244
king, 90, 96, 148, 160, 200, 205, 210, 212ff, 217ff, 221, 223, 235, 256, 364
King James Bible, 14, 81, 82, 139, 382
Kingdom of God, 34, 35, 253, 257, 277, 281 — 286, 292, 334, 344, 352ff, 397; of Heaven, 281
Kings, I and II Books of, 160, 161, 203, 216 — 219, 222, 244; II, 82, 220, 222
Koine Greek, 136
Kugel, James L., 159, 187, 382

Laban, 193
LaHaye, Tim, 100
Lamb of God, 297, 317, 324
Last Judgment, 246, 249, 368; see eschaton
Last Supper, 132, 133, 286, 325
Lazarus, 298
Leah, 193

Levi, tribe of, 193, 200, 218
Leviticus, Book of, 200ff, 389
liberal, 3, 44, 22, 33 — 36, 39 — 45, 49 — 51, 57ff, 60, 77, 92, 243, 398, 405
Limbo, 176
literalism, 13 — 20, 48, 54, 58, 77, 159, 166, 179, 385 — 394
Lord's Prayer, 22, 264
Lord's Supper, 296, 311, 357, see Last Supper
Lot, 79
Luke (evangelist), 137, 251, 273ff, 348, 350, 353
Luke, Gospel of, 69, 98, 101, 128ff, 131ff, 137, 249, 256, 273 — 285, 286, 288, 292, 307, 312 — 318, 320, 322, 324 — 335, 338ff, 341 — 349, 350, 353
Luke-Acts, 276, 277
Luther, Martin, 8, 9, 56, 358

Maccabees, 156, 245
Maccabees, Books of; I, 244, 245, 246; II, 246, 248
Magna Carta, 23
Magnificat, The, 277
mainline churches, 31, 43ff, 50ff
Malachi, 124
Manasseh, 217, 220, 222
Marcion, 129–130
Marduk, 89
Mark (evangelist), 252, 254, 256

233

Supreme Court, 23, 38

synagogue, 250, 252, 270, 279,
    287, 294, 344, 345, 355

Synoptic Gospels, 133, 250 —
    284, 286, 289 — 297, 307,
    316ff, 320 — 335, 339

Syria, 152, 313, 354

Tabernacle, 195, 200, 206

Tacitus, 309

Talmud, 245, 308

Tanakh, 122ff, 130, 234; see
    Scriptures, Hebrew,

Tarsus, 347, 353

tekton, 250

temple, 94, 123, 124, 130, 133,
    154, 155, 160, 161, 200, 206,
    215ff, 227, 228, 245ff, 249,
    257ff, 259, 266, 277, 278,
    289ff, 317, 324, 327, 348, 367

Ten Commandments, The, 23

Ten Commandments, 14, 22ff,
    198

terrorism, 19, 26, 390

Terry, Randall, 67

Tertullian, 45, 86, 390

tetragammaton, 115

theocracy, 210, 212

Theophilus, 274, 341

Theresa, Mother, 71

Thessalonians, I and II Letters,
    310, 349; I, 101, 356, 366; II,
    365ff

Thomas (apostle), 197, 288,
    339ff

Thomas, Gospel of, 131

Thomas Road Baptist Church,
    41

Thomas Aquinas, 407

Tiberius, 278, 313

Tigris River, 150, 172

Timothy, I and II Letters, 127ff,
    349, 363; I, 363ff

tithing, 188

Titus, 349. 363, 365

Torah, 25, 69, 70, 123ff, 130,
    155, 157ff, 192, 195ff, 205,
    224, 230, 244, 247, 249, 250,
    254, 261, 263, 270, 354, 359,
    365, 392

Trajan, 309

Twelve, 255, 276, 279, 281, 310,
    320, 321, 342ff, 351, 353; see
    apostles; see disciples

Tyndale, William, 139

United Methodist Church, 33,
    53ff

Ur, 150; III Dynasty of, 150

Uriah, 216

Uzzah, 224, 226

Vatican, 310

Victorian era, 33

virgin birth, 138, 252, 261, 270,
    279, 314ff

Vulgate, 138, 387

Circle Books

Circle is a symbol of infinity and unity. It's part of a growing list of imprints, including o-books.net and zero-books.net.

Circle Books aims to publish books in Christian spirituality that are fresh, accessible, and stimulating.

Our books are available in all good English language bookstores worldwide. If you can't find the book on the shelves, then ask your bookstore to order it for you, quoting the ISBN and title. Or, you can order online—all major online retail sites carry our titles.

To see our list of titles, please view www.Circle-Books.com, growing by 80 titles per year.

Authors can learn more about our proposal process by going to our website and clicking on Your Company > Submissions.

We define Christian spirituality as the relationship between the self and its sense of the transcendent or sacred, which issues in literary and artistic expression, community, social activism, and practices. A wide range of disciplines within the field of religious studies can be called upon, including history, narrative studies, philosophy, theology, sociology, and psychology. Interfaith in approach, Circle Books fosters creative dialogue with non-Christian traditions.

And tune into MySpiritRadio.com for our book review radio show, hosted by June-Elleni Laine, where you can listen to authors discussing their books.

MySpiritRadio